Contents

Introduction

1 Philosophy of religion

Chapter 1	Philosophy and its methods	2
	1 Introduction	2
	2 Philosophy is a conversation	2
	3 Naming the parts – essential vocabulary for philosophical thinking	4
	4 Sense experience and its problems	9
	5 Metaphysics	11
	6 Study advice – making notes	11
	7 Conclusions	13
	Summary diagram: Philosophy and its methods	14

Philosophical language and thought

Chapter 2	Ancient philosophy: Plato	16
	1 Introduction	16
	2 Understanding of Reality	19
	3 Objections to the theory of the Forms	24
	4 Conclusions	25
	Study advice	25
	Summary diagram: Plato	26

Chapter 3	Aristotle and causation	29
	1 Introduction	29
	2 The philosophical views of Aristotle	30
	3 The four causes	31
	4 The Prime Mover	33
	5 The Prime Mover and Plato's Form of the Good	35
	6 Objections to Aristotle's theories	35
	7 Conclusions	37
	Study advice	37
	Summary diagram: Aristotle	38

Chapter 4	Soul, mind and body	40
	1 Introduction	40
	2 Is the soul a thing?	41
	3 Plato and the soul	42
	4 Aristotle and the soul	44
	5 Substance dualism	46
	6 Other views on the mind–body question	48
	7 Materialism	50
	8 Objections to theories and conclusions	52
	Study advice	53
	Summary diagram: Soul, mind and body	53

The existence of God

Chapter 5   The existence of God: arguments based on observation   56

    1 Introduction   56
    2 The teleological argument   59
    3 Criticisms from Hume   62
    4 Other criticisms   63
    5 Modern versions of the design argument   65
    6 Aquinas' cosmological argument   66
    7 Leibniz and the principle of sufficient reason   71
    8 Objections to arguments from experience   74
    9 Other issues   74
    10 Conclusions   75
    Study advice   76
    Summary diagram: The existence of God based on evidence   78

Chapter 6   The existence of God: arguments based on reason   81

    1 Introduction   81
    2 St Anselm's ontological argument   82
    3 Objections to theories   86
    4 A *priori* and *a posteriori* proofs of God.   90
    5 Conclusion   90
    Study advice   91
    Summary diagram: Existence of God based on observation   92

God and the World

Chapter 7   Religious experience   95

    1 Introduction   95
    2 The nature of religious experience   97
    3 Is personal testimony enough to convince others?   99
    4 Types of religious experience   100
    5 How can religious experiences be understood?   107
    6 Objections to theories   107
    7 Conclusions   110
    Study advice   110
    Summary diagram: Religious experience   111

Chapter 8   The problem of evil   113

    1 Introduction   113
    2 The problem defined   114
    3 Theodicy   116
    4 Soul-making theodicies   120
    5 John Hick's version of Irenaean theodicy   122
    6 Richard Swinburne and didactic evil   125
    7 D. Z. Phillips on soul-making theodicy   127
    8 Conclusions   129
    Study advice   129
    Summary diagram: The problem of evil   129

2 Religion and ethics

Chapter 9 The issues of ethics   134

1 Introduction   134
2 Person and community   135
3 Ethical life   135
4 Theories of ethics   138
Study advice   142
Summary diagram: The issue of ethics   143

Normative ethical theories: religious approaches

Chapter 10 Aquinas and natural law   146

1 Introduction   146
2 Aquinas' four tiers of law   148
3 Aquinas' natural law   151
4 The principle of double effect   157
5 Objections to theories of natural law   158
6 Conclusions   160
Study advice   160
Summary diagram: Aquinas and natural law   161

Chapter 11 Situation ethics   164

1 Introduction   164
2 Joseph Fletcher's situation ethics   167
3 Fletcher on conscience   170
4 Objections to theories   171
5 Conclusions   174
Study advice   174
Summary diagram: Situation ethics   175

Normative ethical theories

Chapter 12 Kantian ethics   177

1 Introduction   177
2 Kant's moral teaching   179
3 Hypothetical imperatives   180
4 The categorical imperative   181
5 Objections to Kant's ethics   186
6 Conclusions   187
Study advice   187
Summary diagram : Kantian ethics   188

Chapter 13 Utilitarianism   191

1 Introduction   191
2 Jeremy Bentham and classical utilitarianism   192
3 Teleology and relativism   193
4 Peter Singer and preference utilitarianism   198
5 Objections to utilitarianism   200
6 Conclusions   203
Study advice   203
Summary diagram: Utilitarianism   204

Applied ethics

Chapter 14   Euthanasia   207

1 Introduction   207
2 A problem of definition   207
3 The law and euthanasia   208
4 Sanctity of life principle   210
5 Quality of life principle   212
6 Voluntary euthanasia   215
7 Non-voluntary euthanasia   218
8 Application of natural law and situation ethics to euthanasia   219
Summary diagram: Euthanasia   221

Chapter 15   Business ethics   224

1 Introduction   224
2 Corporate social responsibility   228
3 Applying ethical theories to business ethics   232
4 Whistle-blowing   233
5 Good ethics is good business   236
6 Globalisation   238
7 Conclusion   242
Study advice   242
Summary diagram: Business ethics   243

3 Developments in Christian thought

Insight

Chapter 16   Augustine on human nature   248

1 Introduction   248
2 The human potential   248
3 Augustine on human nature   249
4 Interpreting Augustine today   258
Summary diagram: Augustine on human nature   263

Chapter 17   Death and the afterlife   266

1 Introduction   266
2 New Testament foundations   266
3 The parable of the Sheep and the Goats   272
4 Developments in Christian eschatological teaching   273
5 Election   279
Summary diagram: Death and the afterlife   283

Foundations

Chapter 18   Knowledge of God's existence   286

1 Introduction   286
2 Natural and revealed theology   286
3 Natural knowledge of God's existence   288
4 Revealed knowledge of God's existence   292
5 The natural–revealed theology debate   295
Summary diagram: Knowledge of God's existence   301

Chapter 19   Jesus Christ   304

1 Introduction   304
2 Jesus Christ's authority   304
3 Jesus the teacher of wisdom   306
4 Jesus the liberator   310
5 Son of God   313
6 Uniqueness   318
Summary diagram: Jesus Christ   320

Living

Chapter 20   Christian moral principles   323

1 Introduction   323
2 Theonomous Christian ethics and practices   323
3 Heteronomous Christian ethics and practices   326
4 Autonomous Christian ethics and practices   330
Summary diagram: Christian moral principles   332

Chapter 21   Christian moral action: Dietrich Bonhoeffer   335

1 Introduction   335
2 Bonhoeffer's life   335
3 Duty to God and duty to the state   338
4 The role of the Church as community   341
5 The cost of discipleship   343
6 Bonhoeffer's relevance today   346
Summary diagram: Dietrich Bonhoeffer   348

Index   351

Photo credits   358

Philosophy of religion

Chapter 1

Philosophy and its methods

1 Introduction

Chapter checklist

This chapter is designed to encourage the correct attitude to philosophical discussion. It begins by pointing out that philosophy is a practice that requires engagement and reflection. It is not simply a list of points to be learned. The chapter briefly discusses the major divisions of the subject – logic, metaphysics and epistemology (theory of knowledge), with some discussion of what we mean by knowledge and when we can claim to have it. It gives guidance on good practice in taking notes in philosophy and theology. Finally, it provides suggestions about the skills required in essay writing.

2 Philosophy is a conversation

'Why did you think that?'
'Is that really a good enough reason?'
'Why did I do that?'
'How did you reach that conclusion?'
'Why on earth do things like that happen?'

We have all heard ourselves and others use sentences like these. We ask questions, both of ourselves and others, and we think about and probe the answers we give. If someone gives a silly reason for an action, we tend to ask more questions and try to probe more deeply.

Key quote

The thing is to understand myself. To see what God really wishes me to do: the thing is to find a truth which is true for me, to find the idea for which I can live and die.

Søren Kierkegaard 1813–55

When we do this, we are conversing – but we are also being philosophers. We are looking for understanding. To understand and to be aware of the questions we ought to ask, and not to be afraid to ask them, is the beginning of wisdom. The word **philosophy** means 'love of wisdom'. In philosophy, we question and think about the answers, then perhaps look for clarification, explanation and justification, just as we do when we are talking to people, so we understand more clearly. Living philosophers talk to each other, and discuss among themselves what other philosophers (including the dead ones) might have meant when they gave their opinions.

Philosophy, including ethics, is not a subject to be learned, but an activity. This is true also in how philosophy relates to theology.

That sounds odd, but understanding this is what makes the difference between doing well in the subject and merely knowing enough to pass an examination. Being good at philosophy is not a question of how much you know, because anyone can, with enough hard work, learn facts. If all you did in the next year or so was learn facts about philosophy, you would have learned the basics to begin philosophy, but no more.

This need not seem so strange. If all you had ever done in mathematics was to learn the meaning of basic arithmetical signs, and learned by heart dozens of different formulas, would you be good at mathematics? Knowing about mathematics is not the same as being a good mathematician. A good mathematician actively uses mathematics, working through problems, using specific knowledge of formulas to work out the solution to problems. This is why the study of mathematics goes beyond mechanical or rote learning. You have to practise it as a set of skills, and in the practice you discover its deeper meanings.

Philosophy is like that. It is quite different from learning something such as the names of the bones in the foot or the periodic table; though good biologists and chemists do more than simply learn these basic facts. They also think through the implications of what has been learned – the meaning of these facts – for understanding the skeleton or chemical structure.

Philosophy, then, requires *engagement*. You should not approach it as you would approach learning a set of notes or a teacher's PowerPoint presentation. Instead, it requires you to think about the issues, reaching your own conclusions – with sound reasoning for the conclusions you reach.

Philosophy discusses big issues. In Ancient Greece, much philosophy, especially as practised by the great philosophers like Socrates, Plato, Aristotle or Pythagoras, was, at its heart, a considered conversation. Perhaps the conservation took place in the market place or, often, during and after a friendly meal.

When a philosopher develops a theory or a new argument, he or she is not saying to the world:

'Learn this!'

Rather, the philosopher asks a question:

'What do you think of this?'

The right response is not to say that you have learned it, but to respond with a considered opinion. You should point out strong or weak points in the argument offered, judging its effectiveness. Sometimes two or three competing arguments are offered, and the philosopher is asking for a reasoned judgement about which of these arguments might most effectively answer the problem they are designed to solve.

If this sounds challenging, there is some practical advice later in this chapter on how to think in the way required. For the moment, it is important to reflect on, and discuss, what you study. Examination questions and essays call on you to reach judgements, not simply to write down what you have learned. It is too late to work out what you think of theories if you have never discussed them or reached a judgement about them before you go into the examination room. Discussion and reflection are habits to be worked on during the study. The same skills apply more broadly in life. In philosophy we need to bear in mind Socrates' idea that:

'The unexamined life is not worth living.'

To live most fully means thinking about the meaning of our experiences, such as our adventures or friendships. Effective philosophising is just an extension of the same activity. By reflecting we discover ways of thinking and being that we had not considered before, and we learn new possibilities. One of the most exciting moments in philosophy is when you can say, 'I never thought of that!' In time you can think about how you have grown since meeting the idea.

There are practical advantages to this type of engagement, and not simply getting better examination results. There are things in philosophy, as in mathematics, that need to be learned. The process of learning is much easier when you have discussed and argued about something than it is when trying to learn cold facts off the page of a textbook. Reflection and discussion engage the whole mind, not just the memory, though memory is stimulated by them.

Of course, there are things which you must learn. It would be absurd to attempt to learn mathematics without mastering the language of mathematics. You have to learn the meaning of arithmetical symbols, of multiplication, division, square roots and all the rest. Without a grasp of that mathematical grammar, the activity is impossible, though the grammar is best learned in practice, using the symbols and concepts by working through problems.

The same is true in philosophy. There are tools of the trade, which need to be understood through use.

This chapter is designed to show you some basic tools and give a little idea of their use in practice. As you work through the chapters of this book, you will learn to use these terms, and you will become more familiar with their correct use.

> **Key quote**
>
> Faced with the complexity of today's world, philosophical reflection is above all a call to humility ... The greater the difficulties encountered the greater the need for philosophy to make sense of questions.
>
> Irina Bokova: Director-General of UNESCO, on the occasion of World Philosophy Day, 15 November 2012

3 Naming the parts – essential vocabulary for philosophical thinking

> **Key term**
>
> **Logic** Branch of philosophy concerned with the structure of ideas and arguments.

(a) Four branches of philosophy

Philosophy of religion needs several disciplines – **logic**, **epistemology** (theory of knowledge), and **metaphysics**. **Ethics** is also important. Religion makes claims about the good life and religious systems are usually, perhaps always, ethical systems. They encourage us to live in particular ways, both individually and in relation to others. In one sense,

Key terms

Epistemology Also known as theory of knowledge. This asks about what we can claim to know. What we truly know is not always the same as what we believe.

Metaphysics Branch of philosophy which asks what it is for something to be, to exist.

Ethics Branch of philosophy concerned with moral questions, not simply what we should do but also such things as the meaning and justification of goodness.

Validity This refers to an argument which is soundly constructed, so that if the premises were true, the conclusion would also be true. An argument might be valid but not true.

Key person

Aristotle (384–322BC): A Macedonian, son of the court physician. He studied at the Academy for 20 years, but disagreed with Plato's theory of the Forms, taking a much more empirical approach to his studies. He created his own school, the *Lyceum*.

Key terms

Syllogism Basic structure of an argument as set out by Aristotle, containing at least one major premise and one minor premise.

Major premise In a syllogism, a sentence which is all or nothing, with no exceptions.

Minor premise In a syllogism, a sentence containing an individual piece of information.

---

ethics can be seen as one of the original tasks of philosophy. Greek philosophers continually asked, 'What is the Good Life for Man?' For the moment, we will postpone discussion of ethics until the next part of the book, when we look at ethical theory in more detail.

There are other branches of philosophy. A philosophical discipline can accompany anything that can be the subject of reflection and questioning. As philosophers, we learn through continual questioning of our beliefs and practices. As long as that is the case, there will be philosophy.

(b) Logic

Logic is about the structure of arguments. Its primary concern is not whether a particular argument is *true*, but rather whether it is *structured to yield true conclusions*. It searches for the **validity** of arguments. An argument is valid if it is in a form that, if the information underlying the argument were true, then the conclusion would also be true.

Until the beginning of the twentieth century, all logic was based on the principles which Aristotle had set out in his logical works. These were known collectively as the *Organon*, comprising six books – *Categories*, *On Interpretation*, *Prior Analytics*, *Posterior Analytics*, *Topics* and *Sophistical Refutations*.

(c) The syllogism

Aristotle's logic is also called 'syllogistic logic', because the **syllogism** is the most basic logical form within the system.

A syllogism has a minimum of three elements: a **major premise**, a **minor premise** and a conclusion.

The most famous example of a syllogism is:

> *All men are mortal. (major premise)*
> *Socrates is a man. (minor premise)*
> *Therefore: Socrates is mortal. (conclusion)*

The first line is a *major premise* because it is an 'all' sentence. The argument would fail if, instead of 'all' we wrote 'a few', 'some' or even 'most'. Socrates might then be one of those men who are not mortal. It could, of course, be 'none' rather than 'all', as long as the term permits no exception. It must include everything of the type because any exception would disprove the rule. The major premise always acts as a universal rule. Just remember that it must always be a case of 'all or nothing'.

The *minor premise* is an individual piece of information. In this case, it is about one particular man, Socrates. Notice that it is the *structure* of the argument that makes the conclusion true. The form of the argument is:

> *All p are q.*
> *r is p.*
> *Therefore r is q.*

We can see that any argument of this form will give us a true conclusion if both premises are true.

Think about a different argument:

> *All Celts have fifteen fingers.*
> *Brian Boru was a Celt.*
> *Therefore Brian Boru had fifteen fingers.*

Here, the minor premise is true, but the major premise is untrue. But we can see that if the two premises were true, then the conclusion would necessarily follow.

Notice that we can say that the conclusion that Brian Boru had fifteen fingers is both *valid* and *logical*. It follows logically from what has gone before in the argument. The term 'logical' does *not* mean the same as 'true' or even 'sensible'. Something is logical when it necessarily follows from certain premises. To sum up: an argument that gives true conclusions when the premises are true is called a *valid* argument.

This type of argument is also called a *deductive* argument. The conclusion is based on the premises and is worked out from them. The conclusion is a necessary consequence.

Here we notice something very important. Checking whether something is true cannot be done from the wording of the premises. We have to look at the world to see whether the premises are true. As logicians, our concern is with the premises. But as philosophers we need to look further. There is a connection with epistemology – the question of knowledge.

(d) Three logical principles

There are many logical principles, but most are simple variants on three straightforward notions:

1   *Identity*. This is easy, because it is assumed in every piece of arithmetic you have ever studied. It is the basic truth that $x = x$, or that *something is (identical with) itself*. We take it for granted when we do a sum such as '2 + 2 = 4', that the terms retain their meaning. The second 2 means exactly the same as the first 2. If it did not, even the most basic mathematics would be impossible.
2   *Non-contradiction*. This is the assumption that a contradiction is not logically possible. Nothing with a quality can have the negative of that quality. If we said that a triangle is not triangular, we would be contradicting ourselves.
3   *Excluded middle*. This simply means that everything either has a quality or the negative of that quality. It cannot have both. Either I am a human or I am not. It is logically impossible for me to be both human and not human at the same time and in the same way. This follows from the principle of non-contradiction. It re-works the same idea.

(e) Epistemology

This is sometimes called *theory of knowledge*. It comes from the Greek word *episteme*, which means 'knowledge'.

Epistemology asks what we can really claim to know. It includes questions such as whether and how I can have knowledge of the world outside my mind. Or can I know, in any way, what goes on in your mind since I can never know your thoughts in the way that you know them?

Key terms

A priori Knowledge which is not dependent on sense experience, such as 'a circle is round' which is true by definition.

A posteriori Any knowledge which is dependent on sense experience.

Sense experience Anything learned through one or more of our five senses. I learn there is an odour through smelling it. Sense experience can be indirect. I know about Julius Caesar from the secondary experience of books, films and hearing about him.

Predicate A grammatical term which refers to the description of a concept. In the sentence: 'Her dress is red', 'is red' is the predicate, adding to the idea of the dress.

Tautology (also called an analytic sentence): A formula that is always true on any interpretation of its terms. 'A square has four sides' is a tautology because four-sidedness is essential to the idea of a square. To have four sides (the predicate) can only mean that what the sentence is about (the subject) is a square.

It also asks questions about the differences between knowledge and belief. This matters for Philosophy of Religion as well as Religion and Ethics. Can we ever be said to 'know' God, or what is truly good? Can I know the effects of my actions on others, or my prayers to God? If I say I believe in God, what kind of claim am I making?

Epistemology asks questions, including what would count as evidence. For example, what would be sufficient evidence to justify the existence of God – or anything else? Questions of knowledge often involve questions of metaphysics (see below), which concerns what might exist. What is the relationship between something's existence and our knowledge – or ignorance – of it?

The distinction between *a priori* and *a posteriori* knowledge is central to epistemology.

(i) A priori

This refers to knowledge which is not dependent on **sense experience**, but on the meaning of words. For example, it is true to say 'a triangle has three sides'. I can know that it is true as long as I know the meanings of all the words in the sentence. A sentence like this is called a **tautology**. This simply means that the meaning of the **predicate** (has three sides), the part of the sentence which describes the subject (the triangle), is a necessary part of the meaning of the subject.

Sense experience is not required to know the meaning of a tautology. This can be confusing, but it matters very much. It is a common mistake to think that *a priori* knowledge is innate. *A priori* does not mean *innate*, as if the ideas were somehow already present in the mind, without any need for learning them. This point becomes much clearer if we think about how we learned basic arithmetic when we were very young. We first needed sense experience to begin to understand. We counted bricks to see that two bricks and two bricks made four bricks. That is how we learned that 2 + 2 = 4. But the truth of the sum is quite separate from how we learned it. If we had learned by adding flowers rather than bricks, 2 + 2 would still equal 4. Once we know the truth, we do not need to keep counting things to see that it is true. And, as we grow in understanding, we learn to understand complicated sums with enormous numbers, without the slightest need to check our mathematics by physically counting millions of bricks. We do not wake up in the night wondering whether two bricks and two bricks still make four bricks.

Other types of sentence, such as 'There is a book on my desk', even if they are true now, would need to be checked again tomorrow, because the book may no longer be there.

There is philosophical debate about what can be known *a priori*. Can anything other than tautologous sentences be known *a priori*? Many modern philosophers, such as A. J. Ayer, think not.

Most modern philosophers restrict the *a priori* to tautologies. As Descartes' *cogito* (I think therefore I am) is not analytic, they would therefore reject it as a tautology because 'existing' is not part of the definition of 'thinking' in the way that having three sides is essential to the definition of a triangle. Mathematics can be seen as *a priori*, because all mathematical calculations are variations on the basic tautological truth that $x = x$. That is, the result of all sums, such as $453 + 247 = 700$, is simply a variation of $x = x$.

Some philosophers, such as St Anselm and Descartes, have attempted to prove the existence of God *a priori*. We will see their theories in Chapter 6.

Philosophers point out two things about tautologies:

1 They tell us nothing about the world. For example, 'A mermaid is half-woman, half-fish' is true, because that is what we mean by the word 'mermaid'. But the only way we can know whether mermaids exist is through sense experience. Tautologies are definitions about the meaning of words.
2 Their truth is certain because we make the rules we are using. That is why mathematics is certain. Mathematicians have made the rules by which $2 + 2 = 4$ is true. If someone showed us a triangle and said 'this is round', we would say 'that's not true'. Without circularity, we would not allow the word 'round' to be used.

(ii) A posteriori

This refers to those things where our knowledge depends on sense experience. Knowledge of this kind is called **empirical knowledge**, from the Greek term *empeiría*, which means 'experience'.

In a descriptive sentence which is not a tautology, some things can be known to be true by using our senses in some other way. Knowing the meaning of the words in 'my cat is playing with a mouse' or 'there are mermaids in the Waters of Leith' is not enough to tell us whether these things are true. Someone would need to look to confirm that it is so. And even if these sentences were true today, we would have to look again tomorrow to see whether they were still true.

Any sense experience has limitations. We can only ever perceive the world with the senses we have. We can never get outside ourselves to check whether our perceptions are accurate. If we look at photographs or see films to check what is out there, we still see those things with our own eyes. We can never certainly know that the world is indeed as it seems to be to us. We can only know that this is how it appears to us.

To think about this a little more, consider the sentence, 'That chair is green.' How do I know whether the chair has any kind of existence beyond my imagination, that outside what-is-me lies this other, not-me object, the chair? I see it as green. All I truly know is that I describe it as green. I may hear you also describing the chair as green. The most I could know is that you use the term 'green' to describe the chair. I do not know what green looks like to you. I cannot get inside your mind to share your understanding of what green feels or looks like, any more than I can know what something tastes like to you. Philosophers call this privacy of experience the 'problem of other minds'.

For a profile of Descartes, see Chapter 4.

Key term

Empirical knowledge Alternative description of *a posteriori* knowledge.

4 Sense experience and its problems

If knowledge of the outside world depends on our observations, then how do we make sense of the information? How do we take our random observations and make general rules of how things work in the universe? Only through making theories of this kind can we have science.

Many philosophers, including David Hume and Bertrand Russell, argue that most of our science – apart from mathematics, which is deductive – is based on making general conclusions from many observations. So, for example, we notice apparently endless instances of the Sun rising every morning, and draw the general conclusion: 'The Sun rises every morning.' This becomes a principle of geography and astronomy. But, of course, the conclusion is at best only probable. There could still be the exception, when the Sun does not rise, because it has burned out. This kind of reasoning, called *inductive*, can only give us probabilities at best.

For a profiles of David Hume and Bertrand Russell, see Chapter 5.

But induction involves the logical problem of induction. The problem is easy to understand. The only proof that events give us probable general conclusions is that we have experienced them enough times to notice a pattern in them. It is this pattern that leads us to probable general conclusions. The only evidence for induction is induction itself.

(a) Philosophical doubt

A posteriori judgements can never be wholly certain. It is unavoidable that they are uncertain, but this need not be a reason for total scepticism or sleepless nights. After all, many things in life are uncertain. We do not withhold friendship because we cannot prove that our best friend will never betray us, and there is no reason to despair of all our knowledge because we are aware of its limitations.

There is an important difference between genuine philosophical doubt and other types of doubt. A good test about doubt is to ask whether a particular doubt is reasonable. If I say a table cannot think, it would be unreasonable doubt to try to suggest tables could think, unless you could give good reasons to suggest that they might. Given that tables have no known brain cells, someone would have to make a remarkable case to justify doubting my original view. Philosophical doubt is always reasoned doubt. The doubt must be supported. We ought not to entertain a doubt when there is no good reason for that doubt. There are good philosophical reasons for doubting arguments for the existence of God – as there are also for rejecting atheism. The philosopher, regardless of personal belief, should take both sets of doubts very seriously.

Key quote

Take the risk of thinking for yourself, much more happiness, truth, beauty, and wisdom will come to you that way.

Christopher Hitchens (1949–2011)

(b) Knowledge and belief

When can we claim that we *know* something and not simply that we *believe* it?

Philosophers generally agree that four criteria must be satisfied in order to claim knowledge:

1 What we believe to be true must in fact be true. I can hardly be said to *know* that Snaefell is the world's highest mountain when it is not.

2 We must believe that what we believe to be true is really true. If someone said: 'I think Paris is the capital of France, but I'm really not sure', we would not say he had knowledge. He has a belief which happens to be true.

3 We must have sufficiently good reasons – not inadequate ones such as, 'it's in the newspaper' or 'my dad says ...'. This is called justification of our beliefs. There is great debate about what counts as sufficient justification. Some say that all attempts at justification ultimately fail.

4 Our belief must not rest on any false information. I could not be said to truly know who the king was who conquered England in 1066 if I believed that every conqueror was named 'William'. In this case I happen to be right, but I believe it for a reason which is mistaken.

It is important to remember these claims about knowledge. On religious matters, as well as on others, such as politics, people claim to *know* things that really they do not. People claim to 'know' there is a God, or to 'know' there is no God, or to 'know' that nationalisation is the right policy for industry. There may be good reasons for those beliefs, and people certainly may be sincere in holding them, but it would be wrong to say they have knowledge. After all, they may be sincere, but sincerely wrong.

5 Metaphysics

The name 'metaphysics' has an odd history.

After Aristotle died, his pupils edited the notes from his course lectures. They had just finished editing the notes about how things move and change, which they sensibly called *The Physics* when they started on a course for which they had no name, so they called it simply *The Metaphysics*, which meant 'beyond the physics'.

Metaphysics is sometimes understood to deal simply with transcendent matters. That is, it deals with things beyond our normal experience. In ordinary language, when people describe something as 'metaphysical', they refer to something beyond our experience. But it is a mistake to think of the philosophical activity on metaphysics in this way.

The central metaphysical question is: What exists? So, asking whether material objects, such as chairs or cats or guinea pigs, exist is as much a metaphysical question as asking whether God exists or souls exist.

Traditionally, metaphysical theories are divided into two kinds:

1 **Cosmological** – this approach refers to theories of the whole of being. They can be found in the work of Plato. He gave a metaphysical account of the entirety of the universe in relation to the Forms (see next chapter). They can also be found in Hegel, in relation to consciousness and the Absolute (covered in Year 2).
2 **Ontological** – these are theories of whether things of a particular kind exist. They do not attempt to make a grand theory of everything. Ontological approaches are piecemeal. So, for example, to ask whether souls exist is an ontological question. It does not ask what other kinds of things might also exist.

6 Study advice – making notes

The art of note-taking is essential to effective study. Remember that your ability in the subject is not determined by the number or length of notes you take, but by how effective they are as a guide to learning. Some students try to write everything the teacher says, but without truly listening, as if they were merely taking dictation, leaving themselves with a mass of notes which – as the examination approaches – they fear they will never be able to learn. You do not wish to finish the course with a daunting pile of notes any more than you should think you have *learned* something just because you have written it all down in class. If you are just writing in class, it becomes mechanical, passive not active.

The key to good note-taking, as to all good learning, is that it needs to be an *active* process. Do not just take notes because everyone else does. Ask yourself all the time what should be noted. Most importantly, *look back at your notes*. Note-taking is not just something to do in class. Really good notes involve taking time (not huge amounts) before and after class. Your aim is effectiveness and reasonable brevity.

(a) Note-taking: general guidelines

(i) Before class

- If you know the subject of the class, it is a good idea to make yourself a skeleton page of main points likely to emerge during the class. For each bit, leave yourself reasonable but not excessive space. If you leave too much space, you think you need to write pages.
- Some lectures are not so clearly signposted in advance. Nevertheless, give thought to what your notes might look like. What structure would you wish them to have? What is a valuable format to adopt? If you simply write down everything the teacher says, are you giving yourself the opportunities needed for you to do some active reflection and learning?
- Think about what your notes need to contain, remembering that you will want to work at and reflect on them. Remember that you will need literal space for reflection: remember to *leave signposted spaces for your own comments and thoughts*.

(ii) In class

- Always *listen* before you take notes. That means, you must always try to express what is said in your own words. Ask yourself, *how would I make this point?* The fact you are putting it in your own words means you are obliged to think about what you say. By all means, make the odd direct quotation, but remember that you need to be the one who can explain the point to someone else, even if that someone else is an examiner.
- Remember in your notes to be prepared to use headings and subheadings, or even, as here, just bullets, to break up the text. This is easier on the eye and makes the text easier to learn and to cross out.
- Use underlining, highlighters or whatever you find easiest for you to break up notes. Remember, these are your notes, and there is not a single right way for everybody. Experiment a bit.
- In general, write in short sentences. Try to avoid too many abbreviations unless they are simple and memorable (such as e.g., i.e., etc.). When reading through your notes, you do not want to be puzzling about what you meant at the time, months before.

(iii) After class

- You should leave class with well-spaced notes with blank areas for further comments. After all, you want to do something with the material you have gathered. Its purpose is not just to sit in a file.
- Within 24 hours, you should go through the notes you have made, not to try to learn them but to begin to use them effectively.

- If, in outlining an argument, you have listed many supporting or opposing arguments, it is useful to edit your list. Think which you find the most significant points and most telling objections.
- Fill in gaps, with examples or comments as necessary. Getting into this habit develops your reflective skills.
- Remember you need your notes as a basis for explaining your ideas to others.

(b) Specific guidelines for philosophy and theology

- In philosophy and theology, you will be introduced to many theories. Remember, any theory is always an attempt to answer a question. Always begin your notes by setting out the question to which the theory is offered as an answer. Remember that the teacher may rather take the question for granted, but leave a headed space in your notes for the time when you have decided what the question is.
- Try to develop a habit of explaining theories by using very short sections, with a sentence or two in each. It is easier to learn things in simple stages.
- Pay special attention to precise definitions of terms, always giving an example of what the definition means in practice.
- For any more difficult points, such as a technical term, leave yourself space to give an example. The teacher may well provide an example, but there is no harm in also thinking of examples of your own. Remember that careful examples both aid accurate understanding and also demonstrate understanding when you use them in your essays and examination answers.
- After each theory, leave a headed space for comments and reflections. Your first comment should always be: How well does this theory answer the question it was supposed to answer?
- Give yourself space for your own comments even if the teacher has given opposing arguments. You need still to reach your own reasoned judgement.

7 Conclusions

Your course is, above all, an activity, demanding thought and reflection. It is a conversation both with those who developed particular theories and with those who study and comment on theories. Be prepared to take a few risks in developing your own reactions to what you hear and learn. By thinking about whether you agree with a theory, you will develop the important skill of supporting your points of view with reasons. If the question you ask yourself is not just 'What do I believe?', but also 'Why do I believe that?', you are thinking philosophically, and in religious matters, theologically too.

Above all, the habits to develop in your learning and thinking are:

- reflection
- careful definition
- asking how well a given theory answers the question it was designed to answer
- using examples to illustrate and demonstrate understanding of ideas in practice.

Summary diagram: Philosophy and its methods

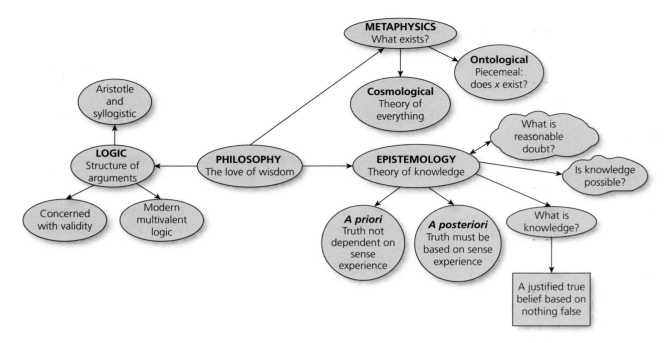

Revision advice

By the end of this chapter you should have a good idea of what philosophy entails. You should be aware that it is a practice and a conversation, and is not simply something to be learned. You should also have some understanding of the principle divisions of the subject and the meanings of logic, metaphysics and epistemology. You should also have some practical knowledge of how to take notes in the subject.

Can you give brief definitions of:
- logic
- metaphysics
- epistemology
- the principle of non-contradiction
- syllogism?

Can you explain:
- the difference between *a priori* and *a posteriori* knowledge
- the difference between validity and truth
- the difference between knowledge and belief
- the problem of induction?

Can you give arguments for and against:
- certain knowledge
- *a posteriori* knowledge
- the belief that the unexamined life is not worth living
- thinking that we understand the minds of other people?

Sample question and guidance

'There is no knowledge so certain that no one can doubt it'. To what extent do you believe that this view is correct?

As a first attempt at a philosophical essay, you might attempt to write about 500–700 words on this title. At this stage, do not worry too much about technical terms, though you may wish to make use of some given in this chapter, especially those on *a priori* and *a posteriori* knowledge and how much we can truly justify. Think also, in ordinary language, about how much we can truly know about what exists outside ourselves. As you write, take care to give examples that illustrate your points.

You need to begin by looking closely at the question. Think about exactly what is meant by '*certain knowledge*'. What counts as knowledge? What is involved in certainty? Is it ever possible to be truly certain? You may wish to look at the idea of justification as outlined in this chapter. It might be helpful to distinguish knowledge from belief and perhaps to consider the point that just because someone says she is certain of her facts does not necessarily mean that she is correct in her beliefs. Sincerity is no guarantee of accuracy.

You might choose to explore the idea that *a priori* knowledge is certain but uninformative about the actual contents of the universe, or you might wish to consider the limits of information gained through sense experience.

The essay title demands some sort of firm conclusion. You might argue either that the statement is true or that it is untrue, or that we can never be certain, but whatever line you take, make sure that you have given reasons for that conclusion, and not just asserted it.

Further essay questions:

To what extent is *a priori* knowledge more reliable and useful than knowledge gained through the senses?

'We can never know what the world is really like.' Discuss.

'In philosophy, questions matter more than answers.' Discuss.

Going further

There are many books which are good as initial reading. It is perhaps best to begin with material which will give you a grasp of epistemology. A brief but reliable guide is: Robert M. Martin: *Epistemology: A Beginner's Guide* (Oneworld, 2010). Another very good introduction is offered by Jennifer Nagel: *Knowledge: A Very Short Introduction* (Oxford University Press, 2014). Longer, but with some valuable insights is: Duncan Pritchard: *What is this Thing called Knowledge?* (third edition, Routledge, 2013).

On philosophy in general; Anthony Kenny: *A New History of Western Philosophy* (Oxford University Press, 2010) is thematic and thorough.

While it is good to read about philosophy, the best way to progress is to engage directly with the writings of different thinkers. Outstanding in this respect is: *Western Philosophy: An Anthology* Ed. John Cottingham (Blackwell, 2008). Not only does it have a very comprehensive range of materials, but it has clear explanatory pieces by the editor. If you only bought one book as a support to your studies, you could do little better than this as a comprehensive guide to the subject.

Chapter 2

Ancient philosophy: Plato

1 Introduction

Plato was a pupil of Socrates

Chapter checklist

The chapter begins by placing Plato in his time and place. Plato's philosophy was shaped by his experience of previous Greek thought and by the events and politics of Athens, where he lived, taught and wrote. It gives a brief overview of the thought of Heraclitus and Pythagoras as well as the ideas of Socrates. It goes on to outline Plato's understanding of reality and his theory of the Forms, including detailed explanations of the similes of the Divided Line and the Cave. Finally, it looks at the objections to Plato's theories, including those by Aristotle as well as some modern ones.

Ancient Greece is often considered to be the cradle of Western philosophy. Socrates (469–399bc), his pupil Plato (427–347bc), and Aristotle (384–322bc) who studied with Plato for twenty years, were undoubtedly three of the greatest philosophers who ever lived. They have had an influence that can be seen throughout philosophical discussion to the present day. What makes a philosopher great is the ability to articulate fundamental questions and to develop lines of thought which illuminate future discourse. Philosophy is, at heart, a discussion in which truth is sought through reflection, consideration, disagreement, refinement of description and study of ideas. The British philosopher A. N. Whitehead (1861–1947) described the whole history of philosophy as a series of footnotes to Plato. What is true of philosophy is no less true of Christian thought. The early Christian Church was influenced by Greek thought, in particular Plato and Aristotle. Their ideas weave their way through the theories of the great Christian thinkers.

Background

It is important to have a setting for understanding any ideas. The information in this box is not required material for the examination, but having an awareness of the context in which a philosopher worked is important for giving depth to your thought and answers.

When we think of ancient Greece, we must be careful not to think of it of as an empire, like the Roman Empire. Instead we should think of it as a civilisation, a set of guiding ideas and shared customs and habits. There was no single centre of power.

There were different states. They were sometimes called city-states, though not all were centred on cities. Famous examples include Thebes, Corinth, Ithaca (an island community, not a city), Samos and Miletus. These were found not just on the mainland of modern Greece, but on the islands of the Aegean and Ionian Seas, in Asia Minor and Sicily. Each of these states was self-governing with its own system of government. They were each known in Greek as a *polis*, from which we take our term 'politics'. Sometimes the states were at war with each other; at other times they were in alliance. But over and above their differences, there were many common features. They worshipped the same gods, spoke varieties of the same language, and came together in religious ceremonies and games, such as the Pythian and Olympic Games. Above all, they thought of themselves as Hellenes (Greeks) as opposed to the outsiders, who were known as 'barbarians'.

Athens and Sparta

Two of the most significant states were Athens and Sparta. Both are important to understanding the thought of Plato and Aristotle. From 431 to 404BC, Sparta and Athens were at war. The Peloponnesian War was one of the bitterest conflicts of the ancient Greek world.

Sparta was a kingdom, based on strictly military lines. Children were trained to be warriors, taken from their parents at a young age and brought up in barracks with strict military discipline. Sparta was not a centre of art or culture. The development of appropriate warrior culture was the focus of the state.

Athens, on the other hand, was a centre of civilisation and the arts. It was also a democracy, ruled by its citizens. This rule was conducted through elections, but also through direct decision of the citizens meeting together in the *agora* (marketplace) in the centre of the city. Here generals were chosen and laws decided. It is worth remembering that this was a direct democracy rather than the indirect democracies found in modern countries, such as the United Kingdom or the United States. In Athens citizens spoke for themselves, rather than electing representatives to decide on their behalf. Of course, citizenship and the right to speak were not given to everyone. Women, children, slaves and foreigners were excluded. Trials were also public affairs, heard by large juries who voted on guilt or innocence and, when necessary, on the appropriate sentence.

Socrates

Socrates was born in Athens and was a stonemason by trade. When he was young, he was a fine soldier. While he was a soldier, he was, on one occasion, struck dumb, standing motionless as the activity of the camp happened around him. He stood through the heat of the day and the coolness of the night, lost in thought. When he came to, he claimed to have been visited by a daimon, a spirit which told him not when he was correct, but when he was mistaken. Socrates claimed that this spirit would return throughout his life. We can date his emergence as a philosopher from this event. When he completed his military service, he returned to Athens to begin his philosophical career. He wrote

nothing, but taught through asking questions and probing the answers given by his listeners, always with the aim of being clear in explaining the good life for mankind.

Unfortunately, Socrates' habit of questioning to find truth could lead to discomfort among his listeners, as he went about the city of Athens. For many young men he was a hero, questioning the certainties of their elders. There were more significant problems, however. Some of Socrates' teaching admired aspects of Spartan life. Most significantly, he was the lover of Alcibiades, the talented and charismatic Athenian general and orator, who fled Athens for Sparta, where he advised the enemies of Athens on strategy. Alcibiades did not admire the Athenian democratic system. According to the Ancient Greek historian Thucydides (*The Peloponnesian War* VI, 89), Alcibiades told the Spartans:

> As for democracy, men of sense among us [the Athenians] – myself as well as anyone, as I have cause to complain about it – knew what it was. There is nothing new to be said about it: it is a patent absurdity.

Taken together with Socrates' seeming provocation of law and order, it is perhaps not surprising that the philosopher came under suspicion. Socrates was put on trial, accused of mocking the Gods and corrupting the morals of the young men of Athens.

His trial, as was usual in the Athenian democracy, was heard by a large jury. The accused were expected to defend themselves. To do so effectively, those who could afford to would consult one of the Sophists, men who would help them to construct an argument that might persuade the jury, and one of the Orators, men who trained others in public speaking and taught the arts of persuading listeners to agree with them.

Socrates made a point of not seeking the advice of the Sophists or the Orators in preparing his defence. His defence seems to have been provocative in tone (even as reported by his disciple Plato, in *The Apology*). It was so provocative so that there is a case for suggesting that he sought his own death. Socrates was convicted and sentenced to die by drinking hemlock. He refused the various schemes his disciples thought up to preserve his life, dying in 399BC.

After his death, some of Socrates' followers wished to honour his memory by writing down his teachings. The most significant of these followers was Plato, who was in his mid-twenties at the time of Socrates' death.

Plato

Plato was both a philosophical and literary genius. He gave up his earlier plans for a career in politics, instead devoting his life to continuing the tradition of philosophical enquiry encouraged by Socrates. He did this in two ways, by founding the Academy in about 385BC, the equivalent of a modern-day university where philosophical teaching would continue, and by writing a series of dialogues capturing and expanding on the thought of Socrates. (The Academy was destroyed by the Roman leader, Sulla, in 84BC, but revived quite soon afterwards, eventually surviving until 529AD when it was closed by the Emperor Justinian as a potential threat to Christianity.)

The Dialogues dramatise ideas in extraordinary ways. It is suggested that these were used for teaching within the Academy. The repetitions within the dialogues suggest that parts were read in groups, then summarised before moving on to the next part. Most of the Dialogues present Socrates as the main speaker, discussing ideas with various followers and opponents. Plato never appears as a participant, though his brothers (or possibly uncles) Glaucon and Adiemantus are major figures. In the *Republic*, the most famous of the Dialogues, Socrates is cast as narrator.

It is important to remember that the Socrates of the Dialogues is not necessarily the Socrates of history. In the earlier dialogues, we may assume that the character 'Socrates' fairly accurately represents the words and ideas of the historical Socrates. From *Gorgias* onwards, the remaining two-thirds of the dialogues, while using Socrates as a mouthpiece, represent the views of Plato himself. This is why we speak of *Plato's* philosophy, ideas, theories, and so on. This is important as the notion of the Forms, central to Plato's ideas, is not mentioned at all in the early dialogues.

Pythagorus

Plato was deeply influenced by the thought of Pythagoras (*c*.570–495BC) and his followers.

Most importantly for our present discussion, the Pythagoreans were fascinated by mathematics, and held a notion of a kind of atomic theory with the basic elements being numbers, which were considered real things. Just as we may think of objects being made of atoms, electrons and various sub-atomic particles, the Pythagoreans thought in terms of things being made of twos, threes and so on. Together with this, they were fascinated with the idea of ratios and how one thing was in proportion to another. Additionally, Pythagoreans made a sharp distinction between the material body and the spiritual soul. All these points emerge in Plato's theory of the Forms. It is interesting that Aristotle, in his *Metaphysics*, talks about the close affinity between Plato and the Pythagoreans.

Heraclitus

Plato was also very aware of the thought of Heraclitus (*c*.535–475BC), who was fascinated by the endless change we find in things. To Heraclitus is attributed the saying 'No man can step in the same river twice.' This is not found directly in surviving works, but Plato, (in *Cratylus* 401d), explains Heraclitus's view as:

> *Everything changes and nothing stays still – you cannot step twice into the same stream.*

Plato did not agree. For him, there had to be things fixed and certain so that there might be fixed and certain knowledge.

In his work, Plato seeks to relate everything to the nature of the good life, the soul, and the nature and purpose of reality. Above all, he seeks a certain basis for all our knowledge of reality. This world is obviously one of change and uncertainty, so Plato assumes there must be another, unchanging, spiritual world where certainty *can* be found.

Key quote

I cannot teach anybody anything.
I can only make them think.

Socrates

Key persons

Pythagoras (*c*.570–495BC): best known to us as the mathematician of the famous theorem, he was also a philosopher who created a school of Pythagoreans who deeply influenced Plato. He held a form of atomic theory, based on number and an almost mystical belief in the power of number.

Heraclitus (*c*.535–475BC): pre-Socratic philosopher best known for his concern with constant change in nature. In later years he suffered from dropsy (oedema) and doctors were unable to help. He tried to reduce the fluid with his own remedy of anointing himself with cow manure and baking himself in the sun. He died within a day.

2 Understanding of Reality

Background

Plato's need to explain the workings of thought and the mind – and to find permanence and certainty in a shifting world – led him to his theory of the Forms, most famously developed in his longest dialogue, *The Republic*.

Key term

The Forms Ideal, eternal single versions of things found on Earth. The Forms are found in the realm of Forms, which is above our daily world, and wholly spiritual. For Plato only the realm of Forms is truly real, and only this, for him, can be described as 'reality'.

Plato is often considered the first great rationalist philosopher. This is true in two senses.

He was a rationalist, as opposed to an empiricist, in that he believed that certain truths about the universe were knowable by mind alone, something the empiricist denies. Through the light of reason alone, and not through any observation, he believed that the enlightened individual – the philosopher – could see beyond the world of the senses, to the real nature of things. For him, to know things like true goodness or true beauty, the mind had to go beyond anything sensed.

But Plato was also a rationalist in perhaps a more usual sense of the word. He believed that the best part of humanity was the power of reason, something that animals lack. For him, as indeed for other Greek thinkers, if only we reason properly then we will always know the right way to live our lives. People do bad things when they do not use their reason and let themselves be carried away by their emotions.

This rationalism raises questions about how we can relate the material, emotion-feeling body with the mind which rises above it.

(a) The Forms

When we try to make something we begin with an idea of what we shall make. If I want to bake a cake, I have in my mind a picture of the finished product, a beautifully baked cake. (This is my example, not Plato's.) But where does this idea come from? I might answer that I have experienced cakes throughout my life, seen cakes of different kinds, and perhaps created a composite picture of the new sort of cake I want to bake. That would also be Aristotle's answer. But Plato's answer is quite different. He would point to the permanence of the idea in my mind. The cake I bake would either be eaten or cease to exist in some other way, but the *idea* of the cake, once in my head, does not suffer the same decay as the material cake.

This thought leads Plato to argue that there must exist an ideal cake. My attempt at baking is simply an imperfect copy. This ideal cake obviously does not exist in this world, so it must exist elsewhere. So Plato suggests the existence of the Realm of the Forms. In this realm there is a Form for everything that exists. There is an ideal cake, chair, vacuum cleaner, textbook and so on. These Forms are spiritual. That is, they are permanent and non-material. We long for the permanence of the Forms and are always dissatisfied with the transience of the world.

Why is this? What is our relationship to **the Forms**? For Plato, our souls belong naturally in the Realm of the Forms, the realm of reality, not this world. For reasons which are not entirely clear, we were trapped in bodies and born into this world. The consequence of this is forgetfulness. We forgot the Realm of the Forms, which was true, good and permanent. But we remember glimpses of it, as when I think of the cake I wish to bake, I remember and aspire to the ideal cake. The more I reflect on the concept of the cake, the clearer my memory becomes. For Plato, all learning is actually recollection of the Forms experienced in a previous life or lives. For him, education does not put anything into a child's mind – it draws out what is already there, hidden by forgetfulness. In the same way, an inventor is not creating something new, but is the first to remember the perfect Form of it. Any subsequent improvement in an invention is the result of people focusing their minds ever more clearly on the original idea.

Certain consequences follow from this understanding. For Plato there are two Realms:

1 the Realm of the Forms, inhabited by spiritual souls and the true beings in themselves
2 the Realm of Appearances, this world in which things look more or less like their originals in the Realm of the Forms.

(b) Hierachy of the Forms

There is a hierarchy in the Forms. The Realm of the Forms is superior in every way to the Realm of Appearances – the latter is a rather pale reflection of the former. As we shall see, even among the Forms there is also a hierarchy, with the Form of the Good above all.

Recall that the Pythagoreans were fascinated by number and by ratio. If we have two numbers, they are in a ratio with one another: 2 and 6 are in a ratio of 1 to 3. If there are two realms, Plato assumes that they are in a ratio to each other. Think of a scale model, such as a miniature model of a famous aeroplane. These models are made in a ratio of 1:72, so an inch on the model I make represents 6 feet on the real Spitfire or Lancaster. From the scale model, we can draw conclusions about the real aircraft.

Plato assumes that if something is true in this world of Appearances, it is even more fully true in the Realm of the Forms. In the world of objects, we need eyes to see them, and we need the light from the Sun to illuminate them so that our eyes can see. In the Realm of the Forms, similarly, we need the 'mind's eye' or the force of intellect to appreciate the Forms. But we also need something like the Sun to illuminate our understanding. This 'Sun equivalent' is the **Form of the Good**, the highest of the Forms. Below it come other 'higher Forms' such as Beauty, and below these are the individual forms of chairs, tables, cakes and all the other objects.

These Forms, then are the perfect versions of the inferior things of this world. As such, Plato believes, they must be eternal, just as our souls are. For him, eternity is part of perfection, because something perfect cannot be destroyed. As we shall see, this idea may be open to objection.

For Plato, most people won't look beyond the trivial to things themselves. Therefore they seek trivial things, such as earthly pleasures, money or fashionable clothes. He gives the example of people who call themselves lovers of beauty. They attend the various festivals and try to see every work of art, but never ask themselves what beauty is in itself. They distract themselves with things that appear beautiful but, as these are material, sensual things, they are imperfect and impermanent. A world-famous painting may be very beautiful, but if we turn it over, we find just rough wood and canvas, with nothing beautiful about it.

Those who think of the meaning of things in themselves are the philosophers. They ask what is true beauty, or true justice. They are capable of knowledge, not opinion. The Greeks thought that if we intellectually knew the good thing to do, we would always do the right

Key term

The **Form of the Good** is the highest form. All other forms have the goodness of perfection from participating in the Good. The Form of the Good also brings enlightenment to the rational mind.

Key question

Does Plato give enough support to justify his case? Is the argument for the Forms convincing?

thing. Plato shared this common view. The Greeks had no word for 'will' and tended, like Plato, to explain wrongdoing as the result of ignorance or incomplete knowledge. If I pursue material things, it is because I am ignorant of the true good. If I know the Form of the Good, I will be good.

Although Plato did not see democracy as the worst form of government, he believed firmly that the best form of government was a society led by the truly wise, the philosophers, with others obeying their lead. In the *Republic*, he sets out his ideas. Children are taken from their families and brought up according to their skills, as in Sparta. Only those carefully selected would be fit for leadership. The Athenian democracy was made up of ordinary people, not philosophers. Therefore it consisted of those taken in by what was apparently good, not what was truly good. This was why they misunderstood Socrates and thought they were doing the right thing by convicting him and sentencing him to death.

(c) The Simile of the Divided Line

Plato develops his case for the Forms in a sequence of three linked similes: the Sun, the Divided Line, and the Cave, in that order. The Simile of the Cave is the most developed and lengthy, as well as the most dramatic of the three similes, but knowledge of the Divided Line is very helpful in understanding the Cave.

Plato's Analogy of The Divided Line
The Four Stages of Cognition

Source of Perception	Things Perceived	Modes of Perception	Classes of Perception
THE GOOD Source of the intelligible order, of the world of reality	**A** *Forms* (Goodness, Reality, Beauty, Truth)	*Reason* (Dialectic)	**KNOWLEDGE**
	B *Mathematical objects* (Hypotheses)	*Understanding* (As in mathematical thought)	
THE SUN Source of the visible order, of the world of appearances	**C** *Physical Objects* (All objects perceptible by the senses)	*Belief* (Accepting sensory perceptions as givens)	**OPINION**
	D *Images of Physical Objects* (Shadows, reflections, illusions)	*Imagination* (Supposition)	

In the Divided Line, Plato asks us to think of a vertical line divided into two parts. The upper part is twice as long as the lower part – a ratio of 2:1. Each part is then further subdivided in the same 2:1 ratio. The upper part represents the Realm of the Forms (A/B on the diagram below) while the lowest part (C/D) represents the world of appearances. Plato notes how the process of observation in the world works in two ways. Sometimes we look at things themselves, as I may look at your car. But sometimes we look at images and shadows, such as my looking at a photograph or painting of your car. In the case of images and shadows, we are not looking towards the objects as they are, but are looking away from them, turning our attention to something which has less reality. For Plato, looking at images is like looking at shadows, as far away from true reality (the ideal Form of the perfect car) as could be. This is why, in the *Republic*, he places artists, who make imperfect copies of material objects which are themselves inferior copies of the Forms, at the bottom of his social hierarchy.

Remember that Plato assumes that if something is true in this world of appearances it is a kind of scale model of the Realm of the Forms. If something is true in the world, it is even more true in the higher Realm of the Forms. So, for Plato, if we have shadows and images ('looking away' from the objects of this world) in this world, then there must be an equivalent in the relationship to the Realm of the Forms. This is found in mathematical reasoning. The mathematician begins with an assumption of something abstract. He assumes a triangle, or numbers, as his starting point. He does not ask what a triangle is, in itself, or what a number is in itself. He considers what calculations he can do with that triangle or those numbers. For Plato, only the philosopher asks what things are in themselves.

Plato makes the assumption that truth and knowledge only apply to what truly exists. So he restricts the term 'knowledge' simply to our awareness of the Forms. He argues that things in our world do not exist as truly as beings in the Realm of the Forms. So we do not have knowledge of them, as they are not real in the full sense. We have only opinion or belief (*doxa* in Greek) about the things in our world. There is nothing to be known about things that do not exist. So Plato calls 'ignorance' the awareness of what does not exist. Plato appears to be confusing states of awareness with the objects of awareness. If I say 'There are no abominable snowmen in my study at present', I would call my awareness 'knowledge'. In Plato's analysis, this would count as ignorance as I am referring to something that does not exist. I am not convinced by his argument.

(d) The Simile of the Cave

This simile demonstrates Plato's literary skill. Writers through the centuries have referred to it, often as a metaphor for their own societies and the process of enlightenment. Different interpretations have been offered, but a straightforward way to understand it would be as dramatising points made in the Simile of the Divided Line.

Plato asks us to imagine an underground cave, connected to the surface by a steep tunnel. In the cave, there is a road which runs across its width. On one side of the road is a wall, running parallel with both the road and the far surface of the cave. Prisoners are chained to the wall, with the road behind them and on the other side of the wall. They have been there all their lives and are chained in such a way that they can only look towards the wall in front of them. They have never been able to see the road. On the opposite side of the road from the wall, and higher up, there is a fire. This fire means that shadows are cast on the wall which the prisoners face. People walk along the road, carrying objects of various kinds. The shadows of these objects appear on the wall in front of the prisoners. The prisoners also hear the voices of those passing along the road. The result is that the only 'reality' the prisoners ever know is the shadow world. They devise competitions between themselves to guess which shadows will appear next. This stage represents the images (D) on the Divided Line – the lowest level of awareness.

Plato asks us to imagine that a prisoner is one day released. He stands up, turns round, and sees the real objects carried by the men on the road. He learns that what he has previously believed was illusion. This represents the seeing of the objects of this world ('looking at' rather than his previous 'looking away') – C on the Divided Line. Then he is at last able to look at the fire. This would be difficult at first as his eyes would be used to seeing only shadows, but gradually he would be able to look at it. The fire represents the Sun in our visible world.

An illustration of Plato's Simile of the Cave

Then the prisoner is forced to make the difficult ascent to the outside world. This difficulty represents the hard road of philosophical enlightenment. At first, the sheer brightness of the outside world would be painful and dazzling, and the prisoner would be able to look only at the shadows of objects in the outside world ('looking away' representing mathematical reasoning (B) on the Divided Line).

As his eyes became accustomed, he would gradually be able to look directly at the objects themselves ('looking at', (A) on the Divided Line). These real objects represent the Forms in themselves. Last of all, he would be able to see the Sun, the brightest object, which gives the light that enables seeing and understanding, and which enables the life of everything else. The Sun in the simile represents the Form of the Good.

Plato then speculates on what would happen if the prisoner were forced to return to the cave. Those in the cave would not be impressed by his adventures. Indeed, they would not believe him. They would deny that there was a more real world. After all, the returned prisoner would no longer appreciate the games they played, having seen the truth, and his eyes would find it difficult to readjust to the shadow world. The others would mock him and might even kill him.

Plato is here trying to show how those with true philosophical insight are not understood by those unable to see beyond the world of appearances, unaware of the true nature of things. The reference to the possibility that the enlightened one might even be killed by the ignorant is an obvious reference to Socrates and his fate.

Key question

Glaucon: You have shown a very strange picture, and they are very strange pictures.

Socrates: They are just like ourselves.

Are they?

3 Objections to the theory of the Forms

(a) Aristotle's objections

One of the first to develop objections to Plato's notion of the Forms was his pupil Aristotle. He lists many reasons for not believing in them. Objections to the Forms in general obviously apply also to the Form of the Good. Some can be summarised as follows:

We may question whether there can be a single Form of the Good. We use terms such as 'good' in so many different ways that there can simply be no single 'good'. Aristotle identifies some of these different ways. A good human does not have the same good qualities as a good horse. A good harpist is one who plays the harp well. We may call her a good harpist but think she is – in another sense – a bad person. Playing a harp well is not the same as living well. We might go further. A good rifle is not morally good – it is good because it is good for shooting with, not because it has moral qualities or because it might be useful for shooting people or shoveling snow.

- Plato assumes that for something to be pure it needs to be eternal. If we consider a quality such as whiteness, we recognise that be white and being eternal are two entirely different things. Something does not become whiter by being eternal. Something might last a few moments, but be perfectly white while it lasted.
- If the Forms were so essential to true understanding, why does no one study them? It seems odd that carpenters, doctors, politicians and others seem to feel no need to study the Forms if they are as necessary to clear thought as Plato thinks.
- The Forms have no practical value. In matters of health there is no 'perfect health'. The health of a seventy-year-old is different from that of a youth. The doctor seeks only what is healthy for an individual. Knowledge of an abstract 'health' does not help in diagnosis or prescription.
- The idea that theoretical knowledge of something leads necessarily to being able to do it is wrong. Practical knowledge is learned through practice and observation, not through intellectual knowledge, which is a different sort of thing. Knowledge of politics comes through careful observation of different constitutions, observation of how policies work out and, above all, knowledge of people and their behaviour. Which is more useful in treating illness – someone who knows that light meat is healthy but has no direct knowledge of white meat, or someone who just knows that chicken is good for you?
- Some things have no Form, according to the Platonists. An example is that there is no Form of Number, but only forms of oneness, twoness, threeness and so on. This raises a further issue, not directly developed by Aristotle. If there are Forms of each number, and there is an infinity of possible numbers, then there is an infinity of possible Forms.

(b) Other objections

Perhaps the most obvious objection to Plato's thought is that he does not justify several of his assumptions:

- A more technical objection is sometimes used against Plato. You would not be expected to know this, but you might wish to do so. Plato assumes both that there are things in the Realm of Appearances and that their perfect counterparts are in the Realm of the Forms. He only says there are. He provides no justification for this assumption. It is not valid to declare that there is a ratio, and, without defining exactly what that ratio is.

- ■ **Empiricists** would object to the various assumptions that we may know anything about the world *a priori,* other than by sense experience.
- ■ There is no empirical evidence for the Forms. Plato argues by assertion and it is easy to be swept along by his imaginative and colourful writing.
- ■ Karl Popper, in Volume I of his *The Open Society and Its Enemies* (various editions, Routledge), argues that Plato is determined to find a certainty that cannot be found in this world. Because he cannot find certainty in a world of continual change, Plato assumes it must exist somewhere else. Many people run from the difficulties of an uncertain world (which is why so many are drawn to the apparent certainties of different types of political and religious fundamentalism). Wanting something to be certain does not make it so.
- ■ Various philosophers have drawn attention to Plato's assumption that because we have a name (noun), such as 'Good' or 'Beauty' there must be something corresponding to that term in reality. After all, nouns name things. A. J. Ayer (1910–89) referred to this assumption as a 'primitive superstition', and the great Polish philosopher, Tadeusz Kotarbiński (1886–1981), argued that certain nouns were *onomatoids*, which means sentences have to contain so-called genuine names (referring to concrete objects) as opposed to abstract objects' names or non-genuine names (onomatoids). For example, if I say 'There is *nothing* in my cupboard', 'nothing' is not the name of a thing called 'nothing' (that would be inherently contradictory) but the name 'nothing' stands for an absence. In the same way, terms such as 'Love', 'Good', 'Justice' are not names of particular things, but stand for qualities of other things. The terms are convenient shorthand when constructing sentences.

Key terms

A priori That which is known by mind alone and whose truth is not dependent on the facts of this world. See previous chapter for a more detailed account.

Empiricism The view that all truth is dependent, directly or indirectly, on what can be known through sense experience. Empiricists are sceptical about the possibility of *a priori* knowledge of things that exist.

4 Conclusions

The greatness of Plato lies, as we have said, in his ability to ask fundamental questions about life, reality and meaning. He sets out on an innovative adventure of ideas, and those ideas, as we shall see in subsequent chapters, have had lasting influence. Plato's search for truth has been inspirational for many, and his vision of enlightenment and the good life, a life lived in accordance with true knowledge, has acted as a model for studying such questions. Few philosophers would accept his ideas about the Forms, although in modern times, Iris Murdoch, in *The Sovereignty of Good* (Routledge, 1970) and *Metaphysics as a Guide to Morals* (Chatto, 1992) has made a spirited defence of a version of the Form of the Good.

Study advice

There is quite a lot of material in this chapter and it is helpful to remember that for the examination, you do not need to know it all. For example, many objections to Plato's theory of Forms are listed.

In the examination, it will simply not be possible in the time to write sensibly and fully about all of them. You may find some of the objections unattractive or may not feel confident about how well you could explain some of them. Think about which of these objections you find yourself most happy to use – perhaps two or three from Aristotle and one or two others, and concentrate on these in your essays and in your revision. The same point is true for the other chapters in this book.

The most valuable advice is always to read original texts for yourself. Examiners often complain of very fanciful renditions of the cave, with references to puppets hanging from the ceiling (there are no puppets mentioned by Plato: his only reference to puppetry is when he describes the wall behind the prisoners as being like the wall in the theatre which hides the puppeteers from the audience) or the prisoner being killed on return to the cave (Plato says only that a prisoner who returned might be killed). Make sure that you are familiar with what the text actually says, here as elsewhere.

Background material is important to your understanding, but be careful in the examination to refer only to points directly relevant to the question. Many examination candidates begin answers with lengthy accounts of the life of a philosopher, with no relevance to the question set, and for that they gain no marks.

Summary diagram: Plato

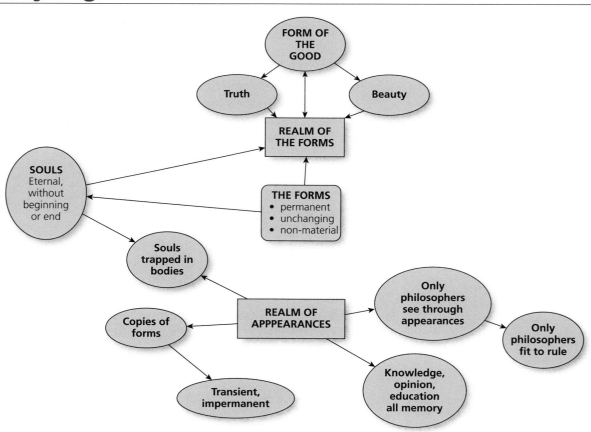

Revision advice

The background to Plato is worth re-reading in order to give depth to your understanding of his ideas. Above all, he seems to have been driven to find certainty in a very uncertain world. Unable to find permanence in a shifting world, he sought it in the Realm of the Forms. Think about whether this is convincing or whether he makes too many unjustified or incompletely justified assertions in developing the idea of the Forms. How effective do you think that Aristotle and others have been in criticising Plato? Thinking about the issues in this way is helpful in learning to justify your own views of Plato – it is a critical engagement in the conversation, in line with the approach to philosophy outlined in Chapter 1. Think about whether Plato truly justifies his view, and think about whether we could ever have innate knowledge of the Forms.

Can you give brief definitions of:
- the Form of the Good
- the Forms
- the Realm of the Forms
- Plato's view of the knowledge

Can you explain:
- how Plato resolves the problems of constant change raised by Heraclitus
- how Plato uses the idea of proportion and ratios to develop his ideas
- the Simile of the Divided Line
- the Simile of the Cave?

Can you give arguments for and against:
- the Realm of the Forms
- the Form of the Good
- the idea that this world is not true reality
- Plato's treatment of knowledge and belief
- Plato's belief that only the philosopher has true knowledge?

Sample question and guidance

'The Simile of the Cave tells us nothing about reality.' Discuss.

This type of question is often asked in the examination, and it can be difficult for students who do not take a moment to think about the title. It does not ask you to describe every detail of the simile, but rather to think about the picture of reality Plato is trying to teach us through it. It is useful early in your essay to write about what Plato's intention is. Although he uses the simile to say something about political life, about knowledge, about education and about the death of Socrates, among other things, the quotation you are discussing picks out the claim that it is a guide to the real world, and, in particular, to the Form of the Good. It is this area which should be the focus of the essay.

The word 'Discuss' in the question is an instruction not to describe the simile, but to consider it. What reasons can be given – what reasons does Plato give – to support his view? What may be argued against his ideas? What is your reasoned opinion on the matter? When you are asked to discuss something, it is hoped that you will weigh both sides of the question and present your own developed conclusion, explaining the factors which have led to your judgement. What matters is not what conclusion you reach but whether you have selected and developed good reasons for your conclusion. Some people try to dismiss Plato by saying that we are too modern to hold such a view. That is hardly a philosophical argument. The belief that $2 + 2 = 4$ predates Plato by centuries and probably millennia, but we do not dismiss the belief because it is so ancient. We must always engage with the idea in itself – there may be something valuable within it. If you think Plato is mistaken, then you need to demonstrate precisely why.

Further essay questions:

To what extent can it be argued that education is about remembering, not learning?

How convincing is Plato's idea of the Form of the Good?

Going further

The literature on Plato is vast with many sound introductory texts. Julia Annas: *Plato: A Very Short Introduction* (Oxford University Press, 2003) can be recommended with confidence as a succinct and clear guide to major ideas.

Plato himself is very readable and it is very useful to look at any text of the *Republic*, especially Books VI and VII, where Plato sets out his vision, including his similes. Reading these should take no more than an hour. Aristotle's criticisms of Plato can be found in various places, notably in his *Nicomachean Ethics*. In Book I, Chapter 6, he lists a series of objections. These take only a few minutes to read (two sides in the Penguin edition) and it will stimulate your own thought to read the criticisms and choose two or three which you think you could use effectively in your own essays. Making this kind of choice is the type of personal reflection which examiners expect.

You might find it helpful to read the first volume of Karl Popper: *The Open Society and Its Enemies* (various editions, Routledge), both for its interesting analysis and criticisms of Plato but also as a model of clear thinking and writing in philosophy.

For a view of Socrates as less than the heroic martyr and proponent of truth of popular myth, you might wish to entertain yourself with the much-read essay, *Socrates Had it Coming,* which may be found at http://christian-identity.net/lindstedt/socrates.html and elsewhere. It is brief, informative and provocative. It is also funny.

Chapter 3

Aristotle and causation

1 Introduction

Aristotle

Chapter checklist

The chapter begins with an account of Aristotle's life and background, followed by a description of aspects of his scientific method. This looks at both his differences from Plato and his specific use of categorisation *per genus et per differentia*. The chapter describes the theory of the four causes, as outlined in *Physics* II.3, leading to the notion of Final Cause and Prime Mover. It distinguishes Aristotle's concept of Prime Mover from that of Aquinas. It develops detailed criticisms, including whether Aristotle is simply naming causes rather than explaining them, questions about whether the universe is truly purposive and possible limitations of his concept of Prime Mover.

Aristotle's philosophy was notable for its extraordinary breadth and range, covering topics from logic and metaphysics to biology, ethics, psychology, physics, dramatic criticism and politics. It was characterised by careful observation of the world, close attention to definition and categorisation of data. In the later Middle Ages, Dante would describe Aristotle as 'Master of Those Who Know'.

Background

Aristotle was an extraordinary man. The important thing to remember about him is that, unlike Socrates and Plato, he was not an Athenian. He was born in Stagira, a Macedonian city, in 384BC. His father was doctor to Amyntas, King of Macedonia. It is interesting to see how often Aristotle refers to the example of medicine in his own writings. Around 366BC, Aristotle went to study at the Academy, where he remained for almost 20 years, until Plato's death. His brilliance and range of interests were remarkable and recognised by Plato. However, in important ways, his approach was different from his master's, and it is not altogether surprising that on Plato's death, leadership of the Academy would pass not to the foreigner Aristotle, but to Speusippus, who was Plato's nephew.

Aristotle left Athens, studied marine biology, spent time as tutor to Alexander (the future Alexander the Great), son of Philip the Great, King of Macedon, and returned to Athens, where he taught at the Lyceum, creating his own distinctive school of philosophy. The Lyceum already existed as a school, but Aristotle gave it a firm basis, using it as the centre of his own activities in learning. It was destroyed in 86BC by Sulla (a fierce Roman General and Statesman), and, unlike the Academy, was not revived as a centre of learning. Its remains, remarkably well-preserved, were discovered in 1996.

Aristotle was tutor to Alexander the Great

Aristotle suffers a little compared with Plato as his work is not so well preserved. Plato's dialogues have come down to us virtually intact. Most of Aristotle's works, with the exception of the logical writings, known as the *Organon*, would be lost to Western philosophy until the twelfth and thirteenth centuries. After Aristotle's death, his disciples edited his lecture notes into the books we have today. The manuscripts went through various adventures, finding their way to the Middle East, where they would become central to Arabic scholarship. Only the *Organon* (*Categories*, *On Interpretation*, *Prior Analytics*, *Posterior Analytics*, *Topics* and *Sophistical Refutations*) were known about in Western Europe, mainly through commentaries by Boethius and Porphyry. Manuscripts, together with commentaries by Arabic scholars, returned to Western Europe during the Crusades and the reconquest of Spain.

Key person

Plato (c.427–347BC): Pupil of Socrates. Created the Academy c.387BC and developed the ideas of Socrates into his own distinctive philosophy, developed in a series of dialogues still central to philosophical discussion.

2 The philosophical views of Aristotle

Key terms

Empiricist One who believes all knowledge is ultimately based on sense experience.
Per genus et per differentia (Latin – through type and difference): Aristotle's method for defining things.

(a) Plato's rationalism versus Aristotle's empiriasm

In looking at Aristotle we find a very different approach to philosophy from that of Plato. Perhaps Aristotle can be described as the first **Empiricist**. He did not look to another realm for an understanding of our existence. Instead, he explored the world and found understanding through a detailed examination of all we find around us.

His method is known as *per genus et per differentia*, meaning *by type and by difference*. Suppose I look at a guinea pig. I would first learn by seeing what kind of animal it is. In this case, it is a kind of rodent. This would establish its type or genus. Then, comparing how it differs from other rodents, I would note the differences between the guinea pig and other rodents such as squirrels, marmots and rats. The more closely I examined these differences, the greater my knowledge would become. Not only would I learn more about the guinea pig, but my knowledge of the other rodents would increase through my study. This process of reflective categorisation would, for Aristotle, lead me to a closer understanding of the thing in itself.

Another difference from Plato was that we learn things in different ways. For Plato, there is one kind of awareness which he calls knowledge – knowledge of the Forms. This knowledge is strictly intellectual, the result of pure thought.

Aristotle's view is quite different. We are not 'remembering' things from the Realm of the Forms. Instead, we are taught things such as mathematics and learn, through practice, the skills of a musician or a great athlete. Notice the differences here. Plato thought education was drawing out of the mind knowledge that lay dormant within it. For Aristotle, knowledge is based on careful observations and reflection on what we have seen. We learn from the outside world, and our knowledge is not innate. This is why some put him firmly in the Empiricist camp. We should notice also that for him, knowledge is gained in more than the single way that Plato thought. We learn to play an instrument through practice. Just because I have theoretical knowledge about music, it does not follow that I know how to play an instrument. Knowing *how* to do something is, for Aristotle, as much knowledge as a theoretical point. I can know the fact of what mathematics is, but I can only learn how to be a mathematician through repeated practice. Some things are learned best by experience; others by practice, book-learning or being taught. The knowledge of an artist is different from that of a mathematician. It is interesting that Aristotle pointed out how infant prodigies all happened in certain disciplines, such as mathematics or music. They never happen in subjects such as politics or history, which require a different type of experience. Even today, when we hear of a nine-year-old achieving an astonishing number of grade As at A Level, the subjects seem invariably to be in the sciences or music, never in the humanities.

A good way of understanding these points is by thinking of what is arguably Aristotle's greatest discovery. He observed an eclipse of the Moon, watching the shadow make its way across the face of the Moon. Beginning with his observation, he reflected on what might cause the effect. He concluded that the shadow was that of the Earth, and that the shape of the shadow could be made only by a spherical object. Hence, he was able to demonstrate that the Earth was a sphere. This kind of knowledge could not be achieved by Platonic means, which would have meant meditating on what the Sun truly was. Instead, Aristotle observed nature, seeing the shadow of the Earth and thinking about it. This empirical method seems particularly useful for discovering the facts of the world.

Key quote

The pleasures arising from thinking and learning will make us think and learn all the more.
Artistotle, *Nicomachean Ethics*

Key questions

Is Aristotle's empiricism, based on sense experience, a more valuable way of understanding knowledge than Plato's rationalist theories about the Forms?

Why is Aristotle's methodology likely to provide different results from Plato's approach?

3 The four causes

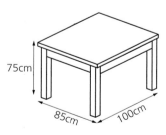

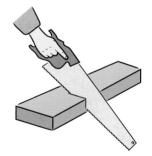

Material cause: the substance of which the thing is made. For example, wood, bricks, nails.

Formal cause: its design that shapes the formal concept. For example, the carpenter/designer's drawings.

Efficient cause: its maker or builder.

Final cause: its purpose or function. For example, a table, a house, a church.

Aristotle was very interested in the nature of the world. The basis of nature is *substance,* the basic matter of things. Any observation of the world reveals that things exist. Aristotle thinks this is self-evident. He uses it as a basic given fact, which requires no further justification. If we are aware of things, then we are aware that they change. They move, they become warm or cold, they may decay and die. Sometimes something quite new and different comes from a thing. From the seed comes the plant, from the caterpillar the butterfly, from the two parents a child. The scientific (and philosophical) question is how this change takes place. Change is – as Hume pointed out – a scientific curiosity. This changes to become that. We have no clear idea what exactly happens at the moment of change. The cause is not a cause until the moment the effect happens. 'Cause' has no meaning – in this sense – unless coupled with 'effect'. At the precise point when the effect happens, it is no longer a cause. It *was* a cause, but *is* a cause no longer. The mystery is what happens in that precise moment.

Hume would attempt to deal with the problem by suggesting that perhaps what we call 'cause and effect' was not much more than our way of explaining things, rather than actually being what happens in the world. Aristotle attempts something different – to demonstrate the nature of things and their causes.

We should notice that Aristotle's notion of cause is wider than what the word means to us. We say that '*x* causes *y*' in the sense that *x* brings about *y*. But Aristotle is trying to probe something slightly different. He wants to know not merely why *x* brings about *y*, but why both *x* and *y*. His enquiry is about not only why things change, but why they are what they are in themselves.

It is important to remember this, because, as we shall see in his theory of the four causes, his use of the word 'cause' is different from ours. Only the **efficient cause** is similar to our usual meaning.

An account of the four causes can be found in *Physics* II 3 and V 2.

(a) Material cause

Here Aristotle begins with the question: what is a thing made from, what material makes it what it is? Examples we might use could be the wood or plastic in a chair, the marble in a statue or the chemicals in a drink. Without the material, a thing could not be. Without the matter something is made from, there would be nothing. According to Aristotle:

> ... *that out of which a thing comes to exist and which continues, is called 'cause', for example, the bronze of the statue, the silver of the bowl ...*

Aristotle: Physics II, 3

(b) Formal cause

To understand this, it is helpful to think of it as the '*Form - al Cause*', that is the shape of a thing. A silver bowl is a silver bowl because it is in the form of a bowl – it would not be a bowl if it was not shaped that way. The silver would just be a lump of silver.

We need to be careful not to confuse Aristotle's idea of the form of a bowl or statue with the use of the word 'Form' by Plato. Here the idea of a **transcendent** single form, of which an individual thing is a more or less good copy, is rejected and replaced by an **immanent** form: the form is in the thing itself. This is a silver bowl because it is in the form of a bowl and not shaped to be something else. The form is not abstract. If there were no silver material, there would be no bowl, but it is only a bowl because it is shaped in the form of a bowl.

See Chapter 5 for a fuller discussion of Hume's 'cause and effect'.

Key terms

Efficient cause What brought it about? This could be a mechanical process or a human, biological, chemical or other process.

Material cause What is it made of? The material – the stuff – of the object.

Formal cause What form does it have? This is something immanent – the shape of the bowl is its form, but it only exists because the material of the bowl is present.

Key terms

Transcendent Beyond our everyday experience of the world.

Immanent Present in the world of our normal experience.

(c) Efficient cause

A statue does not just happen, it takes an *efficient* cause, which in this case would be the sculptor. To put this at its most simple: a statue is what it is because it is in the form of a statue made by something or someone. Something external brings about the effect. This is the closest we come to our normal, modern use of the word 'cause'. It is also worth noting that, for Aristotle, efficient causes are found in nature as well. A rose could be described as having natural processes as its efficient cause.

(d) Final cause

This is perhaps most difficult for us to understand. When we hear the word 'cause' we think of something that begins a process. We say that a cause cannot happen before an effect. Effects *follow* causes.

But Aristotle thought differently. For him, the *purpose* for which something exists is a cause, the *final cause*. The maker of the bowl creates it for a purpose, to be a decoration, to hold plants or fruit. The bowl is made for the sake of its use.

For Aristotle, this is true for everything. We can understand that someone will make things for a reason, because humans have purposes and we do things (generally) for reasons. I listen to music in order to relax. I make a cake to be eaten, a painting to be sold, to hang on a wall. But Aristotle goes much further. He assumes that nature is **purposive**.

Any theory, such as Aristotle's view of reality, which bases its judgements on purpose, is called a *teleological theory*, from the Greek *telos*. The term is used here in relation to Aristotle's theory of nature, but it could equally be applied to his ethics, where the goal is to be a fulfilled person.

Aristotle believed that everything in nature has a purpose and that if we examine the human body we would find a purpose for each of its parts. If I had no feet, my ankles would wear down and I would find it difficult to balance. If I had no eyebrows, sweat would get in my eyes. Given this belief, it is easy to see why he would argue that it is a natural jump to believe that each person also has a purpose. In his *Nicomachean Ethics,* Aristotle uses the concept of final cause to argue that humans have a purpose. For him, a good person is one who fulfils her purpose well. He notes that a good horse is good at being a horse. In the same way, when we describe someone as a good flautist, he is someone who plays the flute well. But there are some people we call 'good' in an unqualified way, not because they are good *at* something (after all, a good flautist might be a bad man), but because we see them as good in themselves. They are good at being people.

Even non-human things, he believes, have purposes. Hence, nature as a whole also has a purpose. Trees, leaves, animals, stones, all exist for a purpose.

Key terms

Purposive Assumes that something has a goal and reason for being.
Final cause What is a thing's purpose? Not a cause in the modern sense, but the reason something exists – its goal.
Teleology A term used to describe any theory in which everything is related to its goal or purpose. *Telos* is the Greek word for goal or target.

Key question

In what ways are Aristotle's ideas of causation different from modern ideas?

4 The Prime Mover

If everything in the universe has a purpose, it would then follow, by analogy with his assumption that if every part of the human person has a purpose, then the person as a whole has a purpose that: the universe has a purpose – a final cause.

Key term

Prime Mover Aristotle's God, indifferent to the universe, contemplating his own perfection, creates motion by drawing all things to himself as ultimate final cause. This concept is particular to Aristotle, for whom the Prime Mover is an attracter, and is not to be confused with Aquinas, for whom the Prime Mover is also a creator. The two versions of the same term therefore mean something different.

Key question

In what ways is Aristotle's God different from the idea of God found in religions such as Judaism, Islam or Christianity?

For Aristotle, this final cause is God.

Here we need to be careful not to envision the kind of God that the Abrahamic religions have given us. Aristotle's beliefs are quite different.

Aristotle did believe that God was 'perfect' and 'everlasting'. For him, God is 'everlasting' in the sense that God and the world are co-eternal. He did not think that the universe had a beginning. Aristotle's God is a completely transcendent God and not the immanent God the Abrahamic religions believe in. So, for Aristotle, petitionary prayer would be redundant. His God is not listening as he is not interested in the world. For Aristotle, 'perfection' in this context means that the only thing worthy of contemplation by a perfect being is perfect being. Perfect thought requires a perfect object of thought. Therefore this God would only contemplate himself. This means that this God, who is not interested in anything else, will spend eternity contemplating his own wonderful being.

So what, then, is Aristotle's understanding of God's relationship with the world? God's relationship with the Earth is as final cause: as 'purpose' or 'goal'. The key word in understanding Aristotle's view on motion is 'change'. In the *Physics*, he defines motion as more than simply something moving from place to place, as when I say I have moved from London to Paris. It includes any kind of change, such as becoming cool or warm or growing older. This is the idea that motion is more than someone hitting a hockey ball with a stick or competing in a heptathlon. When a girl becomes a woman, she has moved from one state to another. Or a piece of wood in a fire moves from one state to another as it burns.

The goal or final cause of the universe may be compared with a cat being attracted to a saucer of milk. We need to be a little careful here. When we speak of someone 'bringing something about', we think in terms of a conscious action. For Aristotle, God attracts by his nature, not because he is interested in things outside himself. Aristotle's God happens to attract, but there is no consciousness in the attraction, any more than the saucer of milk has any awareness of attracting the cat. It just happens to do so.

For Aristotle, the universe does not have an efficient cause. Being eternal, it has no beginning and, if you like, just is. It is there and needs no further explanation. The effect of the Prime Mover is therefore not as creator, but rather it should be understood as something which creates movement and change by exercising a 'pull' on things. If a cart is pulled with sufficient force, it moves. The Prime Mover exercises this pulling power, because it is so powerful, but it does not do so by any act of thought, but rather because the final cause of things is to seek their own perfection.

This concept is often, and perhaps more helpfully, referred to as the Unmoved Mover. This helps to avoid confusion with Aquinas, who, as we

Key person

St Thomas Aquinas (c.1225–74): Dominican friar, perhaps the greatest medieval philosopher, of unparalleled industry. At the forefront of attempts to rethink existing philosophical and theological thought in the light of the Aristotelian revival. Best known for his *Summa Theologica*, *Summa Contra Gentiles* and dozens of other works.

shall see in Chapter 5, uses the term Prime Mover to refer to the one who begins things, who deliberately creates the world from nothing, consciously putting things into motion. It is essential not to confuse the idea of Prime Mover in Aristotle with that in Aquinas.

5 The Prime Mover and Plato's Form of the Good

Although Aristotle was inspired by Plato, and often reflects on that inspiration, as we have seen, he was often to differ from his master. There are few similarities between Plato's Form of the Good and Aristotle's Prime Mover. Neither is directly or personally concerned with the world, and neither created it.

It is not clear – Plato does not tell us – whether the Form of the Good has consciousness of any description. Aristotle's Prime Mover is supremely conscious, but its mental activity is entirely concerned with meditation on its own wonderful nature.

It might be argued that each is assumed to exist in order just to explain why certain things occur in the world. The Form of the Good seems to be a hypothesis to explain what things like goodness 'really' is, to find something permanent in a world of change, while Aristotle derives his Prime Mover to provide his own explanation of change, the problem that had worried Plato (and Heraclitus) in the first place. Plato's Form of the Good seems to provide a *refuge* from the uncertainties of change, while Aristotle's Prime Mover seeks to *explain* them.

But it does not follow that because something seems to fill a gap in a theory, or to explain a theory, that it is necessarily the right solution.

6 Objections to Aristotle's theories

(a) Scientific objections

It would be too easy to use an argument from the modern era against Aristotle's theories. It is certainly true that advances in modern science cast doubts on many aspects of his theory of the four causes.

Aristotle had no access to modern devices such as the microscope or even the magnifying glass. He was attempting astronomy with no telescope, and attempting to analyse the chemistry of things without a laboratory, pure chemicals or heatproof test-tubes in which to heat them. Nevertheless, it is important not to denigrate Aristotle's insights. He recognised, perhaps more fully than anyone of his time, the need not only to be careful in our observations of phenomena, but to find appropriate ways of recording, analysing and sorting the information discovered. This is why we find his account of learning and reflection *per genus et per differentia* so valuable. They were rich in possibilities and provided a groundwork for future debate, on which modern science could build.

(b) Philosophical objections

Philosophical objections to Aristotle's theory are significant, and there are good reasons to doubt the assumptions on which he works. Important objections are:

1 Aristotle's assumptions about efficient cause may be questioned. Aristotle gives the name *efficient cause* to that which brings about a change in things. But it is a mistake often made by people to think that because they have *named* something that they have therefore *explained* it. Something brings about a change, and we call that 'efficient cause', but we know no more than that something brought about the change in the first place, which is where we began. Aristotle's notion of 'efficient cause' does not tell us *what* has happened, only that something *has happened*. The term is used to cover such a wide range of changes, natural, human-made, chemical, physical, biological, those the result of unthinking processes and those determined by thought, that it seems too broad to be informative in any significant way.

2 Questions may be asked about Aristotle's notion of *purpose*. The normal use of the word 'purpose' is to describe a mental intention. People have purposes – that is, they have identified a future state of affairs that they wish to achieve. When I make a cake, I do so having chosen a future state of affairs in which the cake exists to be eaten. Minds have purposes, but do inanimate things? I may have a purpose for the flour, eggs, milk, raisins and icing sugar, but they surely, not being sensate, have no intentions or purposes. Flour has purpose only because we have purposes for which it could be used. In itself, it is just flour, and it is only flour because we chose to grow wheat and turn it into flour. It seems difficult to argue that it has purpose as a natural thing. We are seeing a thing *as having* purpose, but it does not follow that, in itself, it has purpose.

3 The **fallacy of composition** is an error in reasoning. It is the assumption that what is true of the part is true of the whole. Even if it were true that every part of the human body had a purpose, it would not follow that the person as a whole has a purpose. Modern anatomy suggests that not all parts of the body do indeed have a purpose. The appendix may have had a purpose in the past, but it does not seem to have a purpose now. Even more obviously, what is the purpose of a nipple in a male of the species?

4 In the case of the universe, it is even more difficult to assume that it has a purpose. It is not evident that even the parts have a purpose. The universe seems filled with rocky lumps and expanses that serve no end, and fragments that whirl about doing no particular good for anything. Evolution on Earth suggests random and not purposive generation, growth and destruction of species. Many scientists have described evolution as 'blind'. It happens, but does not intend, has no purpose, to go anywhere. Philosophically, questions have been asked about whether it could ever be appropriate to see the universe as purposive. Existentialism, as a philosophical movement, has always denied that the universe has any purpose. Only humans have purposes: the universe just exists. The only meaning it has is the meaning I choose to give it. Outside the Existentialist tradition, other philosophers have seen no reason to assume purpose. Famously during his radio debate in 1948, Bertrand Russell said '... I should say the universe is just there, and that's all.' This view suggests that thinkers like Aristotle – and later Aquinas – are finding purpose where it does not exist.

5 Aristotle uses the idea of the Prime Mover to explain motion and change in the world. But this assumes that there is one, single reason for motion

Key term

Fallacy of composition The error of thinking that what is true of the part is true of the whole. Just because all humans have mothers, it does not follow that humankind as a whole has a mother.

For a profile of Copleston, see Chapter 5.

and change. If we argue that there are many reasons and causes for change, then it is difficult to see how one Prime Mover can be assumed to be the cause of all. If there are many possible causes of change, there seems to be no reason to jump from that to a single explanation.

6 The Big Bang theory and much of modern cosmology would cast serious doubt on a god who brings the world into motion by attracting it to himself. Instead, we are presented with a violent beginning of an ever-expanding universe which some cosmologists would argue has no need for any kind of god.

7 Religiously, it is also possible to criticise the idea of the Prime Mover. Aristotle's god is not the god of the Abrahamic religions. For Jews, Muslims and Christians, God cares supremely about the universe he created and with which he interacts. The way the world is matters. He desires good, and is not indifferent to it or to the world's suffering. Above all, he created the world. The world does not have purpose in itself, as Aristotle assumed, but the believer asserts that God has purpose for the universe, as an action of the divine mind. There would be no point in praying to Aristotle's god, and an indifferent and distant body seems worthy neither of worship nor belief.

7 Conclusions

If Aristotle's views, though interesting, are so flawed, why should we pay attention to them? Obviously, his arguments are an interesting example of a brave attempt to make sense of a complex world. It is also interesting to see this founder of scientific method attempting to make sense of hard questions, and few are harder than the nature of cause. But perhaps most significant is the influence of Aristotle's ideas. When we study Aquinas, we find, for example in his teleological argument for the existence of God, that he adopts Aristotle's notion of the purposiveness of the universe. Many later assumptions in ethics, such as in some versions of natural law theory, have assumed that there is a proper purpose for human life, a purpose which can be determined by human reason.

Study advice

When studying Aristotle, it is important to be clear about major points. Reading will help to reinforce these, but here as elsewhere, such reading must be reflective. Do not just learn about the four causes, but really think about them. Develop your own examples for the different kinds of causes. Examiners are more impressed by material that has clearly come from reflection than learned lists. Work through your ideas on whether or not there are better explanations for the nature of the universe than those put forward by Aristotle.

Be careful not to fall into the trap of confusing the Prime Mover of Aristotle with that of Aquinas. Aristotle's god is not a creator or initiator. Remember that for Aristotle the universe was without beginning, while for Aquinas, as a matter of faith, it was made by God. People sometimes try to Christianise Aristotle. To do so is anachronistic and leads the student into misrepresenting the subtleties of his thought.

Summary diagram: Aristotle

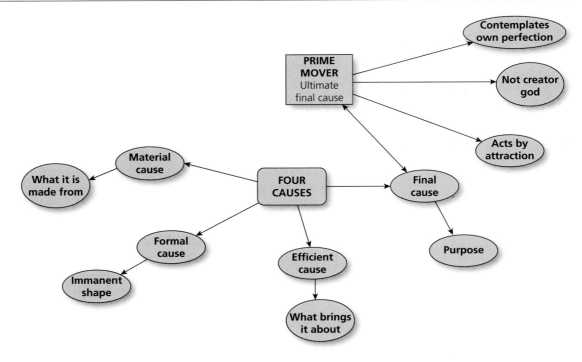

Revision advice

There is not too much material to memorise in the current chapter. Even so, it is important to remember that, as in the last chapter, it is necessary to be selective, especially about objections to Aristotle's theories. Quite a few are listed here. For essay purposes, make sure that you can write confidently about three or four of the objections. There is no need to know them all. But what you learn matters because it is used again in relation to Aquinas on the existence of God, and in some versions of ethical theory, especially of natural law. Being clear about Aristotle will prove both illuminating and helpful.

Can you give brief definitions of:
- material cause
- formal cause
- efficient cause
- final cause
- Prime Mover?

Can you explain:
- how Aristotle's theory of formal cause differs from Plato's theory of the Forms
- how the four causes interrelate
- the connection between final cause and the Prime Mover
- how Aristotle's concept of god differs from that of Aquinas?

Can you give arguments for and against:
- Aristotle's methodology
- his theory of efficient cause
- final cause
- the Prime Mover?

Sample question and guidance

'Aristotle's theory of the four causes explains nothing.' Discuss.

A question like this is very common. It is designed to encourage you to think about what Aristotle's theory actually is but also about whether it is helpful in practice. It is important always to remember that the test of a theory is practice, so you would need to think of examples to illustrate how the theory might or might not have explanatory power.

When an essay such as this is set, it does not mean that the question writer necessarily agrees – or disagrees – with the statement to be discussed. Nor do examiners require a particular answer. They want to know *whether* you agree or disagree, but more importantly, your reasoning in arriving at the conclusions you reach. Make sure you do reach a conclusion. This does not have to be a straight yes or no answer, as you might think the theory has some value but is not wholly satisfactory.

In this essay, it is important to make sure you know and can explain the theory. Do not just refer to it, but demonstrate your knowledge so your understanding can be assessed. Give examples to illustrate the theory and your arguments about it.

A danger in this type of essay is to write just about one aspect of the problem, such as Aristotle's assumptions about the universe as purposive and everything having a final cause, and to ignore others. You might usefully consider whether he needs to postulate a Prime Mover, whether his god is convincing, as well as any issues with other claims, such as his treatment of the efficient cause. You may not have time to develop everything in the same depth, but it is good to demonstrate awareness that there are other issues.

Further essay questions

To what extent has modern cosmology made Aristotle's views on the universe redundant?

'Aristotle's Prime Mover is an unconvincing construction to fill a hole in his theory.' Discuss.

'Aristotle's understanding of the world is more convincing than that of Plato.' Discuss.

Going further

For further reading, Jonathan Barnes: *Aristotle: A Very Short Introduction* (Oxford University Press, 2000) may be recommended with confidence. The literature on Aristotle is extensive, but it is useful, here as elsewhere to take a little time to read some of his original works. These do not have the fluency of Plato's dialogues, as they are in note-form, but they are rewarding to consider and digest. Book 1 of *Nicomachean Ethics* is a good place to start, as Aristotle says much about his philosophical and scientific method. The *Physics* may also be read, perhaps by concentrating on Book II. There are various translations online and Aristotle's complete works are available to read on electronic devices, often with helpful notes. Penguin translations are excellent, largely because of excellent and informative notes, though not all titles are currently available. Perhaps the best book in its field is Mariska Leunissen: *Explanation and Teleology in Aristotle's Science of Nature* (Cambridge University Press, 2015), but it is very dense. A very simple and clear – and brief – guide may be found in *Aristotle in Plain and Simple English,* independently published by Bookcaps (2012).

Chapter 4

Soul, mind and body

1 Introduction

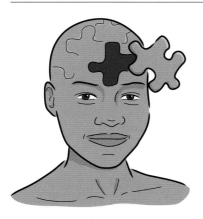

Chapter checklist

The chapter begins with a discussion of the problems of deciding what makes a person 'me'. It then analyses dualism and monism as concepts. It discusses arguments from Plato and Aristotle, then studies Aquinas' and Descartes' substance dualism. It describes Gilbert Ryle's criticisms of substance dualism and looks at them within an analytic framework. The chapter then outlines views of Hick and Anscombe. It discusses Materialism as represented by Dawkins and Skinner. In the conclusions it provides a reminder of the way in which issues remain open.

One of the most important philosophical questions is about what makes a human being. I have a vivid consciousness of myself – at least when awake – and yet I remain something of a puzzle to myself. I look at a hand I call mine and wonder in what sense it is *me*. My consciousness is experienced as somehow and somewhere behind my eyes, and, yet, I feel pain when my hand is hurt.

(a) 'Am I my body?'

Think about that sentence: 'I feel pain when my hand is hurt.' The grammar of the sentence seems to separate the 'I' who has the pain from both my hand and the pain. 'My hand' sounds like a possession, like 'my house'. But is my hand part of what I *have*, or is it part of what I *am*? If I say that the hand is part of what I am, part of what is me, I seem to be saying something useful and true: that *I* am the total sum of what makes up me, hands, brain, hair and all.

Now suppose I have an accident and my leg has to be amputated. My body is less than it was, but am *I* any less 'me'? After all, I am still as conscious as I was, as capable of thought, feeling, memory as I ever was. I might even say I have been enriched by the experience of my accident and injury. This implies that there is now more of me than there was, even though minus a limb. If I suddenly decide to indulge in a six-month eating and drinking spree, I might say there is more of me than there was, by several stones. But I would be reluctant to say that I am more fully myself, even though there is more of me. In my spirits I might actually feel diminished by having become such a glutton. These considerations, contrary to those in the last paragraph, suggest that the real me is not the totality of my body and feelings but a separate thing – my consciousness.

(b) 'Am I my consciousness?'

But that in turn creates problems. Suppose I see a photograph of myself as a baby. I may tell someone, 'That is me at six months old', but I have no recollection of that *me* or my consciousness at that point. The only connection between that baby and the 'me' I experience now is an awareness, largely based on what others have told me, that there is a spatial continuity between that child and me. It is a connectedness that comes from never having at any point disappeared out of the body and appeared unconnectedly somewhere else. But the body of the baby in the photograph has changed almost beyond recognition into what is now the adult 'me'. Original cells have died and been sloughed off by my body. New cells have grown, memories and tastes have changed. Is the current 'me' more truly 'me' than that baby? After all, I hope I have become a little more mature in the intervening decades.

But suppose I develop dementia? My memory would largely disappear. My tastes and character would be other than they now are, but would the person I became be any less 'me'? Sometimes we speak of someone 'not being all there' or 'forgetting himself'. There would be profound moral issues if I were to argue that the person with dementia is less than a full human being.

(c) 'The mind–body question'

There is a famous philosophical question which needs also to be considered in defining 'me'. The 'mind–body' question asks about the relationship between body and mind. If we cut open a body, we find the brain to be just another organ of the body. To be sure, it is a complex organ, but to all intents it is a physical greyish mass. What is the connection between that grey, physical mass, and the vividness of conscious thought? It seems more than merely mechanical, though some have attempted to see the connection in purely physical terms.

Given these difficulties, what am *I*? It has been traditional to see the human as made up of body and soul, with 'soul' somehow as the real me. Many have argued that in afterlife beliefs, the soul is the 'real me' that will live on when my body is dust or ashes. This is something very ancient. Prehistoric tombs, to say nothing of the burial rites of the Egyptians, speak eloquently of the belief in the soul and its eternal destiny. But not everyone has taken this view. There are those who take a strictly materialist view of the person. There is no 'me' beyond and above the meat, bones, muscle and nervous system of my body.

Key question

What do I need for me to be myself?

2 Is the soul a thing?

Before we examine individual theories, we need to consider what we might be talking about when we talk about the soul. Most of us would have little difficulty in describing our bodies as things – bodies take up space, last in time and have physical characteristics. Having these qualities is what we generally mean by describing something as a thing.

But what, precisely, would a soul be? Is it a kind of special object, perhaps a spiritual 'substance'? As we shall see, some philosophers argue that it is. Many religious believers do think of the soul in this way, as a thing in itself.

But others, including many religious thinkers, argue that looking at the soul in this way is a mistake. Certainly we have the noun 'soul' and we may think of the noun as naming some *thing*. It is a problem in philosophy that, as we saw with Plato's forms, we can be tempted to go from thinking we have a name for something to searching for the being that goes with the name. But a name can be fictitious or metaphorical, or it may draw our attention to a specific quality of something. Some philosophers argue that to refer to the soul is not to name some special substance but to draw our attention to the spiritual aspect of the whole person.

> **Key person**
>
> **Socrates** (*c.*469–399BC): Sometimes called the Father of Philosophy, he was concerned with the question of the nature of the good life. He taught in Athens, gathering a group of young disciples, including Plato. He wrote nothing and was executed in 399BC for mocking the gods and corrupting the youth of Athens.

3 Plato and the soul

Plato

Plato was deeply influenced by Pythagorean thought. This emphasised the distinction between the spiritual soul (psyche) and the material body. We can all see in the world around us how things decay. Nothing material is permanent. Plants and animals grow and die, things we make fall apart or decay in other ways. Great works of art may be destroyed. There is no permanence in the visible world of things.

Key question

Is this concept of the soul convincing? What assumptions does it make?

Key term

Psyche Greek term, still used today, which can be used interchangeably for 'mind' or 'soul'.

Plato sought something permanent and certain. If permanence cannot be found in this visible, material world, then it must exist in the realm of the spiritual. From this, he adopted the idea of the soul as immortal. The soul's eternity lies in itself. It is a simple substance and thus cannot be destroyed. To be destroyed is to be broken to bits: as something simple, the soul has no parts into which it can be broken. It was not created: its immortality lies in having neither beginning nor end.

This view of the soul creates a problem. If my soul existed before my current life, and continues after my death, where has it been, and where will it go? In answer to this question, Plato devised his Theory of the Forms.

Pythagoreans believed that people's souls move from one body to another, so that when my body dies, my soul will move to inhabit another body and have no memory of its life in my body.

In the *Phaedo*, which dramatises the death of Socrates, Plato shows Socrates comparing his eternal soul with his body, arguing that as the soul is eternal, he has nothing to fear from death:

> ... the soul is in the very likeness of the divine, and immortal, and intelligible, and uniform, and indissoluble, and unchangeable; and the body is in the very likeness of the human, and mortal, and unintelligible, and multiform, and dissoluble, and changeable.

> Plato: *Phaedo* (Jowett translation)

(a) The relationship of body and soul in Plato

A difficulty with Plato's theory – as with any form of substance dualism – is the question of how the spiritual body interacts with the material body. It is not a question Plato answers with any clarity. Plato's soul ultimately desires to get out of the inferior body in which it is trapped. Yet we need to do things as material beings, such as washing, feeding ourselves and so on. To suggest this is a lesser or more imperfect thing than contemplating the Form of the Good does not answer the question of *how* we direct our limbs to move as they do, in accord with our thoughts, to do what we want. Plato appears uninterested in establishing the link: he seems just to assume it, rather as he assumes that if our minds know the right things to do, then somehow the whole person will do it.

The problem seems to be that he falls into a common philosophical problem, which is assuming that *reasons* are *causes*. When we speak, we use sentences such as 'I am giving you a present because I like you.' But is 'I like you', the *cause* of my action, or just the *reason* for it? A reason is the result of a thought, a mental happening. The *cause* of my action seems to be based on a conscious decision to act on my reason: to get my body to do something about it. The action seems a separate process from any reasoning about it. Plato seems not to make this separation between the reasoning and the action, which perhaps enables us to understand why he believed that if only we knew the right action to take, we would be bound to do it.

For Plato, death is nothing to fear, as it is a shaking off of the temporary shell of the body, and – at least for philosophers who yearn continually for things in their true nature – a chance to return to the pure essence of things.

(b) Plato and Christianity

It should be noted that Plato's view is not a Christian view. For Plato, the soul is without beginning. For the Christian, God creates each soul anew, probably at conception. There have been different views on this. For Plato, the soul is eternal by nature. Nothing can destroy it, because of the kind of thing it is – a simple substance. Christians would argue that to think in this way would be to deny the omnipotence of God. To say nothing can destroy a soul would be to deny the dependence of all existence on God. A Christian believes that any immortality the soul might have would be a gift from God, not something which the soul has by right.

But we should not underestimate the deep influence of Plato in later thought, not only Christian thought. The contrast between a permanent spiritual world of realities, such as Plato's Forms and the temporary and unsatisfactory physical realm is a notion that lies very deeply in our culture. It is found from some of the early Christians to many New Age ideas in circulation today, for example, the School of Economic Science or Scientology. It is easy to see that Plato's view: soul = good / body = not-so-good could be simplified by others into a bald notion of 'soul = good' / 'body = bad'. This is why so many early Christians struggled with the concept of Christ as incarnated and with the concept of *bodily* resurrection. Even today, there are believers who talk about God as saving their souls, or heaven as a place for souls, skipping over what the creeds (statements of faith) mean by the resurrection of the dead.

Key term

Nicene Creed The statement of faith, associated with the Council of Nicea, 325AD, defining the basic beliefs of Catholic Christian belief. It remains an important part of the Sunday Mass, and is used more widely across the Christian denominations.

Key question

Why is it important to think that God created more than just the spiritual?

4 Aristotle and the soul

Aristotle's approach was very different from that of Plato. Remember his notion of the four causes. One of these is the formal cause, that which gives something its shape and nature. The table is a table because it is in the form of a table. In the same way, for Aristotle, I am a person because my body is animated by the soul which gives it life; the soul is the formal cause of the body. Otherwise, I am just matter – bones, meat, gristle and so on – the material cause.

For Aristotle, the soul is not a simple, immortal substance as it was for Plato. When the light goes out and the soul dies, I go back to being a lump of matter. There is no person left. The idea that the soul goes to another world is not part of Aristotle's understanding. He speculates about whether reason in some sense might live on, but he does not believe in personal survival after death. Aristotle is more than a materialist. The soul is not reducible to physics and chemistry. Matter needs the soul to animate it. But his dualism is not the complete separation of types that we find in Plato.

Aristotle's version of the soul is obviously very different from that of Plato. But there are also some similarities. He derives from Plato an idea that he develops in more detail, the belief that the soul has three elements:

- the *vegetative* soul, shared with all living things, including plants
- the *appetitive* soul, in which we find passions and appetites, such as hunger, thirst and sexual desire as well as emotions such as anger, envy or sadness
- the *intellectual soul*, which is rational and directive – it thinks about things and decides the actions we might take. It also includes the powers of memory and reflection on our past and future.

The vegetative soul is found in all living things, including plants. The appetitive soul is just in animals and humans. The intellectual soul belongs only to humans. Aristotle was fascinated by the workings of the human mind, returning repeatedly in his works to questions of psychology, often with immense insight.

(a) Aquinas and the legacy of Aristotle

St Thomas Aquinas, perhaps the greatest medieval philosopher, was at the forefront of those influenced by the Aristotelian revival of the twelfth and thirteenth centuries.

Aquinas tells us:

> ... the soul is defined as the first principle of life in living things: for we call living things 'animate,' [i.e. having a soul], and those things which have no life, 'inanimate.' ... it is the 'first' principle of life ... Now, though a body may be a principle of life, or a living thing, as the heart is a principle of life in an animal, yet nothing bodily can be the **first** principle of life. It is clear that to be a principle of life, or to be a living thing, does not belong to a body as a body; because, if that were the case, **every** body would be a living thing, or a principle of life. Of course, a body is able to be a living thing or even a principle of life, because it is a body. When it is a living body, it owes its life to some principle which is called its 'act'. Therefore the soul, which is the first principle of life, is not a body, but the act of a body; just as heat ... is not a body, but an act of a body.

Summa Theologica (S.T.) I, Q.75.a1.c.

We see how closely he follows Aristotle. He is not saying that the soul *is* me. It is the principle of life, as Aristotle argued. My life needs the body to be animated. He goes on to argue this more precisely:

> ... the human soul, which is called the 'intellect' or the 'mind', is something incorporeal and subsistent.

S.T. I, Q.75.a2.c.

It is not material and should be understood as the mind, not something separate from it. The body is necessary for me to be me:

> Just as it belongs to the notion of **this** particular man to be composed of **this** soul, of **this** flesh, and of **these** bones; so it belongs to the whole notion of man to be composed of soul, flesh, and bones ... Sensation is not the operation of the soul only. As, then, sensation is an operation of man [as a whole] ...

St Thomas Aquinas was heavily influenced by Aristotle

For a profile of Aquinas, see Chapter 3.

it is clear that man is not a soul only, but something composed of soul and body. Plato, because he thought that sensation was simply a function of the soul, was able to maintain that man was a soul making use of the body.

S.T. I, Q.75.a4.c.

Notice how Aquinas is very aware of the difference between his view and that of Plato. Aquinas' view is interestingly developed in various modern discussions, such as those found in G. E. M. Anscombe (see page 50).

5 Substance dualism

(a) Dualism and monism

As we have suggested, it has been normal for many to adopt a form of **dualism**. This is the view that we are made of two separate and different elements, a material body and a spiritual soul. If this is true, a problem remains of how the purely physical body can be influenced or directed by the spiritual soul. There appears to be some link. If my body is hurt, my mind feels it, just as it feels sensations of hunger and thirst when my body needs nourishment. And when I act on a thought I do so through my body.

The alternative view is **monism**. This is the view that we are simply a single being. This is sometimes expressed in the view that 'I am a body', rather than 'I have a body'. In this view, thinking is just something that human bodies do, just as the body of an amoeba splits into two new creatures. This view is not without problems. Amoebae split for physical and biological reasons. Human consciousness, with its qualities of imagination, artistic skill, memory, story-telling and philosophical skills, seems to have capacities which go well beyond those necessary for mere survival or continuation of the species, and which have no obvious biological function. A purely material account seems to struggle to explain such features. **Materialism** (see page 50) is a type of monism, but it is not the only possible type.

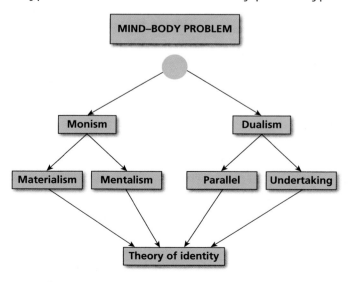

(b) Descartes and substance dualism

René Descartes represents perhaps the most extreme form of **substance dualism**. His views of the soul may be found in both *Meditations* (1641) and a less well-known work, *The Passions of the Soul* (1649). His view of the soul and its relationship with the body represented a dualism as radical as that of Plato. The Aristotelian view, in which the soul was the principle of life, is ignored. This is unsurprising, given Descartes' methods. He begins his philosophical work by asking whether there is any knowledge so certain that no one may doubt it. He notes how sense experience may be mistaken, and speculates about whether his senses might be misled by some malicious demon. This might mean that the material world and even his body might be an illusion. He concludes that there is only one certain piece of knowledge, at least, the *cogito*. This is usually rendered as 'I think, therefore I am.' His method leads to a natural division between body and spirit. The method he has adopted leads to a privileging of the mental and the *a priori* over the doubtable material of things separate from the mind. The body and soul are wholly separate substances. In the *Meditations on First Philosophy*, he argues:

> There is a very great difference between a mind and a body, because a body is by nature divisible, but the mind is not. Clearly, when I think about the mind, that is, of myself as far as I am a thing that thinks, I am not aware of any parts in me – that is, I understand myself to be one whole person. Although the whole mind seems united to the whole body, if a foot, or an arm, or another limb were amputated from my body, nothing would be taken from my mind. Mental faculties, such as 'willing', 'sensing', 'understanding' cannot be called its 'parts', because it is always the same mind that wills, senses or understands. But any corporeal or physically extended thing I can think of, I can easily think of as divided into parts … This reasoning alone would be enough to teach me that the mind is wholly different from the body.

Meditation VI

This approach creates various difficulties. If the mind is simply spiritual and we have bodies which are non-spiritual and material, how do they interconnect? How does my thought of this sentence connect with the working of my hands in typing this sentence? When Descartes writes about the body, he conceives of it in almost mechanical terms, with muscles acting like ropes and cables (In *Meditation VI, 17*, this point is made very specifically).

In *The Passions of the Soul*, Descartes tries to explain the connection by suggesting that:

> There is a little gland in the brain where the soul exercises its functions more particularly than in the other parts of the body.

In his *Treatise on Man*, he claims that the pineal gland is the seat of the imagination and common sense. Here it becomes (perhaps) the link between body and soul. This suggestion, and it is no more than that, is problematic. Saying where the link is, in a physical sense, tells us nothing at all about how the link is made. The conversion of the mental into the physical remains the unexplained point.

René Descartes

6 Other views on the mind–body question

Gilbert Ryle

(a) Gilbert Ryle

> … *Both Idealism and Materialism are answers to an improper question. The 'reduction' of the material world to mental processes and states, as well as the 'reduction' of mental states and processes to physical states and processes, presupposes the legitimacy of the disjunction 'Either there exist minds or there exist bodies (but not both)'. It would be like saying, 'either she bought a left-hand and right-hand glove or she bought a pair of gloves (but not both)'.*

Gilbert Ryle: *The Concept of Mind* (1963), pp. 23–24

Gilbert Ryle (1900–76) was one of the great analytic philosophers of the twentieth century. His influence on others, such as A. J. Ayer, has lasting significance. His best-known work is *The Concept of Mind* (University of Chicago Press, 1949). It is famous for its attempts to refute substance dualism as proposed by Descartes. Ryle used the term 'the ghost in the machine' to describe Descartes' concept of the mind. Descartes himself described – in *Meditation VI* – the mind as the pilot of the body, and the body itself as a sort of mechanism. So Ryle is, when using this description, quite close to Descartes' own language.

It is important to be clear about Ryle's project. As an analytic philosopher he is not attempting to create an alternative theory of the way things are, but is attempting to provide conceptual clarity. He often describes the role of the philosopher as similar to the cartographer who maps the territory but does not create it. It would be crudely inaccurate to label him a materialist, because he considered reductionism to the material to be mistaken. Rather, he saw his work as an exploration of the phenomenon of consciousness.

His complaint against Descartes is that he is guilty of **category error**. He meant assuming, incorrectly, that two terms (in this case 'mind' and 'matter') are of the same logical type, both names of things. They are not, even though sentences about mind and matter might look superficially similar (such as 'there are physical processes' and 'there are mental processes'). In the case of the pair of gloves, it would be an error to think of 'a pair of gloves' as something different from a matching left and right-hand glove. He illustrates his point with three justly famous examples:

1 Suppose a foreign visitor went to Cambridge to look at its sights. He is shown the different colleges, the Fitzwilliam Museum, the library, and so on. At the end of the tour, he then asks, 'But where is the University?' He is guilty of a category error because he assumes that the 'University' is something separate from and other than all those individual bits which collectively *are* the University.

2 A boy watches a military parade. He has been told that a Division is marching by. Someone points out to him different squadrons, platoons, batteries and so on. At the end he asks when the Division will arrive, unaware that all the units he has seen are collectively the Division.

3 A foreigner goes to his first game of cricket, having previously read a book about it. He is shown the stumps and the bails, the umpires, and the various fielding positions. Then he asks, 'But where is the team spirit?' This is a category error.

In the same way, Descartes is guilty of a category error because he assumes that sentences about causes, sensations or events must be *either* mental *or* physical. This presupposes an unjustified assumption that they cannot be both. To describe an action as mental is not to suggest that it is something different from what I as a whole do. When I think I shall stop work, *I* am thinking I shall stop work. To say 'my mind thinks I should stop work' does not mean the mysterious separate something is telling my body to stop work.

Ryle's argument is holistic, not a denial of the mental or saying that the mental is just material. His opposition is to the needless and improper – as he sees it – separation of the two. His philosophy is possibly monist but not materialist, though even to say he is 'monist' probably over-simplifies the issue.

Such a view would not be contrary to Christian or other religious thought. Aquinas, as we have seen, argued that 'my soul is not me'. In the analytic school, the devout Roman Catholic, Peter Geach (1916–2013) argued:

> It is a savage superstition to suppose that a man consists of two pieces, body and soul, which come apart at death; the superstition is not mended but rather aggravated by conceptual confusion, if the soul-piece is supposed to be immaterial. The genius of Plato and Descartes has given this superstition an undeservedly long lease of life; it gained some accidental support from Scriptural language, e.g. about flesh and spirit – accidental, because a Platonic–Cartesian reading of such passages is mistaken, as Scripture scholars now generally agree. In truth, a man *is* a sort of body, not a body *plus* an immaterial somewhat; for a man is an animal, and an animal with one kind of living body; and thinking is a vital activity of a man, not of any part of him, material or immaterial. The only tenable conception of the soul is the Aristotelian conception of the soul as the form, or actual organisation, of the living body...

Peter Geach: 'What Do We Think With', *God and the Soul* (2001), p. 38

Key person

Peter Geach (1916–2013): British philosopher, married Elizabeth Anscombe in 1941. They had seven children and both converted to Roman Catholicism. Professor of Logic at University of Leeds. Books include: *Logic Matters* (1972) and *God and the Soul* (1969).

Key question

Would the views of Geach and Ryle be acceptable to a religious person?

Reductionism The belief that everything can be reduced to statements about physical bodies.

Behaviourism The belief that all mental states are simply learned behaviours of bodies. To say that I feel sad or angry means that I am behaving sadly or angrily.

Key persons

John Hick (1922–2012): British philosopher of religion, based at the University of Birmingham. His major works include *Evil and the God of Love* (Macmillan, 1966), *Death and Eternal Life* (Collins, 1976), and *An Interpretation of Religion* (Macmillan, 1989). His views on religious pluralism became increasingly controversial.

G. E. M. (Elizabeth) Anscombe (1919–2002): She worked closely with Wittgenstein at Cambridge, subsequently becoming one of his executors. Appointed Professor of Philosophy at Oxford, she was prolific in a range of areas, including linguistic philosophy, ethics and philosophy of mind.

(b) John Hick

John Hick (1922–2012) approached the question in a similar way. He strongly opposes the Platonic view of the soul, as un-Christian, not least for assuming that the soul is immortal in itself. For Hick, as for Aquinas, 'my soul is not me'. His outlook is not dissimilar to that of Aristotle, and is often described as 'soft materialism'. We are our bodies, but those bodies have a spiritual dimension. There is no mind without matter. To be a person is to be a thinking material being. Thinking in this way is not **reductionist**. The mental depends on the body, but is more than simply a **behaviourist** reaction to stimuli. That we are necessarily material beings does not mean that we are *just* material beings.

Hick is very opposed to any approach which assumes that to die is something not to be feared. For Plato's Socrates, as the soul cannot die, death is simply like moving from one room to another. But for the Christian, to die is to be before God. He alone can bestow eternal life. It is something to be prepared for.

(c) G. E. M. Anscombe

In her essay 'Analytical Philosophy and the Spirituality of Man' (see G. E. M. Anscombe: *Human Life, Action and Ethics*, Imprint Academic, 2006, pp. 3–16), she considers the phenomenon of pointing. If I point at something, the mere action of the body is not the whole of its meaning. If I point at the king on a chessboard, my bodily action is what it is – a gesture. But the meaning of the gesture, that I am pointing out that it is this piece here, and not that bishop, or that I am indicating that it is this colour, or has this texture or design feature, cannot be indicated by that bodily gesture alone. The meaning and the significance could not be deduced from even the most complete physical description of my actions. A description of my bodily actions might fully describe *how* my body is working, but not *why* it is working. Just looking at the action of a body, in this case my pointing body, does not *explain* the action. For that, we need to have a description of the thought: 'I am pointing at the chess piece because ....'. But it is still my body that does the pointing: the action would be impossible if I were not a body. A disembodied soul could not point. It is my body that points. She argues that 'this bodily act is an act of man *qua* spirit', the act of a human as a whole.

7 Materialism

Materialism is the philosophical view that there exists only physical matter. In the case of human beings, this means that there is only flesh and blood, nerves and cells. This means that anything said about a person is absolutely reducible to sentences about physical processes. So, if I said that I intended to paint a painting, write a novel or go for a pint in the public house, each statement could be reduced to a statement about the behaviours of brain cells, neurons and electrical activity within the brain.

Some philosophers question whether every act of what we call consciousness is reducible in this way.

As we have seen, rejection of substance dualism does not entail materialism as a necessary consequence. Often those described as materialists turn out to be less materialist than they appear.

(a) Richard Dawkins

Richard Dawkins (b. 1941) is often cited as an example of a materialist thinker. Yet on analysis, his approach is much more subtle than crude reductionism. Unsurprisingly, he rejects any notion of the disembodied soul espoused by Plato and Descartes – and many religious believers. He finds no empirical evidence for such an entity and mocks religious believers for supporting such a bizarre notion. Nevertheless, he acknowledges the mystery of consciousness, while asserting his faith that it should be possible for scientific enquiry into DNA eventually to explain the phenomenon. To do so will be difficult as the phenomena of consciousness – imagination, scientific research, art and so on – are so various and do not always have obvious evolutionary value.

Dawkins makes an interesting distinction between what he calls *Soul One* and *Soul Two*. Soul One is the separate substance of much traditional thought. Dawkins rejects this notion as primitive superstition. Soul Two is intellectual and spiritual power, higher development of the moral faculties, feeling and imagination. Of course, these are rooted in the body and their precise nature is yet to be scientifically explained. The point, however, is that there is something to be explained.

(b) Behaviourism

Another type of materialism is behaviourism, which sees human thoughts as simply learned behaviours. Probably the best-known behaviourist was B. F. Skinner (1904–90). He believes that what we consider mental events are simply learned behaviours. The idea of a mental state separated from the body, in any sense, is a radical misunderstanding. Animals learn behaviours – are conditioned to particular behaviours – as we know from the study of Pavlov's dogs. For Skinner, mental acts are caused acts, explicable at a physical level. He says:

> The position can be stated as follows: what is felt or introspectively observed is not some nonphysical world of consciousness, mind, or mental life but the observer's own body. This does not mean … that introspection is a kind of psychological research, nor does it mean (and this is the heart of the argument) that what are felt or introspectively observed are the causes of the behavior. An organism behaves as it does because of its current structure, but most of this is out of reach of introspection. At the moment we must content ourselves, as the methodological behaviourist insists, with a person's genetic and environment histories. What are introspectively observed are certain collateral products of those histories.

B.F. Skinner: *About Behaviorism* (1974), p. 18

Skinner supported his arguments by much scientific work, especially experiments in relation to animal behaviour.

(c) Objections to behaviourism

Various philosophical objections have been made, perhaps most notably by Daniel C. Dennett (b. 1942), especially in his article 'Skinner Skinned'. Dennett argues that Skinner over-simplifies human consciousness, not

Key person

B. F. Skinner (1904–90): American behaviourist psychologist and thinker. Appointed Professor at Harvard in 1948 where he remained for the rest of his career. His behaviourism has been attacked as reductionist.

Key questions

Are purely materialist views capable of explaining human consciousness?

What is the difference between materialism and Ryle's position?

Key person

Daniel C. Dennett (b. 1942): American philosopher and cognitive scientist. Major figure in current philosophy of mind; Author of *Brainstorms* (1981), *Consciousness Explained* (1992) and many other works.

least because he assumes that what is true of the consciousness of a pigeon will apply also to humans. An animal want or desire may be explained as a learned behaviour. But, argues Dennett, the same is not true for the human. If I am asked why I am reading a book, simply saying it is a learned response misses the point. If I say, 'because I want to', I am providing an *explanation*. If I went further and said something such as 'I enjoy this author's books and I am interested in the period he writes about', I am taking my explanation even further. To reduce this to a learned behaviour misses the point. My reason for reading the book excludes certain other reasons. I am not reading the book to keep fit or to get rich, but for other chosen goals. Dennett argues that Skinner would be right only if my explanation stopped with the fact I had a desire. But human thinking moves beyond Skinner's 'basic theory':

> ... *Insofar as 'the basic analysis' proves anything, it proves that people are not like pigeons, that Skinner's unmasking explanations will not be forthcoming. Certainly if we discovered that people only handed over their wallets to robbers after being conditioned to do this, and, moreover, continued to hand over their wallets after the robber had shown his gun was empty, or when the robber was flanked by policemen, we would have to admit that Skinner had unmasked the pretenders; human beings would be little better than pigeons or wasps, and we would have to agree we had no freedom and dignity.*

Daniel C. Dennett: 'Skinner Skinned', *Brainstorms* (1978), p. 69

If Dennett is right, there is something more to human consciousness than something simply explicable as a material cause-and-effect. What that something is remains elusive.

8 Objections to theories and conclusions

Perhaps the most that can be said, after a review of some of the literature, is that we have a continuing mystery of the nature of soul, and what we mean by soul. The persistent danger is of simplification of a complex and difficult area. Even established assumptions may be challenged. For example, John Cottingham (b. 1943), perhaps the greatest contemporary Descartes scholar, has challenged traditional readings of Descartes as a dualist (see his *Cartesian Reflections*, Oxford University Press, 2008, especially Chapter 9). He argues instead that we are made up of body, soul and spirit. If we are made of two substances, mind and body, an area of human experience including passions, emotions and sensations cannot be straightforwardly reduced to either category.

Cottingham's point directs us to other considerations. There are no straightforwardly precise definitions of body and soul, mind, consciousness, and so on. Philosophers and theologians slide between one term and another. We might consider whether the type of answers thinkers have offered to these questions is shaped by the models chosen to create those responses. Plato's view is largely the consequence of his seeking certainty in an uncertain world and needing to posit a separate type of existence. Descartes' view flows from his model of enquiry, which begins with consciousness and contrasts it with the external world. Skinner is clearly basing his interpretation on animal experiments.

Study advice

Careful definition is an essential skill in all philosophy, but never more so than here. It is essential to be clear about concepts such as materialism or dualism. It is important also to be clear that just because someone does not endorse a particular view it does not follow that he or she holds the opposite. Someone opposed to substance dualism is not necessarily a materialist, as we have seen. Views on body and soul are more nuanced than simply cases of either/or.

As always, it is important to take time to think through issues carefully, wherever possible taking a little time to look at pieces of original texts. Sometimes the process of explanation by others can falsify original statements, through a kind of Chinese whispers or the desire to put a thinker into a neat category.

Summary diagram: Soul, mind and body

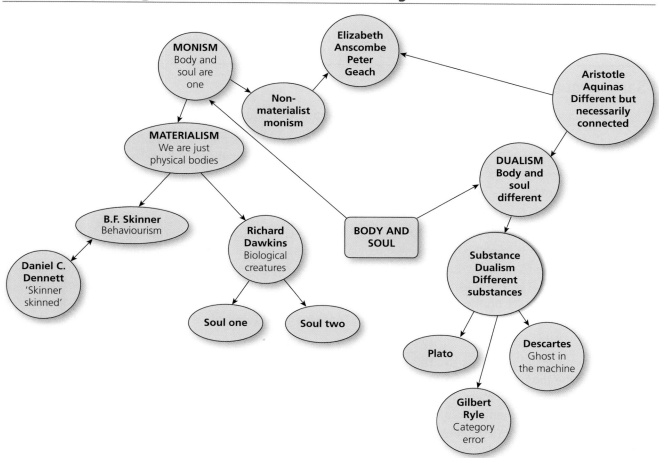

Make sure that you have a good understanding of the key philosophers mentioned in this chapter, reflecting on, and not merely learning, the arguments they have used. Think about your own views on the ideas explored in this chapter and beyond, thinking about whether views stated do justice to the richness of human experience as thinking creatures.

Can you give brief definitions of:
- monism
- dualism
- materialism
- substance dualism
- category error?

Can you explain:
- the differences between Plato and Aristotle on the nature of the soul
- Descartes' substance dualism
- Gilbert Ryle's reasons for rejecting substance dualism
- Richard Dawkins' theory of Soul One and Soul Two?

Can you give arguments for and against:
- Plato's theory of the soul
- Aquinas' notion that my soul is not me
- materialist ideas of the soul
- substance dualism?

Sample question and guidance

Assess whether substance dualism is a convincing approach to questions of body and soul.

This question is relatively straightforward, as long as you focus on substance dualism. If you mention other views of body and soul, this should be within the context of using them if you believe that another theory is more or less convincing than substance dualism. It should not be because you have learned those other theories and want to show that you have learned them. If you mention another theory, you must say specifically why it is relevant to the question.

Obviously, you will need to explain what substance dualism entails. Try to give both a definition and look at the arguments of those who have argued in favour of this view, probably Plato and Descartes. You might then find it fruitful to look at criticisms of these theories, perhaps drawing on the arguments of Aquinas, Anscombe, Geach, Ryle or Dawkins. It is unlikely that you will have time or space to develop each of these thinkers, so concentrate on the one or two whom you think most significant for your argument. There is no requirement to list everyone you have learned. There is a need to deploy the material you have selected effectively.

Notice the command word 'Assess'. This requires you to weigh up points, to *consider* arguments and not just to describe them, and to reach some sort of reasoned conclusion. Therefore, you should be commenting thoughtfully on each argument as you describe it, stating what you find stronger or weaker points, with reasons for your judgements as you work through the material. An essay should not read like a list of everything you have learned followed by a hasty judgement at the end. You must show you are reflecting on and weighing material as you work through relevant points.

Further essay questions:

To what extent is Plato's belief in a separate body and soul convincing?

'It makes more sense to say 'I am a body' than to say 'I have a body'.' Discuss.

'Religious faith demands belief in a separate body and soul.' Discuss.

Going further

The Religious Studies course is not a course in the Philosophy of Mind, but you should be familiar with those ideas which bear on the religious concept of the soul. If you have time, read the *Phaedo* of Plato. It is freely available online, or may be found in the Penguin Classic, *The Last Days of Socrates*. It is brief and clear, and reading this will also act as useful revision on Plato and the Forms. On Aristotle, his classic work on the soul is *De Anima*, but *Nichomachean Ethics*, Book I Chapter 13 and Book VI give a very good sketch of Aristotle's insights. Also look at *Meditation VI* of Descartes, and try to read Gilbert Ryle: *The Concept of Mind*, Chapter 1 (University of Chicago Press, 1949, Penguin, 2000). The latter is noted for its elegance and will remind you not to fall into the trap of seeing Ryle as a materialist.

Other books discussed in this chapter are:

- Dennett D. C. '*Skinner Skinned*', *Brainstorms* (Bradford Books, 1978).
- Dennett D. C. *Consciousness Explained* (Little Brown, 1992).
- Geach P. '*What Do We Think With*', *God and the Soul* (second edition, St. Augustine's Press, 2001).
- Ryle G. *The Concept of Mind* (Penguin 1963).
- Skinner B. F. *About Behaviorism* (Macmillan, 1974).

Chapter 5

The existence of God: arguments based on observation

1 Introduction

> ### Chapter checklist
>
> This chapter concerns what many consider to be the most important question in the philosophy of religion – whether or not God exists. This chapter considers those arguments based on alleged evidence from the world, to see whether what we learn through sense experience permits us to infer the existence of God. It begins by outlining some of the difficulties of any attempt to prove God's existence, noting that the search for God is different from other types of existential questions. The teleological argument of Aquinas and the design argument of Paley are discussed. Objections, especially those of Hume, are summarised and considered. The chapter also considers modern versions of the argument from F. R. Tennant and Richard Swinburne, then discusses Aquinas' cosmological argument and Leibniz's idea of Sufficient Reason. Various objections are considered, such as that to Aquinas' appeal to imagination and Hume's objections to causation, as well as more general discussion of whether and how God might explain the universe. The chapter concludes with discussion of whether traditional proofs of this type do justice to the lived experience of believers.

Throughout history, many have attempted to demonstrate beyond doubt that God exists. Whether such an attempt can ever be wholly successful may be doubted. The First Vatican Council (1869–70) decreed that it was possible to know the existence of God by reason alone:

> *If anyone shall say that the one true God, our Creator and Lord, cannot be certainly known by the natural light of human reason through created things: let him be anathema [rejected by the church].*

> Vatican Council I: *Dogmatic Constitution on the Catholic Faith*: Canon II: 1

However, no attempt was made to suggest that any attempt to prove the existence of God had been successful. The Fathers asserted that a proof was achievable, but endorsed none. Indeed, they were careful to point out that:

The divine mysteries by their own nature so far transcend the created intelligence that, even when delivered by revelation and received by faith, they remain covered with the veil of faith itself, and shrouded in a certain degree of darkness, so long as we are pilgrims in this mortal life, not yet with God; 'for we walk by faith and not by sight.'

Dogmatic Constitution on the Catholic Faith: Chapter IV

Herein lies the fundamental problem. God is not a being among beings. The God of believers is not simply another *thing* in the universe.

This raises several issues. Suppose I ask whether the Loch Ness monster exists. I may not believe in the existence of the Loch Ness monster, but I know what it is I do not believe in. I also have a fairly clear idea of what sort of evidence would prove my scepticism mistaken. When we ask whether the Loch Ness monster is real, we are asking whether it is a creature in the universe in the way that a zebra, an elephant or a marmot may be. We know the methods of finding animals through trapping or fishing, we know the methods of zoological research and we know how to analyse DNA. We are clear about the kinds of evidence of existence we are seeking.

None of this is the case with God. We do not know God in himself. As he would be unlike anything else we know, we cannot straightforwardly use the methods we have developed to detect the existence in this world of things of known types. In the case of the Loch Ness monster, we can make a comparison with existing mammals and reptiles. God is, by definition, incomparable.

Therefore, we need to be aware that when we ask 'Does God exist?', we are asking a very different question from whether the Loch Ness monster or the tooth fairy exists. Even the word 'exist' creates problems. We understand 'existence' in terms of what it is to be a physical object in the universe. But God is not a physical object in the universe. Whatever it means for God to exist is not identical with what it means for a physical object to exist. This is important when you think about these issues. Both believers and non-believers can fall into the trap of thinking that because 'Does the Loch Ness monster exist?' and 'Does God exist?' have similar grammatical forms they are questions of the same type. When we ask about God, we are not clear either about what it is we seek, nor the appropriate method of finding him.

This can be an issue which makes proving there is a God more difficult than normal issues of proof. Generally, we can assert with confidence that it is easier in principle to prove the existence of something than to demonstrate its non-existence. Take the case of a mermaid. If I want to prove that mermaids exist, all I have to do is to find a mermaid. Once I have done so, my search is at an end. But if I want to prove that mermaids do not exist, I could continue not finding mermaids forever. There might always be a mermaid behind the next rock, on another island, on another planet or beyond. Unless I looked in every place, I could not be sure beyond every conceivable doubt that there were no mermaids.

But the case of God is different. Someone says that he has found God. Others accuse him of delusion. He claims 'proof' in his own experience, but I do not share that experience. He cannot produce a body and say: this is God. I may reject both his evidence and the methods used to find that evidence and have reasonable grounds for doing so. However, if he produced Nessie on a lead, my rejection of it would seem utterly irrational.

Philosophers attempting to demonstrate the existence of God have generally chosen one of two routes. Some have sought to claim *a priori* that God exists, that is, from first principles, without reference to sense experience. Kant has called their arguments 'ontological arguments'. See an example of this in Chapter 6.

Others have chosen to seek evidence of God in the world. After all, if God is creator of the world, surely we can find evidence of the creator of the world? After all, if I see an anonymous painting or read a book without knowing the author, I can deduce something about the artist or writer from the evidence of the book. Certainly, there is much I cannot know, such as his shoe size, personal life and so on, but I can draw inferences about his ability and intentions from what he has produced. Might not the same be true of God's work?

Arguments of this kind are based on observation, and therefore are *a posteriori*. They offer less apparent certainty than *a priori arguments*, outlined in Chapter 1, but they have the merit of drawing on our everyday experience. Arguments of this type tend to be of two kinds:

- *teleological* arguments, sometimes called arguments from design as they are based on the apparent order of the universe
- *cosmological* arguments, which base themselves on some perceived general quality of the universe, such as cause and effect.

The most famous philosopher to argue for God from the evidence of the world was St Thomas Aquinas (*c.*1225–74) in his famous Five Ways, from his *Summa Theologica*.

Background

What follows in this box is not required material for the examination, but having an awareness of the context in which a philosopher worked is important for giving depth to your thought and answers.

After his death in 322BC, Aristotle's own books disappeared almost completely. The only things to survive were notes of Aristotle's various courses in the Lyceum, perhaps his own teaching notes supplemented by his students. This is why his major works read like notes rather than polished prose. But they are very detailed.

These works themselves were largely lost to Western Europe, but went east, where they were fundamental to Arabic thought and to the growth of science. By the year 1000AD, none of Aristotle's work was available in the West in anything approaching its original form.

Aristotle's works would eventually come into Western Europe during the twelfth and thirteenth centuries, as texts brought back during the Crusades, but, more particularly during the reconquest of Spain. Greek scholars began to teach throughout Europe, and translation of the range of texts, beyond the purely logical ones, was undertaken at the University of Toledo and elsewhere, including Oxford. Perhaps the finest translator was William of Moerbecke, who provided St Thomas Aquinas with his texts.

St Thomas Aquinas (*c.*1225–74) was astonishing, not merely in the sheer number of words he produced, but in the range of topics he discussed. When asked towards the end of his life about the greatest gift God had given him, he replied that he had never read a page he had not at once understood. Yet there was also a simplicity to this great intellect. The monk who heard his final confession left his room saying he had just heard the confession of a little child. This huge, very quiet man remains a central figure in the history of thought.

Key person

St Thomas Aquinas was born at Roccasecca, near Aquino, in Italy of aristocratic stock. He studied at the great Benedictine monastery of Monte Cassino, before entering the University of Naples. He was perhaps as young as nine years old. While at Naples he decided to join the new Order of Preachers, the Dominicans. His family had other ideas. They wanted him to become a Benedictine monk, perhaps to become Abbot at Monte Cassino. For a while they imprisoned him, but eventually he was able to fulfil his wish. Aquinas was a Dominican, and hence a friar – not a monk. Monks commit themselves to a monastery, to live there probably for the rest of their lives. Friars, such as Aquinas committed to the Order, to live and work wherever instructed. He went to Cologne, where he was a pupil of St Albert the Great (Albertus Magnus, 1200–80). St Albert's intention was to provide a systematic account of the newly discovered and translated work of Aristotle, using it to interpret Christian thought. When Albert moved to the University of Paris, Aquinas followed. He began study for the degree of Master of Arts. Among the many tasks required was – as it would remain for several hundred years - to write a commentary on a fairly short theological text known as *The Sentences of Peter Lombard*. Aquinas' commentary ran to about 1,750,000 words. But he completed it before he was 30, so only the pope could grant him the degree of master. That thesis established his reputation as the finest mind in Europe. Thereafter, his output was prodigious. He died in Fossanuova in Italy, but his bones now rest in Toulouse, in France. He wrote commentaries on all the major books of Aristotle and on other authors, including Boethius. Other works included many volumes on disputed topics as well as monographs on particular questions, hymns, prayers, masses and others. He is best known for his two great Summas, *Summa Contra Gentiles* and *Summa Theologica*. The latter was unfinished at his death. It is a monumental attempt to rethink the whole of Christian Faith, question by question, in the light of the revived Aristotelian learning.

2 The teleological argument

(a) Aquinas' Fifth Way

In Greek, the term *telos* means a goal or an end. It is from this that the **teleological** argument of Aquinas gets its name. Aquinas takes over from Aristotle the theory of the four causes, in particular the idea of the **final cause**, which is the purpose of things. Aristotle assumes in his physics and biology that everything in the universe has a purpose, and this is clearly reflected in his teleological argument. The name was not given by Aquinas. It is a later description.

Aquinas' version of the argument is briefly given as the Fifth of his Five Ways. It seems to have been the least significant of his arguments. He deals with it briefly, and hardly returns to it. He writes:

Key terms

Teleological Any argument which is cast in terms of the end (telos) or purpose of something.

Final cause Aristotle's idea of the ultimate purpose of a thing.

> *The fifth way is taken from the governance of the world. We see that things which lack knowledge, such as natural objects, act for a purpose, and this is evident from their acting always – or nearly always – in the same way, to obtain the best result. It is plain that they achieve their end by design and not by chance. It is obvious that something without intelligence could not move towards an end so unerringly unless it were directed by a being with knowledge and intelligence, just as an [inanimate] arrow is directed by an archer. Therefore, some intelligent being exists which directs all natural things to their end. This being we call God.*

S.T., I, q.2, a.3,c.

Here we see directly the influence of Aristotle's notion that nature is teleological, where everything serves a purpose. This argument is sometimes described as a version of the **design argument**, but it is important to notice that Aquinas is less concerned with how things fit together than with what they are for. Aquinas claims that not only is there purpose in the universe, but that, that purpose comes directly from the will of God.

The obvious question is whether it is actually true that everything has a purpose. Modern biology, in the light of evolutionary theory, would deny this. Much is the result of chance. Some things show no significant purpose, and even if we see purpose in things, is the purpose in the thing itself, or do we just see it as having purpose? The word 'purpose' implies a mental state. People have purposes. But can we properly say that material things have purposes? Surely 'purpose' implies a mind to have the purpose. And if objects do not have minds, then the purpose is not in the thing but in the mind that has the purpose for the thing. In Aquinas' example, the arrow does not have any purpose at all. It is the archer who has a purpose for it.

A further consideration is that we may see things as having a purpose because we like to find reasons for why things are as they are. But the purpose may just be in our own minds.

Even if it were true that things have a purpose, it does not follow that that purpose is a good one. Some might argue that there is evidence of design in the way that a bed of nettles is often found close to dock leaves. Dock leaves are an antidote to nettle stings. This looks like purpose in nature, but we may still ask the purpose of nettles. Why do they sting us? Of course, we can find a purpose for nettles, perhaps in medicine or soup, but it does not follow that that purpose is *in* the nettles themselves. It seems implausible to suggest that they evolved *so that* they could be made into soup.

If we look back at the quotation, Aquinas inserts, 'or nearly always'. This suggests some hesitancy. If there is purpose in everything, then it would always be found. Does this mean that Aquinas was unsure of his argument, or was he merely saying that he could not work out the purpose of some things? We might find it difficult to see a good purpose in a mosquito. If there are things in the world that have no good purpose, do we think they are designed? If God is creator of all things, then why do things with no point exist?

(b) The design argument of Paley

Perhaps the most famous argument from design is known as Paley's watch. This was an analogy used in William Paley's wonderfully titled *Natural Theology: or Evidences of the Existence and Attributes of the Deity Collected from the Appearances of Nature*, which was published in 1802, and which is referred to generally as *Natural Theology*.

Background

Paley's book draws on the science of his day, which was an *Enlightenment* science, deeply influenced by the example of Isaac Newton (1642–1727) who viewed the world as a machine-like system. In *Philosophiae Naturalis Principia Mathematica* (1687), Newton, using mathematics and classical geometry, demonstrated how the universe follows mathematical principles. Newton claimed to demonstrate 'the system of the world.'

The intellectual effect of this was considerable, shaping the approach of scientists for the next three hundred years. Suddenly it appeared as if the entire universe was in principle knowable to human reason. In Alexander Pope's famous epitaph:

William Paley (1742–1805)

Nature and Nature's laws lay hid in night;
God said, 'Let Newton be! and all was light.

Newton seemed to have demonstrated that the universe ran according to a few simple rules, rather like a machine. And, like a machine, it seemed predictable. If the world is like a giant machine, running on predictable lines, according to certain simple laws, then it is reasonable to assume that it has been constructed, as a machine is constructed, and constructed by someone. The Enlightenment period was one when design arguments had their heyday, and there were many examples, such as found in the *Bridgewater Treatises*. This series of eight books, published by distinguished authors between 1833 and 1840, was designed to demonstrate 'the Power, Wisdom, and Goodness of God, as manifested in the Creation'. (The project was endowed by the eccentric Earl of Bridgewater, an Anglican cleric who lived in Paris, with his pets fed by uniformed waiters off silver plates.) Another book was added to the series in 1838 by Charles Babbage, best known for his invention of the difference engine, the first mechanical computer. In this book, the universe is seen most evidently as a machine. Throughout his life, he would return to mechanical models, frequently in a theological context.

Paley, like other Enlightenment thinkers, uses a mechanical model. He points to the complexity of the human brain where millions of cells co-ordinate together. In the same way, the human eye is a device of extraordinary flexibility and ability. The fin of a fish and the wing of a bird are perfectly engineered to allow movement through water or flight. The planets rotate on their axes, the seasons advance and recede, with astonishing order. The extent of this regularity surely points to design, and hence, to a designer.

This point is illustrated by his famous analogy, known universally as *Paley's watch*. (Note that Paley is talking about a analogue watch and not a digital watch.)

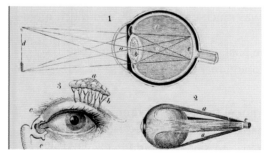

The complexity of life led Paley to conclude that there must be an intelligent designer

Suppose I were walking in a wilderness and I came up on a rock lying on the ground. I could easily account for its existence, by reference to natural causes such as water, wind, erosion, volcanic activity etc.

But, suppose instead I came upon a watch. I could not account for it in that natural way. A watch reveals an array of intricate, beautifully made cogs, levers, springs etc. Such a design could not have come about by chance – something must have made it to fit together. There must be a watchmaker.

Paley adds three vital comments:

1 Our inference would remain valid even if we had never seen a watch before. The watch is so obviously different from the rock, it must have a different type of origin.

2 Even if the watch did not work perfectly – just as the world seems to function imperfectly – there is enough design, indeed overwhelming evidence of design, to enable us to deduce the watchmaker.

3 In the same way, our inference would still be correct even if there were parts of the machine whose function we could not work out.

> ## Key persons
>
> **Isaac Newton** (1642–1727): British scientist, best known for his discovery of gravity. Influenced Enlightenment by showing how the universe might be rationally explained by a few simple laws.
>
> **William Paley** (1743–1805): was born in Peterborough and studied in Cambridge, where he lectured in moral philosophy, divinity and Greek New Testament. English clergyman and defender of religion, he held several significant posts in the Church of England, eventually becoming Archdeacon of Carlisle. Best known for *Natural Theology* (1802), which contains the argument known as 'Paley's watch'.

However, the most we could infer from the existence of a watch is that there *was* a watchmaker. We do not and cannot know whether he is still active or even still alive. We cannot say whether he made the watch alone or had some help.

3 Criticisms from Hume

> ## Key person
>
> **David Hume** (1711–76): Scottish philosopher and historian, perhaps the greatest British philosopher, noted for his empiricism and religious scepticism. Major works include *A Treatise of Human Nature*, *An Enquiry Concerning Human Understanding* and *Dialogues Concerning Natural Religion*.

Perhaps the most convincing criticisms of the type of argument offered by Paley can be found in David Hume's *Dialogues Concerning Natural Religion*, published posthumously in 1779.

It is essential to note that Hume was not responding to Paley, as he wrote more than twenty years before the appearance of *Natural Theology* (1802). There is no evidence that Paley was familiar with Hume's criticisms of design arguments in general, perhaps because in the eighteenth century, Hume was much better known, and much more widely read, as a historian.

Despite his writing before the publication of *Natural Theology*, his objections are fully applicable to arguments such as those of Paley. Hume makes three key objections:

1 **Aptness of analogy:** The model used by Enlightenment thinkers, of a machine-like universe, shaped their arguments. Hume's argument points to this. What we choose to say the world is like shapes the outcome of the argument. A watch is a machine, and machines have machine-makers. But, consider a cabbage. If we examine its leaves, they fit together perfectly and they serve a purpose as a very healthy form of food. But, if we found a cabbage, we could not (and would not) draw the inference that there exists a cabbage-maker. Cabbages we know as natural things, like grass or dandelions. Is the world any more like a watch than it is like a cabbage or a dandelion? We can see the world as a complex natural object at least as easily as we might see it as a machine. By choosing a machine as their analogy, thinkers like Paley have already determined the result they want.

2 **The Epicurean thesis:** Any world has to fit together, at least up to a point, in order to continue. Any significant existence requires a degree of stability and mutual adaptation. The question is whether such a stable order could arise at random. If something could display order without being made to do so by a grand designer, we would have an alternative way of explaining the phenomenon. Hume suggests one such way by reference to the ancient **Epicurean thesis**. Suppose we have infinite time. Now suppose that a huge but finite number of particles exist, freely moving around. In infinite time, these particles would undergo every possible combination. Every possible combination might very well include one – or more – which is relatively stable, that is, one which fits together quite well. That could be where we are living now, in a universe with at least some apparent order. An easy way to remember this argument is to think of the old tale of monkeys in a room full of typewriters. In infinite time, they will type every possible combination of letters, including the Bible and the works of Shakespeare.

3 **Argument from effect to cause:** We cannot go from an effect to a cause greater than that needed to produce the cause. Hume gives the example of a set of scales. Suppose we can see only one pan, which has a known weight in it. The pan is in the air, so we know that what is in the other pan is heavier, even though it is hidden from our view. What else can we deduce? We have no idea whether what is in that pan is heavier by an ounce or by a ton, and we have no idea what that heavier thing might be, whether it is a ton of feathers or an elephant holding the pan down with his big toe. In the same way, we cannot go from the evidence of this world, with all its limitations, to the infinite, all-loving, all-powerful, all-knowing God in whom most believers believe. Hume suggests that perhaps this world is the discarded effort of an infant deity or the work of a committee of gods. We simply cannot know.

4 Other criticisms

(a) John Stuart Mill

John Stuart Mill (1806–73) pointed to the amount of evil in the world as a fundamental objection to design. He argues:

> *Not even on the most distorted and contracted theory of good which was ever framed by religious or philosophical fanaticism, can the government of nature be made to resemble the work of a being at once good and omnipotent.*

> John Stuart Mill: *Three Essays on Religion: Nature, the Utility of Religion, Theism* (1874), p. 38

His criticism is about the problem of evil, but his argument is that from a flawed universe, the most we can infer is a flawed creator. There is real evil, not merely the result of people's free choices (known as *moral* evil), but also, and more significantly, *natural* evil. This includes deaths from illness, plague, volcanoes, earthquakes, fog at sea, and so on, which seem part of the structure of the world. If these were designed, it seems a very

Charles Darwin (1809–1882): British naturalist and scientist, best known for his theory of evolution first published in *The Origin of Species* (1859).

John Stuart Mill (1806–73): British philosopher noted for his contributions especially to Utilitarianism, Liberalism and empiricism. Pupil of Jeremy Bentham. M.P. for Westminster until defeated by W. H. Smith.

Sir Anthony Kenny (b. 1931): Former Catholic priest, now agnostic, best known for his work in analytical Thomism, Wittgenstein studies and general philosophical questions.

Charles Darwin

faulty sort of design, and a designer who lets such things happen would be morally flawed. I would not be described as a good shipbuilder if my ships were leaky buckets at the mercy of storms and wild waves.

Anthony Kenny has said that Paley's type of argument 'leads to a God which is no more the source of good than the source of evil. The God to which this argument of rational theology leads is not supreme goodness: it is a being which is beyond good and evil' (Anthony Kenny: *The Unknown God*: Continuum, 2004, p. 100).

(b) Evolution

For many people, the most significant reasons for rejecting design arguments were to be found in the scientific discoveries of Charles Darwin and others. Darwin, rightly revered as one of the most significant scientists in human history (Marx notoriously believed the three greatest scientists to be Newton, Darwin and himself), published his famous book *On the Origin of Species* in 1859, and followed this with other significant works, including *The Descent of Man* (1871). His theories were based on his five years touring the world on HMS Beagle, between 1831 and 1836, when he examined various species in their native habitats, perhaps most famously in the Galapagos Islands.

Some would choose to argue against established religion on the grounds of elements of evolutionary theory. Darwin himself never did so. In his early life, he was a devout Anglican. As he grew older, his position became more agnostic, apparently not because of his evolutionary theory, but rather because of his encounters with other religions, held just as sincerely by their adherents as the Christianity in which he had been brought up. Despite his doubts, he was buried in Westminster Abbey.

The basics of evolutionary theory are probably familiar to you. It is often described as 'the survival of the fittest' a phrase not used by Darwin himself but by T.H. Huxley (1825–1895). The key to the theory is the idea that species develop rather randomly. Those creatures which happen to be best suited to their environment survive, while those which are not, die out. The name given by Darwin for the process was Natural Selection.

For Darwin, there are more creatures born in any species than can survive, so there is a struggle for survival, both within and between species. The weakest examples within a species, and the weakest in the struggles between species, lose in the battle for life. Those who happen to have features well-adapted for survival will be best able to survive.

All this points us to a world where survival is a matter of pure chance. The idea that there might be some *purpose* behind it all seems very strange indeed – this is rather 'nature, red in tooth and claw', in Tennyson's memorable phrase from Canto 56 of *In Memoriam*. The world of evolution is one of random survival, lucky chance and endless strife and threat.

Evolutionary theory also questions design. If Charles Darwin is correct, survival of species depends on their ability to fit in, to adapt to the world. Creatures that survive might look as if they were made to fit in, but they survive *because* they fit in. Countless numbers of species (think of the dinosaurs, the mammoths, the aurochs or the dodo) have not survived because they could not adapt, or could not adapt quickly enough, to a changing environment. If this represents design, it is an extraordinarily wasteful process.

Modern science in terms of evolutionary theory, quantum theory, the theory of relativity, chaos theory and so on offers a view of the universe less congenial to teleological and design arguments than the purposive universe of Aristotle or Newton's simple mechanistic model. Some philosophers, such as Richard Swinburne and F. R. Tennant. For some fundamentalists, continue to use variants on design arguments, but those who do so represent a minority view.

5 Modern versions of the design argument

(a) F. R. Tennant and the anthropic principle

> **Key term**
>
> **Anthropic principle** The view that the universe exists for the sake of humankind and is particularly adapted to that purpose.

F. R. Tennant in *Philosophical Theology* (Cambridge University Press, 1930) developed the **anthropic principle**. This argues that the world is so exactly right to create the precise environment for man to evolve that it must surely have been planned. If the Earth were closer to or further from the Sun, if the elements had been different, human life would not have been possible. The chance of our lives occurring in such a well-adapted world as this one is so remote that it must have been planned.

But, consider the huge space of the universe. The Earth is a tiny dot in this vastness. Most of the universe is bleak, cold and barren. In this unimaginably vast space, with so many possible events, the chances that somewhere something odd happens are much improved. Tennant's view seems to assume that the entire universe exists for the sake of this little Earth. This seems unlikely. We need to ask ourselves where the evidence for design exists in remote uninhabited and uninhabitable galaxies. Why are they there? What purposes do they serve? What possible design do they fit?

> **Key persons**
>
> **F. R. Tennant** (1866–1957): Anglican theologian. Studied mathematics, physics, biology and chemistry before changing his focus to theology, which he taught at Trinity College, Cambridge. His major work was *Philosophical Theology* (1928–30).
>
> **Richard Swinburne** (b. 1934): British philosopher of religion, based at Oriel College, Oxford. Nolloth Professor of the Philosophy of the Christian Religion 1985–2002, now Emeritus. Prolific author of *apologetic* works, including various attempts to demonstrate the validity of proofs for the existence of God. Involved in various controversies, notably with the non-believer, Richard Dawkins and with the Christian D. Z. Phillips. Interested in probability theory which he applies to demonstrate the reasonableness of faith. Former Anglican, joined Orthodox Church in 1986.

> **Key term**
>
> **Apologetics** Theological attempts to defend the Christian faith.

(b) Richard Swinburne and simplicity

A more modern version is suggested by Richard Swinburne, whose interest is the simplicity of the universe. There are few elements operating to the same simple laws. The same hundred or so elements can be combined in so many ways, each following the same sets of simple physical laws, yet leading to such richness. Swinburne argues that the simplest and most economical explanation would be that God planned it. William of Ockham, in the fourteenth century, believed that when we have two or more competing theories, the one with the fewer or fewest hypotheses is the most likely to be true. This theory is called 'Ockham's razor'. Swinburne appeals to this principle.

However, it does not follow that because the simplest explanation is the most likely to be correct that it *is* correct. It might just be that by chance there happens to be a combination of elements which can function in complicated ways. That they follow a few simple laws is no more surprising than that they might follow many and complex rules. It is just the way they are. In any case, modern science has found particles that behave in apparently random ways. Theories such as quantum theory point to a much more complex universe than one run on simple, Newtonian lines.

However, we may question whether God really is a simple explanation at all. For an explanation to work, we have to understand the explanation. We do not know the mind of God, and his ways are unknown to us in their fullness. We cannot assert that God is the explanation when we cannot show with any precision what type of explanation God might be, given his difference from any type of explanation offered by physics, chemistry or biology. Further, the objections made by Mill and Hume seem to apply with equal force here. Evil remains a problem, as do the many bits of the universe that either work not very well or function to no obvious purpose.

Swinburne has devoted much of his scholarship to a study of probabilities, and he uses a weight of probability theory in his arguments about God. At the heart of his version of the design argument is a fascination with what he calls 'temporal order'. By this he means the 'all-pervasiveness' of regularity in the universe, the idea that physical objects 'throughout time and space have some general powers identical to those of all other objects'. He argues that we accept induction as the basis of the laws of nature, and that nature conforms so well to 'formulae recorded in the scientific laws formulated by men' (*The Existence of God*: Clarendon, Oxford, 1979: p. 148). For Swinburne, such regularity is incredible unless there is a cosmic designer to ensure regularity.

> **Key term**
>
> **Ockham's razor** (sometimes called *Occam's razor*) Refers to the idea that theories should not be multiplied beyond necessity. If we have to choose between two or more theories, the one with the smallest number of assumptions is the one most likely to be correct.

> **Key question**
>
> Is it possible to claim that there is design in the world, and therefore a designer, when there are so many things we cannot explain and so many things that seem to work not very well?

6 Aquinas' cosmological argument

Cosmological arguments, as the name implies, are arguments based on some claimed common feature of the whole universe, such as movement or cause and effect. The name was never used by Aquinas, but was coined by Kant to distinguish this type of *a posteriori* argument from the *a priori* ontological arguments of Anselm and Descartes.

Key terms

Cosmological arguments
Arguments for the existence of God based on God's alleged ability to create the universe. Arguments generally refer to God as first cause, Prime Mover or explanation.

Prime Mover In Aristotle, that which creates movement as a final purpose, by attraction; but in Aquinas, the divine initiator of all change and motion.

Motion For Aristotle and Aquinas, motion includes not just movement in the modern sense but also change of any sort, such as becoming warm or cold.

First cause The uncaused beginning of all other beings, initiating all other causes. Posited by Aquinas in the second of his Five Ways.

Necessity Something that has to be the case.

Contingency Something is contingent if its existence is dependent on something else in order to exist.

In Part I of the *Summa Theologica*, Question II, Article 3, Aquinas gives his famous Five Ways for the existence of God. He claimed that we can only get to God from evidence that we find in the world. This is very Aristotelian. Aristotle always begins from observed features of the world, which means that Aquinas follows him in looking at what we find in our experience. The first Three Ways are collectively known as the cosmological argument. The titles in square brackets refer to the titles by which these arguments are traditionally known. These titles were *not* given by Aquinas. In his words:

> [**Prime Mover**] *The first and most obvious way is the argument from* **motion**. *It is obvious that in the world some things are in motion. Whatever is moved is moved by another … It is impossible that in the same respect and in the same way a thing could be both mover and moved, i.e., that it should move itself. Whatever is moved is moved by another. If that by which it is moved is itself moving, then this must also be moved by something else, and that by something else again. But this cannot go on to infinity, because there would then be no first mover, and, consequently, no subsequent mover, as subsequent movers move only insofar as they are moved by the first mover, just as a staff moves only because it is moved by the hand. So there must be a first mover, itself unmoved; and this everyone understands to be God.*

> [**First cause**] *The second way is from the nature of efficient causes. In the world of sensible things we find an order of efficient causes. There is no case known (it would be impossible) in which a thing is found to be its own efficient cause; to be so it would have to exist before itself, which is impossible. In efficient causes we cannot go on to infinity, because in any order of efficient causes, the first is the cause of the intermediate and the intermediate of the last, whether there are several intermediate causes or only one. Without a cause, there is no effect. Thus, if there were no first cause … there would be no intermediate causes, and no last. If we could go to infinity in efficient causes, there would be no first cause; if that were true, there would be no intermediate cause, and no present effects for us to see. Plainly this is not the case. So we must admit a first efficient cause [itself uncaused], which everyone calls 'God'.*

> [**Necessity** and **contingency**] *The third way is taken from possibility and necessity. In nature we find things that are possible to be and not to be – they are found to be generated and corrupted – and so it is possible for them to be and possible not to be. It is impossible for them always to exist, for that which is possible not to be at some time does not exist. If everything is like that, at one time nothing existed. If that were true, there would be nothing in existence now, because things only come to exist because of things already existing. If at some time nothing existed, there would be nothing today, which is obviously false. So, not all things are merely possible – there must exist something whose existence is necessary. Every necessary thing either has its necessity caused by something else, or it does not.*

*As we saw when we considered efficient causes, it would be impossible to go on to infinity in a chain of things which have their necessity caused by another **necessary being**. We have to admit the existence of some being whose necessity lies in itself, (and not received from something else), which is the source of necessity in others. This all men call God.*

(a) Prime Mover

Perhaps this argument comes first because it is a basic observation that things move about in the Universe – we see things moving at almost every moment. Remember that for Aristotle and Aquinas, movement includes things such as changes; for example, things becoming hotter or colder, or growing older.

Despite the similarities there is a crucial difference between Aquinas and Aristotle – as we saw in Chapter 3. For Aquinas, there is an uncaused cause who initiates all movement in the universe by a deliberate act of will. For Aquinas, this motion is the consequence of a creative act of God. Aristotle's Prime Mover acts by attraction – he is indifferent towards the universe, has no intentions for it – but just happens to attract everything in the universe.

(b) First cause

This is a particularly appealing, but rather problematic, argument. It is the closest to the one we hear most commonly, which is when people ask, if there is no God, where did the universe come from? Cause is something we see all the time. Everything is caused by something else, that in turn, by something else, and so on. Surely, the argument says, there must be a first cause, different from the others in requiring no cause. It makes no sense to ask the question, 'What caused God?' The very term 'God' refers to something that does not have a cause, different from any object within the universe. A 'caused God' would be a contradiction in terms.

There are three particular difficulties:

- David Hume identified problems with the very notion of causation. We speak of 'cause' and 'effect', and assume we understand the ideas, but, scientifically, they remain problematic. Consider the moment when the cause is succeeded by the effect. Immediately before that moment, the cause is not yet the effect. Immediately after, the effect is no longer the cause. What happens in the precise moment when cause is not yet the effect and the effect is no longer the cause? Science will tell us what went before, and what came after, but the moment itself remains a deep intellectual puzzle. The ease with which we talk of 'cause and effect' disguises the complexity of the notion. Hume suggests that what we call 'cause and effect' may simply be our way of reporting what is just a statistical correlation. Instead of saying, 'x causes y', precisely the same phenomenon might be described by saying, 'whenever x, y'. In this case, we describe the phenomenon without any mention of cause. If we can do this, 'cause' is not the obvious notion which Aquinas assumes.
- Whatever is meant by 'cause' in relation to God, cannot be cause in the ordinary scientific sense. God is not another cause in the way that my moving is the cause of a ball's movement or the mixture of certain chemicals is the cause of the explosion which blew up a safe.

God and Adam, part of ceiling in Sistine Chapel, Rome

If God is a cause, then he is a cause of a very different kind from anything in my experience. I may properly ask on what evidence I can posit a cause of a sort outside my experience, or, indeed, any earthly experience. I know what a biological cause, a chemical cause, might be. But I have no direct experience of divine cause, so have I any right to assume the existence of such a thing?

■ If God is to be understood as a cause at the beginning of the universe, problems are compounded. If he is a cause of no known type – not chemical, physical or biological – then we have no known process for understanding that about which we are talking. Physicists can create experiments which they believe model the beginning of the universe, such as with the Large Hadron Collider near Geneva. Chemists can construct experiments to analyse possible reactions. But nothing can model this unknowable cause. This means that we can have no direct observational experience of either the original event or of any models we might create of that event. Further, if we argue that God's creation is not simply a 'back then' original event, but is an ongoing process, then again it must be outside the normal scientific processes we are able to observe by known methods.

Some of these difficulties have been noted by Dorothy Emmet (1904–2000). In a book written towards the end of her life, she argues:

> 'First Cause' is not, I think, the first member of a causal sequence, although this is suggested in the Five Ways … It is an eternal non-temporal activity on which everything else depends. 'Cause' is now recognised to be a problematic notion, even in its normal use. How much more so in this abnormal use?

Dorothy Emmet: *Outward Forms, Inner Springs* (1998), p. 71

(c) Necessity and contingency

Aquinas' argument, in essence, appears to be that everything in our experience is contingent, but not everything can be so contingent. There

Key question

Why is the idea of cause so problematic?

Key person

Dorothy Emmet (1904–2000): Professor of Philosophy, University of Manchester 1946–67, best known for work in metaphysics and religion.

Key persons

Bertrand Russell (1872–1972): British mathematician, peace activist and prolific author (winner of Nobel Prize for Literature, 1950). Major works include *Principia Mathematica* (1910–13), a revolutionary work in both mathematics and logic.

William Temple (1881–1944): British churchman, *ecumenist*, social activist and philosophical theologian. The only son of an Archbishop of Canterbury to become Archbishop of Canterbury (1942–44). Works include *Nature, Man and God* (1934). Coined the term, 'Welfare State'.

Key terms

Infinite regress An endless sequence going backwards through time, without beginning.

Ecumenism The attempt to bring unity between religious denominations.

Key question

Why is the distinction between what can be imagined and what can be thought about so important when thinking about Aquinas' arguments?

must be something necessary, not dependent on anything else, on which everything else depends.

The problem that most immediately occurs is Aquinas' assumption about a time when once there was nothing. There is no reason to assume that there need have been such a time. There could be overlapping chains of contingent beings, so that there never was a period when nothing existed.

A further problem has been raised, by among others Bertrand Russell. The question is whether it makes sense to speak of a 'necessary *being*'. In logic, a proposition may be described as 'necessary'. It is, for example, a necessary truth that a square has four sides. But can a *thing* be necessary? Whatever we mean here by the term 'necessary', it is a special usage. But, if nothing else than God is necessary, and we cannot see his necessity directly, it seems impossible to argue that we have any concept of necessary being that we can attribute to God in the way Aquinas does here.

(d) The appeal to imagination

A very important criticism is that Aquinas and others appeal to the alleged impossibility of an **infinite regress**. There is however a very important distinction to be drawn between something being impossible to picture in our minds and actually being impossible.

In *Mens Creatrix* the future Archbishop, William Temple, commented that '... it is impossible to imagine infinite regress. [but] it is not impossible to conceive it.' (William Temple: *Mens Creatrix*, 1915, p. 271). What he meant by this is that while it is impossible to imagine infinity we can understand the concept. Infinite regress is logically possible even if it is difficult to understand. The concept of a square circle is inconceivable because the two words contradict each other. But 'infinite' does not contradict 'regress'. I cannot imagine infinity, but I can think of it. I know what the word means and I understand the idea. This would not be true in the same way about the *logically* impossible. A square circle is not only unimaginable. It is unthinkable. I cannot attribute any significant meaning to the words. But words and phrases such as 'eternity' or 'infinite regress' have significant meaning. After all, religious people will talk significantly about the infinity of God or the possibility of eternal life. If 'infinite' or 'eternal' can be understood coherently in the context of God, surely they can be used with equal coherence about terms such as 'universe' or 'being'. To say it is impossible for me to imagine something says something about the limits of my imagination, but not about the limitations of things. I cannot assume that because I cannot imagine four or five or six dimensions that I cannot think about the possibility. Indeed, mathematicians today, recognising that mathematics is a system of definitions, quite happily do multi-dimensional geometry, even though they are quite unable to draw the diagrams, or even to imagine them.

This objection, based on the fact that infinite regression is logically possible, may be used about each part of Aquinas' cosmological argument and you should be able to develop this in your essays.

7 Leibniz and the principle of sufficient reason

Just as there have been developments of modern versions of Ontological Arguments, so there have also been with Cosmological Arguments. Perhaps the most significant development has been the move from understanding Cosmological Arguments in terms of disputed ideas such as motion, causation or necessity and contingency to the idea that only God really *explains* the universe. Of course, this is Aquinas' underlying assumption, but the more modern attempts make this assumption explicit. This is why, when thinking about the arguments of Aquinas, it is helpful to consider this assumption in the later literature.

As we have seen, there are problems of arguing for God as first cause, necessary being or Prime Mover, just as there were with versions of the teleological argument. In consequence, many philosophers have preferred to argue in terms of God as ultimate explanation of the universe. A significant problem of arguments from Prime Mover or first cause is that they appear, at least at first glance, to be about the beginning of things – that there *was* a cause or mover or designer. But most religious people see God's relationship with the world as one which is not just about the beginning of the universe but about how it is sustained – how it continues to be. For the believer, God sustains and holds the world in a continuous loving embrace. The German-American theologian Paul Tillich (1886–1965) speaks of God as the 'Ground of Being'. To speak this way is to talk of God in terms of his continued action.

This approach, common among recent philosophers, sees God in terms of explanation, developing the idea that God alone explains what exists. Explanation is a concept which does not confine us simply to past events. Explanation involves not only origins but intentions, plans, contingency and so on. When we ask for an explanation, we ask why things are as they are, and not just how they began.

Key persons

Paul Tillich (1886–1965): German-American Lutheran theologian and philosopher. Professor of philosophy at Frankfurt University and then moved to the USA in 1933 where he taught at first at the Union Theological Seminary in New York, then Harvard Divinity School and finally at the University of Chicago. His theology was strongly influenced by existentialism as can be seen in his influential three-volume *Systematic Theology* (1951–64).

Voltaire (1694–1778): Born Francois-Marie Arouet, French writer, philosopher, deist and historian. Famous for his wit, attacks on the Catholic Church and support for freedom in thought and expression. His *Candide* is famous for its wit and philosophical insights.

The concept was developed by the great German philosopher and mathematician, Gottfried Wilhelm Leibniz (1646–1716). An important part of his thought was that the universe is a harmonious whole, which is essentially good. God created this world for a particular reason as the best of all possible worlds. This view of Leibniz is savagely satirised by Voltaire (1694–1768) in *Candide* (1759), in which the hero insists that all the disasters that happen to him are for the best of things in the best of worlds.

Eventually he learns otherwise, taking a more pragmatic and realistic view. Voltaire use examples to demonstrate the foolishness of assuming explanations, or that we know what they are: 'It is demonstrable that things cannot be otherwise than as they are; for as all things have been created for some end, they must necessarily be created for the best end. Observe, for instance, the nose is formed for spectacles, therefore we wear spectacles.'

A fundamental idea is the principle of **sufficient reason**. As Leibniz says in *Monadology* (§53):

> As there is, in God's ideas, an infinity of possible universes, yet only one can exist, there has to be a sufficient reason for God's choice, a reason which makes him make one choice rather than a different one.

This assumes that the universe is in principle rational and open to human intelligence to understand.

Behind this principle lies the belief that everything has an explanation and can be fully (sufficiently) explained. We may put this more formally by saying:

1 For any entity that exists, there is a sufficient reason to explain its existence.
2 For every event, there is a sufficient reason to explain the occurrence of the event.
3 For every sentence that is true, there is a sufficient explanation for why it is true.

Such notions seem to be needed in any attempts to see God as explanation.

It is an understandable assumption, though, as we shall see, it raises many questions. At first sight, the notion seems to fit with normal scientific practice. Scientists, on coming upon something strange, do not hold up their hands and say 'It's a mystery!' and think they have provided a satisfactory or sufficient reason for what they have found. Science works on the assumption that there is an explanation for all phenomena, and thus, that scientists are, in principle at least, capable of finding it. If each individual phenomenon is explicable, is it not reasonable to ask whether the whole *universe* has an explanation? As we shall see, the assumption involved here is a large one.

It is interesting to note that Leibniz does not carefully distinguish in his work between *causes* and *explanation*. The same trait may be noted in a modern philosopher arguing from sufficient reason, F. C. Copleston (1907–94) in a famous BBC radio debate with Bertrand Russell (1872–1970) in 1948. He makes specific use of the principle of sufficient reason:

> '... we know that there are at least some beings in the world which do not contain in themselves the reason for their existence. For example, I depend on my parents, and now on the air, and on food, and so on. Now, secondly, the world is simply the real or imagined totality or aggregate of individual objects, none of which contain in themselves alone the reason for their existence. There isn't any world distinct from the objects which form it, any more than the human race is something apart from the members.

Gottfried Wilhelm Leibniz 1646–1716

Therefore, I should say, since objects or events exist, and since no object of experience contains within itself the reason of its existence, this reason, the totality of objects, must have a reason external to itself. That reason must be an existent being. Well, this being is either itself the reason for its own existence, or it is not. If it is, well and good. If it is not, then we must proceed farther. But if we proceed to infinity in that sense, then there's no explanation of existence at all. So, I should say, in order to explain existence, we must come to a being which contains within itself the reason for its own existence, that is to say, which cannot not exist.'

When Bertrand Russell asks Father Copleston about whether he considers 'cause' to be an explanation, Copleston agrees that he does.

Russell points to the incidence of uncaused — and hence, in principle unexplainable — beings in the universe. He cites individual quantum transitions in atoms as examples. Copleston also mentions indeterminacy (the view that some things happen at random, with no obvious cause), but does not see this as damaging his argument.

(a) A logical fallacy that cannot be overcome?

At the heart of Russell's argument against Leibniz and Copleston is the belief that they are guilty of a logical fallacy, known as '**the fallacy of composition**'. This is also mentioned in discussions of Aristotle. The fallacy was pointed out by Hume. This fallacy is the assumption that because something is true of the parts, exactly the same must be true of the whole. Aristotle is perhaps guilty of this error when he argues that because every part of the body has a function, man as a whole must also have a function. Russell suggests that we cannot go from saying that all mankind has a mother to the assumption that the universe has. He is also, perhaps, pointing to a psychological fact. We may wish there to be an explanation, just as we always want reasons, but we cannot go from our desire for something to be the case to the assumption that therefore that something is indeed the case. We cannot assert that there *must* be an explanation unless we have some evidence that there *is* an explanation. In the case of the universe, we cannot get outside it to see what explanation there might be outside it, and because we cannot get outside to see any possible explanation, we are unable to assert that there *is* an explanation.

Again, we need to be aware of the difference between what we can imagine and what we can conceive. We cannot *imagine* that there is no ultimate explanation of things, but it does not mean that an inexplicable object is *logically* excluded.

Bertrand Russell

Key term

Fallacy of composition The logical error, cited by Hume, of assuming that what is true of the part is true of the whole.

Key question

Is it possible to claim that God explains the universe if we cannot understand the nature of God and therefore cannot claim truly to understand the explanation?

8 Objections to arguments from experience

Over the centuries, many points have been made, and many arguments developed, both for and against these theories. Some of these arguments have been pointed out in the exposition of particular arguments, but there are further considerations. The following arguments might also be mentioned:

- A problem which has to be addressed is whether God can ever be the stopping point in explanation. Is God a sufficient reason which explains everything? To say 'God did it' seems not to end questions, but to create more. Why did he make this or that, allow this or that, make people die, allow there to be deserts, make the universe so wretchedly big with so many parts apparently barren and useless, create mosquitoes, give life to evil men and women? To answer those questions, we would need to know the mind of God, and that, religious people say, is a mystery we shall never know.

- Underlying the last question is the problem of evil. Voltaire, both in *Candide* and elsewhere pointed to the Lisbon earthquake, which struck on All Saints' Day, 1755. It was one of the worst earthquakes in history, killing tens of thousands and destroying 85% of the buildings in the city. Its effects stretched across the Algarve to Morocco and it was accompanied by a tsunami. Voltaire's question about how such an event could happen in 'the best of all possible worlds' remains no less valid today.

- An explanation really needs to explain something to the person to whom it is addressed. If I cannot understand the explanation of something someone gives me, then nothing has been explained to me. If no one can understand an explanation, then can it even be called an explanation? To say something is explained or caused by something we cannot understand is surely no explanation at all. There seems little advance beyond saying: 'It's a mystery!' Explanations must be understood.

9 Other issues

(a) Sheer chance

For many we have studied the arguments outlined in this chapter, there is an underlying problem, which touches on issues raised by both evolutionary theory and the objection made by Hume in his suggestions about the Epicurean thesis.

As humans we seek explanations for why things are as they are, or as they seem to be. We simply do not like things to be left unexplained. Not to know what is going on makes us uncomfortable. When we need something – or think we need it – we are tempted to grab at the most obvious solution offered. We are baffled and perhaps uncomfortable about the idea of things being the result of random chances, but the fact that we are uncomfortable with something we find unpalatable does not itself mean that the unpalatable is an error. It may be the uncomfortable truth.

Russell's suggestion that 'the universe just is' – it happens to exist, inexplicably, might be correct and needs to be considered seriously.

(b) The leap to the transcendent

In a similar vein, we need to ask whether arguments such as the Cosmological make too much of a leap when they go from arguing that there is a First Cause or Necessary Being, to arguing that this being must be the transcendent being of religious belief. We saw how Hume, in response to design arguments, argued that even if we could rightly infer a Designer, such as being would be far less than believers mean by God. The same point is applicable also to Cosmological Arguments. The First Cause might be an undiscovered immanent being, as yet undiscovered by science. If God is strictly unknowable, we cannot be sure that the universe is explained by the inexplicable God any more than we can be certain it does not come from some other unknown source.

10 Conclusions

That there are so many objections to the arguments whether around infinite regress, problems of causation or of what is logically possible, would seem to indicate that these arguments are failures. Saying this, however, may be unjust. We cannot accuse someone of failing in a task if she had never attempted the task in the first place and had no intention of doing so. What did Aquinas intend to do in the Five Ways? After all, if any one of his arguments were conclusive, he would surely have no need to give the other four. Indeed, his use of language is interesting. In Latin, he begins his Five Ways:

> *Respondeo dicendum quod Deum esse quinque viis probari potest*
>
> *S.T.* I,2 a.3c

This is usually translated as 'I answer that God is able to be proved in five ways.' The key word is *probari* from which we get the English 'prove'. But in Latin it is more ambiguous. It may also mean 'demonstrate' or 'show'. This is much weaker than the modern sense of 'prove', which is usually taken to mean something absolute. Of course, the notion of 'proof' in English has changed. It once meant 'to test', a sense rarely heard except in calculating the strength of alcoholic drinks or in the saying, 'It's the exception that proves the rule', which means 'It is the exception which *tests* the rule', not that it demonstrates the rule to be true. That would be silly! Aquinas wrote as a believer, and one who had already said that we could only come to God by indirect routes. To see him as offering a modern scientific proof is to mistake his intention. Rather, he seems to be offering indications to point his reader towards God.

It is worth considering whether many believers believe *because* they are persuaded by a philosophical argument. They may attempt to construct arguments to justify their belief, but the belief seems prior to any arguments for the existence of God. Aquinas was already a believer. In a series of books, John Cottingham has argued that:

> *Believers may perhaps find the traditional proofs reassuring as formal confirmation of the intellectual respectability of the religious outlook (or alternatively they may have doubts about the proofs' soundness); but they will often admit that other factors were of more immediate importance in making them turn to God – perhaps some deep crisis in their lives, perhaps something overwhelming or inspiring in their experience of the natural or the human world, or perhaps a growing sense that religious commitment satisfied some profound fundamental human need or yearning.*

> John Cottingham: *Philosophy of Religion: Towards a more Humane Approach* (2014), p. 28

Religious people often have the sense that somehow the arguments miss both the point and the lived experience of belief in God.

It is important also to remark that it does not follow that because a particular argument may fail that there is or is not a God. It merely means that that argument fails as a proof. Equally, poor arguments against the existence of God do not indicate that there is a God. Francis Galton in the nineteenth century argued that because members of royal families lived on average less long than other professionals, such as clerics and doctors, then clearly there was no God, as royal families are prayed for in church more often than others. It is weak at every level, presupposing that prayer works in a mechanical way. As we have seen, mechanical models of the universe may be doubted. Religion is not magic, but it seems not reducible to science, either.

> ## Key person
>
> **John Cottingham** (b. 1943): Emeritus Professor of Philosophy at the University of Reading, with an international reputation as a Descartes expert. In recent times has concentrated on Philosophy of Religion.

Study advice

Obviously there are points for reflection throughout this lengthy chapter, together with encouragements to develop your thoughts much further. In your reflections, it is worth concentrating on the issue of whether we should consider the question of God's existence as a scientific question – whether in terms of the Aristotelian science of Aquinas or in terms of more recent questioning of the universe. Some philosophers would argue that to treat questions about God's existence as a scientific enquiry is an error. The famous atheist Richard Dawkins argues that he treats the existence of God as a failed scientific hypothesis. Many theists might agree with him, arguing that God's reality is not a scientific hypothesis at all.

You might find it interesting to think about and discuss the approaches of different philosophers such as John Cottingham, mentioned on page 76.

You might consider also philosophical interest in the concept of religion without explanation. D. Z. Phillips believed that to seek an explanation was a mistaken enterprise:

> Just as there are unquestionable propositions in certain contexts, such as our talk of physical objects, so ... there are, in one sense, unquestionable beliefs in religion. This is why religion must remain, in a way I try to make clear, without explanation.

D. Z. Phillips: *Religion Without Explanation* (1976), p. 10

He argues that to ask whether God exists is not a theoretical question. If it means anything it is about wonder and praise and prayer. It is life-changing, but as a question which is unanswerable.

From a different perspective, the great Jesuit theologian, Karl Rahner (1904–84) argued:

> [Faith is] ... a letting go of oneself into the incomprehensible mystery. Christianity is far from a clarification of the world and existence; rather it contains the prohibition against treating any experience or insight, however illuminating it may be, as conclusive and intelligible in itself. Christians have [fewer] answers (at their disposal) than other mortals to hand out with a 'now everything is clear'. A Christian cannot enter God as an obvious item in the balance sheet of his life; he can only accept him as an incomprehensible mystery in silence and adoration, as the beginning and end of his hope and therefore as his unique, ultimate and all-embracing salvation.

Karl Rahner S.J.: *Theological Investigations* (1979): Vol. 16, pp. 14–15

It is essential, here as elsewhere, to concentrate on two things: precise and careful definition of terms, and reflection on the arguments outlined. You need obviously to know the content of arguments and criticisms of them but it is important also to be aware of wider context and to reflect not only on whether an argument is flawed but whether it is an appropriate argument to use. For instance, design arguments appear to presuppose a very mechanistic view of the universe, a view significantly undermined by modern physics, but they also point to an **anthropomorphic** type of God, a Grand Designer or Great Architect of the Universe. Are such models appropriate either to God or the world?

Key term

Anthropomorphism Projection of human characteristics onto a non-human being. In religious terms, this could be seeing God as simply a super human being. The term would also apply in fiction, when the author treats animals as if they were human beings, as In *Toad of Toad Hall* or *Watership Down*.

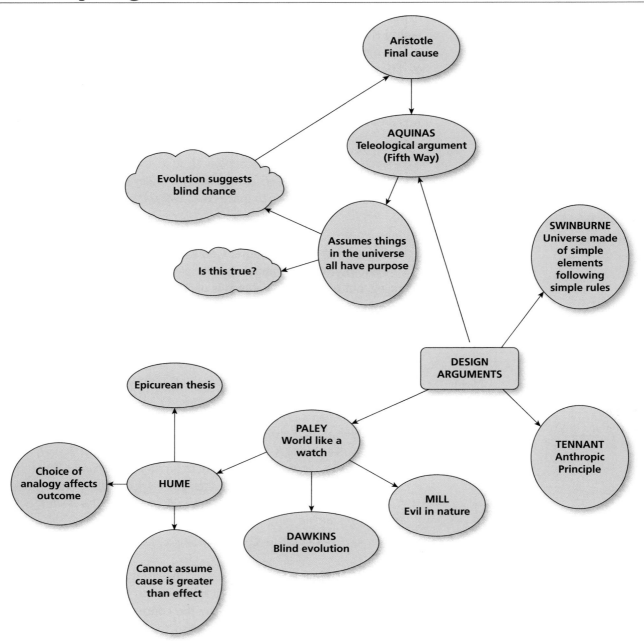

Revision advice

There is much to learn in this chapter, and there is a strong possibility – though not a certainty – that there will be a question on the existence of God in the examination. Whenever you discuss such a question, it is important to remember the difficulties outlined in the opening part of the current chapter. Remember that the question of whether God exists is a question of a different order from whether the tooth fairy exists.

It is important to be sure which points go with which argument. Reading the question is crucial here. Do not think in the examination that just because you have learned a great deal of material that the examiners wish to see everything you have learned. They will want to see the right material, that is, the material relevant to a specific question.

Can you give brief definitions of:
- cosmological arguments
- design arguments
- contingency
- necessity
- infinite regress?

Can you explain:
- how Paley develops his version of the design argument
- Aquinas' version of the cosmological argument
- Hume's objections to causation
- Hume's reasons for rejecting design arguments?

Can you give arguments for and against:
- the argument that the universe must have a first cause
- the argument that because everything in the universe is contingent, there must be a necessary being on which it depends
- the argument that God is the only explanation of the universe
- the argument that there is evident design in the universe?

Sample question and guidance

'There is no design in the universe.' Discuss.

This question is obviously about design arguments and not other justifications for the existence of God. It would be helpful to outline the claims made for design in the universe, perhaps looking particularly closely at one argument, such as that of Paley. Notice, however, that the focus of the question is not design arguments in themselves, but whether there is in the universe the evidence of design on which such arguments depend.

You may go on to consider whether we see the universe as designed or whether it really is. You might want to consider examples from nature of evil or things which have no evident purpose. You might want to think about Hume's Epicurean argument that apparent design could have come about because of random events. A particularly relevant argument could be developed on the basis of evolutionary theory. These points should be the central thrust of you answer, because the question's focus is the nature of the universe rather than whether it demonstrates that God exists.

As in all 'Discuss' questions, it is essential to go beyond mere description of arguments, developing considered opinions. When you describe an argument, such as one from Hume, be prepared to comment on its effectiveness, stating why you consider it a good point or otherwise. Also, reach an overall, justified conclusion, stating what has led you to reach the conclusion you have drawn. Here as elsewhere, what matters is the quality of your argument, not the conclusion you have reached.

Further essay questions

To what extent is Aquinas' first cause argument successful in proving that God exists?

How true is it to say that only the existence of God would provide a sufficient explanation for the existence of the universe?

'The universe is just there: it neither has nor needs an explanation.' Discuss.

Going further

The literature on arguments for the existence of God is vast, and we can give only a few suggestions. Aquinas' Five Ways are discussed in depth in Anthony Kenny: *The Unknown God: Agnostic Essays* (Continuum, 2005). A more sceptical approach may be found in Robin Le Poidevin: *Arguing for Atheism: An Introduction to the Philosophy of Religion* (Routledge, 1996). Brian Davies: *An Introduction to the Philosophy of Religion* (third edition, Oxford University Press, 2003) may be recommended with confidence, and some approaches in the present chapter are developed in Michael B. Wilkinson with Hugh N. Campbell: *Philosophy of Religion: An Introduction* (Continuum, 2010). As mentioned in the text, John Cottingham: *Philosophy of Religion: Towards a More Humane Approach* (Cambridge University Press, 2014) is a thoughtful essay on wider approaches to the questions in this chapter.

Other books discussed in this chapter are:
- Emmet D. *Outward Forms, Inner Springs* (Macmillan, 1998).
- Phillips D. Z. *Religion Without Explanation* (Blackwell, 1976).
- Rahner K. *Theological Investigations* (Darton, Longman and Todd, 1979).
- Russell B. *Principia Mathematica* (with A. N. Whitehead, Cambridge University Press, 1910–1913).
- Mill J. S. *Three Essays on Religion: Nature, the Utility of Religion, Theism* (Henry Holt & Co, New York, 1874).
- Temple W. *Mens Creatrix*, (Macmillan, 1915).
- Temple W. *Nature, Man and God* (AMS Press, 1934).
- Tennant F. R. *Philosophical Theology* (Cambridge University Press, 1928–1930).
- Tillich P. *Systematic Theology* (University of Chicago Press, 1951–1964).

Chapter 6

The existence of God: arguments based on reason

1 Introduction

Chapter checklist

This chapter concentrates on the ontological argument of St Anselm, as well as criticisms by Gaunilo. It begins by describing the nature of ontological arguments, and some issues with them. It then looks in detail at the text of the ontological argument of Anselm, given complete in a new translation, examining both Chapters Two and Three of *Proslogion*. It describes and considers the objections of Gaunilo and the Response of St Anselm. Then the chapter describes and develops Aquinas' objections to Anselm, and explains Kant's objections to ontological arguments. The chapter concludes by discussing whether it is ever possible to move from a definition to an existential statement.

In Chapter 5, we saw various arguments for the existence of God based on human experience of the world. St Thomas Aquinas was well aware that there are limitations on arguments from experience. The objects of experience might enable us to infer the existence of God, but, inevitably, any understanding will only be partial. If we found someone's footprints, and nothing else, we would know only a little about him or her. We might deduce whether the prints came from a human, perhaps even male or female, light or heavy, but we would know little else about appearance. Big footprints might not necessarily mean they came from someone tall. They might be from a little person with unusually big feet. For Aquinas, God was, in himself, unknowable, at least during earthly life.

Others, however, have speculated about whether we can prove God's existence not from sense experience but from the very idea of God.

The **ontological argument** attempts to argue for God without reference to sense experience. Various philosophers, including St Anselm and Descartes, through to the present day have developed versions, believing that it is valuable in demonstrating the way to God. Others, including many believers, such as Aquinas, have dismissed these arguments as misconceived.

The argument is *a priori*. This means that it claims that the very definition of God necessarily entails his existence, just as the definition of a square necessarily entails having four sides. A square without four sides, it is argued, would not be a square. In the same way, God without existence would not be God.

The obvious question to think about is whether we can go from a *definition*, which is verbal, to a *fact* about the universe. That squares have four sides, by definition, does not mean that squares exist, just as we cannot say that because a mermaid is by definition half-woman, half-fish, that mermaids must therefore exist. This is important, as it will be argued that whether something exists is a different question from its definition.

Key terms

A priori Something knowable without reference to sense experience.

Ontological argument An argument for the existence of God from his definition. Such an argument does not depend on sense experience.

St Anselm of Canterbury (1033–1109): One of the most significant and interesting thinkers of the Medieval period. He was aware of the logic of Aristotle which he knew about, second-hand, from the commentaries of Boethius, and he uses aspects of the logic of Boethius in his argument. His major works include *Monologion, Proslogion, De Grammatico, De Fide Trinitatis* and *Cur Deus Homo*?

Anselm was born in Aosta in Northern Italy. He became a monk, joining the abbey at Bec, in Normandy, one of the most significant monasteries in Europe. Founded in 1034, it produced three Archbishops of Canterbury. Anselm became prior, second in importance after the abbot, and was responsible for the day-to-day running of the monastery. In 1066, William the Conqueror invaded England from Normandy and installed the Abbot of Caen, Lanfranc, as Archbishop of Canterbury. Anselm became Abbot of Bec in 1078. The next King of England, William II (William Rufus), was not interested in religion, but, after pressure, in 1093 appointed Anselm Archbishop of Canterbury. The relationship with William was fractious. Bad relations continued between Anselm and Henry I after William's mysterious death (by an arrow of unknown origin) in the New Forest in 1100.

St Anselm of Canterbury

Bec Abbey today

2 St Anselm's ontological argument

Anselm's 'ontological argument' (the title was given by Immanuel Kant) may be found in his brief work, *Proslogion*. It is important to remember that Anselm believed that true understanding was a consequence of faith. His personal motto was *Credo ut intelligam* ('I believe so that I may understand'). This means that if we have faith, that which we need to know can become clearer. Understanding of God is a consequence of belief, not something that precedes it. We do not begin by knowing who God is, and then finding him. We need to believe in God before we can have any understanding of him.

The entire text of *Proslogion* is a prayer. The book is directed to and addressed to God. Anselm's intention in the book is twofold: to demonstrate that God exists, the subject of Chapter Two, and then, in the remaining chapters, to show that God is indeed the type of God in whom Christians believe. He examines the traditional beliefs about God's qualities to demonstrate that it is rational to believe in these.

(a) *Proslogion* Chapter Two

In philosophy, close attention to the text is an important skill. It is therefore helpful to consider what this text can teach us, paying attention not only to the main part in which Anselm sets out his argument, but also to his preliminary remarks which point us to an understanding of his entire project.

Chapter Two

That God Truly Is

Therefore, O Lord, who gives to faith understanding, give to me, as far as you know it to be expedient, that I may understand that you exist, as we believe, and you are what we believe you are.

And, indeed, we believe you are something than which nothing greater can be thought. Or is there no such nature, as the fool has said in his heart: 'There is no God?'

But certainly that very fool, when he hears what I now say: 'something than which nothing greater can be thought', understands what he hears and what he hears is in his understanding, even though he does not understand it to exist.

Now, there is a difference between a thing's being in the understanding and its being understood to exist. For when the painter thinks ahead to that [the painting] which is to be made, he truly has it in his understanding, but does not yet understand to exist that which he has not yet made. When, however, he has made the painting, he has in his understanding and understands to exist that which he has now made.

So even the fool is therefore bound to admit that there at least exists in his understanding something than which nothing greater can be thought, because when he hears this he understands, and whatever is understood is in the understanding.

And certainly, that than which a greater cannot be thought is not possible to be in the understanding alone, for if it is at least in the understanding alone, it can be thought also to exist in fact, and this is more great.

*For this reason, if that than which a greater cannot be thought is in the understanding only, then the very thing than which a more great is **not** able to be thought is that than which a more great **is** able to be thought.*

But obviously, this contradiction cannot be.

So, therefore, without any doubt that than which a more great is not able to be thought exists both in the understanding and in fact.

(author translation)

The argument of Chapter Two is straightforward – and brief – but it is useful to take time to read it, thinking about each part. Notice how Anselm uses an example – of a painter – to make clear his important distinction between having an idea of something and thinking that it exists.

The entire argument rests on the logical impossibility of a **contradiction**. Anselm refers to the fool in the Psalms (Psalms 13 and 52 in the Vulgate of St Jerome, used by Anselm, Psalms 14 and 53 in modern editions) who says in his heart that there is no God. In an age of faith, it would be difficult for Anselm to pick an argument by a named atheist. What he then does is to offer a definition which, he claims, the fool himself would accept, that God is: 'something than which nothing greater can be thought'. He then explains the difference between things in the understanding and those which are understood to exist. For instance, I understand what a mermaid is. I have the idea of a mermaid in my understanding, but it is not my understanding that mermaids actually exist as beings in the world. It is important to take a moment to think about this. His argument depends on this point, which is why he repeats it so carefully. This is what Anselm shows in his example of the painter. Before he paints the picture, the idea is in his understanding, in his mind, but he does not think it exists. He thinks it exists only when he has painted it.

This illustrates the position of the fool. He knows the definition of God, but he does not think that there is in the universe anything equivalent to the definition. He knows what God is supposed to be. Otherwise he would have no reason to deny his existence.

But, says Anselm, the fool is contradicting himself. If God is the greatest thing we can think of *and* he does not exist, he would not be the greatest thing we can think of, because a real thing is greater – being more real – than something that does not exist. To put it crudely, a real ten million pounds in my bank account is greater – being more real – than a purely imaginary ten million pounds. Reality is presumed to be a good worth having. This appeals very much to the intuition that it is much better to exist than not to exist. According to Aristotelian logic, a contradiction is impossible. So, thinks Anselm, God must exist. Avicenna, also known as Ibn Sina (980–1037AD), the Arab philosopher said: 'Anyone who denies the law of non-contradiction should be beaten and burned until he admits that to be beaten is not the same as not to be beaten, and to be burned is not the same as not to be burned.'

If he did not exist, then God would not be the greatest thing we can conceive, yet the fool has already conceded that God must be the greatest thing we can conceive. A real God would be greater than an imaginary one.

(b) *Proslogion* Chapter Three

Chapter Three concerns the first quality of God that it is not even possible for him to be thought not to exist. This is often interpreted to mean that God is a *necessary* being, one who *has* to exist and cannot not exist. This is unlike *contingent* beings, such as ourselves, who might or might not exist. If our parents had not met, for instance, we would not be here. *Contingent* beings depend on other things for their existence. It is sometimes mistakenly argued that the argument is designed to show that God, unlike our parents – is a necessary being. Such an interpretation is too limited. Anselm is going much further than this.

Chapter Three

That he cannot be thought not to be

Which indeed is so true that it is not possible *for it **to be thought** not to be.*

Because something is possible ***to be thought*** to be *which is* not possible ***to be thought*** not to be,

and the latter is greater than that which is possible ***to be thought*** not to be.

Wherefore, if that than which a greater cannot be thought is possible ***to be thought*** not to be, *then*

the very thing than which a greater cannot be thought is not *that than which a greater cannot be thought;*

but this cannot be consistent.

So real therefore is the thing than which nothing greater can be thought that it is not even able to be thought not to be.

And this is what you are, O Lord our God.

Therefore, so truly do you exist, O Lord my God, that you are not even able to be thought not to be.

And rightly so, because if a mind could think of something better than you, the creature would rise above the creator, and would judge the creator, which is the height of absurdity. And truly, whatever else exists, apart from you alone, can be thought not to exist, because anything else does not exist so truly, and therefore has less being.

Why therefore has the fool said in his heart 'God is not', when it is obvious to the rational mind that you have being in the highest degree? Why, unless he is stupid and a fool?

(author translation)

To understand Anselm's point fully we need to know that Boethius, in his Commentary on Aristotle's Categories, argues that everything that we can think of comes into at least one of four categories:

- possible to be
- possible not to be
- not possible to be
- not possible not to be.

You and I – and most things around us – fall into the first two categories. This means that we/they both could and could not exist. Square circles are impossible. They are a contradiction in terms, and thus fall into the third category. The fourth category is *necessary beings*, things that have to be.

If you look back at Chapter Three of *Proslogion*, you will see that the language of the categories is there, not *italicised* in my translation, but you will notice also the addition of '**to be thought**' in every usage. Knowledge of the science of the eleventh century is helpful here. In Anselm's day, scientists thought that necessary beings included all permanent things. To them, this included the Earth, the Sun, and the stars. This idea can be seen in Ptolemy's *Almagest*, the standard astronomical textbook used by medieval scholars. They were created by God, but as necessary beings. They were necessary because they show no sign of decay, unlike contingent beings. What Anselm is doing is to show, using the same pattern of argument as in Chapter Two, that God is not simply another necessary being, but is even more significant. He alone cannot even be thought not to exist. This is reinforced by the wording of the final sentences of the chapter. He relies again on the impossibility of a contradiction. It is impossible to argue at the same time that God *is and is not 'not possible not thought not to be'*. Anselm points out the character of God's existence when he says that God's existence has a special truth which is not available to any other being.

3 Objections to theories

(a) Gaunilo's criticism

Gaunilo of Marmoutier, a Benedictine monk and contemporary of Anselm, thought there was something wrong with the argument. He argued that Anselm's argument was an exercise in wishful thinking, in that it permitted anything to be thought into existence. Notice that Gaunilo (sometimes called Gaunilon) was a believer as much as Anselm was. He was asking whether this argument was philosophically sound, not questioning God's existence. In his *In Behalf of the Fool*, Gaunilo puts himself in the position of a rational non-believer. In doing so, he engages in good philosophical practice.

Too often people take a position on something and view opposing arguments from that perspective, rather than thinking through how the original argument appears from the perspective of the opponent. In medieval universities, it would become standard practice to teach through disputations in which the students were required to argue from different positions. These positions which were frequently contrary to their own beliefs.

Gaunilo asks us to consider the mythical Lost Island, which was considered to be the perfect island. If the perfect island did not exist, it would be a contradiction to call it the perfect island, for the perfect island would not be perfect if it did not exist. Therefore the perfect island, and anything else we think of as perfect must, by definition exist, because if the perfect thing did not exist, it would not be perfect.

To Gaunilo, this is absurd. The perfect island does not exist, just as perfect pens, books, tables and so on do not exist. Here Gaunilo appeals to his own empiricist views. He asks his readers to look at the evidence of the world. There is no trace of these perfect beings — no perfect island, tables or

Key person

Gaunilo of Marmoutiers
(*fl.* eleventh century): Benedictine monk, known only for his response to St Anselm, *In Behalf of the Fool*.

Marmoutier Abbey, Tours

books. He argues that if parallel arguments from perfection are absurd, then the original ontological argument is absurd.

(b) St Anselm's response

Anselm wrote a careful response. He pointed out that an island is contingent. Its very existence is contingent. That is, it depends on things like sea and earth. Islands do not have to exist, so their existence cannot be necessary. For there to be an island there must be other conditions fulfilled. This is true of any contingent being. There is nothing in the universe – as far as we can tell – that exists wholly independently of anything else. A table would not exist were there no materials or table-makers. Anselm argues that God is supremely necessary. He is not dependent on anything else, so the argument applies to him alone.

He might have added, as some modern philosophers such as John Hick have done, that the idea of the perfect island does not make sense. It is indefinable. If I add one grain of sand to the perfect island, does it become imperfect? Or is a perfect island plus a million extra grains of sand or an extra palm tree even more perfect? But, if we keep adding billions of grains of sand, it ceases to be a perfect island and becomes Australia, instead. When does an island become a continent? Also, your perfect island might not be mine. As someone with a lifelong hatred of the taste of coconut, I would not wish to have coconut palms on my island. You might think otherwise.

In Chapter 9 of his reply, Anselm gives an important further clarification, which needs to be understood. Occasionally, people have argued that if God cannot be thought not to be, how is it possible for the fool to think in his heart that 'There is no God'? Anselm here directly addresses the issue. The verb he uses throughout the argument is *intelligere*, that is, 'to understand'. It is not merely that the concept of God needs to be thought of. It needs to be really understood. That is why, at the end of Chapter 3, Anselm says that the fool says what he does because he has not really understood the thought he had.

We can *say* anything, in that we can produce the words. But it does not follow that either we understand the words or that the words in themselves make sense. I can talk absolute nonsense, perhaps without even realising that I am talking nonsense. For example, I might tell you about an art exhibition I visited and say that there were amazing sculptures, some in eight dimensions, and an extraordinary picture of a nine-sided circle. If you were paying attention, you might point out that what I said was complete nonsense. The fact that I can use the words does not mean either that they make sense in themselves or that the way I use them entails any understanding on my part. So it is with the fool. His sentence, 'There is no God', would be nonsense to any rational mind. The rational mind would think matters through.

A weakness in Anselm's response is that even fools do not, generally, deny what is truly self-evident.

Key question

Is Anselm successful in refuting Gaunilo's criticisms?

(c) Other criticisms

Thoughts along these lines were developed by St Thomas Aquinas:

> *A thing can be self-evident in either of two ways: on the one hand, self-evident in itself, though not to us; on the other, self-evident in itself and to us. A proposition is self-evident because the*

Key term

Predicate A grammatical term which refers to the description of a concept. In the sentence: 'Her dress is red', 'is red' is the predicate, adding to the idea of the dress.

predicate is included in the essence of the subject: e.g., Man is an animal, because 'animal' is contained in the essence of 'man' ... If ... there are some to whom the essence of the predicate and the subject is unknown, the proposition will be self-evident in itself, but not to those ignorant of the meaning of the subject and predicate of the proposition. Therefore, as Boethius says, there are some concepts which are common and self-evident only to the learned, e.g. ... Incorporeal substances are not in space. Therefore, I say that the proposition God exists is in itself self-evident, because God is his own essence ... [But] because we do not know the essence of God, the proposition is not self-evident to us, but must be demonstrated by things that are more known to us, though less evident in themselves – namely, by his effects ...

Summa Theologica: I, q.2, a.1, c.

Aquinas argues that something is self-evident in two ways: in itself and for us. We, as humans, need to be able to see the self-evidence to assert that we understand the self-evidence. I know that it is self-evident that a square has four sides because I really understand the meaning of the word 'square' and know what a square is. The proposition about the square is self-evident to me because I speak English. It would not be self-evident to someone who spoke no English. One has to be in the right place to see the self-evidence. In the case of God, so much is unknown to us. Aquinas, throughout his work, is insistent that the nature of God is strictly unknown to us. We can have an idea of him, but only in human terms, with all the limitations of human language and human knowledge. We simply do not know enough of about God to be able to understand the full meaning of the proposition. If the very nature of God's existence is hidden from us – even precisely what it means to say that 'he exists,' as he would be so beyond the limits of human comprehension – then we cannot have any vantage point from which we could demonstrate his self-evidence. I am able to demonstrate clearly and precisely why it is necessary for a square to have four sides, but I cannot point to God and tell you to see the reasoning for yourself, as something self-evident to us.

Aquinas uses Boethius to argue against Anselm, though, interestingly, throughout the article, he never names Anselm. Often in his writing, we find him using philosophers' own sources to argue against them.

We should also notice Aquinas' final comments. He argues that the only way to God is, for us, through his effects in the world. He indicates that our way to God is an indirect one. This is an important qualification when we consider his Five Ways.

(d) Descartes' development of Anslem's argument

Later philosophers also attempted to reformulate Anslem's argument, including Descartes in the seventeenth century, Norman Malcolm and Alvin Plantinga in the twentieth, and David Smith in the twenty-first.

For the examination, you are not required to know these arguments, but knowledge of Descartes can be valuable, as the criticism directed by Kant to Descartes' argument applies with equal force to Anselm.

For a profile of Descartes, see Chapter 4

Can existence be treated as a predicate?

Descartes builds his arguments, which may be found in the *Meditations*, on two points:

- God is by definition perfect. An imperfect God would not be God. So, if God is perfect, he must contain all perfections, including the perfection of existence. If he did not exist he would not be perfect. So, he must exist.
- Existence is a *defining predicate* of the concept of God in exactly the same way that having three sides and three angles is necessary to the concept of a triangle. Without three sides there can be no concept of a triangle. A defining predicate is a description something has to have to be itself. A square that did not have four sides would not be a square. A God who did not exist – according to Descartes – would not be God.

(e) Kant's critique of Descartes

In the *Critique of Pure Reason*, Immanuel Kant (1724–1804) develops two criticisms of Descartes. These objections also apply to Anselm's version of the ontological argument:

- Suppose Descartes is right, and existence is indeed a defining predicate of the concept of God. There is no contradiction – and hence no impossibility – in someone rejecting a concept together with all its defining predicates. To take an earlier example, I can accept that being half-woman and half-fish is a defining predicate of the idea of a mermaid. I would not be contradicting myself if I said I did not believe in mermaids or creatures that are half-woman and half-fish. I would only be talking nonsense, and contradicting myself, if I said that I believed mermaids exist but did not believe in the existence of creatures that are half-woman and half-fish. In the same way, I could say that I accepted that *if* God existed, *then* he would necessarily exist, but that I did not believe in him *or* his necessary existence. There would be no contradiction here.
- Kant's second objection argues that existence is not a predicate at all, and therefore, cannot be a defining predicate. Remember that a predicate adds a description to a concept. So, if I say, 'my cat is tabby', the 'is tabby', tells us something about the idea of my cat. But when I say '*x* exists', I am not adding anything to the *concept* of *x*. Instead, I am asserting that in the real world there exists an object which corresponds to the concept of *x*. Think about this for a moment. Suppose I believe in the existence of mermaids and you do not. There is actually no difference between us about what a mermaid might be. We agree that it would be half-woman, half-fish. What we differ about is not the idea of the mermaid, but whether something just like the mermaid concept could be found in the real world. Our *concept* of the mermaid is identical. So, if Kant is right, to say something exists adds nothing at all to the *concept* or idea of a thing. Kant illustrates this with the example of the conceptual difference between a hundred real and a hundred imaginary *thalers* – a common currency in Middle Europe at the time. The number of thalers is identical in the thought of the imaginary set as may be thought about in the real set. The idea is the same. When I say something exists, I add nothing at all to the idea but attempt to say something about the world. As predicates add to a concept, then, because saying '*x* exists' adds nothing to the idea, 'exists' is not a predicate.

Defining predicate A description that is necessary to the concept. In the sentence, 'A square has four sides', 'Has four sides' is a defining predicate: the idea of a square necessarily entails four-sidedness.

Key question

Is Kant as successful in refuting Anselm as he appears to be with Descartes?

Key person

Immanuel Kant (1724–1804): Philosopher from Konigsberg in East Prussia. One of the greatest thinkers in history, attempted to reconcile the insights of the Rationalists, such as Descartes and Leibniz, and the Empiricists such as Locke, Hume and Berkeley. Author of *The Critique of Pure Reason*, the *Critique of Practical Reason* and *Groundwork of the Metaphysic of Morals*.

4 *A priori* and *a posteriori* proofs of God

At the end of two chapters on arguments for the existence of God, it is helpful to pause to consider whether the *a priori* arguments you have studied are any more likely to be persuasive than the evidentiary arguments of Aquinas, Paley and others.

Each type of argument involves its own problems.

A priori arguments, notably the Ontological Argument, tend to be precise and to promise certainty in the way that a mathematical formula does. If we could prove God by definition, then one of the deepest – and perhaps the deepest – of all mysteries would be solved.

But the question is whether we can actually define God in the way I can define the geometrical concept of a triangle. A triangle is a human concept in the human system of geometry. We can define a triangle because we know precisely what we mean by the term 'triangle'. From the knowledge, we can make our definition. But that knowledge is exactly what we do not have if we imagine we can define God. Even a formulation such as 'that than which nothing greater can be thought' can be questioned as a *definition* of God. It doesn't define at all what God is, in himself. The definition is actually a statement about the limits of human thought, coupled with an acknowledgement of God being at or beyond the limits of thought. We may question whether it is possible to argue from an unknown to something knowable as existing.

There is the further issue, identified in Chapter 1 of this book, that many philosophers argue that all we can know *a priori* is the truth of definitions, not whether they refer to things that exist in reality. Existential questions seem to require actual evidence, based on sense experience.

This is why, as we saw, Aquinas rejected Anselm's arguments for what he describes as more indirect ways which are more accessible to us – the evidence of God's handiwork in the world. The advantage of this approach is that it begins from something known rather than something unknown. The question, however, is how far that approach might then take us towards God. The problem here is the point in any line of reasoning from the known to the unknown. Even if the starting point of the reasoning, based on this world, is more secure, there is a point in the argument when a leap of faith is made into the arms of an unknown God.

5 Conclusion

The ontological argument, in different forms, continues to fascinate philosophers. Attempts have been made to construct versions which avoid the types of criticisms made by Aquinas, Kant and others.

The major problem, of course, is whether it is possible to make the leap from what is said to what exists. However exact my description of God – or anything else – the existence of the description surely does not entail the necessary existence of that which is described. In the case of God, things are further complicated because human words cannot encompass the unknown nature of God, a God who surpasses human understanding. John Cottingham has recently suggested a different way of thinking of the ontological argument:

> ... *[Arguments for the existence of God]... are best understood not as ways in which any impartial inquirer can be led to conclude that*

*God exists, but rather as throwing light on the **content** of theistic faith. Such a construal [reading]... would be in broad harmony with the 'faith seeking understanding' tradition. Thus the ontological argument would serve to underline the unsurpassable perfection of God ... [For] those who already are committed or inclined towards theism, reflection on the arguments could succeed in deepening the reach of their faith and illuminating its object.*

John Cottingham: *Philosophy of Religion: Towards a More Humane Approach* (2014) pp. 34–35

Cottingham argues that the argument makes sense only within the context of faith. He reminds us of how God transcends any human conception. On his reading, it would seem that the argument makes sense only *within* a life of faith. This reading would seem consistent with Anselm's *Credo ut intelligam*, which treats true comprehension in terms of faith seeking understanding. This suggests that a non-believer would not be likely to be convinced, because the argument begins from a perspective of faith.

Study advice

Reflecting on what you have learned

It is always good practice to compare the merits of particular arguments, weighing the strengths of different arguments against each other. Consider the significance of ontological arguments compared with those based on experience.

At first sight, ontological arguments appear to be more precise and more complete. As Aquinas acknowledges, arguments from experience offer a route that is more indirect but begins with premises that we can understand better. This goes to the heart of the issue of whether we may claim to be able to define God, because he is of an order quite different from anything in human experience. In a sermon, St Augustine warned:

... if you claim that you have grasped him, what you have grasped is not God.

St Augustine: *Sermones*, 52:16

We may go further, reflecting on the view that the only way we can check the truth of a proposition about what exists is by observation of the world. Sometimes, of course, we make existential claims based on inference. When I find a hole in my window I infer that something must have broken it. I may infer that the cause of my window being broken was the action of the child next door, and I may (properly) be questioned on the justice of such an inference. But the origin of my train of thought is observation – the observation of the broken window. If I assumed that my window had been broken, and the culprit had been the child, without ever checking that I did indeed have a broken window, something would seem to have gone horribly wrong with my reasoning. Indeed, my neighbour (the parent of the child) might argue that I had lost my reason. The thought of something and its reality – as Kant implies – are quite different questions.

As noted, careful study of the text is invaluable. Make certain that you are familiar with the original text of St Anselm as well as Gaunilo's arguments and Anselm's response. It will deepen the quality of your argument to know Descartes' arguments and especially Kant's two responses, which are applicable also to Anselm.

In your criticisms, it is very important to be conscious not simply of the content of arguments, but, especially in the case of the ontological argument, their style. Think about whether it is a legitimate form of argument to use to demonstrate the reality of God. Gaunilo, Aquinas and Kant all find the form of the argument inappropriate.

Examiners routinely point to errors of understanding. Two particular misconceptions stand out:

■ Many candidates think that Chapter Three of *Proslogion* is Anselm's response to Gaunilo. It is not, because it was part of the original book. The reply to Gaunilo is a separate work.
■ A second problem is that many candidates misunderstand the notion of a *predicate*. The term does *not* refer to the quality of a thing. It is a grammatical notion. It refers to part of a sentence which describes the quality of the subject of the sentence. Things do not have predicates, but nouns and subjects of sentences often do.

Summary diagram: Existence of God based on observation

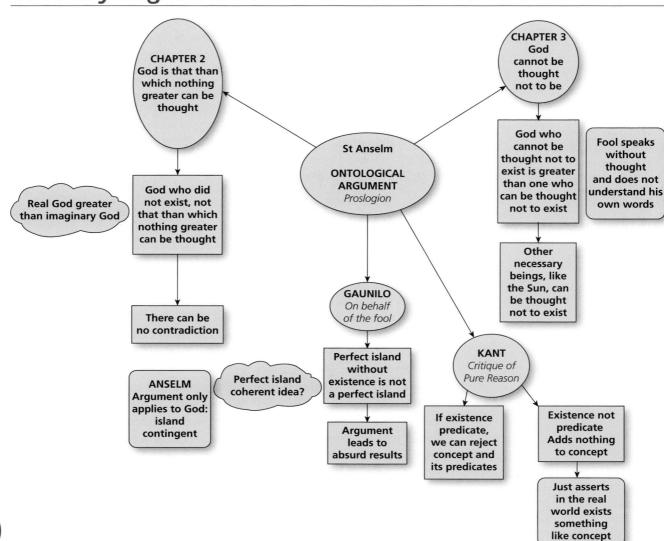

Revision advice

It is important to be thoroughly familiar with the text of the argument so that you can describe Anselm's points with confidence. Make certain that you can distinguish the arguments of Chapter Three from those in Chapter Two, and understand how Anselm relies on the principle of non-contradiction. Be certain also that you can confidently describe Gaunilo's objections and Anselm's response, and that you are familiar with the arguments of Kant.

Can you give brief definitions of:
- the *a priori*
- the principle of non-contradiction
- a defining predicate
- a necessary being
- a contingent being?

Can you explain:
- Chapter Two of *Proslogion*
- Chapter Three of *Proslogion*
- Gaunilo's objection
- Kant's objections to ontological arguments?

Can you give arguments for and against:
- God as a necessary being
- Gaunilo's objection to Anselm
- God's existence as self-evident
- existence as a defining predicate of the concept of God?

Sample question and guidance

To what extent does St Anselm's ontological argument prove the necessary existence of God?

This question goes to the heart of the issue of whether Anselm's argument works. Before beginning, notice the wording of the question. 'To what extent ...?' needs an answer in terms of wholly / quite a lot / somewhat / not very much / not at all. This is a little more nuanced than just asking whether it works or not. Bear this in mind as you construct your answer because the invitation is there to consider whether the argument has any merits, even if you conclude that it is flawed.

The question is specific to Anselm's argument, so there is no need to look at any other version of the argument. It would be helpful to outline the argument as well as to say something about what is meant by the 'necessary existence' of God. You might consider here Anselm's argument from Chapter Three of *Proslogion*. You might then choose to consider those arguments aimed directly at Anselm by Gaunilo and Aquinas. In doing so, be sure that you are considering and commenting on these arguments and not just describing them. You might then consider whether any other points in relation to ontological arguments in general are relevant to this question. Unless you can make points directly relevant to Anselm's version, there is no point – and no merit – in including them.

In reaching your conclusions, remember the precise wording of the question. Even if you consider that the argument as a whole fails, you might nevertheless think that it has some valuable features. In reaching your conclusions, be careful – as always – to ensure that you have justified your arguments and not merely stated them.

Further essay questions

'We cannot derive the existence of God from his definition.' Discuss.

'As existence is never a defining predicate, it cannot be a defining predicate of the concept of God.' Discuss.

Chapter 7

Religious experience

1 Introduction

Chapter checklist

This chapter considers both religious experience in general and as evidence for God. It begins with an account of reports of religious experience, including issues of interpretation and the problem of other minds. It looks at John Hick's theory of religious experience as 'experiencing as' before going on to specific discussion of William James, Richard Swinburne's notions of credulity and testimony, and Rudolf Otto's theory of numinous experience. The chapter specifically considers mystical and conversion experiences. Throughout, it offers examples of experiences to illustrate arguments.

Key person

Rowan Williams (b. 1950): Welsh theologian, poet, philosopher and bishop. Lady Margaret Professor of Divinity, Oxford, 1986–2000; Archbishop of Wales 2000–02, Archbishop of Canterbury 2002–12; Appointed Master of Magdalene College Cambridge 2013. Gave the Gifford Lectures 2013–14.

Key quote

The touch of God is dangerous, in that it can be a light too sharp to be borne without hurt or breakage; and when the perception is skewed and redirected, it may run close to the destructive and the hellish … For God to come near us is for God, it seems, to 'risk' God's own integrity, in the sense that God puts himself into our hands to be appallingly misunderstood, to become the justifier of our hatred and fears, our madness. And it is to put us at risk, since the disorientation we thus experience can unleash some very dark things in us. Revelation itself, as the Church's history shows, is bound up with tragic possibilities.

Rowan Williams: 'The Touch of God', *Open to Judgement: Sermons and Addresses* (1994), pp. 114–115

It has been common throughout human history for people to claim to have religious experiences. All religions seem to have had mystic cults, whether those of ancient Rome, such as the cult of Mithras through to various mystical groups around New Age ideas. Of course, it does not follow that because a claim is made, what is claimed to have been experienced actually happened. In any experience, there are at least two main factors: the experience itself and the interpretation of that experience. I may sincerely believe I have experienced something, but the error lies in my interpretation of the event.

When we think about it, we often experience things in incorrect ways. In ordinary life, we misjudge what we see, mistaking something for something else, getting speeds and distances wrong. Sometimes we

Wittgenstein used puzzle pictures to explain his argument

experience a dream so vividly that we do not realise that we were asleep. The great English philosopher, Thomas Hobbes, in Chapter 32 of *Leviathan*, raised an interesting question by asking the difference between a man saying that God spoke to him in a dream and a man dreaming that God had spoken to him. Bertrand Russell suggested that some people drink too much and see snakes, while others fast too much and see God.

Wittgenstein developed the concept of 'seeing-as' in his *Philosophical Investigations* (1958, p. 194). We interpret our experience in a particular way. For example, I see someone in the street and *see* her *as* an old friend. When I call out, she turns, only to be a stranger, to my embarrassment. In this case, the way I saw that person was incorrect, though sometimes I interpret my seeing correctly, if the person I thought was my friend actually turned out to be the right person. He drew attention to the phenomenon of puzzle pictures. An example might be the famous drawing which could be a rabbit or a duck, depending on which way you look at it. Another example is the picture which might be an old woman or a young girl, depending on your perception at a specific time. John Hick explored these issues and developed Wittgenstein's idea of *'seeing-as'* into a rather richer notion of *'experiencing as'*. For Hick, the important point here is that the world and everything in it can be experienced in different ways, even though the facts experienced are the same for the two — or more — experiences. We know this in our lives, when, for example, we go to the cinema. My friend and I see the same film. She experiences it as the funniest thing she has ever seen in her life, while I find it simply juvenile and lame. We have seen precisely the same thing. There is nothing she has seen that I have not, but its significance is quite different. Two people may see the same beautiful sunset. Each sees it in its splendour. Each agrees it is a thing of beauty. But one experiences it as mediating the greatness of God, and feels touched by the divine, whereas the other believes it to be just an extraordinary natural event. Again we find a difference of experience, not a difference of fact.

If we apply this to religious experience, we can see why some might see evidence of God in everyday life or interpret a particular experience in their lives as religious. However, in the real world we have the problem of truth claims. When people claim that they see something, they also are saying that they believe they are seeing the world as it really is. We think we get things right when we report our experience. Vincent Brümmer (*What Are We Doing When We Pray?*, 2008, pp. 85–87) has pointed out that the problem with the duck/rabbit picture is that it is neither a duck nor a rabbit. It is truly just a line drawing. He notes also that people want to go further than just to be content with saying that they interpret an event religiously (or otherwise). They make the crucial additional claim that theirs is the correct claim. Neither the believer nor the unbeliever is saying that it is just a matter of interpretation.

This can be where problems begin. Sometimes, the issue is not the experience but the certainty with which someone interprets that phenomenon. We know very well that people want certainty. In practice, certainty can lead to fanaticism of the type described by Rowan Williams.

Some people just want life to be tidy, with simple answers. This is the appeal of fundamentalism, which can be of many types. There are fundamentalist atheists, just as there are fundamentalist believers. A curiosity, which we shall explore, is that often a fundamentalist of one type will suddenly be converted to another. The committed Christian gives it all up and becomes a committed and militant atheist. The left-wing communist becomes the right-wing free marketeer. In some cases, the new cause is followed as fanatically as the old. Of course, not all **conversions** are of this type. Many are gradual and are the result of a variety of experiences and reflections. To assume that just because someone is believer or atheist he is therefore fanatical would be absurd. Fanaticism only occurs when there is refusal to deny the possibility that he might be wrong.

> **Key term**
>
> **Conversion** Change from one set of beliefs to another, with life-changing consequences.

2 The nature of religious experience

It is difficult to take a single example of religious experience, and to say 'this is what religious experience is'. Like people, experiences of all sorts are of different kinds. Two people will have very different experiences of an art exhibition, even when they have visited it together. Each has some sort of artistic experience, but each will be very different from the other. If this is true of aesthetic and other experiences, we should not be surprised to find it just as true of religious experience.

It is worth remarking, by way of preliminary discussion, that much literature on religious experience concentrates on dramatic experiences, such as the conversion of St Paul or the visions of St Teresa of Avila. It is important to remember that not all religious experience is so dramatic, any more than ordinary life experiences will always be dramatic. Some people claim direct awareness of God, but that is probably not true of most believers. For many, the experience of faith is an experience of belonging in some way to a community of believers or the habit of following certain practices. God is found, for most believers, most of the time, in the ordinary and the everyday. It is found perhaps in the different types of love or the kindness of strangers, perhaps in the beauties of the natural world. This experience is seen as indicative of God, rather than *proof* of God. After all, nature has its ugliness and pain, and there is human cruelty and callousness as well as kindness.

(a) William James and *The Varieties of Religious Experience*

The great American philosopher and psychologist, William James, elder brother of the novelist Henry James, gave the Gifford Lectures in Edinburgh, in 1901–02. These were subsequently published as *The Varieties of Religious Experience*. This text, drawn from a variety of case studies, has remained a central work in the philosophy of religion. James acknowledges the variety of experiences, but tries to find some common threads that all significant experiences have in common.

William James

Background

Key person

William James (1842–1910): Philosopher and psychologist, was Professor at Harvard University. He was the brother of novelist Henry James, and a major philosopher in the American *Pragmatist* tradition. His Gifford Lectures of 1901 and 1902, perhaps the most famous in the series, were published as *The Varieties of Religious Experience*.

Key terms

Pragmatism A philosophical movement, largely in the United States, that believes that a theory may be treated as true if it works satisfactorily in practice. William James and Charles Sanders Peirce are the best-known philosophers in the tradition.

Ineffability Unable to be expressed in words.

Noetic quality James' term for the way that religious experience imparts knowledge unlike any other.

Passivity The idea that we contribute nothing to true religious experience: we are taken over by it.

Transience For James, a quality of religious experience, lasting only a brief time but with life-changing significance.

He sought common characteristics of religious experience, partly to separate significant from bogus claims. His research led him to four characteristics which mark the genuine experience:

1 **Ineffability:** these experiences are beyond the ability of our words to express. He describes the experiencer entering a mystical state of mind which is 'negative'. This means that no words can begin to describe the nature of what she is experiencing.
2 **Noetic quality:** it gives a kind of knowledge unlike the knowledge of any other human experience. In his own words:

> *They [religious experiences] are states of insight into depths of truth unplumbed by the discursive intellect. They are illuminations, revelations, full of significance and importance, all inarticulate though they remain, and as a rule carry with them a curious sense of authority for aftertime.*

William James: *The Varieties of Religious Experience*, Lecture XVI

3 **Transience:** meaning the experiencer has the experience for a very short time, rarely more than half an hour, but the effects of the experience are life-changing.
4 **Passivity:** meaning that those in the grip of such an experience claim that they have no will of their own because they are under the influence of a superior power.

Just because James found commonality between descriptions of religious experiences, this does not mean that he is saying that these experiences are either all real or divine in origin. Instead, he claims that they are *genuine*, in the sense that the one who experiences in this way is making an honest claim. He argues that claims should be tested and not just accepted. We need to discount the possibility of delusion or the presence of mind-altering substances.

He notes that these experiences take place within a conceptual framework that already exists within the experiencer's mind. What we see, therefore, from the outside, is the effects of what James describes as 'over-beliefs'. Those who speak of these 'events' find that their descriptions are aimed at supporting their own beliefs. A Roman Catholic is unlikely to see Ganesh and a Hindu is unlikely to see the Blessed Virgin Mary. Indeed, the fact that these experiences fit into the culture of the person's worship is one of the most regular objections to their being real.

James' response to this type of criticism is to argue that there is a valuable distinction between the experience in itself and the way it is

For a profile of Swinburne, see Chapter 5.

Key question

Is it possible to think of experiences which we would consider genuinely religious but which would not meet all four of James' criteria?

experienced. We interpret experience – as Kant pointed out – in ways that fit with our own understanding of the world. If my experience is Christian or Hindu, then the stories I have learned and the concepts I have been taught will provide the framework within which I interpret the experiences I have.

3 Is personal testimony enough to convince others?

This leads to the question of what would count as evidence that might convince others that the experience was real. It does not matter how convinced the individual is of the experience: most people would find it hard just to accept someone's word.

(a) Richard Swinburne on Testimony

Key terms

Principle of credulity Swinburne's principle that people should be believed unless we have good reason to disbelieve them.

Principle of testimony Swinburne's principle that people in general are truthful. There need to be good reasons to doubt their honesty.

There are different ways of approaching the question of accepting someone's word about accepting her experience. Richard Swinburne has attempted to address these questions using the principles of credulity and testimony. The **principle of credulity** argues that if someone believes that she has experienced something then she probably has. If we saw a helicopter fly past a window, there is a good chance that we did indeed see that, and we ought to believe that, unless there is very good reason not to do so. We rarely question claims like this and, in general, neither would we be questioned about making them. The **principle of testimony** argues that, all else being equal, we believe the testimony of others. Swinburne argues that unless someone is a liar or disturbed, her description of a religious experience is probably true. If our default position is to doubt everything that a person says, then conversation would become almost impossible. In practice, we do not, without very good reason, doubt the experiences of others. Swinburne is suggesting that if there are those who doubt the word of those who have experienced something religious, then the questioners should be asked to prove their testimony wrong. If they cannot do this, then the description of a religious experience should be believed.

Key question

To what extent are Swinburne's principles of testimony and credulity really applicable to religious experiences?

The issue with Swinburne's position is that testimony about religious experience is not like testimony of ordinary experience. The testimony is almost certainly about something which is by definition rare and unusual. I know what a helicopter is, and I understand everyday occurrences. It is quite difficult to conceive of an adult in an advanced society not knowing what a helicopter was. Few are likely to confuse a helicopter with a butterfly or an airliner. There are not likely to be many observational errors.

But religious experience is not like that. No one knows exactly what God is, and the possibilities of error are many. God is not reducible to ordinary experience, nor is he simply definable. I can define a helicopter. I cannot define God. When I cannot define something clearly, there are opportunities to describe it mistakenly. Swinburne's point is predicated on a question of whether people are truthful. People can be truthful in only saying what they believe to be true, but it does not follow they have correctly grasped the truth of their perception. Swinburne is answering a different question from whether that which is experienced is true. He goes little further than asserting that people are generally honest. But in identifying religious experiences as accurate accounts of God, there is a different question.

(b) The problem of other minds

Another issue to remember is the epistemological question known as 'the problem of other minds'. When I meet people, I assume that they have minds of their own. I think this, because their behaviour leads me to believe they direct themselves. They show the behaviours which indicate they appreciate things differently from the way I do. They do not do as they are told. They 'do their own thing'. But all I see is their behaviour. I cannot see into their minds, nor they into mine (for which they, and I, may well be deeply grateful). I make the inference that they have minds of their own – it seems the easiest way to explain their actions – but I cannot get inside their minds. I do not know how things taste or what blue looks like to them, and I cannot know exactly how they experience their worlds.

This matters in the present discussion of religious experience. If you claim to have a particular experience, you may well be telling the truth, but I cannot experience your experience as you do. I may know you as a truthful person, not given to fanciful notions, but I cannot say that you have interpreted your experience – which is not my experience – correctly. I may doubt your experience without doubting your honesty. Of course, if I did not trust you, I might also doubt your honesty. But, in either case, I am not acquainted with your experience as you are. This means I am at one remove from the point at which you are drawing whatever conclusions you have reached. If I cannot share your experience, in what sense can it be evidence for me? Even if I trust you, and accept your sincerity, that is not enough for me to be able to assert that your experience is correct. You may be sincere – but sincerely wrong. There are sincere people of all faiths and none, sincere Nazis, sincere members of the Ku Klux Klan, sincere vegetarians and sincere slaughtermen. But that is not reason for me to become a Nazi, a vegetarian or anything else. The sincerity of a belief is not to be confused with the validity of a belief. This matters when we consider those who claim to have experiences of all kinds, and not simply the religious.

Key question

To what extent should we trust reports by people who claim to have religious experiences?

4 Types of religious experience

There are many different ways of characterising religious experience. They can be personal or corporate. They may be mystical or conversion experiences. It could be argued that there are as many types of experience as there are individuals and groups having them, and, indeed, one person may have experiences of more than one kind. We change over the course of our lives, and when we look back at our experiences, we may see them differently from the way we did at the time. We continually rethink and reconsider our experiences. We may at one point in our lives think of something as coming from God, only later to reconsider it and think of it as purely natural or the result of our mental state at the original time. It is worth noticing that we were not dishonest in the first place or now. We honestly reported our understanding of our experiences both then and now, but we have changed our minds about what we saw and felt.

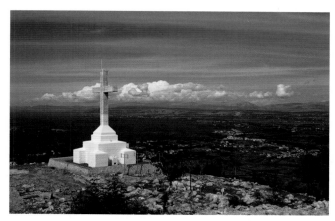

Medjugorje in Bosnia is the site of a famous corporate religious experience

(a) Corporate religious experiences

Religious experiences shared by a group of people are know as corporate. As we clearly cannot see into other people's minds, we should remember that even those experiences believed to be corporate can only be actually experienced by the individual. Other people who claim the same experiences as me still have their own perceptions, which are never, and can never, be mine. My life, to me, can only ever be lived as I know it. It may be that people may genuinely believe they are having an experience while they are actually being carried away in some sort of mass hysteria.

By looking at two such corporate experiences, we can see why they evoke both belief and suspicion. Apparitions of Our Lady, Queen of Peace, have been reported since 24 June 1981 in Medjugorje in Bosnia Herzegovina. Six children in the town made the reports. Since then, news of the messages delivered to them has drawn millions of pilgrims to the area. Many of these pilgrims find their lives have been changed. Some leaders in the Roman Catholic Church have expressed discomfort at the alleged visions and experiences. But the official view of the Roman Catholic Church is that: 'It is undetermined at this time if it is of supernatural origin.' This was stated by the Yugoslav Bishops in 1991. At the time of writing, the Vatican has reached no firm conclusion about these events, though the official line has been sceptical. Cynics may say that a whole industry has grown up around this previously poor area, casting doubts on the original claim. Just because people claim to have felt themselves to be closer to God, or even to change their lives, it does not mean that they interpreted events correctly or that they were given correct information. I might very well change my whole attitude and way of living because of what someone tells me, but he might even so have told me a lie or got the facts wrong. People have been changed, but it does not follow that they are correct in their judgement of the original events.

Another claim to corporate religious experience is those events alleged to have taken place and to be still taking place at the Toronto Vineyard Airport Church (now called Catch The Fire) in Toronto, known as the Toronto blessing. The church is evangelical in outlook, with a strong emphasis on personal testimony and direct intervention of the Holy Spirit. One of the phenomena associated with this type of experience is known as 'holy laughter', believed to be a sign of the presence of the Holy Spirit. The experience itself involves members of the congregation breaking into spontaneous uncontrollable laughter, most commonly during solemn worship. People weep, fall to the floor in ecstatic trances or make animal noises, roaring like lions or barking like dogs. Others wander around the church looking drunk. All these behaviours are called 'holy laughter'.

These two modern examples of corporate experience are perhaps at the extreme edge of the range of possible experience. For most people, including religious people, corporate experience is of a more ordinary type. Corporate religious experience is, generally, experience of community, perhaps the congregation of a church they attend, or the faith found within a family or a school. As humans, we tend to mix with people we find of like mind. Intense religious experiences, for those who claim them, are brief events (see William James on transience, further on). They may then support those experiences with their everyday life as part of the community. Intense experiences, such as those claimed by mystics such as St Teresa of Avila, are reported as brief events. There are some religious groups, such as some types of 'born-again' Christians, who demand a particular and intense type of experience to authenticate someone's religious faith, but this is not the understanding of the majority of religious outlooks.

(b) Issues with corporate religious experiences

Corporate experiences raise particular issues. People do not behave in groups in the same way that they do as individuals. If we see groups enjoying themselves, laughter becomes infectious. Teenagers and adults will behave in ways they would never do if they were alone. Mass hysteria is a well-recognised phenomenon. Critics suggest that the kinds of people attracted to evangelical/charismatic worship are already pre-disposed to both this sort of behaviour and the effect of group suggestion. A particular kind of atmosphere is created by the preaching about the Holy Spirit and the kinds of prayer and singing common to these meetings. Critics – not necessarily atheist – might suggest that some sort of group hallucination is taking place during these worship sessions.

Some religious believers who accept the power of the Holy Spirit have suggested that the behaviour demonstrated in the Toronto blessing might be the work of demons, keen to make fun of believers, rather than of God. Believers point to the Acts of the Apostles, and the actions of the Holy Spirit during Pentecost. Here the 'speaking in tongues', claimed at the Toronto blessing, was actually something much more comprehensible. Jerusalem was full of people who had come from all over the world to celebrate the Passover. The crowds assembled in the city spoke many different languages but they all understood the message the apostles were inspired to preach as if they were hearing their own language. There is no evidence in scripture that 'speaking in tongues' was anything but comprehensible. There is no sense of people behaving like animals or hysterically.

Why would God make people behave in these laughable ways? There is, at least, some sort of logic in a God who delivers the 'gifts of the Holy Spirit' to a Church just beginning to grow. The same cannot be said for a small group in an obscure Church seemingly making fools of themselves and claiming that God is moving them to do so. If God is trying to reveal himself in this way, what might he be trying to tell us? Does God, on the one hand, give us free will to choose to believe or not and on the other take that free will away so that he can make fools out of us? Is the Holy Spirit more interested in 'playing' with a small group of people than challenging all the dreadful things which are being done in our world in the name of religion? It could be argued that rather than helping the faithful, if this is an act of God, then it is not a god worthy of human worship.

(c) Personal religious experiences

Of personal experiences, **mystical experiences** are perhaps the most intense. There are different definitions of 'mystical experiences', but a common thread is the sense of something which reveals – or seems to reveal – the transcendent, something that goes beyond any normal experience of the everyday world. The experience is not rational in any normal understanding of the term, yet it seems to reveal something very important about the divine. Those who report such experiences find them life-changing.

(i) Rudolf Otto and *The Idea of the Holy*

Many of the experiences reported by William James are clearly personal, intense and fully mystical. Perhaps the writer who has most fully explored these is Rudolf Otto in his book *The Idea of the Holy*, published in German in 1917 and in English in 1923.

He explores the idea of the **numinous** to describe an encounter with God, an encounter with the **wholly other**. The term 'wholly other' signifies that God is not a being among beings but rather of a completely different order from anything in ordinary experience. He describes the meeting as a kind of seduction, using the phrase *mysterium tremendum et fascinans*. This means 'a mystery tremendous and fascinating'. We must be careful here. We often say in conversation that something is 'fascinating' as a synonym for 'interesting'. Otto returns to the older usage – to be fascinating is to draw someone in, to compel by attraction. The experience he suggests is immensely powerful, an experience which at its centre has the fascination which comes from loving something. There are no adequate words with which to describe this event. The *holy* cannot be described in language taken from our ordinary lives. After all, our language is based on the experience of our earthly lives. The wholly other is unlike anything in our everyday lives, not simply as a different sort of thing, but rather as of a different order from anything we have experienced. Otto points us to a special kind of experience which is simply religious. Commenting on this, Ninian Smart says:

> We discover ... that religious experience has its own kind of logic. The holy Being, for instance, is the source of grace in virtue of its being both terrifying and fascinating. For men cannot without blasphemy presume to become God: but at the same time they feel drawn toward that which is holy ... in such ways one can observe patterns of thought and practice rising out of the numinous experiences. We might put this in another way by saying that the pattern of religious language has its own peculiar and special structure, just as other areas of language ... possess their own characteristic forms of inference. So ... we have good reason to accept Otto's thesis that religious language cannot simply be reduced to other forms of discourse. It follows that an important task for the philosopher is the analysis of this area of discourse.

Ninian Smart: *Philosophers and Religious Truth* (1969), p. 117

Rudolf Otto

Key person

Rudolf Otto (1869–1937): German Lutheran theologian and student of comparative religion. Professor of Divinity at Marburg 1917–29. Best known for *The Idea of the Holy* (1917).

Ultimately, we are talking about experience which has no language capable of describing it. This is consistent with James' use of the notion of ineffability. It also points us to a weakness of Swinburne's principles of credulity and testimony. The criteria we use of ordinary experience seem wholly out of place here.

(ii) Teresa of Avila

On mystical experience, James made great use of the writings of St Teresa of Avila. In her book the *Interior Castle* and her *Autobiography* she describes a series of visions which she had undergone in her 39th year, and, more importantly the effect these had on her life. Against accusations that these experiences might have been psychologically driven or the result of sexual frustrations, she looked to her self-examination. She looked at the evidence of her feelings afterwards. She argues that if they were simply sexual frustrations, they would have left her with a feeling of disgust.

Using a similar approach to the unsought vision, she argues:

> *... a genuinely heavenly vision yields ... a harvest of ineffable spiritual riches, and an admirable renewal of bodily strength. I allege these reasons to those who so often accuse my visions of being the work of the enemy of mankind and the sport of my imagination ... I show them the jewels which the divine hand had left me: they were my actual dispositions ... this improvement, palpable in all respects, far from being hidden, was brilliantly evident to all men.*

> St Teresa of Avila: *Autobiography*, Chapter xxviii

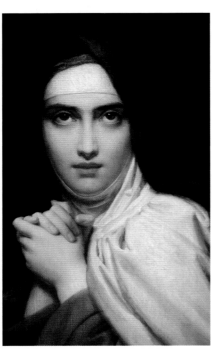

Teresa of Avila, by François Gérard

Key persons

Ninian Smart (1927–2001): Best known for his work in comparative religion, he was made full Professor at Birmingham University, at the age of 34. He went on to create the Department of Religious Studies at the University of Lancaster in 1967. He gave the Gifford Lectures of 1979–80.

St Teresa of Avila (1515–82): She was a Catholic saint, Carmelite nun, mystic and theologian. Her major works include her autobiography, *The Life of Teresa of Jesus* and *The Interior Castle*. She underwent a series of visions of Jesus, which she used in her spiritual writings. She was canonised in 1622, and was named Doctor of the Church (with Catherine of Siena) in 1970, the first two women to receive the honour.

For mystics such as Teresa, there are always tests of these experiences. These include whether these visions leave us with the kinds of feeling we would expect from God and whether they fitted with the teachings and beliefs of the Church. Her argument was that the religious experience happens within a tradition with norms and teachings. Anything contradictory to those would be suspect if God were truly present in the Church. Existing teaching and tradition are the test of experiences, not the other way round.

Like James, Teresa asks whether we see a genuine change in character in the person who claims to have had the religious experience. Mere

Key question

If mystical experiences refer to things beyond normal human experience, can we claim to make any sense of them?

change is not enough. We need to see clearly that it is a change for the good. Someone who reacted with pride, or who sought to make money from his vision would be suspect. Of course, while this change for the good may count as supportive evidence, it falls short of proof. A change for the good could happen because the person sincerely believed she had encountered God, not because she had really done so.

(d) Conversion experience

In simple terms, a conversion experience is one in which a person alters her way of life from one set of convictions to another. A non-believer may become a believer, or someone committed to one religion may adopt another. A committed Anglican might join the Roman Catholic Church, a Christian become a Muslim, or someone might move from no faith to religious belief. This change is not simply a change of views. To change my religious beliefs is to change the entire framework in terms of which I see and relate to the world. The behaviour of someone moving from one religion to another, or from none to religious belief, alters perspective in fundamental ways. Once cherished beliefs are viewed in different ways, perhaps as noble but mistaken, perhaps as ignoble, perhaps as useful in a journey of faith. The change which conversion brings affects my habits of thought and speech, my manner of praise and worship. In short, it changes my entire behaviour. My diet may change. I will meet different people in new environments. Friendships may change or be lost. My family may treat me as an outcast, but certainly differently.

William James' particular view of conversion may be questioned. James assumes that a conversion to religious life will provide a sense of wholeness and integration. But the movement could be other way. One might be converted from religion to **atheism** or **agnosticism** and feel a sense of liberation if the practice of faith had seemed oppressive, mistaken or absurd. That change would be as life-changing as any leap into faith.

(e) Examples of conversion experiences

Perhaps the most famous example of a conversion was that of St Paul. According to the *Acts of the Apostles*, he was leading a group to Damascus to persecute the embryonic Christian community there. He was thrown from his horse, and heard a voice saying, 'Saul, Saul, why do you persecute me?' (*Acts 9:4*). He was blinded and taken to Damascus, where he was tended by Christians until he came to the truth of Christian faith. Then he could see again. Saul became Paul, ceased persecuting Christians, became their greatest missionary and was martyred for his beliefs. Whatever happened to him, whether he truly heard God or suffered an epileptic episode, his life was truly changed. What he believed before, he now treated as error. He moved in new circles, and believed new things.

> **Key quote**
>
> William James says of conversion:
>
> To be converted, to be regenerated, to receive grace, to experience religion, are so many phrases which denote the process, by which a hitherto divided, and consciously wrong inferior and unhappy, becomes unified and consciously right superior and happy, in consequence of its firmer hold on religious realities.
>
> William James: *The Varieties of Religious Experience*, Lecture XI

Conversion of St Paul, by Caravaggio

Atheism The belief that there is no God.

Agnosticism The view that we cannot determine whether there is a God or not, and that therefore we can commit neither to God nor to atheism.

It is important to note that not all conversions are of this kind. Many who convert describe the process as gradual. William Vecera was a young British soldier who served in Afghanistan during the recent conflict. Writing of his experience he says:

> ... I loved being a soldier; the problem was I wasn't living for God. The world had taken over and I lived for the adventure. I was living for myself ... Sometimes I would feel guilt and shame because of the way I was living .... When I was home and safe, I would forget about God and go on living the way I wanted to again. But this soon changed after I left the Army. I wanted to get to know Him properly and this was a desire to change my life. This desire led me to talk to Him more in prayer and I remember saying, 'Don't give up on me.' I was also reading scripture and coming to know who Jesus is in the Scriptures. I then started to go to Mass regularly ... I also went to confession for the first time in years and experienced God's mercy and forgiveness in the sacrament.

William Vecera: 'Who Do You Say That I Am': The Journey of Mercy 2016, Wonersh, pp. 9–10

Key person

St Ignatius Loyola (1491–1556): A knight of Basque origin, he underwent a religious conversion in 1521, and founded the Society of Jesus (Jesuits) as soldiers of Christ, taking the lead in the Counter-Reformation and performing whatever tasks the pope required of them. He was canonised in 1622, and the Jesuits remain a major order within the Catholic Church. Pope Francis was the first Jesuit to become pope.

This account is philosophically interesting at several levels. The process described by Vecera is gradual. The way he describes his experiences shows his conversion to a new way of life as something which entails a continued reinterpretation of his life. There is no sudden, single moment in which all becomes clear. Things have actively to be thought through. Neither is his experience wholly passive in the ways writers such as James describe. Vecera has to make the effort to go to Mass, to go to Confession and to read scripture. Certainly something profound happens to him, but it was desired. He wanted to change his life and determined to do something about it. He calls on God not to desert him, but clearly feels sustained by God through the process.

Conversions can be as much about lifestyle as religion. St Ignatius of Loyola was always nominally Catholic – he had been brought up as a Catholic – but not always devout in his practice. His conversion to the saint he became in his later life was something which happened over a long period. It was also something that happened because of a long recovery from a war wound, a wound which needed three fairly horrific surgeries. Some might say that a divided and wildly searching man became psychologically, as well as physically, whole while recovering from the cannon ball injuries to his legs. The change in his personality is interesting. What he had once wanted for himself he projected onto God. As a young man, he wanted 'glory' for himself as a great military leader. The order he founded, The Society of Jesus (the Jesuits) has as its motto, *Ad Maiorem Dei Gloriam* – 'For the Greater Glory of God'. The drive to seek glory was still important to him, but now it was for God and not himself. After the experiences which led to founding the Society of Jesus, he spent the rest of his life administering the order, never seeking personal glory.

5 How can religious experiences be understood?

(a) Union with a greater power

Part of any mystical experience seems to be a union with some being or power infinitely greater than ourselves. The philosophical question is what would be such a union, and the extent to which it is genuine. To feel oneself in the presence of God is not like being in the presence of another human being – the mode of sensation must be different. I do not 'see' God as I see my friends or partner. Nor is there the sense of this as a union between equals, for I am not God's equal. Nevertheless, people feel a sense of closeness, even though in doing so, they report their sense of being overwhelmed by something infinitely greater, as we noted in our discussion of James' notions of ineffability and passivity.

(b) Psychological effect – an illusion?

One of the difficulties in considering such events, perhaps because they are so unusual, is that they may be interpreted as illusions. As humans, we know our minds play tricks. Some children have imaginary friends, who become as real a part of their lives as any people they know. They hold imaginary conversations, and confide in the friend who never was. Some adults who are psychologically disturbed believe they hear voices speaking to them. People with no obvious psychological condition sometimes have a sudden and deep sense of foreboding, perhaps expecting something awful to happen to someone they love. Sometimes people want – or fear – something so much that they imagine its reality. We are prone to so many perceptual errors, that perhaps those who want God and think so hard about him see him in their imaginings.

(c) A physiological effect?

Bertrand Russell tells us in his autobiography that he remarked to Beatrice Webb, the socialist thinker, who was apparently keen on fasting, 'if you eat too little, you see visions; and if you drink too much, you see snakes' (Bertrand Russell: *Autobiography*, 2000, p. 75). This point is important. Drink, drugs, tiredness, illness, depression, fasting from food, dehydration all change the ways we think and experience the world. Our mental states are deeply affected by our physical states. If we deprive someone of sleep, he will start to have hallucinations. Many of the great mystics – and many of the lesser ones too – underwent periods of fasting and other self-imposed disciplines to bring them closer to God. St Teresa of Avila, prior to her visions, suffered from illness and was given to intense self-mortification. To what extent might such things have led her to believe that she was in the presence of God?

6 Objections to theories

The common feature of conversion experiences is how they change lives. Philosophically, the issue is whether or not religious experiences can ever be used as a proof of the existence of God. Given that the experiencer is the only one who has undergone the experience, and it cannot be known

Key question

Are conversion experiences of others of any evidential value to the non-believer?

by others as he knows it, and also that we know the phenomenon of misinterpretation of what we think we have seen, the evidential value seems limited. It might convince the one who has the experience, and might well change her for the better, making sense to her of her belief, but it is difficult to see how this event can be used as general evidence of, or for, God.

Many objections may be brought to instances of religious experience.

1   Most significant is the privacy of experience, as mentioned above. We cannot know the content of the mind of another. We often make assumptions about how others interpret things, what they are enjoying, what things look like to them. We are surprised when they tell us we misinterpreted their behaviour, intentions and feelings.

2   We must beware of thinking that because someone is sincere, he is correctly interpreting what has happened to him. Making mistakes is part of the human condition, and an unavoidable one. Sincerity is about honesty, but it is no guarantee of truth.

3   David Hume, writing of miracles, draws attention to the ways in which humans are drawn to the unusual and the bizarre, and no less to the enthusiasm with which tales of these things are passed on, often growing in the telling and retelling. The hairy monster grows larger, grows horns and even extra heads as the news is passed on. People add details when they tell their own tales, so that by the umpteenth repetition, the teller remembers what he said rather than what he experienced. It is said that the Prince Regent, the future George IV, retold the tale of the Battle of Waterloo so often that by the end of his life he truly believed he had been present. Police are aware when they interview witnesses to a crime that there can be as many versions of events as there are witnesses. This leads many to mistrust the memories of others and, in some cases, even their own.

4   The ineffability of religious experience creates further problems. It is difficult to know how much weight to give to a tale that by its nature cannot be properly told. We are always likely to misinterpret that which cannot be clearly expressed.

5   Our knowledge of the mind-altering qualities of various chemicals is significant. Alcoholics have a deficiency of vitamin B in their blood when they are drinking. This causes *delirium tremens*, a condition which can lead to hallucinations. It has been argued that St Francis Xavier's aesthetic diet was deficient in vitamin B. When he prayed long into the night, it is not unreasonable to think that his 'heavenly visions' were caused by his diet rather than God. St Francis was seeking God and perhaps the chemical imbalances in his body supplied him with the visions he sought. This of course is just speculation and St Francis may well have had visions.

6   People are sometimes just mistaken, whether through ignorance, lack of vocabulary to describe a phenomenon, or lack of scientific knowledge to explain it. Sometimes, people are not ignorant in this way, but they tell lies to appear better than they are.

7   It is easy to assume, from much of the literature, that for an experience to be experienced as 'numinous', it must be religiously interpreted. This is not necessarily true. People have experiences of art and nature which go beyond the everyday, and which may be properly called spiritual, but they are not understood as coming from or pointing towards God. As John Cottingham notes:

> ... the suggestion is that so-called 'transcendent' aspirations and experiences are available to the non-believer as well as the believer. On this view, the 'spiritual' dimension of experience, the dimension of the 'sacred' as it has often been called in religious parlance, does not in fact require religious belief at all, but simply arises from [a] certain kind of special sensitivity to the purely natural world we live in.

John Cottingham: *How to Believe* (2015), p. 31

8   People often say of disputed events that they are 'a matter of interpretation'. In the case of religious experience, everything hangs on the interpretation made by the experiencer. In his lecture, *Existentialism and Humanism*, Jean-Paul Sartre gives a fascinating example:

> While I was imprisoned, I made the acquaintance of a somewhat remarkable man, a Jesuit ... In his life he had suffered a succession of ... setbacks. His father had died when he was a child, leaving him in poverty, and he had been awarded a free scholarship in a religious institution, where he had been made to feel continually that he was accepted for charity's sake, and, in consequence, he had been denied several of those distinctions and honours which gratify children. Later, about the age of eighteen, he came to grief in a sentimental affair; and finally, at twenty-two – this was a trifle in itself, but it was the last drop that overflowed his cup – he failed his military examination. This young man, then, could have regarded himself as a total failure: it was a sign – but a sign of what? He might have taken refuge in bitterness or despair. But he took it – very cleverly for him – as a sign that he was not intended for secular successes, and that only the attainments of religion, those of sanctity and faith, were accessible to him. He interpreted his record as a message from God, and became a member of the Order. Who can doubt but that this decision was his, and his alone? One could have drawn quite different conclusions from such a set of reverses – as, for example, that he had better become a carpenter or a revolutionary.

Jean-Paul Sartre: *Existentialism and Humanism* trans. Philip Mairet (1978), pp. 38–39

This suggests the distinction between the event of the experience and its interpretation. We decide what experiences mean to us. Gwen Griffith-Dickson refers to such a possible understanding in these terms:

Experience and interpretation can be seen as separate, either conceptually or in practice. One might see experience as something that happens, which is then interpreted. Concepts, beliefs, language and other forms of organising one's thought and one's experience can be applied or withheld.

Gwen Griffith-Dickson: *Human and Divine: An Introduction to the Philosophy of Religious Experience* (2000), p. 91

7 Conclusions

It is difficult to argue that religious experience is proof of God, even though it might be sufficient to convince the one who experiences the event. If, as suggested, everything depends on the interpreter, any interpretation presupposes an intellectual framework in terms of which the interpretation is made. I cannot describe an experience as being of God revealing himself without language which includes notions such as 'God' and 'self-revelation'. I might not believe in God, but familiarity with the meaning of the term 'God' lets me use it properly as a tool of description in my attempt to make sense of my experience. If it is religious language which enables sense to be made of the experience, it is not unreasonable to suggest that religious experience should be understood not as justifying faith but as a means by which those within faith, or converted into faith, find justification and authentication.

Study advice

Religious experience is a more diffuse topic than many: there is no one sort of religious experience, and no certainty that a given experience is genuinely religious. It is not possible to treat a single experience like a single philosophical theory. But, very helpfully, scholars such as James and Otto provide us with schematic ways of considering those experience. It is important to be familiar with their ideas but also to reflect on them. What exactly do they teach us? Are their ideas ways of categorising experiences rather than either explaining them or demonstrating their value as evidence of God? Are there ways of looking at experience which go beyond these categories? Would an experience be invalidated if the believer had contributed to it in some way?

However you approach these questions, it is important to think about them in relation to examples. William James provides many of these and you may well be aware of others which you can choose. Unfortunately, some reported experiences seem trivial, such as people seeing the face of Jesus in a piece of toast, something closer to magic than genuine or life-changing. As we do not know what Jesus looked like, though scholars suggest he would have been short and clean-shaven, if a typical Galilean of the time, the attribution seems unlikely.

Summary diagram: Religious experience

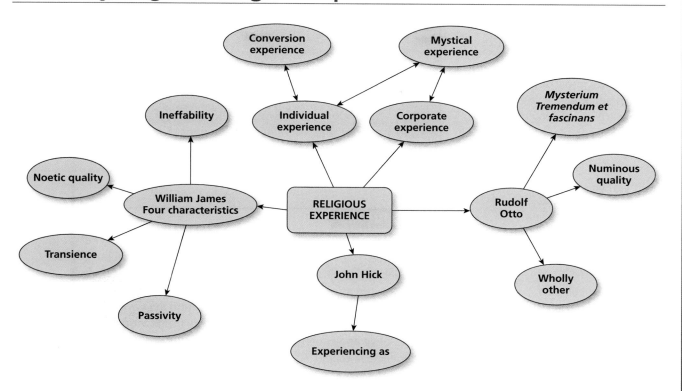

Sample question and guidance

To what extent are the ideas of William James helpful in understanding religious experience?

This is a 'to what extent ...' question requiring you to reach a judgement, carefully considered and justified, about whether James is completely, very, somewhat, a bit, not at all helpful, explaining why you have reached your conclusion. You need to think about whether he misses some significant features of experience, perhaps arguing that something which you consider genuine has features James overlooks.

Of course, in your essay you need to demonstrate understanding of what James says and to explain what his theory of religious experience actually is. Remember that James is not attempting to prove the experiences and their interpretation correct but to provide criteria for determining those experiences most likely not to be bogus. Be careful not to suggest that the different criteria apply to different types of experience. Significant experiences, for James, exhibit all four characteristics.

You might find it helpful to compare James with the views of others, especially if you believe someone else has a better account, but there is no requirement to do so.

Revision advice

As noted, it is important in your revision not only to know the theories of James, Otto and Hick, but to be able to illustrate them with good examples. As you revise, reflect on what you have learned, thinking about advantages and limitations of religious experiences for the existence of God.

Can you give brief definitions of:
- noetic experience
- transience
- the wholly other
- ineffability;
- the numinous?

Can you explain:
- Hick's theory of religious experience as 'experiencing as'
- the nature of conversion experience
- the concept of mystical experience
- transcendence and immanence?

Can you give arguments for and against:
- religious experience as evidence for God
- different religions having different religious experiences
- correct interpretation of religious experiences
- William James' categorisation of religious experience?

Further essay questions

'Conversion experiences are the most convincing form of religious experience.' Discuss.

'… religious experience has its own kind of logic' (Ninian Smart). Discuss.

How satisfactory are religious experiences as proof of the existence of God?

Going further

There are many editions of William James' *The Varieties of Religious Experience*. The Penguin edition of 1985 contains useful introductory material. Rudolf Otto: *The Idea of the Holy* is briefer. The Oxford University Press edition from 1956 is still available as a Galaxy paperback. A fine set of material can be found in *Divinising Experience: Essays in the History of Religious Experience from Origen to Ricoeur* Eds. Liven Boeve and Laurence P. Hemming (Peeters, Leuven, 2004). *Religious Experience: A Reader* Ed. Craig Martin and Russell T. McCutcheon with Leslie Dorrough Smith (Routledge, 2012) is also recommendable. Very interesting are the works of John Cottingham, especially his *The Spiritual Dimension: Religion, Philosophy and Human Value* (Cambridge University Press, 2005) and *Philosophy of Religion: Towards a More Humane Approach* (Cambridge University Press, 2014). Well worth reading are books by Mark Wynn, especially *Emotional Experience and Religious Understanding: Integrating Perception, Conception and Feeling*, (Cambridge University Press, 2005) and *Faith and Place: An Essay in Embodied Epistemology* (Oxford University Press, 2009).
Other books discussed in this chapter are:
- Russell B. *Autobiography* (One volume edition, Routledge, 2000).
- Brümmer V. *What Are We Doing When We Pray?* (second edition, Ashgate, 2008).
- Cottingham J. *How to Believe* (Bloomsbury, 2015).
- Griffith-Dickson G. *Human and Divine: An Introduction to the Philosophy of Religious Experience (Duckworth, 2000)*.
- Sartre J-P. *Existentialism and Humanism trans.* Philip Mairet (Methuen 1978).
- Smart N. *Philosophers and Religious Truth* (second edition, SCM, 1969).
- Vecera W. *Who Do You Say That I Am': The Journey of Mercy* (The Evangelist, St John's Seminary Magazine, 2016)
- Williams R. 'The Touch of God', *Open to Judgement: Sermons and Addresses* (Darton, Longman and Todd, 1994).
- Wittgenstein W. *Philosophical Investigations* (Oxford University Press, 1958).

Chapter 8

The problem of evil

1 Introduction

Key quote

Let my eyes run down with tears night and day,

and let them not cease,

for the virgin daughter – my people – is struck down with a crushing blow,

with a very grievous wound.

If I go out into the field,

look – those killed by the sword!

And if I enter the city,

look – those sick with famine!

Jeremiah 14:17–18

Chapter checklist

The chapter looks at the issues of evil, in terms of scope and the difficulties of explaining why evil, and human suffering, happens. It explains the philosophical and religious issues of evil, including the inconsistent triad, and explores unsuccessful approaches, such as the denial of evil or the aesthetic claim that somehow we need evil to appreciate goodness. The chapter explains and develops Augustinian theodicy, and considers objections. It gives an account of Irenaean soul-making theodicy, followed by that of Hick. It points out differences between Hick and Irenaeus, especially in terms of universal salvation. It gives a brief description of Swinburne's soul-making theodicy, noting differences between him and Hick, and develops and explains D. Z. Phillips' objections to soul-making theodicy.

As the quote from Jeremiah reveals, there has always been evil and suffering. The Black Death in the fourteenth century killed a third of the population of Europe. In the seventeenth century, the Thirty Years War wiped out a third of the population of Germany. The Irish Potato Famine of the 1840s killed over a million – about an eighth of the then population of Ireland. The flu pandemic of 1918 killed far more people than the First World War – between 50 and 100 million.

Evil and pain are part of the very fabric of the world. The twentieth century produced suffering on an industrial scale, whether in the Civil War in Russia, in Stalin's cruelties (perhaps 30 million dead), Hitler's death camps and murder squads (18 million dead), Mao's China (100 million dead) or Pol Pot's Kampuchea (2 million dead – 25% of the population). We have weapons of mass destruction, terrorists kill indiscriminately, and there are uncounted smaller cruelties.

Evil is perhaps the greatest objection to the existence of God. Evil as an experience goes to the heart of who we are. Pain is the essence of the tragedy of human existence – whether in the damage from nature – storm, disease, whirlwind, quicksand, plague, malaria, earthquake, avalanche – or in human cruelty. As persons, we are capable of great kindness, but also of genocide. Some people are made bitter by the anguish they have suffered. Others appear to rise above suffering, not merely facing adversity with cheerfulness, but apparently better for the experience.

Is there any kind of answer to the immensity of human suffering which does not involve God being accused of neglecting the world, or at least not apparently caring about it?

No answer can be simply theoretical. If evil is *my* suffering or *your* anguish, then any answer has to be addressed to the place where the suffering exists. The innocent victims – the man shot as a hostage, the schoolgirl brutally assaulted, the victim of terrorism – need an answer that speaks to their suffering. Is any answer possible?

(a) The evidential problem of evil

We must remember that evil is always suffered by someone. The reality of pain is always experienced individually. When a million people die in an African famine, there are a million individual agonies, as well as the grief and anguish of those who survive to mourn them. Evil is not a theoretical problem but part of living.

It is normal to divide evil into two kinds:

- **moral evil**, the evil that comes from human choices, which raises the question of why God permits humans to behave as they do
- **non-moral evil** or **suffering**, sometimes called **natural evil**, the evil that follows from natural sources, such as famine, drought, hurricanes, earthquakes and much illness.

It is not always easy to separate the two types of evil. If I choose to live in an earthquake zone, or voluntarily live in a mosquito-ridden swamp, then there is at least an element of moral evil in any harm that happens to me. We cannot be too general about this. It is important not to be facile about this. I have some choice about where I might live, but, if I had been born poor or a slave, in a land of poverty, with no freedom of movement, it would make no sense to say that I *chose* to live in such a place, that the death of my family in the flood or earthquake or epidemic could be blamed on my free choices, because, in those circumstances, I would have none.

Key terms

Moral evil Evil done as a result of human choices.

Non-moral evil Evil – such as found in nature – which owes nothing to human choice. Examples might be earthquakes or storms.

Suffering Another term for non-moral evil.

Natural evil Any evil that arises in nature without reference to human agency, such as earthquakes or hurricanes.

2 The problem defined

(a) The logical problem of evil

The problem of evil is traditionally defined as an **inconsistent triad**. In ancient times, it was posed by Epicurus and David Hume would return to it. It may be expressed like this:

Key term

Inconsistent triad God is all-powerful, so he could prevent evil. He is all-loving, so that he would want to prevent evil, yet evil exists. How is it possible that these three claims could all be true?

1 If God were all-powerful, he would be able to abolish evil.
2 If God were all-loving, then he would wish to abolish evil.
3 But evil exists.

Therefore, God is not all-powerful, or not all-loving, or both.

For more information on Hans Küng, see Chapter 20.

This is not an objection to any kind of God. It would not be an objection to a **deist** creator, who made the universe but gave nothing to it. Aristotle's self-regarding God is indifferent to human suffering. One could imagine an idle God who injected pain and anguish into the world to make it more entertaining for himself, to amuse himself with the bizarre antics of all those little people. However, the God of Abraham, Isaac and Jacob, the God of Jewish, Christian and Muslim faith is a God who is intimately bound up with his creation, who loves and cares for all he has made.

(b) Responses to the problem

One line of defence, that evil is not real, will be unacceptable to the great **Abrahamic religions**. The Church of Christ Scientist – not to be confused with L. Ron Hubbard's Scientology – founded in 1879 by Mary Baker Eddy (1821–1910), does argue for the illusory nature of evil, but is not considered a Christian Church by other denominations, and has not been admitted to the World Council of Churches. If I experience a pain as a pain, even if it is a figment of my imagination, it is nonetheless a pain. The cause of the pain might – at least sometimes – be unreal, but the pain itself never is. The Bible presents evil as brutally real. The Old Testament is filled with famines, massacres, murders and all kind of evils, natural and human-made. If the suffering of Christ were merely illusory, his death would offer no redemption. The New Testament shows his death in bloody and absolutely real terms. Crucifixion was used by the Romans precisely because it was a hideous, excruciating and terrifying way to die.

Trivial responses are sometimes given. Perhaps the cruellest and most thoughtless – and it is a remarkably common one – is that we need the black to appreciate the white, the darkness to see the light, or the evil to see the good. This response is morally inadequate, and says nothing to the victim. An ideal observer outside the world might look down and appreciate a picture, noting the contrasts. This is not how evil is experienced by those who suffer. Evil is not a picture seen by a distant observer. It involves real harm to real people. To say that Gypsies or Jews were exterminated during the Second World War so that good could grow out of their suffering – a good they could not experience – or so an observer could truly appreciate the good, says nothing to those who died so horribly. D. Z. Phillips has argued that this type of response adds to the evil in the world, not least in the callousness it displays towards the suffering of others.

Some theologians argue that what Jesus shows is that God does not remove suffering but shows the world that he will never desert humanity in its suffering: this seems to be the promise of Jesus. Hans Küng claims that God suffered on the cross so that he could look suffering humanity in the face. This might be an important religious truth about how God relates to the world, but it does not explain the question to which Epicurus wanted an answer. Why does God allow the evil in the first place?

3 Theodicy

St Augustine of Hippo

An attempt to justify the goodness of God in the face of evil is known as a **theodicy**. Of theodicies, probably the best known is that by St Augustine.

(a) The theodicy of St Augustine

St Augustine of Hippo, in North Africa (354–430AD) was one of the most influential Christian thinkers. In his younger days – as he tells us in his *Confessions* – he was a Manichaean. The Manichees were very influential in North Africa, where he lived. Their doctrine was a perversion of Platonism. For Plato, the material was inferior to the spiritual, but good insofar as it participated in the Realm of the Forms. For various heresies this would be over-simplified into the notion that things spiritual were good, those material were evil. For the Manichaeans, matter and spirit had different origins, coming from different gods. The task of the believer was to liberate the good spirit from the wickedness of matter. The logical consequence, of course, was suicide, but, in practice, it was the denial of the material aspects of life. Manichaeanism was perhaps the most extreme of that body of heresies that make up Gnosticism. The **heresy**, created by the Persian prophet Manes (c.216–276AD) was at its height in North Africa – Augustine's home – between the third and seventh centuries.

In all its forms, the main idea of Gnosticism is that physical matter is evil. It follows that God, if he is good, cannot be responsible for matter. Equally, Jesus, if truly the Son of God, could not have a material body. Against this, Irenaeus would hold that everything is from God – the position later upheld at the Council of Nicea, in 325AD, formalised in the Nicene Creed and part of Christian orthodoxy.

But if matter is of God, and not evil, then evil needs another explanation. If God made the world, then how is evil to be explained?

(b) Original perfection

After his conversion to Christianity, in 387AD, St Augustine adopted the view that the universe was made good. *Genesis* 1:31 says:

God saw everything that he had made, and indeed, it was very good.

Augustine believed that everything made is good, as Genesis tells us, but it is not good in the same way as the goodness of God. If God makes that which is not God, he makes it good, but *in its own way*. Think of a simple example, such as a stone. A stone may be good, but only in the way a stone can be good – good for building or for other uses. A stone can only be good as a stone can be. It cannot be good in the way a cat or a meal is good. Cats and meals are different in kind from stones and are good in quite different ways. The goodness of humans is different again. A stone cannot be a good author and an author is (probably) no good as a building material. If God makes things in all different ways, then although each thing good is good itself, there will be a scale of goods. Some things will be better than others because they have more capabilities. The creation of such a variety of things entails the creation of beings more or less good in different ways.

If everything God made was good, Augustine concludes that evil must be the going wrong of something itself made good. He writes:

> By the Trinity, which is supremely and equally and unchangeably good, all things were created. These things are not equally, supremely and unchangeably good, but they remain good, even taken separately. Taken together, they are very good, because they make up the universe in all its wonderful order and beauty.
>
> In the universe, even that which we call evil, when it is regulated and put in its own place, only enhances our admiration of the good; for we enjoy and value the good more when we compare it with the evil. For almighty God, who, as even the heathens admit, has supreme power over all things, being Himself supremely good, would never permit the existence of anything evil among what he has made, unless through his omnipotence and goodness that he could create good even from evil. For what is that which we call evil but the absence of good? In the bodies of animals, disease and wounds mean nothing except the absence of health. When a cure is achieved, that does not mean that the evils – namely, the diseases and wounds – go away from the body and live elsewhere. They completely cease to exist; for the wound or disease is not a substance, but a defect in the fleshly substance. The flesh itself is a substance, and therefore something good, of which those evils – that is, privations of that good we call health – are accidents. In exactly the same way, what are called vices in the soul are nothing but privations of natural good.
>
> St Augustine: *Enchiridion* 10–12

Augustine then develops this idea that evil is a privation in something itself good. We must be careful – he is not denying the reality of evil. Father Herbert McCabe used to say that nothing in the wrong place is just as real as something in the wrong place. If someone drives his car over a cliff, it is the nothingness under his car he has to worry about. Someone whose mind turns to evil has become a human being gone badly wrong. Adolf Hitler was good insofar as he was a human being. The evil came when he became less than what a good human being could become.

Augustine's argument here is that even a sinful person is more good – because more fully human – than a mere puppet. A truly good human has all his great gifts working well, but even if he does not use those gifts well, the possession of the gifts is more valuable than not having them.

(c) The Fall

To explain the evil in a world itself made good, Augustine concentrates on two events – the Fall of Angels and the Fall of Man. Certain angels, led by Lucifer, chose to reject God. In their choice – which was not the choice of God – they introduced the evil of denying God and fell into hell. Later, Adam and Eve in the Garden of Eden chose to reject God's command, eating the forbidden fruit from the tree of knowledge. For their defiance they were punished by expulsion from the bliss of Eden and suffered the pains of struggling to live 'by the sweat of the brow' and all the anguish of childbirth.

Augustine's theodicy is described as a **soul-deciding theodicy**. The choice is ours. We decide whether to obey God or not.

Augustine believes the punishment continues through history, for all generations. Evil is either the *result* of sin or punishment *for* sin. We are punished because all humankind was seminally present in the loins of Adam. Natural evil is the result of the disorder brought into the universe by the original sins of our ancestors, both human and angelic. God does not stop loving us, despite our wickedness, and he offers redemption, for those who seek it, through the saving work of his son, Jesus.

(d) Augustine and free will

Important to St Augustine's philosophy was his concept of *will*. Plato lacked a word for 'will' and explained wrongdoing as ignorance of the good. Augustine thought we could know the good, yet still not do it. We have *will* (*voluntas*). We can choose what we do. This is important to theodicy, and not only to Augustine. We have free choice and this is essential to being truly good.

Imagine a young man and a girl. He pours out a tale of his love for her. He tells her that she is the light of his life and that he wishes nothing more than to be with her. She asks why he loves her so much. He tells that her father said he would be shot if he did not marry the daughter. If he does marry her, he will be given money, and save his own life. It would not be too odd for the girl, unless completely naïve, to doubt the sincerity of the young man's love. In a genuine relationship, love has to be freely given to mean anything. If we are to have a genuine love for God, it must be freely given. That is why freedom of the will is so important. Augustine thinks that a world with the evils that follow from free will is better than one without it:

> *But God, in the bounty of his goodness, did not shrink from creating even that creature whom he foreknew would not merely sin, but would persist in willing to sin. For a runaway horse is better than a stone that stays in the right place only because it has no movement or perception of its own; and in the same way, a creature that sins by free will is more excellent than one that does not sin only because it has no free will. I would praise wine as a thing good of its kind, but condemn a person who got drunk on that wine. And yet I would prefer that person, condemned and drunk, to the wine that I praised, on which he got drunk. In the same way, the material creation is rightly praised on its own level, but those who turn away from the perception of the truth by immoderately using the material creation deserve condemnation. And yet even those perverse and drunken people who are ruined by this greed are to be preferred to the material creation, praiseworthy though it is in its own order, not because of the merit of their sins, but because of the dignity of their nature.*

St Augustine: *On Free Choice of the Will* Trans. Thomas Williams (1993), p. 81

Augustine's use of free will to explain that the responsibility for evil is not the consequence of any choice by God, has come to be known by philosophers as *The Free Will Defence*, as it is a theodicy, defending God's goodness.

In his article 'Evil and Omnipotence' (*Mind*, April 1955, p. 209), J. L. Mackie questioned this. Some people have free will and yet we know that because of their character they will always do the right thing. We describe some people as reliable because we know their characters are trustworthy and they always do the kind and fair thing. Mackie says that an **omnipotent** God could make creatures with free will but, because of the character he had given them, always guaranteed to freely choose the right thing. This is not logically impossible, and if God's omnipotence means that he can do everything not logically impossible, then he could have made people this way and prevented a great deal of suffering. Against this we might argue that if God made people guaranteed to do the right thing, they would feel free to themselves, because they would experience themselves as choosing the right thing, but they would not be free in the relationship with God, the one that really mattered.

(i) Objections to St Augustine

1   The obvious problem is that Augustine depends on a very literal reading of scripture. He treats Genesis as history of actual events. Secondly, his science is flawed. In ancient times, there was a theory of *homunculi*, which believed that a man contained, in his sexual organs, large numbers of little people. In successful intercourse, a little person was planted in the woman's womb. Medical textbooks from the Middle Ages show – sometimes with delightful pictures – a man's loins populated with little people. This view is now rejected. We do not pre-exist conception and we were not present in Eden. Even if we were, it is unjust that we should bear the blame for the actions of someone else. We do not – now, anyway – punish entire families for the crimes of one of their members. It seems inconceivable that a just and loving God should punish us for a sin that you and I had no say over. Modern theologians often treat Original Sin simply as the inclination in all people to get things wrong – to sin – rather than taking the Eden myth literally.

2   If creation were really made perfectly, it would not go wrong. The notion of perfection surely entails the inability to go wrong. If, as Augustine thinks, God had made hell as a place to send the wicked, then he had built into the universe not only imperfection but also a place of torment and suffering, a place of eternal suffering that is neither good in itself nor will ever make its inhabitants good.

3   Does it make sense to describe a stone, or anything of such a type, as *good*? A stone might be good *for* something, but not in itself. It might be seen *as* beautiful, or *as* useful, but this beauty or usefulness is the judgement of someone else. It is not something found *in* the stone. Minds value things, but the stone has no mind: it just exists. This would be argued to be the case by all existentialist thinkers, but it is a telling point. Even Genesis refers merely to God finding his creation very good. The goodness is in the mind of God, not necessarily intrinsic to the thing. It is also questionable that we can find a way of saying that a horse, good in itself, is more good than a stone. We are not comparing like things and the term 'good' seems to be used here with subtly different meanings. A horse is good if it functions well; but a stone does not function. It just is.

Key term

Omnipotence Literally, 'all-powerful'. In relation to God, this is understood to mean his ability to perform any possible action.

Key term

Original Sin Traditionally understood as the disobedience of Adam and Eve that led to all humanity being flawed thereafter. Many theologians who do not take scripture as literal history tend to use the term to refer to the universal human tendency to commit evil.

4 Augustine was very inconsistent in his free will defence. In Book I of *De Libero Arbitrio* (*Of the Freedom of the Will*), as we have seen, he supports freedom of the will, arguing that the responsibility for an action lies with the person who performs it. It is his responsibility, not God's (Book I.11). By Book III Augustine talks of the humans' ignorance, saying that we cannot overcome our wretched condition (*De Libero Arbitrio* III.18). On this reading, the free will defence is not obviously justifiable. If we are ignorant, then it is impossible to say that we make genuine and *informed* choices.

Is it right to punish people for ignorance they could do nothing about? Aristotle argued, as Aquinas would, that to be truly responsible for an action, we need full knowledge (that is, we must be informed) and full consent. We must act with awareness, by our own choice. Without these we cannot be justly punished. Neither condition, whether knowledge or consent, is met in my relation to Adam's sin. If it is said we sin because we are ignorant, then that seems monstrous as a justification of punishment. If I am not responsible for my state of ignorance, and I have not contributed to my ignorance, then any punishment that I suffer for my sins would seem as cruel as thrashing a two-year-old for knowing no better. Augustine's views on predestination, the idea that God knows in advance and determines our eventual fate, also weaken his version of the free will defence. For Augustine, our election to heaven is a matter for the inscrutable will of God. His intention was to oppose the heresy of Pelagianism, which argued that humanity could achieve salvation by its own unaided efforts. But, in responding to this, Augustine appears to have undermined his own theodicy.

Key question

Is God spared blame for evils in the world by Augustine's view of the origins of moral and natural evils?

4 Soul-making theodicies

St Irenaeus

(a) The theodicy of Irenaeus

St Irenaeus was born early in the second century, probably in Smyrna (Izmir), in Turkey, and was almost certainly of Greek origin. He came from a Christian family and was a protégé of Polycarp, who, by tradition, was a member of the circle of St John the Evangelist. Irenaeus spent time in Rome, but the main part of his life was spent in Lyons (then called *Lugdunum*), in Gaul (France) as both priest and bishop. He died in about 200. His major work, still extant, is *Adversus Haereses* ('Against Heretics'). Fragments of other works are known. We know that he wrote *On the Monarchy, or How God is not the Cause of Evil*, now lost.

In recent years, particularly since the publication of John Hick's *Evil and the God of Love* (1966), there has been a revival of interest in what is called **Irenaean theodicy**. The emphasis of such theodicies is on 'soul-making', the idea that there is evil in the world to provide opportunities for people to develop in goodness and character.

Key person

St Irenaeus (*c*.130–202AD): Early Church Father and apologist, taught by Polycarp. Greek-born, became Bishop of Lyons and opponent of Gnosticism. Possibly a martyr, his tomb at the Church of St John, Lyons, was totally destroyed by Huguenots in 1562.

(b) Reaching divine likeness

The key text for this approach is *Genesis* 1:26. And God said 'Let us make man in our image, according to our likeness.' This means that we are made in God's *image* but need to grow, throughout history, into his *likeness*. We need to become like God, mature and self-directed. Irenaeus treats Adam and Eve as children in their moral immaturity. Like children, they disobeyed a simple rule. He does not treat this as a catastrophe. It is part of growing up. He does not have the sense of Original Sin found in later writers, such as Augustine. God wanted humankind to mature over a lengthy time, not just a single lifetime, but through history as a whole. He sends Christ to help us to learn.

For Irenaeus, we must recognise that the evil of the world can serve a purpose. Irenaeus' theodicy is therefore described as *soul-making*, as opposed to the *soul-deciding* theodicy of Augustine.

God sends evil also to help us. We learn the right way through experience, in the way that Jonah learns repentance through his time in the belly of the whale (*Jonah* 2:1–9). Without evils like death and other suffering, we would not learn the need for goodness and repentance. If everything required no effort, there would be no virtue. Worthwhile things are gained with difficulty. Only then do we fully realise their value, and increasing our understanding makes us become better people. We need to learn that we must be patient, to give God time to make his world as he chooses. A favourite image of Irenaeus is God as a potter moulding his clay. Irenaeus says:

> *You do not make God: God makes you. As God's workmanship, you should wait for the hand of your Maker who makes everything in his time. For yourself, your creation is being carried out. Offer to God your heart in a soft and mouldable state, preserving the form in which the Creator first made you. Keep yourself moist so you do not become too hard for his fingers to work. By keeping this structure, you will rise to perfection, for your moist clay is hidden by God's workmanship. His hand fashioned your being. He will cover you on the inside and outside with purest silver and gold. He will adorn you so well that 'the King himself will take pleasure in your beauty.' But, if you let yourself be hardened, then you reject the work of his skill. Your ingratitude, ignoring his goodness in creating you human, will mean you have lost his work on you, and with this, you will lose your life.*

Against Heresies: IV.xxxix.2

Key term

Pelagianism A heresy from the fifth century, named after the Briton, Pelagius. The heresy denies Original Sin and believes that we can attain heaven by our own unaided efforts – we do not depend on God. It was described by William Temple as 'the only intrinsically damnable heresy'.

The work of God is ongoing, in Christ helping us with our efforts. What St Irenaeus puts into balance is the free choice of humanity together with the working of God. These are essential to our salvation. He avoids any hint of **Pelagianism**, which argued that we can be worthy of God wholly through our own efforts, almost two centuries before that particular heresy arose.

Irenaeus suggests the continuation of soul-making into the next life, a theme developed by John Hick. But, he is in no doubt that those who reject God will be damned. God made hell as a place of eternal suffering for those who do not co-operate with God's plan. Irenaeus says:

> It is one and the same God who prepared good things with himself for those who seek his fellowship and obey him, and who has created eternal fire for the devil, the leader of apostasy and those who fell with him. Into this fire he will send those men who are on his left hand, having set themselves apart ... [He makes] peace and friendship with those who return to him, bringing unity, but prepares for those who reject the light, impenitent, eternal fire and outer darkness, which are truly evils for those who fall into them.

Against Heresies: IV, xl,1

5 John Hick's version of Irenaean theodicy

For a profile of Hick, see Chapter 4.

John Hick

In *Evil and the God of Love* (Macmillan, 1966), the distinguished British philosopher of religion, John Hick (1922–2012), developed this theodicy. He takes the basic idea of soul-making, but spells out its implications.

Central to Hick's theory is the place of genuine freedom. He accepts the free will defence, arguing that God wants genuine relationship with us. He argues that the only relationship worth having is one which is freely chosen. Its precondition is free choice. If we are genuinely to have real choices, then real consequences must be possible. If it is impossible for you to be hurt, then I am not free, in any meaningful way, to choose to hurt you. If we turn things round, if everything in your life is wonderful and nothing I choose to do could damage you, neither could I do you any good. A perfect life needs no improvement. If I can become a good person only by performing genuinely good acts, then good (or harm) must be real and felt as real. If I can do you no good to improve your life, not only am I unable to improve through performing good acts, but you will not learn gratitude; and if I cannot harm you, then there is no opportunity for you to learn qualities such as tolerance, patience or forgiveness.

Hick says that God creates an *epistemic distance*, a gap in knowledge between ourselves and God, that permits us to come to our own, rational conclusions.

Hick's view about natural evil follows from these considerations. He develops a *counter-factual* thesis, asking what the world would be like if it were not like ours, with its pain. Such a world, he argues, would be like that shown in Tennyson's poem, *The Lotos-Eaters*, a meaningless, empty haze, in which we drifted about aimlessly, like zombies, not suffering, but not thinking or caring, either. We would be less than we are capable of being. Generosity, fellowship, concern, courage, patience, charity – virtues which enable people to become better, to be more themselves – would be impossible. Many ordinary activities, even those harmless ones, would become impossible. A cricket match in which the ball was hard to be hit, but soft when caught, where the bowler never failed to take a wicket, but the batsman was never out or missed the ball would be no cricket match at all. It would be of no interest and would be no fun to play. In such a world, there is little room for true human life. Life would be without suffering at the cost of being dull – and we would be dull creatures, as we would never need to learn anything.

What would be the point of such a life? Hick's view is that in a world with God's hand continually intervening, there would be no genuinely self-chosen activity. More importantly, none of us would grow into the likeness of God, as we would lack his creative freedom.

(a) Instrumental good

The underlying idea of Hick's argument is that something's goodness may depend very much on its purpose. He argues that a world with no pain or no possibility of pain might be a very good world in itself, but it would not be a good world for making us better people, or for soul-making, in the sense of development of our natures. If God made this to be a world in which we could develop, then this creation, with all its problems and pains, suits that purpose very well. What Hick argues is that the world, as it is, is *instrumentally* good. An instrumental good occurs when something is good *for* something, as a good carving knife is good for carving cooked meat. Such knives – and such a world – obtain their goodness from how suited for purpose they are.

This world is therefore described by Hick, rather poetically as 'a vale of soul-making'. The phrase comes from a letter written by the poet, John Keats, on April 21st 1819 to his brother, George, who had emigrated to America. Keats did not believe that we live in a world of perfect nature. Rather we have to learn, in the face of life's sorrows, how to become better people. For Hick, this world as it is, works supremely well as a way of making us better – enabling us to become finer persons. As Keats says in his letter:

> Do you not see how necessary a World of Pains is to school an Intelligence and make it a soul? A Place where the heart must feel and suffer in a thousand diverse ways?

This appears to get around the issue of intrinsic good. There is no attempt, as in Augustinian theodicy, to claim that the goodness of a thing is wholly intrinsic. It makes little sense to argue that an earthquake is good in itself if it hurts people. It might make more sense to argue that it is good for something, not in itself, in the opportunities it creates for people to become better. It should be remembered, however, that while such an approach is perhaps more promising than arguing in an Augustinian way, it is still not easy to argue that every evil either serves, or potentially could serve, a good purpose. Hick himself recognises the problem of purposeless or **dysteleological** evil.

(b) Freedom and knowledge

This is not just a matter of freedom of action. It is also essential to developing real understanding of the world. If no harm could come from any of my actions, then God would need continually to intervene. Sometimes the knife in my hand would be hard and sharp, when I needed it to cut my bread, but blunt (and soft) if it could otherwise cut someone. To keep this continual change, God would need to act at every moment to change the world. Nature would have no regularity. Things would be sometimes sharp and sometimes blunt, sometimes soft and sometimes

Key question

Does God's need to create a *'vale of soul-making'* justify the existence or extent of evils?

Key term

Dysteleological Something that serves no purpose.

123

hard. Without regularity, there would be no possibility of science. Science constructs its theories on regularity in things.

If there were no science, there would be no explanation for anything. Probably we would not even look for a purpose. But if we did, we would find that the only thing approaching an explanation would be some sort of benevolent God. Without the possibility of alternative explanations, there would be no freedom to choose or reject God. The free will defence presupposes genuine freedom to see the world in ways that do not involve including God in our explanations.

To this extent, Hick has simply developed Irenaeus. But, in one important area, he rejects Irenaeus. Hick believes in universal salvation, which Irenaeus rejects.

(c) Universal salvation

For Hick, hell is part of the problem of evil. If the evil exists to produce good, then, argues Hick, we cannot explain hell. It does no good except to cause pain and punishment. Those condemned for eternity to stay there will stay there in perpetual suffering. Even in the view of St Thomas Aquinas, who rejects the idea of hell as a place of torture, the pain of permanent separation from God would remain, without hope of redemption.

Hick takes a view of hell that is essentially purgatorial. Roman Catholics believe that when people die, those who have chosen God, but are not yet worthy to be with him, go to a place of purgation, or cleansing, where they undergo further preparation for their eternal glory with God. Such is Hick's view of hell – a place of temporary suffering. Hick is not saying everyone goes to heaven when they die. There would be no justice if all people went to heaven, regardless. But he claims that further opportunity is given for soul-making. God does not ever despair of us, but gives further opportunities to get ourselves ready for him.

This view has its own problems. The idea of further soul-making is appealing. Even the great villains, provided they eventually repent and purge their evils, are not outside the love of God. This seems to fit a view of a God of love and mercy.

However, if the whole purpose of soul-making is to permit us the freedom to choose or reject God, then if we spend all eternity with God because eventually we will choose him, what was the point of free will in the first place? Even if we accept Aquinas' argument that hell is our voluntary separation from God, there is still, on Aquinas' account, no hope of improvement. Some have argued for *annihilationism*, the idea that if we reject God, we are not rewarded with eternal life. There is nothing. We do not suffer, but simply stop being. However, this would seem not to work for Hick's argument. If we just stop, we get no better. God wishes us to be special creatures, beloved by God. If there is nothing left of us, there is nothing for God to love. God would be destroying something he had made.

Hick is very aware that his theodicy might seem too glib. He is aware that the most he can do is to justify suffering in general. There is a weight of suffering on Earth that seems to serve no purpose. He speaks of pains where:

> *… we can see no gain to the soul, whether of the victim or others, but on the contrary only a ruthlessly destructive purpose …*
> *Instead of ennobling, affliction may crush the character and wrest from it whatever virtues it possessed.*
>
> John Hick: *Evil and the God of Love* (1968), p. 331

This dysteleological evil remains a problem which Hick does not claim to explain. He offers hope of a future so great and good that it makes sense of even the greatest pain, but he is clear that he cannot properly justify such a claim – it is a hope, not a philosophical answer.

6 Richard Swinburne and didactic evil

Richard Swinburne

For a profile of Swinburne, see Chapter 5.

Following Hick, Richard Swinburne has developed his own version of soul-making theodicy. There is no requirement to know Swinburne in detail, but this is useful background as for critics of soul-making theodicy, it brings out very clearly the issues that arise from the **instrumental view** of evil. It is helpful to be clear about instrumentalism so that we can understand the force of the criticisms made by Phillips and others to soul-making approaches.

(a) Another soul-making theodicy

Background

One of the most controversial modern theodicies is offered by Richard Swinburne. Its basic premise is that natural or physical evil is a precondition of moral evil, a view different from the traditional idea of St Augustine that natural evil is a consequence of, or punishment for, sin. Swinburne argues that natural evils are logically necessary for people to *know* how to create evil or prevent it. They need this knowledge if they are to have a genuine choice between doing evil and doing good.

There are seven stages to his argument which supports his view:

1   People gain knowledge by induction from present events about what will happen in the future.
2   If people are knowingly to bring about or prevent certain circumstances, they must understand that consequences follow from their actions.
3   People can only know that certain actions will have bad consequences if they have previous knowledge of those consequences.
4   We can only know about these bad consequences if others have suffered them before.
5   For any evil act (such as murder or assault), there must have been a first instance. The first murderer cannot have known the consequences of his action from seeing someone else murdered.
6   Therefore, the first murderer must have gained his knowledge from having seen or heard of this action killing people (e.g. a rock falling on someone's head and killing him).
7   There have to be many natural evils for us to know the range of possible evils, and many instances of these to give us sufficient inductive knowledge.

Swinburne argues that by providing this wide range of evils in nature, God provides the opportunity for people to exercise responsibility. Only by allowing great horrors is he able to give us the gift of full freedom. Many argue that the sheer scale of the horror of Auschwitz or Hiroshima is simply too great to justify God.

Swinburne argues against this:

> *What in effect the objection is asking is that a God should make a toy-world, a world where things matter, but not very much; where we can choose and our choices can make a small difference, but the real choices remain God's. For he simply would not allow us the choice of doing real harm, or through our negligence allowing real harm to occur. He would be like the over-protective parent who will not let his child out of sight for a moment.*

Richard Swinburne: *The Existence of God* (1978), pp. 219–220

At a theological level, there are several objections to Swinburne's argument:

- God is seen as a teacher of truths, providing unlimited lessons in the possibility of evil. A Christian might ask: where is the God of love and justice? Could we defend a parent who let his child play on the railway line in order to learn that it is dangerous? If he said he did not want to be over-protective, we might very well want to argue that he was morally (and legally) negligent.
- If the purpose of evil is to teach, where is the mercy and justice if people still have not learned and still cause great evils?
- Does this theodicy provide the answer which has to be given to the victim? An answer has to be directed to the person who suffers. As noted above, suffering is not an intellectual puzzle which makes sense to an ideal observer. An answer has to be at the level of the victim, because suffering is always something experienced by a person. To Swinburne's world picture, the victim has suffered the evil so that others can learn their responsibilities. Much has been said about Swinburne's frequent assertion that those who suffer have one consolation, that they have been *of use* to others, as a lesson to others. He argues that the worst thing of all would not to have been of use. This has seemed to critics both coldly utilitarian and no answer to the Auschwitz prisoner herded into the gas-chamber with her child as one among millions of victims. She does not tell herself that she is of use, so this is no answer to her, and even less to her child. The horror would not have been mitigated or the lesson any less if that one mother and child had been spared.
- He appears to underestimate the capacity of the human brain to extrapolate from experience. I do not need to see a person's skull crushed by a rock to know how to end a human life. I could see that breaking an egg damages it, then think that a similar action with a human head might have the same effect.
- Swinburne argues that God shows his mercy to people in giving us death when suffering becomes too great. That does not lessen

Utilitarianism is discussed in Chapter 13.

the suffering before unconsciousness intervened, nor does death follow every type of acute suffering. Grief or other types of mental anguish can last a lifetime. It is no answer to a young mother with terminal cancer to say that in her final days, her pain will be eased with morphine, or that her suffering will end: the agony is above all her concern for her children.

■ Swinburne does not attempt to answer John Hick's worry about his own Irenaean theodicy:

> *... if we ask whether the business of soul making is worth all the toil and sorrow of human life, the Christian answer must be in terms of a future good great enough to justify all that has happened on the way to it.*
>
> John Hick: *Philosophy of Religion* (1973), p. 43

Swinburne does consider the idea that God will use an afterlife to compensate people for the evils of life. He says that he sees strong reasons for this view, but says that to include it in his argument would reduce the overall probability of his theory.

In the second edition of his *The Existence of God* (2006), Professor Swinburne responded to objections by arguing in more detail the ways in which evil permitted moral growth, but some critics claim that this does not sufficiently answer the questions about instrumentalism.

7 D. Z. Phillips on soul-making theodicy

In 2004, D. Z. Phillips (1934–2006) published *The Problem of Evil and the Problem of God* (SCM), challenging many assumptions of twentieth-century theodicy, in particular the views of Hick and Swinburne.

In earlier writings, Phillips had argued that 'to ask of what use are the screams of the innocent, as Swinburne's defence would have us do, is to embark on a speculation we should not even contemplate' and he asserted that this 'is the sign of a corrupt mind'. (D. Z. Phillips: 'The Problem of Evil II', *Reason and Religion* Ed. Stuart C. Brown, Cornell, 1977, p. 115.)

Phillips' philosophical approach has a deep awareness of the inability of the human mind to understand the divine and a strong sense of both the tragedy and the wonder of human existence. He protests against tidy moral assumptions – as found in utilitarianism, Kantianism, and situation ethics. In *The Problem of Evil and the Problem of God*, Phillips develops at length the theme of the overwhelming evils that face mankind. His account of the Holocaust is very moving, and his anger against any theodicy – such as those of Hick and Swinburne – which tries to justify God by looking at the usefulness of evil in the world is evident throughout the text. For Phillips, such accounts (and he includes Hick) are *instrumental* uses of evil – evil as a means. The claim of Swinburne is that the suffering of the Holocaust victim means that she is *of use*. But no one can justify torture because it might lead to some good. The torture is still evil because it is immoral. We cannot justify God in this way:

For more detail about moral assumptions, see:
Utilitarianism, Chapter 13
Kantianism, Chapter 12
Situation ethics, Chapter 11.

127

... I am opposed to instrumentalism in ethics. To rescue sufferings from degradation by employing cost-benefit analysis, is like rescuing a prostitute from degradation by telling her to charge higher fees.

D. Z. Phillips: *The Problem of Evil and the Problem of God* (2004), p. 71

His criticisms of inadequate theodicies are developed at length in Chapter 3. Phillips gives various morally insufficient reasons for evil. These include claims that:

■ Evil gives opportunities for character development.
■ Evil is logically necessary.
■ Evil acts as a spur to greater effort and to be better people.
■ Things are not as bad as they seem.
■ Suffering is never more than we can bear.
■ All will be redeemed after death.

The flavour of Phillips' argument is evident in the following passage:

... Swinburne's analysis leads to the vulgarisation of the concept being analysed. It would make it possible for the Good Samaritan to say, on coming across the victim of the robbers, 'Thank you, God, for another opportunity to be responsible.' ... the sufferings of others are made instrumental to the self. Our moral growth is presented by Swinburne as the justification of those sufferings which he treats as the means of achieving it. We cannot speak of moral growth in this way ... Swinburne's instrumentalism worsens when he tries to justify the existence of horrendous evils, by saying that we need them in order to grow deeply in responding to them. Apparently, God knows this as well as we do, and wants to separate the men from the boys ... But would the world not be better off without such attitudes to the suffering of others, attitudes that are a denial of the very moral concepts they claim to be elucidating? Here is a clear instance where a theodicy, in the very language it employs, actually adds to the evils it seeks to justify.

The Problem of Evil and the Problem of God, pp. 59–60

(a) John Hick's response to D.Z. Phillips

Hick has responded to Phillips (John Hick: 'D. Z. Phillips on God and evil', *Religious Studies* 43, December 2007, pp. 433–441) by arguing that he pays too little attention to his own frank admission of the problem of dysteleological evil, and by pointing out that he would never claim any justification of the Holocaust. He broadens his argument into a general critique of Phillips' entire philosophical approach, but does not seem to address the important criticism of instrumentalism in his own work. Of course, Phillips' main target is Swinburne, but the general question is still whether allowing actual suffering to individuals, especially when the suffering is so great, can ever be justified. This needs to be considered carefully in any analysis of soul-making theodicy, which seems to justify goodness at the cost of great evil. The great evil does not stop being evil, whatever goodness there may be in future.

Key terms

Instrumentalism The belief that something's value depends on its usefulness as a means to bring about something else.

Soul-making theodicy Any theodicy, such as those of Hick, Swinburne and Irenaeus, which argues that we need pain and adversity to build character.

8 Conclusions

Any frank discussion of the problem of evil has to avoid simple answers. There are no simple answers, and it would be foolish to attempt to explain evil away. The problem can be understood, which is different from being answered.

It is perhaps useful to reflect that in the Abrahamic religions, evil is not denied, nor is any promise made that there will be an end to it in this world. Jesus offers his disciples no promise that their lives will be made painless by belief. Instead, he talks of persecution and martyrdom. The only promise is that God will be with his people in their troubles, and, at the end, there will be reward. The character of God's relationship with the world is a promise of never letting his people go, never lacking in his love – but not a promise of a comfortable or easy life. In Judaism and Christianity, this relationship is expressed as a covenant of keeping faith.

The philosophical issue is that the language of faith and covenant is a *response*, not an answer which *explains* the mystery of evil, or the mystery of God. *Explanation* seems always incomplete.

Study advice

It is important to be very clear about what evil and its problems involve. Do not underestimate the depth of the problem or be satisfied with glib answers of the 'need-the-black-to-see-the-white' variety. Remember that evil is not a theoretical issue but one which affects everyone. Death, illness, grief, unfairness are part of the life of all of us. Be ready to explain your thoughts with specific examples of actual harms that occur to people. As always, careful thought and reflection matter very much, but here there are special issues, so be prepared for the incompleteness and uncertainty of the issues, being careful not to be too dogmatic.

Summary diagram: The problem of evil

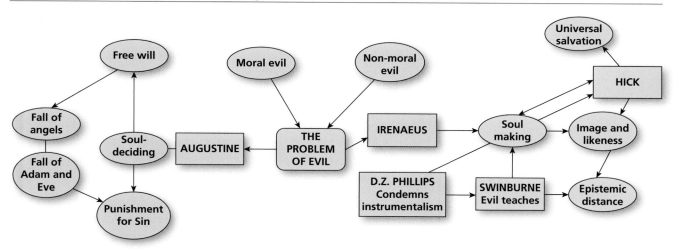

It is important to be clear in your definitions and not to confuse soul-deciding and soul-making theodicies. Be clear about the differences between Augustine and Irenaeus, and be very careful not to attribute to Irenaeus all the views of Hick or *vice-versa*.

Can you give brief definitions of:

- theodicy
- soul-making theodicy
- soul-deciding theodicy
- moral evil
- non-moral evil?

Can you explain:

- instrumentalism
- evil as privation
- the free will defence
- dysteleological evil?

Can you give arguments for and against:

- Augustine's use of *Genesis* in his theodicy
- Irenaeus' argument for evil as soul-making
- Hick's concept of hell
- D. Z. Phillips' opposition to soul-making theodicy?

Sample question and guidance

'There is no satisfactory answer to the problem of evil.' Discuss.

The important thing to notice is that this is a very provocative question. Think first about what the problem is. It is important to state what any problem is if you are to judge the adequacy of any attempted answer.

In a question of this type, you cannot be expected to know every theodicy ever devised. You would however be expected to know those specified for study – Augustine and Hick – and to have some awareness of their strengths and weaknesses to assist you in reaching a judgement. Remember that you are not asked to write a detailed description of each of these theodicies. What matters is your ability to pick out the salient features and to demonstrate that you have reflected on these. You might, for instance, want to consider the relative merits of soul-making versus soul-deciding theodicies as answers to the problems. You would need to give examples of each, but there is no need to tell the reader everything you know about Irenaeus and his life and times. What matters is whether you can explain *your* reasons for preferring one type of theodicy over the other or for thinking that neither is satisfactory.

Notice that the question is about evil in general, so you would need to consider both moral and non-moral evil. Always be careful, on a question about evil, to ask yourself whether it is concerned with all evil or just one type.

Further essay questions

'The free will defence resolves some but not all the problems created by evil in the world.' Discuss.

To what extent is St Augustine more successful than Irenaean theodicy in explaining evil in the world?

Discuss the strengths and weaknesses of John Hick's theodicy.

Going further

There is a huge literature on the Problem of Evil. John Hick: *Evil and the God of Love* (Palgrave Macmillan, 2010) remains a classic overview, and, like all Hick's work, is very readable. Kenneth Surin: *Theology and the Problem of Evil* (Blackwell, 1986) is brief and admirable in its insights. Marilyn McCord Adams: *Horrendous Evils and the Goodness of God* (Cornell University Press, 1999) is a very useful text. Michael B. Wilkinson with Hugh Campbell: *Philosophy of Religion: An Introduction* (Continuum, 2010) outlines other approaches to theodicy, including process and protest theodicy. Alvin Plantinga: *God, Freedom and Evil* (Eerdmans, 1974) is brief and accessible, with particular reference to the relationship of God and human freedom. D. Z. Phillips: *The Problem of Evil and the Problem of God* (SCM, 2004) is essential reading for anyone interested in soul-making theodicy.

Other books discussed in this chapter are:
- Hick J. *Philosophy of Religion* (second edition, Prentice-Hall, 1973).
- Swinburne R. *The Existence of God* (second edition, Oxford University Press, 2006).
- Williams T. *St Augustine: On Free Choice of the Will* (Trans. Thomas Williams) (Hackett, 1993).

Religion
and ethics

Chapter 9

The issues of ethics

1 Introduction

> ### Chapter checklist
>
> This chapter gives essential background to the understanding of ethical discussion. It begins by seeing how ethics affects and permeates daily life, not only in making decisions about actions but in making judgements about others, giving advice and developing good character to live a good life. It relates ethical thought to practical reasoning and the nature of the person. The chapter then deals briefly with issues of ethical language, the relationship between morality and religion, before giving an overview of the subject, explaining some main technical issues. It briefly defines concepts which will be used in both AS and full A Level Studies. As in any subject, knowledge of terminology matters.

When we hear or think of the term 'ethics' we recognise that we are talking about the good life, and how we might live – that is, the question of morality.

It is essential when embarking on ethical studies to be conscious of what is involved in the ethical life. When we hear that we should be moral, we think at first of what we are expected to do, or what we ought ourselves to do. But that is not the total of what is required by the ethical life. To be sure, we do have to act. There are things we need to do, and things we should do. There are also things we ought not to do, as well as things we ought to do, but which we leave undone. Each of these involves moral judgement.

Even when we have listed all these, there are other activities which are part of the moral life. We raise young people. How should we do that? What is the good we want those children to have? Sometimes we are asked to advise others. What is the right thing to seek when doing this? Should we advise for our own good, or for the sake of others?

Beyond this, we sometimes have to make judgements on the actions of others. These judgements are not simply about whether someone has performed a right or wrong act, but whether he or she should be held responsible for that action. Aristotle argued that we cannot hold someone responsible for an act if that person acted in unavoidable ignorance or through being forced to do so. This view was subsequently adopted in Catholic moral teaching.

> ### Key person
>
> **Aristotle** (384–322BC): A Macedonian, son of the court physician. He studied at the Academy for 20 years, but disagreed with Plato's theory of the Forms, taking a much more empirical approach to his studies. He created his own school, the *Lyceum*.

2 Person and community

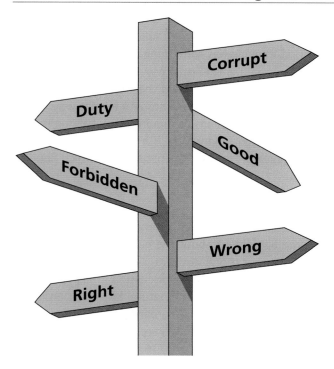

Discussion of this kind reminds us that morality arises from the fact that we are social creatures, living in community. Living in community has so many advantages, because we are not self-sufficient. A baby cannot look after herself but depends on the care of others. In the same way, I cannot provide for all my physical and emotional requirements. I need to relate to others who help to supply my needs, just as I find I must contribute to their needs. If I treat my neighbour without concern, with contempt and ingratitude, he may feel less inclined to give me the help I need. Therefore, I need to constrain my behaviour in various ways.

It can be argued, as it has been throughout the history of moral thought, that ideas of duty, responsibility, rights and obligations must arise out of this mutual need. Alan Gewirth gives a detailed justification of this approach in *Reason and Morality* (1978). It is interesting to consider whether someone living alone on a desert island could be considered capable of living a genuinely moral life. He presumably has no duty to others, and there is no one to have a duty towards him. Does he perhaps have duty towards himself? Even if he can be said to have moral demands, these will fall short of the full moral life. He is beholden to no other human being. He has no one other than himself to educate, counsel or judge.

If these considerations are true, the moral life entails life in community.

3 Ethical life

(a) Ethics and practical reasoning

If our ethical life is something lived in community, then it follows that it requires certain types of skill. This will be developed further in Chapter 10, but it is helpful to think carefully about the type of understanding entailed in the moral life.

Plato attempted, not successfully, to argue that the moral life flowed properly from our understanding of the Form of the Good. His was an essentially intellectualist account. For him, wrongdoing is always the result of ignorance. This is psychologically unconvincing. I can know that some activity, such as smoking, is harmful, but still do it anyway. The smoking habit is not the result of ignorance of why it is harmful but must have some other explanation.

If this is true, simply knowing what is right or wrong is not enough to direct our behaviour. Aristotle and a rich tradition since his time argue that moral life requires a kind of practical reasoning, just as art does. Knowing what a good painting is will not make me a good artist, and, in any case, there is no one 'right' painting to paint. The painter has to make judgements not only about what to paint but how to paint it. He may be

Plato (c.427–347BC): Pupil of Socrates. Created the Academy c.387BC and developed the ideas of Plato into his own distinctive philosophy, explained in a series of dialogues still central to philosophical discussion.

See Ingolf Dalferth: 'Religion, Morality and Being Human: The Controversial Status of Human Dignity', in: P. Jonkers and M. Sarot (Eds.), *Embodied Religion* (2013), pp. 143–179.

restricted in the size of canvas he may use, and by many other factors. He brings not only intellectual skill to the creation of his painting, but accumulated experience of materials, awareness of his own painting abilities and their limitations, as well as years of practice and experiment.

If Aristotle is right, moral thinking has something of the same character, although there are differences. In art, the artist may make a deliberate error as part of the art (Josef Haydn loved to do this in his music). But deliberate error seems not to be acceptable in morality in that way. Nevertheless, moral judgement does seem to require careful thought and the ability to work out what is right and wrong. But it also needs to work out what is practically manageable, in the circumstances in which people find themselves.

(b) Ethics and the person

If, as suggested, ethics is about the person in community, then it follows that we need to have some agreement about the nature of the person and what he or she is owed in our moral duties.

Agreement on this is hard to find. In ethical discussion, there is a large literature on natural human rights. In the natural law tradition (see Chapter 10), thinking about 'right reason in accordance with nature', it is assumed that we have rights simply because we are human. The United States Declaration of Independence, from July 1776, is unequivocal:

> We hold these truths to be self-evident, that all men are created equal, that they are endowed by their Creator with certain unalienable Rights, that among these are Life, Liberty and the pursuit of Happiness.

The assumption that we are endowed with rights makes for much discussion. The claim, 'I know my rights!' seems to follow every perceived injustice that someone suffers.

Yet it is not self-evident to philosophers that we have such rights. What is their origin? What are these rights? When you study utilitarianism you will discover that the theory dismisses any theory of natural rights, arguing that a notion of natural rights interferes with the goal of achieving the best possible outcome. From a different perspective, the American philosopher Ronald Dworkin (1931–2013) argued that rights were not to be understood absolutely. In *Life's Dominion: An Argument About Abortion, Euthanasia and Individual Freedom* (1993), he argues that we should instead see a human life in investment terms, and think of rights incrementally. If a young person dies at 20, it is an immense tragedy. So much has been invested in her by way of care and education, but little return has been given. This life is so much more significant than that of an old person who has paid back society through all she has given, or a baby in whom little investment has been made.

Against such views, Ingolf Dalferth (b. 1948) has argued that basic rights, and above all human dignity, are central. Human dignity is not a possession that can be taken away, as freedom may be in some circumstances. We are dignified in being ourselves. It is the essence of being human.

Religious views emphasise that we are children of God. From this they derive an insistence on the sacredness of life and the infinite value of the human person.

However, the question of the status of the person is developed, it seems at least clear that ethics makes sense only in terms of human activity. It is about persons and for persons.

(c) Ethics and language

If we are social persons, much of that sociality comes through language. We use language to frame the ideas we use to understand the world. We use language to tell others our memories and activities. We also use it when we think out the meaning of what we are doing or have done. We use language to reach judgements, to advise, to give instructions or to make requests. We use language to give thanks, whether to other people or to God. We use it to teach and learn, to encourage or to condemn, to complain or to praise.

Being human and being speaking persons are intricately entwined. If we are in constant relationship with each other, and we speak in but also about those relationships, then we cannot think about morality without thinking about the language we use.

The questions to think about in relation to language are not simply questions about the meaning of words or sentences. They are questions about how they are or should be used. If I describe someone as 'good', what am I saying about her? After all, 'good' is used in so many ways. Sometimes we use it as a term of moral approval: for example, when I say 'Mother Teresa was a good person', or 'Giving to the poor is good'. But sometimes I use the term in non-moral ways, such as when I praise someone for being good *at* something: 'Picasso was a good artist' or 'Marin Alsop is a good conductor.' Again, I may use it to express pleasure: 'That was a good meal.' Sometimes I use 'good' as a description, sometimes as an encouragement on a student's piece of work.

Both moral and non-moral uses of 'good' are significant for ethics, but there are also deep questions to consider about whether 'Giving alms to the poor is good' is a descriptive sentence like 'Everest is a high mountain'. These questions are called metaethical, and will be important in your Year 2 work.

Ethics
Ethics in business
moral principles
rules and regulations
of right conduct
values that guide

(d) Ethics and religion

Ethics is often taught in schools in conjunction with, or as part of, the subject of religious studies. Such a connection has value. All the great religions make ethical claims and provide guidance, and sometimes firm directions, on what it means to be moral.

This connection can sometimes have an unfortunate side-effect of leading people to imagine that there is a necessary condition of the ethical, that morality somehow *depends* upon a religious basis. This assumption leads to misunderstandings. People sometimes say of an action that it is wrong *because it is forbidden by the Ten Commandments*. Many Christian philosophers, including St Thomas Aquinas, Martin Luther and Pope St John Paul II, would argue that this interpretation gets things the wrong way round. Murder, theft, adultery and lying are forbidden by the Ten Commandments *because they are wrongful acts*. In other words, they are wrong in themselves, and can be known to be wrong in themselves by reason. Natural law theory argues that what is right and wrong is knowable by reason. On this view, the Ten Commandments simply sum up what we should know by reason.

This view seems to have a good biblical foundation. The Jews behave badly and God gives Moses the Ten Commandments. He does this not to tell his people something new but forcibly to remind them of what they ought to have known very well. Evil and wrongdoing happen in Genesis before the Commandments are promulgated, as we can see in the tales of Noah and the Flood or Abel's murder by Cain. These actions are not presented as those of people acting in ignorance – the wrongdoer is not given the excuse that he couldn't know he had done wrong because the Ten Commandments had not yet been set out. Much later, in the New Testament, St Paul says:

> When Gentiles, who do not possess the Law do instinctively what the Law requires, these, not having the Law, are a law to themselves. They show that what the Law requires is written in their hearts, to which their own conscience also bears witness; and their conflicting thoughts will accuse or perhaps excuse them on the day when, according to my gospel, God, through Jesus Christ, will judge the secret thoughts of all.

Romans 2:14–16

Notice the mention of the law written on men's hearts, by which they can work out what is right and wrong. Closer to our own time, the future Archbishop of Canterbury, William Temple, was categorical:

> In its nature, the moral judgement is quite wholly independent of Religion.

William Temple: *The Kingdom of God* (1914), p. 42

Of course, some religious people insist that their beliefs rest simply on the commands of scripture, thinking that *x is wrong* just because the Bible or the Qu'ran says so. But this belief might not always be more than skin-deep. Suppose a critic were to say, 'So if God changed his mind and decided to make murder, pillage, adultery and lying compulsory, then we should all do them?' Most, perhaps all, would almost certainly say, 'But God would not do that!' If that is their reply, it suggests that there really is something intrinsically wrong about those actions. This is why a good God would not command them. These are things knowable as wrong in themselves.

Archbishop William Temple

4 Theories of ethics

Philosophers generally distinguish three areas of enquiry: **normative**, **applied** and **metaethics**.

Metaethics concerns the theory of ethics. It involves questions such as what we mean by terms like 'right', 'wrong', 'good', 'bad', and important issues such as the justification of ethics or the relationship between ethics and law. Some especially significant metaethical theories include:

■ **Emotivism:** the view that ethical sentences simply evince [exhibit] an emotion and have no factual justification. 'Killing is wrong' is logically equivalent to 'Killing – boo!' This theory was held by, among others, Rudolf Carnap and A. J. Ayer.

- **Subjectivism:** the view that x is right because I say so and for no other reason. This view is held most notably by **Existentialists** such as Jean-Paul Sartre or Martin Heidegger.
- **Relativism:** the view that rightness is culturally or religiously determined. Incompatible positions are justifiable by their cultural roots. This view is surprisingly common today, especially in the form of **vulgar relativism**, which holds that as all beliefs are relative, all should be tolerated. The theory has only to be stated for its absurdity to be apparent: if there is a requirement to be tolerant, then there is, after all, a universal principle of tolerance. If there is a single universal principle, then this version of relativism is contradictory.
- **Divine command theory:** the view that x is right because God commands it. This view is rejected by most Christian philosophers, including St Thomas Aquinas, Martin Luther and Pope St John Paul II. It is sometimes found in some – but not all – Evangelical circles.
- **Natural law theory:** believes that moral rightness can be determined through careful reflection on the facts of the world: 'right reason in accordance with nature'. Aristotle, Cicero, St Thomas Aquinas, Richard Hooker, Hugo Grotius and, today, John Finnis, support this view.

Metaethics will be studied in more depth in the second year of the course. For the moment you need only to understand what metaethical questions are about.

The main concern of the first year of your course is normative ethics. It consists of particular theories of how we ought to live. An important division is between **deontic ethics**, which emphasises what we should do, and **aretaic ethics** (virtue ethics), which emphasises the type of persons we should strive to be.

Categorical imperatives are discussed in Chapter 12.

Aretaic ethics are associated with Aristotle and his followers, both ancient and modern. Alisdair Macintyre, Philippa Foot, G. E. M. Anscombe and Martha Nussbaum are key writers in the modern tradition. The perception that it is not enough to perform a good act is crucial to this school of thought. One might perform a just act for an unjust reason. One can never be a just person without performing just acts. But performing just acts does not make one a good person. Motivation and character are crucial.

Deontic ethics are normally split into two kinds:

1   **Teleological theories** (often called consequentialist) determine what is good by outcomes: *x* is seen as good because it leads to good results. Some well-known theories of this kind include:

- **Utilitarianism** which holds that we should seek always the greatest balance of good over evil. This does not mean 'the greatest good of the greatest number' as the theory is sometimes inaccurately described. It is important to notice that this theory stresses the idea that we should always follow this one principle. The theory has no room for any view of natural rights. Rights get in the way of utility. Supporters of this theory include Jeremy Bentham, John Stuart Mill, Henry Sidgwick, and, more recently, Derek Parfit and Peter Singer.

- **Egoism** (not egotism, which is not a moral theory, but simply refers to complete selfishness) is an ethical theory which believes that we should all seek to act in our own best interests. It argues that if everyone did this, we would all achieve the best results. This approach is presupposed in many theories of economics, including some types of free market theory.

- **Situation ethics,** generally associated with Joseph Fletcher, argues that in each situation we should do that which will produce the most loving outcome. This approach is sceptical about rules, arguing that always following rules can lead to cruel and unloving consequences.

2   **Deontological** theories argue that something is right in itself:

- **Kantian** ethics are often understood to emphasise the primacy of doing one's duty regardless of consequences. The categorical imperative emphasises in its first form that we should act only on that maxim we can at the same time will to be universal law, in its second that we should so act as to treat people always as ends and never as means only. What matters above all is having a good will.

- **Agapism** stresses love. It holds that we should just love. 'Love is all you need.' This theory has few philosophical adherents – Archbishop William Temple dismissed it as 'fatuous bleating' – but it is sometimes heard. The absence of a specific theory of justice appears to make it impractical and emphasises its distance from other views, including those of Christianity.

- **Divine command theory** also sometimes appears in this category as well as under the guise of a metaethical view.

is GOD NECESSARY FOR MORALITY?

See Chapter 12 for a discussion of Kantian ethics.

Key persons

John Stuart Mill (1806–73): English utilitarian, Liberal politician and social philosopher. Brought up on utilitarian principles by James Mill, his father, and Jeremy Bentham. Major works include Utilitarianism (1863) and On Liberty (1859). His marriage to Harriet Taylor greatly influenced his thinking on social policies. Supported womens' legal rights. His basic philosophical position is that all knowledge is based on experience and that our desires and beliefs are products of psychological laws. Ethics, for example, are based on the psychological law that all humans desire to be happy (although he famously differed from Bentham in that he considered that intellectual pleasures are higher than other forms of happiness). MP for Westminster 1865–68, until defeated by W. H. Smith (of the bookseller's). Godfather to Bertrand Russell.

Immanuel Kant (1724–1804): Philosopher from Konigsberg in East Prussia. One of the greatest thinkers in history, attempted to reconcile the insights of the Rationalists, such as Descartes and Leibniz, and the Empiricists such as Locke, Hume and Berkeley. Author of *The Critique of Pure Reason*, the *Critique of Practical Reason* and *Groundwork of the Metaphysic of Morals*.

Background

Teleological and deontological theories: a word of caution

The division between deontological and teleological theories is best understood in terms of orientation rather than dogmatic categories.

The American philosopher William K. Frankena (1908–94), especially in his very influential textbook *Ethics* (1973), devoted attention to systematic categorisation of ethical theories, especially in the distinction between teleological and deontological theories. The result of the distinction was to create a climate of discussion in which people became needlessly wrapped up in whether a given theory is deontological or teleological, often at the expense of concentrating on what the theories said.

An obvious example was in Kantian ethics. Frankena labelled this deontological, which has led many to understand Kant as strictly unconcerned with consequences. But this is to misread him. As you will see when you study him, he says that we should always do our duty because it is our duty, not because it leads to good outcomes. This is deontological, but, at the same time, when he comes to working out what our duty is, he becomes consequentialist. The principle of universalisation says that we can only treat as

moral an action that we are willing for everyone to do. Also we should treat people always as ends, never as means only. Both these principles are consequentialist, and do not make sense without thinking about outcomes. William Temple always treated Kant consequentially and there are interesting essays taking this view in *Essays on Derek Parfit's On What Matters* (2009). Perhaps we can say of Kant that the right-making feature of his theory is whether we have done our duty, which is deontological, but determining that duty requires a teleological approach.

In the same way, natural law is occasionally rather oddly described as a deontological theory, though it is much more commonly understood as a teleological one. For Aristotle and Aquinas, 'right reason in accordance with nature' is to be understood in terms of the consequences for human flourishing.

The important thing to remember is that philosophers who devise or outline ethical theories do not begin their work by thinking 'I am going to write a deontological theory about how to live'. They set out what they believe is right. Any categorising comes later, and by others.

The best way to think of Frankena's categories is that they illuminate the general direction of theories. They are not definitive pigeonholes.

For more detail on the thought of Aquinas, see Chapter 10.

For a discussion of act utilitarianism, see Chapter 11.

Background

A note on relativism and situationalism

Among commonly found terms are 'relativism' and 'situationalism', often contrasted with 'absolutism'. People often confuse the two concepts and it is important to be clear about the difference.

A **relativist theory** is one which believes that all ethical judgements are relative, whether to culture or to some set of beliefs. There are no absolutes in ethics because nothing is definitively right or wrong.

A **situational theory** is one where particular judgements are relative to situations, but there is some principle which it is always right to apply. In natural law theory, one must always use right reason in accordance with nature. In act utilitarianism, one must always follow the general principle of seeking the greatest balance of good over evil, though what that will be has to be determined in each situation. In situation ethics, there is an absolute command always to perform the most loving act. It would be a mistake to describe any of these theories as relativist.

Study advice

This chapter contains a large number of 'isms'. As with many things, it is not easy to learn them in one go. It is better in your learning to go back to them as you work through ideas in the following chapters. Seeing how the ideas work out in practice is the best way of making sense of more abstract concepts.

The question of practice matters very much for developing the skills of reflection on the ethical theories mentioned in the next chapters. Sir Karl Popper, one of the greatest philosophers of the twentieth century, used to become very cross when people said: 'It's fine in theory, but it won't work in practice.' His objection to people saying this was an obvious one. If a theory doesn't work in practice, it is a bad theory, because the test of a theory is how it works out in practice. It is very helpful, when you think about ideas you will study, such as utilitarianism or natural law, that you think about actual circumstances and instances, to see whether a particular theory of right and wrong would give the kind of guidance people want. Giving specific examples and instances is good practice in all writing about philosophy, but invaluable in ethics.

Sometimes it can seem difficult to reach a conclusion in ethics. Very often, teachers find students concluding their essay with statements such as 'It is all relative', or 'It is all a matter of opinion' or even 'If it is right for you, then it's right.' When students write in that way, it is just an assertion, not a philosophical argument. What is needed here to do well would be a justification of your point of view.

Take just one of these assertions: 'It is all a matter of opinion.' The point being made here is that we can make no certain ethical judgements and it is a personal matter to decide. In philosophical terms, the student is arguing for subjectivism, the theory that something is right for me because I say so, or choose it as right, and for no other reason.

There is no requirement not to hold the position you have taken, but you need to defend the point. It is not a self-evident truth that there are no objective reasons for moral judgements. Your case has to be made and sustained. How should you go about doing so?

The best way is to think about what someone who disagrees with you might argue. What might she say?

Suppose she said: 'I cannot agree with you. Are you saying that I am wrong to say that a man torturing children for his own gratification is doing something objectively wrong, and that my condemning him as immoral is no more than a personal opinion? Surely I can show that torture is bad for people psychologically and physically? Can you demonstrate how someone could really argue that torture is absolutely fine? In the same way, I think that incest is really wrong, because it can have no good results for people and many truly bad ones. And I don't think it is just my opinion that rape, stealing or putting arsenic in someone's coffee just because I don't like her are wrong.'

Now, if you think she is wrong to say these things, and you believe that ethical judgements are just matters of opinion, then the challenge is to show in the specific instances she has mentioned why she is wrong and why it would be legitimate for someone to say these acts were not really wrong in themselves. You would need to justify your conclusion, that these were just matters of opinion, with reasons. If you are able to do so, you are arguing well. If you find that you cannot give good reasons, then perhaps you might want to modify the original assertion. In good philosophical work, we should be prepared to change our minds if we think there are better arguments than we have considered.

Summary diagram: The issue of ethics

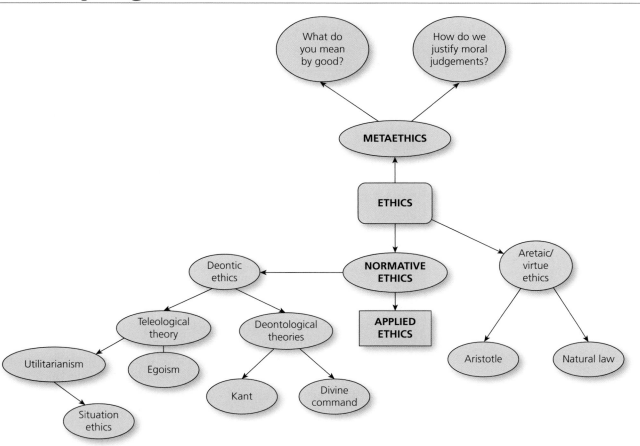

It is worth remembering that many terms used in this chapter will recur throughout the course, which means that you will learn about them in more depth through practice. Nevertheless, it is really helpful to have some certainty about key terms before you continue with your studies, recognising that your understanding will gradually deepen as you move beyond basic definition.

Can you give brief definitions of:
- metaethics
- normative ethics
- divine command theory
- natural law theory
- aretaic (virtue) ethics?

Can you explain:
- the difference between metaethics and normative ethics
- the difference between deontic and aretaic (virtue) ethics
- the difference between teleological and deontological approaches to ethics
- relativist and situational approaches to ethics?

Can you give arguments for and against:
- relativism
- subjectivism
- teleological approaches to ethics
- the idea that ethical theory presupposes religious belief?

Before you begin a detailed study of ethics, it is really helpful to begin the habit of thinking reflectively about ethical issues for yourself. Think about specific instances in life and how they might illustrate issues. Perhaps you will find it helpful, in order to begin thinking ethically, to try one or two of the following essay titles, which are designed to get you in the habit of thinking reflectively about questions.

Sample question and guidance

'There is nothing in life which is truly evil.' Discuss.

This essay requires initial thought before you begin writing. The title makes a very bold claim, but it provides an opportunity to think about those who argue that ethical judgements are just subjective matters of opinion. It also requires you to begin to think about what we mean by ideas of right or wrong. You might like to think about whether to describe something as right or wrong means that it is good or bad for people or sentient beings in general. Think perhaps about whether certain actions are always right or wrong, such as helping the poor, or incest.

You might choose to think a little more widely. Is ethical behaviour what we mean by describing something as morally good? People will sometimes describe a dagger or a nuclear weapon as 'evil'. Does this actually make sense? Surely a nuclear weapon is an inanimate thing, made from neutral ingredients? Someone might argue that the human actions of making or using weapons is evil, but does it make sense to speak of the object itself as evil?

This is a very open question, and it is difficult, as so often in philosophy, to say it has a right answer. The question is designed to encourage you think hard and deeply about issues, but it is also designed to develop the use of examples. The question cannot be answered without using examples of things and actions you might want to argue really are evil, or really are not.

Further essay questions

'If there is no God, then nothing is right or wrong.' Discuss.

To what extent would someone living alone on a desert island have moral responsibilities?

When India was a colony, the British authorities did not attempt to prevent people from practising their beliefs. However, they banned the practice of *suttee,* used by a minority of Hindus, in which the widow of a deceased man was burned on the funeral pyre with him. To what extent do you consider the colonial authorities were correct to interfere in people's beliefs in this way?

Going further

There are many books which give general introductions to ethics. Most are rewarding in various ways. One of the finest is Julia Driver: *Ethics: The Fundamentals* (Wiley–Blackwell, 2006). Piers Benn: *Ethics* (Routledge, 1997) provides a solid introduction, and William Frankena: *Ethics* (second edition, Pearson, 1988) remains invaluable despite reservations one might have about his insistence on particular categorisation of theories. His insights on utilitarianism and other theories are penetrating and important. Michael J. Sandel: *Justice: What's the Right Thing To Do,* (Penguin, 2010) is justly popular and wide-ranging, also touching on political philosophy. Simon Blackburn: *Ethics: A Very Short Introduction* (Oxford University Press, 2003) is interesting and useful for developing your own ideas. For any student of ethics, an invaluable source is *A Companion to Ethics (Blackwell Companions to Philosophy),* Ed. Peter Singer (Blackwell, 1993).
Other books discussed in this chapter are:
- Dalferth I. `Religion, Morality and Being Human: The Controversial Status of Human Dignity', in: P. Jonkers and M. Sarot (Eds.), *Embodied Religion* (Utrecht: Ars Disputandi Supplement Series Vol. 6, 2013).
- Dworkin R. *Life's Dominion: An Argument About Abortion, Euthanasia and Individual Freedom* (Knopf, 1993).
- Gewirth A. *Reason and Morality* (Chicago, 1978).
- Suikkanen J. and John Cottingham J. *Essays on Derek Parfit's On What Matters* (Wiley-Blackwell, 2009).
- Temple W. *The Kingdom of God* (Macmillan, 1914).

Chapter 10

Aquinas and natural law

1 Introduction

Natural law theory is misunderstood, partly because of the writings of some who have claimed to support it, and partly because it has often been seen as a distinctly Catholic and religious approach to ethics. It is true that Catholicism has taken natural law theory into its moral teaching, but it does not follow on from this, that it is dependent on Catholic belief for its justification. It has been adopted by non-Catholic thinkers such as the Anglicans Richard Hooker (1554–1600) and, in the twentieth century, William Temple (1881–1944). As a theory it predates Christianity and, because it does not depend on any specific reference to teachings revealed by God (though some have argued otherwise), it could, at least in principle, be defended without reference to religious belief.

The Roman jurist Cicero (106–43BC) would write:

> ... *[natural] law is right reason in agreement with Nature; it is of universal application, unchanging and everlasting; it summons to duty by its commands, and averts from wrongdoing by its prohibitions. And it does not lay its commands or prohibitions upon good men in vain, though neither have any effect on the wicked. It is a sin to try to alter this law, nor is it allowable to attempt to repeal any part of it, and it is impossible to abolish it entirely. We cannot be freed from its obligations by Senate or People, and we need not look outside ourselves for an expounder or interpreter of it. And there will not be different laws at Rome and at Athens, or different laws now and in future, but one eternal and unchangeable law will be valid for all nations and for all times ...*

Cicero: *De Republica*, III, xxii, 33

Cicero says that this understanding, true everywhere, is promulgated by God. But it would be perfectly feasible to suggest that right reason can work it out without reference to God.

Natural law appeals to the sense that certain things can clearly be known by anyone to be wrong. As we are rational creatures, we are capable of knowing that certain things are right or wrong. Take, for example, incest. The horror against incest seems universal and, by observation, we can see that it is harmful to human flourishing. In-breeding perpetuates disability, illness and various ailments, and is psychologically damaging for its victims. Societies might differ about what counts as incest, but the general principle is clear. If it is objected that in ancient Egypt, the Pharoah was expected to take his sister as first wife, the justification was that they were Gods, not humans. The penalties for everyone else who indulged in incest were severe. Tutankahmen we now know to be the product of incest: he was disabled and died very young. The same appears to be true for theft, murder, torture, rape and so on. The natural law theorist claims that we can by use of reason alone, know that these are bad for human happiness and human flourishing. Societies with no contact with Christianity have similar prohibitions against these acts.

Is it possible to uphold the theory without reference to God? This approach has a long history. It is implicit in Aquinas' theory and explicit in Hugo Grotius (1583–1645):

What we have been saying would have a degree of validity even if we should concede that which cannot be conceded without the utmost wickedness, that there is no God, or that the affairs of men are of no concern to Him.

De Iure Belli ac Pacis, Prolegomena, §11

Hugo Grotius (Huig de Groot) (1583–1645): Protestant Dutch legal theorist, best known for his *De Jure Belli ac Pacis* (The Law of War and Peace) (1625), a major contribution to both natural law and just war theories.

Background

A note on natural law and the manuals

After the Middle Ages, and after the Council of Trent (1545–63), the thought of Aquinas became central to teaching within the Catholic Church. The natural law tradition was emphasised in some contradiction to the more scripturally based approach to ethics found in the Reformers, although Martin Luther did make use of natural law theory in his writings, and acknowledged this.

The Council of Trent also created seminaries for the proper training of clergy. These institutions remain today. Those training to become priests had a lengthy education in theology, scripture and philosophy. Even today, the normal course of training at a seminary lasts six years. To support these courses various thinkers produced manuals, including manuals of moral theology, normally in Latin. Examples include the four-volume *Theologia moralis* of St Alphonsus Ligouri (1697–1787) and the very commonly used *Compendium*

theologiae moralis of Jean-Pierre Guy (1801–66). The tone of these books was very much in terms of discussion of moral requirements as fixed laws, with much discussion of how to interpret individual cases.

These manuals often read more like law books than discussions of morality. This is especially true of the work of Heribert Jone (1885–1967), which was very widely used in seminaries in the English-speaking world. This overall approach led many to argue that natural law theory was absolutist and *deontological*, not concerned with situation or outcomes: *x* was right because 'natural law said so'. That was how it was taught and it led some to imagine – incorrectly – that the same was true of Aquinas' original teaching.

The Catholic moral theologian, Servais Pinckaers (1925–2008) called for a return to an understanding of Thomist natural law within the principle he had used, based on what was the goal of true happiness for humans. Of the manuals he wrote:

Because of the focus on obligations, moral theology ... detached itself from everything that goes beyond legal imperatives ... The moral theology of the manuals lost sight of the essential question: ... happiness and the destiny of the human person ... Obedience to law encroached upon charity and the virtues; the theme of friendship was lost ...

Servais Pinckaers: *Morality: the Catholic View* (2001), p. 40

The British Thomist scholar – and fellow Dominican – Herbert McCabe was even more blunt:

The manuals show no serious interest in the development of Christian life, the growth in grace by which people are educated in the moral dispositions, virtues, so that they mature into being their true selves. In place

of the truth involved in Aquinas' account of action (recognition of relevant factors in the judgement of means and the discovery of the self in decision) there is an appeal simply to obedience – thought to be the work of a quite unpredictable and almost random free will. For Aquinas, by contrast, the basis of the moral life is prudential (prudence), right practical reason in the development of caritas (charity)...

Herbert McCabe: *The Good Life: Ethics and the Pursuit of Happiness* (2005), pp. 93–94

It is crucial to the study of Aquinas on natural law not to see him through the prism of **manualist** interpretations, but to concentrate on his own views.

Manualist approaches to natural law, stressing obedience, were clearly deontological. But Aquinas' natural law emphatically was not. The goal is always the good for persons.

> **Key terms**
>
> **Deontological theory** Any ethical theory that argues that the goodness of an action lies in itself, regardless of consequences.
> **Teleological theory** Any ethical theory that argues that the goodness of an action is determined by whether it has good consequences.
> **Manualist** Author of one of the manuals (principally written 1600–1960), textbooks normally in Latin, used for instruction in Catholic seminaries. Often legalistic in tone.

2 Aquinas' four tiers of law

At the heart of Aquinas' treatment of law is the concept of a fourfold division: *Eternal Law*, *Divine Law*, *Natural Law* and *Human Law*.

(a) Eternal Law

Eternal Law should not be confused with divine command theory, or the Ten Commandments. Manualist approaches (see note, above) tended to emphasise natural law in relation to the commandments. For Aquinas, the commandments reveal what can be known by the light of human reason. Adultery does not become wrong because the Ten Commandments say so. The wrongness of adultery can be seen in its effects and is knowable by reason, as Aristotle, with no knowledge of the commandments, knew very well.

> **Key quote**
>
> Repeal the Missouri compromise ... repeal the Declaration of Independence, repeal all past history, you still can not repeal human nature. It still will be the abundance of man's heart, that slavery extension is wrong.
>
> Abraham Lincoln

What Aquinas means by Eternal Law is that God has willed that the universe is of this kind and not something different. Because he is all-powerful, God could, for example, have made humans immortal, or naturally solitary. Instead, he made them mortal and social. Why God willed things this way, we cannot know, but he presumably had his own good reasons for doing so. So, Eternal Law is best interpreted as the principles by which God created and controls the universe.

> … law is nothing but a certain dictate of the practical reason 'in the leader' who governs any perfect community. It is clear, however, if we presuppose … that the whole world community is governed by divine reason. And thus the rational guidance of things in God, as in the existing ruler of the universe, has the significance of law… It is fitting to call a law of this kind the Eternal Law.
>
> *Summa Theologica (S.T.) I–II, q.91, a.2, c*

Human beings cannot fully understand God's Eternal Law but it does not follow that that they cannot work out, through reason, its meaning in human life.

(b) Divine Law

Divine Law in Aquinas is something of an oddity. As a believer, he knows that God has taught certain moral truths in revelation, in the Ten Commandments and in other ways, including Jesus' answers to particular questions.

In the Sermon on the Mount, Jesus introduces us not to a specific set of answers but rather to the need for developing the appropriate virtues. He is very much telling us the dispositions we should cultivate, describing the types of people we should be:

> Blessed are the poor in spirit, for theirs is the kingdom of heaven.
> … Blessed are the meek, for they will inherit the earth.
> Blessed are those who hunger and thirst for righteousness, for they will be filled.
> Blessed are the merciful, for they will receive mercy.
> Blessed are the pure in heart, for they will see God.
> Blessed are the peacemakers, for they will be called children of God.
>
> *Matthew 5:3, 5–9*

When Jesus speaks of the law, he emphasises always the spirit of the law rather than precise adherence to the letter. It is perhaps this insight which is most important to the understanding of the application of law.

As we shall see, Aquinas believes that moral requirements are knowable by human reason. If this were not so, then the basis of Natural Law would fail. Nothing in Divine Law contradicts Natural Law. The opposite is true. For Aquinas, Divine Law makes clear and confirms that which we can know by reason and it is a help to those trying to work out what reason teaches. In scripture, God reveals the Ten Commandments, not as new teachings, but to bring back the people of Israel to what they should have known for themselves. Aquinas is well aware that those without Christian revelation are just as capable as believers in working out the need to preserve life, to educate the young, and so on. Aquinas' position is often described, with some accuracy, as Christian Humanism because it makes the good of the human person central, in a way that can be understood by anyone, while remaining true to the Christian belief in the dignity of the person as the beloved child of God. It is important not to make the mistake of thinking that his view *depends on* the Ten Commandments or other teachings. For Aquinas, these revelations, including the Ten Commandments, should be understood as *affirmations* of what is knowable by reason.

(c) Natural Law

Natural Law therefore follows the direction of Eternal Law. It is an essentially rational exercise, a 'thinking along the grain of nature' to work out what is good for human flourishing. It must be noticed here that Aquinas means *human nature*. It would be an error to think that because some creatures in nature devour their partners after mating that humans should do so. God has willed that man has a natural inclination to do good, but also that he has a rational capacity to work out what it is right and proper to do.

The Primary precept is often simplified to:

Do good and avoid evil.

This is a useful way of remembering the point made by Aquinas, as it sums up the essence of what we have just seen, though it is important to remember that we still need to work out what the goods to be done and the evils to be avoided actually would be for human beings.

(d) Human Law

Human Law arises out of the reality that man is a social animal. We need regulations in order to function co-operatively. This is why societies establish governing authorities who set rules on how their citizens should behave. Nevertheless, Aquinas does not accept any notion of the divine right of kings in the sense later claimed by James I or Charles I of England. His basic principle is that a Human Law's value is essentially prudential, but its validity is dependent on not contradicting Natural Law. As an example, if the king says that we should all kill our first-born children, that would be bad for human flourishing and contrary to the preservation of life. The same would apply to an order to commit genocide. These contradict Natural Law and cannot be justified. But if government required us to drive on the right instead of the left, that contradicts no Natural Law but is a simple matter of prudence. This seems to fit with a deep instinct. If someone argues that she will not assist in abortion our instinct is to see this as an issue of conscience, even if we disagree with her; but if she refuses to obey the rule not to park on a double yellow line, then we would see her behaviour as odd, not conscientious objection. The issue of double yellow lines contradicts no Natural Law.

Key question

How valuable is Aquinas' theory for judging the actions of governments?

If a regulation is contrary to Natural Law, then it loses its validity:

Human Law has the quality of law insofar as it is according to right reason; and accordingly it is clear that it flows from an Eternal Law. Insofar as it deviates from reason, it is called an unjust law, and thus it has the quality not of law but more of violence.

S.T. I-II, q.93, a.3, ad.2

This concept enables Aquinas to develop a theory of civil disobedience. A ruler who persistently breaches Natural Law may be disobeyed or even removed:

Man is bound to obey secular rulers to the extent that the order of justice requires. Therefore if rulers have no just title to power, but have usurped it; or if they command unjust things, their subjects are not obliged to obey them, except perhaps in some cases in order to avoid scandal or danger.

S.T. II-II, q. 104, a.1, ad.3

3 Aquinas' Natural Law

For a profile of Aristotle, see Chapter 9.

Key person

The Stoics: Included both Greek philosophers like Zeno 9 (c.334–262BC) and Romans including Cicero, Seneca (c. 4 –65BC) and Marcus Aurelius (121–180AD). They believed that as we can do nothing to change human fortunes, we must cultivate the right attitudes of self-control and acceptance.

For more on Aristotle's and Plato's thought, see Chapters 2 and 3.

The idea of natural law is very ancient. It may be found in Aristotle (e.g. in *Nicomachean Ethics* Book V) and it informed much of Stoic ethical thought. At its core is the insight of St Paul (*Romans* 2:15) of 'the law that is written on men's hearts', the belief that all humanity can find a common idea of rightness which will be the same for all peoples and nations.

We should remember that, influenced by his master, Albertus Magnus (St Albert the Great, c.1200–1280), Aquinas would attempt the reconstruction of all thought in the light of the new learning represented by Aristotle and his followers. He believed in the light of reason. As a result, he believed that what morality requires is knowable by reason alone.

He rejected divine command theory – the belief that something is right *because* God commands it – arguing that God commands what is right. Its rightness is knowable in itself. Anyone who studies nature ought to be able to determine what is right and wrong. The result of this was a sort of Christian humanism in Aquinas – the idea that morality is rooted in reason rather than scripture, although it is justified and developed in scripture.

To this Christian humanism, he would bring something of Aristotle's **situationalism** (*Nicomachean Ethics* II) and a new factor – an understanding of 'will'. Ancient Greece had lacked a word for 'will'. Right or wrongdoing was variously described by ancient thinkers. Plato had tried to explain human psychology in terms of knowledge or ignorance. Aristotle, more subtly, referred to the nurturing of good or bad habits.

Only in the Christian centuries had the idea of 'will' grown up, most evidently developed by St Augustine of Hippo (354–430AD). For Aquinas, the idea of 'will' would enable him to move beyond Aristotle, not least in his determination to demonstrate how the world is wholly dependent on God's will for its existence.

Natural law, as developed by Aquinas, is a version of virtue ethics. It is tied very much to the virtues, which Aquinas discusses at length. He agrees with Aristotle that cultivating the virtues is essential to the good life. He emphasises the central role of practical reason (prudence) in determining what it is right and proper to do in each situation.

Background

Virtue ethics

Virtue ethics, also known as aretaic ethics, from the Greek *arête* (virtue), takes a holistic approach to the moral life. Some theories, such as utilitarianism, treat ethics as concerned only with the actions we perform. We are ethical if we have performed a good action. However, as Aristotle pointed out, we could perform a good act for a bad reason. To be a good person, it is not enough to do good things. I must do them for good reasons, based on a good character. For a virtue ethicist, it is essential to develop good character, both by practising moral virtues such as courage, generosity and so on, but also developing the correct intellectual virtues, such as good judgement, understanding and awareness. For Aristotle, to live the good life, we need to develop good habits, so that good behaviour becomes part of our characters. In particular, we need the intellectual virtue of *prudence*, which consists of understanding (the ability to grasp a situation), good judgement (the ability to work out what it is right and proper to do) and good deliberation (the ability to work out how to achieve what our judgement tells us we should do). This ability is different from purely theoretical understanding. It cannot just be grasped, in the way an infant prodigy might understand mathematics, but requires experience and practice.

These ideas deeply influenced Aquinas. When you study his notion of double effect, you will see how important *intention* is to his moral teaching. As you read through the remainder of this chapter, notice how the ideas outlined in this box recur.

Of course, Aquinas is not satisfied with Aristotle's list of virtues. For him, as for St Ambrose, the theological virtues of *faith*, which entails intelligence and knowledge, *hope*, which also includes proper fear of the Lord, and *charity*, which includes the gift of wisdom, all need to be added. After these, for Aquinas and Ambrose, come the cardinal virtues: *prudence, justice, courage* and *temperance*.

(a) The telos

For Aquinas, as for Aristotle, the universe is purposive. Things on Earth seek to achieve their goal – in Greek, their *telos*. Plants do so blindly. Seeds grow into plants, without consciousness. Animals follow their instincts. Only humans have fully rational thought. Using reason, we can both work out what is good for us, but also work out how to achieve our goals in life. For Aristotle, our earthly goal is to flourish in community. He had no belief in personal survival after death. But Aquinas believed that we are only able to be fully what we should be – what God meant us

Is it true that human nature is purposive? Do we all have a clear idea of what the purpose might be?

Key person

St Thomas Aquinas
(*c.*1225–1274): Dominican friar, perhaps the greatest medieval philosopher, of unparalleled industry. At the forefront of attempts to rethink existing philosophical and theological thought in the light of the Aristotelian revival. Best known for his *Summa Theologica, Summa Contra Gentiles* and dozens of other works.

Key term

Lex Latin term from which we derive 'legislation.' Refers to specific rule or regulation.

Key term

Ius Latin term which refers to the general principle of law, not to specific regulations. Sometimes translated in terms of rights, and the word from which we derive 'justice'. In Latin, natural law is always '*ius*'.

to be – in the next life. To achieve that goal, we need to live this life in faithful service of God, by the light of reason.

For Aquinas, as for Aristotle, the goal of human life is flourishing, which leads to true happiness. For Aristotle, that happiness was to be understood as *eudaimonia*, a full flourishing of the human person and his abilities. That is not sufficient for Aquinas. As a Christian, he sees happiness in the fullest sense as union with God in the bliss of heavenly life. The desire to be with God is the centre of our natural destiny. It is for this that we were created and to which our intellect directs us. Our goal is our heavenly home.

This can be a little difficult to appreciate. For Aquinas, we are fulfilled only when we are most complete and at our best, with God. For him, earthly happiness is a foretaste of heavenly bliss, though it lacks the same permanence. However, Aquinas does not treat life on Earth as irrelevant or of little regard. It matters that we live on this Earth as well as we can, using our reason. This is why he writes so much on topics such as politics and ethics.

It should be noted as you work through this chapter that Aquinas' view is much more situational and much more rooted in what leads to the good life than some later interpreters who have attempted to explain the natural law in more theoretical and abstract terms have allowed. This separates Aquinas from the manualists.

(b) Ius and lex

An important distinction has to be made before embarking on detailed study of natural law theory. It is a frequent mistake of English-speaking writers to think of natural 'law' as a set of regulations. Partly this is because of the British and American tradition of statute law, in which law consists mainly of specific regulations which permit or forbid.

In Latin, there are two words for the English word 'Law' – *ius* and *lex*. By *lex* is understood a specific regulation – **the letter of the law**, as in statute law. By *ius* is meant **the principle of law** rather than the exact wording of a given regulation. It is important to remember that theorists such as Grotius, Cicero and Aquinas are talking always of *ius* (from which we derive English words such as 'justice' or 'jurisprudence').

In the seventeenth century, the great British philosopher Thomas Hobbes (1588–1679) pointed out the significance of the distinction:

> *… though they that speak of this subject use to confound ius and lex, rights and law: yet they ought to be distinguished; because RIGHT consisteth in liberty to do, or to forbear: whereas LAW determineth, and bindeth to one of them: so that law and right differ as much, as obligation and liberty.*

Thomas Hobbes: *Leviathan*, Part 1, Chapter 14

Hobbes recognises that Natural Law must always be understood as *ius*, not as a legalistic system of precise regulations. Aquinas' invariable use of the word *ius* emphasises the point very clearly. However, as a matter of history, we find that the Catholic Church in particular, following the manualist tradition, has in the past very much treated natural law as a set of regulations, sometimes pronouncing on particular actions as 'licit' or 'illicit', words derived from *lex*. You will see some examples of this in Chapter 14 on Euthanasia. It is interesting that the two most recent popes, Benedict

XVI and Francis, and perhaps especially the latter, have in their moral pronouncements moved back to the original *ius* interpretations of Aquinas.

(c) Primary and secondary precepts

Key quote

The order of the precepts of the Natural Law is the order of our natural inclinations. For there is in man a primary and natural inclination to good, which he has in common with all things, inasmuch as every thing desires the preservation of its own being (*esse*) according to its nature. Through this inclination the Natural Law pertains to everything that makes for the preservation of human life and all that impedes its death. There is in man a secondary inclination to more specific ends according to the nature he has in common with other animals. According to this inclination, those things are said to be of Natural Law 'that nature has taught to all animals', instincts such as the union of husband and wife, the education of children, and so forth. Third, there is in man a certain inclination to good according to his rational nature, and this is proper to man alone: thus man has a natural inclination to know about God and to live in society. And in respect to this, there come under Natural Law all actions pertaining to such inclinations: notably that a man should avoid ignorance, that he must not offend those with whom he deals, and all other actions of this kind.

S.T. I-II, q.94, a.2

This passage needs careful study. We notice the *primary precept of Natural Law is the natural inclination to do good*. Other points, including the secondary precepts, follow from this initial insight. The value of stable relationships and good education of children is evident because not only do they help to preserve life but they enable a flourishing within life. There is more to the quality of life than merely being alive. And, thirdly, humans are social creatures. We do not flourish in a state of constant strife with our neighbours any more than we truly flourish if we are ignorant. Implicit in all of this, and explicit elsewhere in Aquinas, is the need to cultivate those virtues which encourage the right habits of both mind and behaviour.

Based on the thought of Aquinas, commentators have implied five broad areas of moral conduct:

- preservation of life
- ordering of society
- worship of God
- education of children
- reproduction.

A moment's thought enables us to recognise how these precepts are intrinsic to the very idea of doing good and avoiding evil. They are spelling out not something added to the original demand to do good, but what this means. For this reason, they are often referred to as 'the five primary precepts', though the phrase is not used by Aquinas himself.

From these ideas, we can then derive further, secondary precepts. Think about an issue such as reproduction or education. It is clear that we are made to reproduce. It does not follow that we should spend our lives just seeking members of the opposite sex, mating with them whenever possible. We need to consider also the needs of education, preservation of life and the good order of society. From these we can derive rational principles about family life, sexual conduct and so on.

It is important to remember that Aquinas himself does not write so specifically. Notice his 'and so forth'. Neither in the *Summa*, nor elsewhere, does he ever offer a definitive list. The tendency to be so specific – these are definitively the five – is a manualist one, not found in Aquinas himself. But those points given as the list of five secondary precepts are certainly part of his approach. This is a very good example of how Aquinas' insights have been treated in more legalistic terms than he would have chosen for himself.

We may note also in this passage the influence of Aristotle's discussion of the soul in *Nicomachean Ethics*, Book I, xiii. It is clear, as we noted, that Aquinas is not saying that Natural Law is simply what we share with the animal kingdom. There is a distinctly human nature – characterised by rationality – which informs what is right for humans.

(d) Prudence and natural law

The need for intellect – the virtue of prudence or practical reason – becomes apparent in Aquinas' discussion of particular cases. We do not know by a kind of intuition what we should do. Neither is it a gut feeling. Intrinsic to human nature is that we are *rational* creatures, capable of directing our behaviour through a process of thinking. The general precepts of Natural Law are invariable, but their application is not: we need to look at the results of our actions in a rational way. The implication here is that there is a necessary process of reasoning to be gone through in particular cases – these cannot be resolved by gut-feeling:

> *... practical reason is used in the contingent affairs in which human actions are located. Here we see that although there is a certain necessity in the general principles, the more one descends to the particulars, the more is the conclusion open to exception.*

> *...When we come to the particular conclusions of the practical reason ... there is neither the same standard of truth and uprightness for all ... [For example] All people realise that it is right and good to act according to reason. From this principle it follows as an individual conclusion that debts ought to be paid. In most cases this is true, but it could happen in some individual instance that it would be harmful and therefore irrational to repay a debt (if, for example, the money were to be used for a war against one's own country). Such exceptions are more likely to occur the more we get down to concrete cases, such as when it is we say that debts are to be paid with a particular precaution or in such a way. The more specialised the conditions stated, the greater is the possibility of an exception arising ...*

S.T. I–II, q.94, a. 4c.

Key question

Can we rationally determine what is good for human beings? Think about human actions which would not obviously be good for people.

This is a very important part of Aquinas' theory. Here he shows us specifically that the use of reason does not end at the formulation of the general precepts. We need to go much further, looking at each application of those precepts in a rational way. The need to be rational matters in each situation. This is why Natural Law has to be understood situationally.

The concept of prudence is taken directly from Aristotle. Aquinas tells us:

> Prudence entails not only consideration of the reason but also the application to action, which is the goal of practical reason.

S.T. II-II, 9.47, a. 3c.

Background

Prudence entails three intellectual skills: *understanding, judgement* and *good deliberation*.

Understanding is the ability to grasp the overall picture of what is going on in a given situation. It has been described as a 'touchline' skill. If I watch a sporting event, I describe myself as having understanding if I can grasp clearly what is happening on the field. But this, by itself, is enough merely for me to be a capable spectator. The manager needs judgement, the capacity to know what is the right thing to do in the circumstances, determining what is right and proper.

But knowing *what* the right thing to do is pointless unless one knows *how* to do this. This is where we need to be able to deliberate well. The process of deliberation involves using what is available. When there are no means available, we need to know what we cannot do and give up an impossible enterprise. The football manager may work out that he needs to be playing a stronger team, but with half his players injured and no money in the budget, there is nothing he can do to win the league.

John Finnis (b. 1940): Australian-born Oxford philosopher and natural law theorist, best known for his *Natural Law and Natural Rights* (1980) and *Aquinas: Moral, Political and Legal Theory* (1998). Also known for his friendship with Aung San Suu Kyi, whom he nominated for a Nobel Prize for Peace (awarded 1991).

(e) A modern development of natural law theory

In modern times, John Finnis is well-known for his development of natural law theory. His *Natural Law and Natural Rights,* first published in 1980 (2011), has proven itself a central text.

Finnis' theory of natural law is based on strongly Aristotelian principles, and on what Finnis calls 'basic forms of human flourishing'. He believes these forms are used – more or less reflectively, more or less adequately – by everyone who considers what to do. These include life, knowledge, play, work, aesthetic experience, friendship, practical reasonableness and religion. By the last he means the spiritual aspect of ourselves. For Finnis, each of these aspects of ourselves has its own rights. Men deprived of leisure and play do not flourish. But neither do those deprived of work. These areas of flourishing are supported by 'basic methodological requirements', such as:

- pursuit of goods
- a coherent plan of life
- no arbitrary preferences among values, detachment and commitment
- 'the (limited) relevance of consequences'
- 'respect for every basic value in every act', the requirements of the common good
- following one's conscience.

From these goods and requirements we can derive the unchanging natural law. Objective knowledge of morality is possible and we can define justice in terms of the concrete requirement to promote the common good.

Common good is defined as people realising their own basic values as well as other reasonable personal objectives. Precise details will necessarily be circumstantially determined. But the notion of basic goods and methodology enables us to rule out many types of injustice. Certain absolute duties and correlative absolute rights are therefore derivable, such as:

■ rights not to be tortured
■ not to have one's life taken as a means to another end
■ not to be lied to when factual communication is proper and expected
■ not to be condemned on charges known to be false.

For Finnis, and other philosophers, natural rights are the logical follow-on from of natural law theory.

4 The principle of double effect

Key term

Principle of double effect An act may have more than one effect, and be known to have more than one. An example might be an action to save one person's life, which means harming someone else. What matters is intention. The aim of the act was not harm to the second person but the (good) intention of saving the first.

One of the clearest ways of understanding the relationship of natural law theory to virtue theory in general and its concern with consequences is through the **principle of double effect**.

The point is that many actions have more than one result. If I work all night marking students' homework, I might complete it by tomorrow. But another effect is that I shall be very tired and work badly tomorrow. Aquinas, in accordance with his virtue, ethics and Natural law ideas has two concerns. What is the motivation and what does reason tell us to do? Any judgement about an action should be a judgement on intention and the use of right reason in reaching that decision. This has been much debated and its practical implications have been very important in discussion of medical dilemmas.

Aquinas' point provides the basis for subsequent discussion:

> *Nothing hinders an act from having two effects, only one of which is intended, while the other is beside the intention. Moral acts take their character from what is intended, not from what is outside the intention, as this is accidental … For example, the act of self-defence may have two effects; one is the saving of one's life, the other is the killing of the attacker. Therefore this act, since one's intention is to save one's own life, is not unlawful, as it is natural to everything to keep itself in 'being,' as far as possible. However, an act might have a good intention but still be wrong if it is not proportional to the end. If a man, in self-defence, uses more violence than necessary, it will be unlawful: but if he repels force with moderation, his defence will be lawful … It is not necessary for salvation that a man omit the act of moderate self-defence in order to avoid killing the other man, because one is bound to take more care of one's own life than of another's.*

S.T. II-II, q.64, a.7, c.

We need to consider both intention and results of an action. An important part of moral life is making judgements about intention and behaviour. We do not condemn someone just because she has committed a particular action. We consider – if we are fair-minded – what she intended to do. Did she make a mistake? Was her intention good? We make similar distinctions in law.

In medicine, a doctor may, to relieve suffering prescribe something that will shorten the patient's life. The intent of the medication or treatment is the avoidance of suffering. It is not the doctor's intention to kill. This has been central to debates about euthanasia. Natural law theorists argue that it is wholly wrong for a doctor to give lethal drugs to kill when the intention is killing the patient. This is why, for example, in the United States, when someone is sentenced to death by lethal injection, no doctor may administer the drugs.

In natural law approaches, four conditions are normally required in the principle of double effect:

1 The act must not be evil in itself. Killing is not intrinsically evil in the way murder (wrongful killing) always is.
2 The evil and good that come from the act must be at least equal, and preferably the good must outweigh the evil.
3 The intention of the agent must be good. The agent must not want to bring about an evil result.
4 A proportionately serious reason must be present to justify allowing the indirect bad effect.

The last point is very significant. Aquinas insists on proportion, as we saw in the quotation on double effect. As a general rule, people should not perform acts which are in any way harmful. Circumstances have to be serious before we do something with bad side effects. An example might be a risky operation, which could kill the patient, when the only alternative is a lingering painful death.

The agnostic (formerly Catholic) philosopher, Anthony Kenny argues:

> ... I believe that a principle of double effect must form part of any rational system of morality, and it has many everyday applications. There are cases where it makes a huge difference whether an outcome is intended or merely foreseen. For instance there is nothing wrong with appointing the best person for the job even though you know that by doing so you will give pain to the other candidates. It would be a very different matter if you appointed A (even though the best candidate) for the express purpose of giving pain to B.

Anthony Kenny: *What I Believe* (2006), p. 90

This is a very good way of understanding Aquinas' idea. The test of a theory is always how it works in practice, and in this case we can see clearly the importance of intention.

5 Objections to theories of natural law

■ **Vagueness**. Perhaps the most significant argument against natural law theory is that it suffers from the same vagueness about what should be done as other versions of virtue theory. It does not enable us to be precisely certain what to do in significant cases. If we are to say that life should be preserved, there are hard cases when it is very far from easy to determine whose life is to be saved. Arguments rage about a case in which one life can only be preserved by taking the life of another. Simply knowing the general principle that we should preserve life does not tell us whose life ought to be preserved. Such dilemmas arise in wartime, when the cost of saving lives is taking others, perhaps of entirely innocent people. If we believe that the infant in the womb is a person as much as her mother, then who is to be privileged if the continued pregnancy means the mother will die?

- **Unclear conclusions**. This issue of vagueness means that it may be possible to construct natural law arguments that point in opposing directions. A good example can be seen in the controversy surrounding *Humanae Vitae*, Pope Paul VI's encyclical which argued that obedience to natural law, in its insistence on preserving and encouraging life, meant that it was wrong to use artificial methods of birth control:

> *The Church, nevertheless, in urging men to the observance of the precepts of the Natural Law, which it interprets by its constant doctrine, teaches that each and every marital act must of necessity retain its intrinsic relationship to the procreation of human life.*

Pope Paul VI: Humanae Vitae, 1968, para. 11

Opponents argued that natural law could be understood in a different way. Part of the purpose of human nature requires that we use our intellect to determine what is best for human flourishing. If over-population is damaging to the preservation of life, then it would seem to follow that the primary precept of natural law leads us to justify artificial birth control, either in terms of the use of reason to a right end or, because those using these methods might wish to preserve and protect the lives of existing children or to avoid the harm to communities of over-population. What we should notice here is that opponents did not reject natural law teaching but thought it pointed in a different direction. The French-American natural law theorist Germain Grisez argued that opponents of Pope Paul's interpretation misunderstood natural law theory, but the issue remains unresolved.

- **An un-Christian theory**. Many, but not all, Protestant thinkers have argued against natural law as ultimately unbiblical. John Calvin looked to scripture as the Word of God as the principal source of moral teaching. Nevertheless, various non-Catholic thinkers, including, as previously mentioned, Martin Luther, Richard Hooker and William Temple incorporated large elements of natural law thinking into their moral teaching.
- **Acceptance**. An issue in natural law theory is one of acceptance. If it is true that it is 'right reason in accordance with nature', then, if it is accessible to all, one would expect people to accept the teaching more widely. But the ambiguity of its understanding of law leads many to doubt this:

... it is ... not a law in any known sense of the word, not an 'is' but an 'ought', a 'pattern laid up in heaven', and thus inaccessible save through (dubious) interpreters. Christians may answer that it is a law, a law laid down by God in pre-Christian days and not abolished, though crowned, by the Christian revelation with its laws. We shall certainly not be able to convince non-Christians, or even all Christians, that such a law exists, and the most difficult part of the argument revolves around its content.

Bernice Hamilton: 'Some Arguments Against Natural Law Theory', in *Light on the Natural Law* Ed. Illtud Evans (1965), pp. 49–50

■ **A purposive universe?** An important area of potential criticism of Aquinas' approach is its reliance on Aristotle's belief that everything has a purpose, and so human nature has a purpose. Is any theory of natural law doomed if the metaphysic on which it rests is mistaken? Later natural law theorists, such as Grotius, Grisez and John Finnis, among many others, have attempted to deal with this problem by arguing in terms of the nature of the human as she is, rather than in terms of purpose. Whatever her purpose may be, she still needs food, safety, education, protection and so on just to make the best of her life.

See Chapter 3 on Aristotle's four causes.

6 Conclusions

Key term

Positive law the belief that the law does not depend on any wider principle than the authority of those who make the laws or the existing codes of law. Among British thinkers, Jeremy Bentham argued for a command theory of law, in which laws are simply commands of the state, while H.L.A. Hart (1907–1992) argued that the study of law was simply the study of its rules.

Natural law is a rich if controversial type of moral argument. Many problems have arisen because of attempts to over-simplify its theories, whether into an absolute set of rules, applied without concern for consequences, or in terms of some vague intuition that mysteriously just knows what is right. Neither of these approaches does justice to the theory, especially as articulated by Aquinas. His approach may be summarised, perhaps crudely, but not inaccurately, as: 'God gave you a brain – now use it to work out what is best for human good in each situation. Work on the virtues that help you to act fully as God wishes.' This type of insight tended to be lost among some of the manualists.

That natural law remains central to Catholicism, and not only to Catholicism, suggests that it has lasting significance. In jurisprudence, the philosophy of law, the debate between natural law theorists and **positive law** theorists, remains a live one.

Study advice

As always, careful reflection is at the heart of any successful approach to the issues.

Do not worry too much about trying to classify the theory as absolutist or situational, deontological or teleological. It does not fall neatly into categories, though it is fair to say that for Aquinas it is teleological and always concerned to find the best outcome in the circumstances.

In the case of natural law, always remember the *ius/lex* distinction to keep issues clear in your mind.

Do not fall into the traps of treating the theory as just knowing, without any thought, what is right or as being necessarily religious. Avoid, when talking of Aquinas of using a manualist approach that suggests it is based on the Ten Commandments. Concentrate always on the implications of 'right reason in accordance with [human] nature'.

Summary diagram : Aquinas and natural law

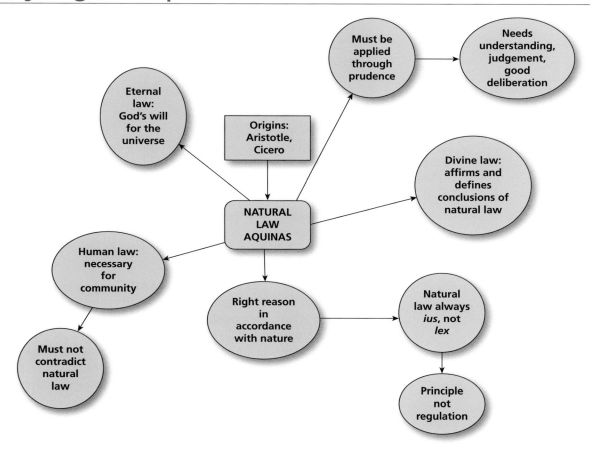

By the end of this chapter, you should find it possible to explain how natural law relates both to general virtue ethics and to questions of whether specific belief in revelation is essential to acceptance of the theory. You should be clear about the nature of *ius* in Aquinas' theory and be able to distinguish the differences between Eternal, Divine, Natural and Human Law.

Can you give brief definitions of:
- *ius*
- Eternal Law
- Divine Law
- Divine Law
- Human Law
- prudence?

Can you explain:
- how Aquinas' theory of Natural Law relates to and differs from Aristotle's notion of *telos*
- how natural law is a variant of virtue ethics, involving good intellectual and moral habits
- How natural law theory can be applied independently of religious belief
- how the notion of double effect relates to the application of natural law?

Can you give arguments for and against:
- natural law as a religious theory of ethics
- natural law as giving specific and clear moral guidance for each situation
- natural law's claim that right reason will always arrive at the same general precepts
- double effect as a useful notion in determining right action?

Sample question and guidance

To what extent is natural law the best way to resolve moral problems?

It is important to remember from the outset that the term 'the best way' in the question requires you to make a comparison with other approaches to moral decision-making, such as utilitarianism or Kantianism. It is unwise to try to list every theory you have studied, working through each one in turn. This type of question partly tests whether you have thought through the issues as part of your study. When studying natural law, have you thought about how this approach compares with others, and whether you have reached a judgement about the merits of the theory compared with others? If you have already made that type of judgement, then you can compare and contrast *one* chosen theory – one you think better or worse than natural law – with natural law. You may usefully mention other theories you have studied, in not more than a sentence or two, but as long as you have stated why you have selected this one theory for reaching your judgement, that is sufficient.

The essay might begin by explaining the claims of natural law theory, outlining the claims of Aquinas. It is helpful to concentrate on the parts of the theory which directly affect decision-making – the use of right reason, understanding, prudential judgement and the end in terms of true human flourishing. The question does not ask you to write everything you know about natural law. It is specifically about those parts of the theory entailed in moral decisions, so concentrate on those.

When you consider comparisons, you might wish to discuss the view that natural law is considered by some to be too religious, or you might, perhaps more helpfully, consider the argument that it is too vague and situational compared with Kantianism or utilitarianism, though you might also consider the argument that only such situationalism truly does justice to the complexities of life, arguing that natural law is more fully moral than other theories as it considers the agent and her intentions as well as the action itself.

Whatever way you answer the question, it is essential to conclude with clear and argued reasons whether or not natural law really is the best way to resolve moral problems.

Further essay questions

'Natural law theory succeeds because it takes human nature seriously.' Discuss.

'Natural law's situationalism means that it does not offer precise answers to difficult dilemmas.' Discuss.

'Double effect is simply a trick. If we know something we do will have a bad effect, we cannot excuse ourselves by saying we did not intend to cause that effect.' Discuss.

Going further

The literature on natural law is huge. It is good always to go back to the roots and to read Aquinas, whether on the internet or elsewhere.

On natural law, various books can be recommended. A valuable one, which takes account of modern as well as classical ones, and is excellent on both the *ius / lex* distinction and on the relationship of natural law theory of natural rights is: A. P. d'Entrèves: *Natural Law: An Introduction to Legal Philosophy* (third edition, Transaction Publishers, 2006). This is brief but has been a central text since its original publication in 1951. It wears its considerable learning very lightly.

In modern times, John Finnis is well-known for his development of natural law theory. His *Natural Law and Natural Rights,* first published in 1980 (second edition, Oxford University Press, 2011) has proven itself a central text. Other books discussed in this chapter are:

- Finnis J. *Aquinas: Moral, Political and Legal Theory* (Oxford University Press, 1998).
- Hamilton B. '*Some Arguments Against Natural Law Theory*', in *Light on the Natural Law* Ed. Illtud Evans (Burns & Oates, 1965).
- Kenny A. *What I Believe* (Continuum, London, 2006).
- McCabe H. *The Good Life: Ethics and the Pursuit of Happiness* (Continuum, 2005).
- Pinckaers S. *Morality: the Catholic View* (St. Augustine's Press, 2001).

Chapter 11

Situation ethics

1 Introduction

Advice to teachers

It is helpful, when looking at the ideas of situation ethics, also to pay attention to some of the problems of Act Utilitarianism outlined on pages 200–202. Many observations made about Act Utilitarianism apply equally to Situation Ethics.

Chapter checklist

This chapter begins with a brief account of the life of Joseph Fletcher, considering how he relates to situationalism in earlier authors. It then explores his reliance on the thought of Archbishop William Temple, because Temple could be argued to be the true originator of situation ethics. It then describes Fletcher's version in some detail, looking at his overall beliefs and his use of the four working principles and six propositions. The chapter then analyses the relation between religion and Fletcher's thought and his controversial treatment of conscience. Finally, the chapter develops objections to his theory in some depth.

Situation ethics is most commonly associated with the American ethicist, Joseph Fletcher (1905–91), whose 1966 book, *Situation Ethics: The New Morality* (Westminster Press), caused enormous controversy among theologians and philosophers.

Fletcher believed that he was following the logic of many previous writers. Aristotle, in *Nicomachean Ethics* is quite specific that right judgement requires that we pay particular attention to circumstance. We cannot lay down firm rules on what will be true in every situation, but judgement has to be individual and situational:

> *For this reason it is a difficult business to be good; because in any given instance to find [the right action] … it is easy to get angry – anyone can do that – or to give and to spend money; but to feel or act towards the right person to the right extent at the right time for the right reason in the right way – that is not easy, and it is not everyone who can do it. Hence to do these things is a rare, laudable and fine achievement.*

Aristotle: *Nicomachean Ethics*: Book II, ix

(a) Joseph Fletcher and William Temple

Fletcher had deeply studied the thought of Archbishop William Temple (1881–1944), and published one of the most developed accounts of Temple's work – *William Temple: 20th Century Christian* (Seabury, 1963). Temple's approach to ethics very closely prefigures that of Fletcher. Temple's ethic was personalist and love-centred:

> *There is only one ultimate and invariable duty, and its formula is 'Thou shalt love thy neighbour as thyself.' How to do this is another question, but this is the whole of moral duty.*

William Temple: *Mens Creatrix* (1917), p. 206

Temple's interpretation of this was situational:

> *Universal obligation attaches not to particular judgments of conscience but to conscientiousness. What acts are right may depend on circumstances … but there is an absolute obligation to will whatever may on each occasion be right.*

William Temple: *Nature, Man and God* (1934), p. 405

In an article published in 1940, Temple would further develop this idea of situationalism, especially in relation to war:

> *The general principle is that relative terms are absolute in the appropriate relations. To kill is right, if at all, relatively and not absolutely; that is, it can only be right in special circumstances. But in those circumstances it is absolutely right.*

> *It is doubtful if any act is right 'in itself'. Every act is a link in a chain of causes and effects. It cannot be said it is wrong to take away a man's possessions against his will, for that would condemn all taxation, or the removal of a revolver from a homicidal lunatic;*

For more information on St Thomas Aquinas, see Chapters 5 and 10.

neither of these is stealing – which is always wrong; though high authority [A reference to St Thomas Aquinas: Summa Theologica: II–II, q.66, a.7, c (author's note)] *has held that a starving man should steal a loaf rather than die of hunger, because life is of more value than property and should be chosen first for preservation if both cannot be preserved together.*

The rightness of an act, then, nearly always, and perhaps always, depends on the way in which that act is related to circumstances; this is what is meant by calling it relatively right; but this does not in the least imply that it is only doubtfully right. It may be, in those circumstances, certainly and absolutely right.

William Temple: 'A Conditional Justification of War': *Religious Experience and Other Essays and Addresses*, Ed. A. E. Baker (1958), pp. 173–174

Temple's view is apparently consistent with Aquinas' judgement:

… if we speak of the moral act as an individual act, then every particular moral act must be good or evil by reason of some circumstance, for the singular act cannot take place without circumstances making it right or wrong. If anything at all is done when it should, where it should, as it should, etc., then this kind of act is well-ordered and good; but if any of these be defective, the act is badly ordered and evil. This may be chiefly examined in regard to the circumstance that is the end, for whatever is done because of a just need or a pious usefulness is done in a praiseworthy way, and is a good act; but whatever has no just need or pious usefulness is an idle act.

St Thomas Aquinas: *De Malo*: q.2, a.5, c.

It is arguable that what Fletcher does is to work out in more detail the implications of a thoroughgoing situationalism. He shares with Temple certain key assumptions. Most significant of these is the belief that there is a fundamental axiom:

*There is only one thing that is always good and right, intrinsically good regardless of the context, and that one thing is love … It is the **only** principle that always obliges us in conscience. Unlike all other principles you might mention, love alone when well-served is always good and right in every situation. Love is the only universal. But love is not something we **have** or **are**, it is something we **do**. Our task is to act so that more good (i.e., loving-kindness) will occur than any possible alternatives … It is an attitude, a disposition, a leaning, a preference, a purpose.*

Joseph Fletcher: *Situation Ethics* (1966) pp. 60–61

Key question

Is it true that only love is always right? Could it ever be wrong to be just, or to avoid murder?

Key term

Metaethics The branch of ethics concerned with the justification of ethics and the meaning of the language used. It would be a metaethical question to ask what we mean by the term 'good'.

It is important to notice here that Fletcher is not arguing for the **metaethical** theory of relativism, which holds that every ethical judgement is relative. Relativism holds that there are and can be no universals. Fletcher plainly states in the passage just given that there is one universal, which is love. Particular judgements are relative to that invariable and absolute maxim.

The second idea shared with Temple is the notion that justice is love in action. Temple argued consistently that simply to say to people, 'Love one another' would be, in particular circumstances, of little value. In one book, he describes it as 'fatuous bleating':

> *It is axiomatic that Love should be the predominant Christian impulse, and that the primary form of Love in Social organisation is Justice. No doubt this latter truth is sometimes ignored by those who wish to apply Love, so to speak, wholesale and direct. But it is hard to see how this works out. Imagine a Trade Union Committee negotiating with an Employers' federation in an industrial crisis on the verge of a strike or lock-out. This Committee is to be activated by love. Oh, yes, by all means – but towards who? Are they to love the workers or the employers? Of course – both. But then that will not help them much to determine what terms ought to be either proposed or accepted. The fact is that these problems arise only so far as perfect love is not operative. That is a reason why both sides should confess their sin, but still the problem is unresolved.*

William Temple: *Christianity and Social Order* (1984) pp. 78–79

For a profile of William Temple, see Chapter 9.

Key term

Personalism The belief that all good is always good for a person or persons, and never abstract. Goodness must always be experienced as good by someone.

The third common feature is the insistence of both men on **personalism**. Good has to be experienced to be good, and thus is applicable only to or for a person.

2 Joseph Fletcher's situation ethics

Key terms

Legalism An approach which reduces the moral life to a system of regulations.
Antinomianism The view that rules and principles should be rejected.
Pragmatism Seeking workable, practical solutions rather than trying to find something abstract.
Relativism The belief (according to Fletcher) that the moral act should always be relative to the needs of both the performer and the situation.

Fletcher argues that there are three possible approaches to the moral life:
- **Legalism** believes that there are fixed moral rules which are universal and always to be followed. He believes that this approach to morality has been a major fault in Catholicism, Protestantism and Judaism. It leads to Puritanism, making the rule something with greater dignity than the person. If we are to have a truly ethical approach, the person must come first.
- **Antinomianism** is the denial of the possibility of any rules. This can be found in the ideas of Nietzsche or Sartre, and some other existentialists, who believe that there are no rules to follow but only our own choices.
- **Situationism** (Fletcher's position) believes absolutely in the rule of love, but believes that it needs to be applied situationally.

(a) The four working principles

In applying situation ethics, Fletcher outlines what he calls four working principles:

1 **Pragmatism**, by which he means that we must seek practical solutions which work to achieve success. Fletcher makes explicit his debt to American pragmatism as represented by Peirce, Dewey and, especially, William James.
2 **Relativism**, he argues that whatever we do must be related to both the facts about ourselves and what we are able to do and the

particular facts of the situation. In this, he is situational; the absolute demand to do the loving thing remains.

3 **Positivism**, the belief in a God of Love (or, for non-Christians, a higher good) is posited, then supported by logic. As we have this belief in the supremacy of love, we must then reason out what supports that love in the situation that faces us.

4 **Personalism,** requires that we place people, not principles or rules or things, at the centre of all our moral considerations.

(b) The six propositions

These principles support the six propositions which should be followed in all our judgements of what to do:

1 'Only one 'thing' is intrinsically good; namely love: nothing else at all.'
2 'The ruling norm of Christian decision is love: nothing else.'
3 'Love and justice are the same, for justice is love distributed, nothing else.'
4 'Love wills the neighbour's good whether we like him or not.'
5 'Only the end justifies the means; nothing else.'
6 'Love's decisions are made situationally, not prescriptively.'

These propositions are variations on the theme of always considering the most loving result. Proposition 5 reveals how absolutely **teleological** this theory is. Everything is geared to the goal of making life as good as it could be for people, for this is what love requires. It suggests there is room, as we shall see, for arguments about how we are able to know certainly what the right thing to do will be.

It could be argued that the insistence of proposition 1, that love is the only thing intrinsically good, leaves rather open how questions about forgiveness, humility and other virtues might be seen under the general description of love, although Fletcher does go some way in his work to try to demonstrate how such virtues are contained in the commandment of love. It should be noticed here than Fletcher is more categorical than Temple was. Although Temple saw justice as love in action, or love distributed, he was not so categorical that everything was reducible to questions of love. Perhaps this is why Fletcher described Temple's approach as 'timid' (*Situation Ethics*, p. 59) and accuses him of making too sharp a distinction between love as directed at the individual, and justice, which is concerned with the group (*Situation Ethics* pp. 93–94).

(c) Faith and situation ethics

An important question is about the relationship of faith and situation ethics. Fletcher's book is filled with references to Christian literature, philosophy and thought, but it is not clear that situation ethics requires Christian belief. In the Bible, Jesus makes love central. When asked to say which commandment is first:

Jesus answered, 'The first is 'Hear, O Israel: the Lord our God, the Lord is one; you shall love the Lord your God with all your heart, and with all your soul, and with all your strength.' The second is this, 'You shall love your neighbour as yourself.' There is no other commandment greater than these.'

Mark 12:29–31

Key terms

Agape A Greek word meaning love. Very early on the word *agape* was adopted by Christians to refer to Jesus' sacrificial and generous love for others.
Altruism Any theory which puts the needs of others before those of oneself.

The Gospel of John emphasises the theme of love very strongly. What is meant here is love of neighbour, not erotic love. The point is developed by St Paul:

> *And now faith, hope and love abide, these three; and the greatest of these is love.*

> *1 Corinthians* 13:13

When Fletcher gave up his Christian belief, he did not give up his situation ethics. In his book, he states that the difference between a Christian and non-Christian situationist is that the former clearly and directly equates the good with *agape* (altruistic love), while the non-Christian will find some other account, such as Aristotle's flourishing. (*Situation Ethics*, pp. 30–31)

Background

Agapism

When we speak we often use the term 'love' very loosely, and in many ways. The cashier in the supermarket may say, 'thank you, love', as a polite endearment, just as she may say 'thank you, duck', or 'thank you, my dear'. We may use 'love' as a term of enthusiasm, when we say, 'I love that music' or 'I love spaghetti and meatballs'. For some, it may be almost without any deep significance, as when someone says 'love you' as a way to finish a phone call, though the same phrase, used to a special person, may mean much more than that.

There are many possible usages, but a division is made by scholars between love as *eros* and love as *agape*. These Greek terms are very useful for pointing us to different aspects of the notion of love.

Eros (from which we get the adjective 'erotic') refers to the love which is tied up with sexual desire. It has a physical quality, where people's care and desire for one another goes beyond the spiritual, and has a bodily aspect. True erotic love – as opposed to lust – involves much more than simply bodily desire, but that bodily desire is a central part of it.

Agape refers to the love people feel for human kind. It entails ideas like fellowship, fraternity, altruism, concern for the dispossessed and the stranger. There is no bodily desire entailed, but it may be no less intense an emotion. The love is closely tied to the idea that we must do actual good for people, the virtue of charity, and not simply have nice feelings about them.

It is to this sense of *agape* that Jesus appeals in the New Testament when he tells his disciples that they must love God above all things and their neighbours as

themselves. It is this profound and universal love which the Gospel writers make central to their accounts of his life. Jesus is portrayed as demonstrating this love in his actions, in his healing miracles and in the crucifixion, where he lovingly lays down his life for all people. At the Last Supper, according to John, he says;

> *I give you a new commandment, that you love one another. Just as I have loved you, you also should love one another. By this everyone will know that you are my disciples, if you have love for one another.*

> *John* 13.3435

St Paul emphasises the idea in a very famous passage:

> *Love is patient; love is kind; love is not envious or boastful or arrogant or rude. It does not insist on its own way; it is not irritable or resentful; it does not rejoice in wrongdoing, but rejoices in the truth. It bears all things, believes all things, hopes all things, endures all things. Love never ends … And now faith, hope and love abide, these three; and the greatest of these is love.*

> *I Corinthians*: 13. 4–8, 13

Fletcher's appeal is therefore to *agape*, thought of as an active love, involving us in doing as much good for people as possible.

3 Fletcher on conscience

Fletcher's comments on conscience have attracted some attention. He notes that various thinkers have offered different accounts of conscience. Some people have treated it in terms of an inner voice that somehow just knows what is right. John Henry Newman thought that our consciences were somehow the voice of God. St Thomas Aquinas, following Aristotle, treated conscience as the practical reason, essentially prudence, which enables us to work out what we ought to do, and which enables us to look back on previous actions to reflect on whether we have acted rightly.

For Aquinas, conscience has many aspects, and he notes the variety of ways in which we speak about it:

> ... conscience is said to witness behaviour, to bind us to action or to incite us to do something, but also to accuse, rebuke or torment us [for our actions]. All these follow the application of knowledge to what we do. This application is done in three ways. One way happens when we recognise that we have done or not done something: 'your heart knows that many times you have yourself cursed others' (*Ecclesiastes 7.22*). In this way, conscience is said to witness to our actions. In the second way, we judge what should or should not be done: in this sense, conscience is said to bind us to action. In the third way, when we use our conscience to decide whether something is well or badly done: in this sense, we say that conscience excuses, accuses or torments us.

S.T. I, q79, a.12c

In brief, what is argued here is that we use conscience to reflect on actions we have done and to examine our actions but also to determine what we should do when we are faced with particular choices.

Aquinas treats conscience as a faculty of the mind, covering different aspects of thought. Fletcher rejects such an approach entirely:

> The traditional error lies in thinking about conscience as a noun instead of as a verb. This reflects the fixity and establishment-mindedness of all law ethics as contrasted to love ethics. There is no conscience; 'conscience' is merely a word for our attempts to make decisions creatively, constructively, fittingly.

Joseph Fletcher: *Situation Ethics* (1966), p. 53

Key question

Does Fletcher use the term 'conscience' in a satisfactory way?

Fletcher pushes to one side the question of judgements of conscience about actions we have committed. His interest is only in the reasoning for future actions.

By arguing that conscience is to be understood as a verb, Fletcher means just that it describes our performing an act in a particular way, doing so bearing in mind all the aspects of circumstances that we have seen in his treatment of Situation Ethics.

This seems to mean that all the Fletcher means by 'conscience' is that we should act 'conscientiously'. His remarks on conscience are remarkably brief, and seem to leave much unanswered.

He seems also to want to use conscience in a way very different from normal usage. When most people talk of conscience, they seem to speak in a way which is much closer to Aquinas' usage. For example, they may say that they have 'a bad conscience' over some action they have performed. It is certainly true that we do reflect on our actions, and sometimes look back and think we did some things quite well, while we regret others, especially when we believe we may have acted badly. If this is not part of 'conscience' then how ought such thoughts to be treated? Fletcher does not tell us. Critics argue that in failing to do so, he leaves a significant part of the moral life insufficiently considered.

4 Objections to theories

Many objections have been brought against Fletcher's situation ethics.

See Chapter 13, Utilitarianism.

Key terms

Utilitarianism The moral doctrine that one should always seek the greatest balance of good over evil.

Act utilitarianism Believes that we should always perform the act which will lead to the greatest balance of good over evil.

- Situation ethics seems to have all the problems of **act utilitarianism** so it is important that you are familiar with the issues about this. Philosophers have paid particular attention to proposition 5. They point out that situation ethics is strictly teleological and therefore suffers from the associated problems of determining outcomes, having time to make decisions, possessing the necessary skills, having all relevant information and so on.
- One particular issue with situation ethics is that it doesn't define what constitutes a 'situation'. Is it the particular circumstance or does it stretch into the future? If so, how far into the future? For example, I see a man drowning and, out of love for a fellow human being, jump into the water to save him. A life is saved, and a good thing apparently done. But a year later, the man I saved wantonly guns down 50 people in a terrorist killing. Is my act, initially seen as loving, an unloving one after all? Ought I to have left him to drown as a loving act, in case he turned out to be a bad man?
- Fletcher seems equally vague in defining what the good for people actually is. He speaks loosely of 'welfare', but is vague in providing a definition beyond that.
- Is it true that no actions are intrinsically wrong regardless of circumstance? To use an example suggested by Anthony O'Hear, could it ever be right to throw living babies onto bonfires? This seems simply an act of cruelty and one cannot imagine it as a good act. It does not follow that because many actions are situational in their rightness, that all are. Fletcher attempts to argue that there could even be circumstances when an action such as adultery could be right and loving (*Situation Ethics*, pp. 164–165). He gives the example of a married German lady who encouraged a German prison guard to impregnate her so that she could be released and rejoin her family. Some would question this, and many might argue that the case cited by Fletcher in support of this argument is an uncertain one. It could be questioned whether this is 'adultery' within the normal meaning of the term. Aristotle remarks that the term 'adultery' means it is a wrong act, and it would be contradictory to argue that a wrong act could ever be right. Even if this woman's action was justifiable in these circumstances – and a case can certainly be made – it seems not to invalidate a general principle of avoiding adultery. There are other factors which might lead us to argue that this lady was not an adulteress.

- Many have pointed to a few sentences from a later work by Fletcher:

People [with children with Down's syndrome] ... have no reason to feel guilty about putting a Down's syndrome baby away, whether it's 'put away' in the sense of hidden in a sanatorium or in a more responsible lethal sense. It is sad; yes. Dreadful. But it carries no guilt. True guilt arises only from an offense against a person, and a Down's is not a person.

Bernard Bard and Joseph Fletcher: 'The Right to Die',
(April 1968), pp. 59–64

It is not obvious that killing such children is a loving act. Is it loving to decide that a human being is not a person? Where ought we to draw the line – if at all – between persons and non-persons? Is it loving to declare that a group of humans has no rights?

If Fletcher is right, there would, in principle, be situations in which actions such as cruelty, using children for sexual pleasure, genital mutilation, date-rape, pillage, torture or incest could all be seen as right or loving acts. Is it really possible to argue that there can ever be righteous cruelty?

- There is an interesting philosophical question raised by the last three points, and especially the case of the German woman. Fletcher assumes that the difficulty of being certain in some situations leads to a position where we need an alternative to rule-based ethics without falling into antinomianism. He assumes that those who talk about following rules are absolutist and never allow for any exceptions. Most ethicists make allowances about when it is not appropriate to be rigid about obeying in all circumstances. His method is to point to hard cases, where the right thing to do is not clear, usually because different rules seem to point in different directions.

Lawyers often point out that hard cases make for bad laws. In morality, there are similar concerns. It is true that there are cases where it is not clear that we should tell the truth or take someone's property. But it does not follow from that that the rules of truth-telling and avoiding theft are invalidated in general. In most cases, there are overwhelming good reasons for telling the truth and not being a thief, and very few, if any, bad ones.

In *The Right and the Good* (Oxford University Press, 1930), the great Scottish philosopher, W. D. Ross (1877–1971) argued that we have *prima facie* (at first appearance) duties such as fidelity, justice and beneficence which should always be followed unless there were, in a given situation, overwhelming *moral* reasons for performing another sort of moral duty. This approach appears more credible than Fletcher's denial of rules and gives some useful guidance about how to act morally.

- A virtue ethicist might argue that Fletcher gives too little weight to character in stressing the outcome and the action so strongly. By concerning himself just with outcome and actions, he seems to ignore the wider aspects of being a moral person, acting in the right way for the right motivation.

- Aquinas would treat conscience in a very different way from Fletcher's account. Fletcher's interest only in the decisions we make in the future seems to miss a crucial aspect of human experience. As a simple matter of fact, most people do review their lives and actions. We

Key person

W. D. Ross (1877–1971): Scottish-born Oxford philosopher, knighted in 1938 as Sir William David Ross. Major Aristotelian scholar and author of *The Right and the Good* (1930).

wonder whether we did the right thing and consider where we did well or poorly. Doing this is partly curiosity, but it also enables us to function better. The habit of reflection on the things we have done and the motives we had builds character and is important for future decision-making. Fletcher's reductionism towards conscience seems to impoverish a valuable part of human experience.

- D. Z. Phillips has raised the question of whether we can, in moral dilemmas presented by situations, ever be truly confident that we have done 'the right thing'. This kind of knowledge may be beyond us:

> *When one finds oneself in situations where, whatever one does, one is going to hurt someone, talk of arranging goods in an order of priority often seems out of place ... On the contrary ... even after a person has decided what he must do in these situations, he may still feel remorse for having committed the evil which his decision inevitably involved. When one lies to save a friend from suffering despite the fact that one's whole relationship with him has been characterised by absolute straightforwardness and honesty; when one has to go against the wishes of parents who have sacrificed a great deal for one in deciding to marry a certain girl or to take up a certain job; when a man is forced to kill another person to save a child's life; talk about establishing an order of goods would be a vulgar falsification for many people. They did what they had to do, but they did not glory in it. In the cases I have mentioned, a trust in truthfulness has been betrayed, great sacrifice has been considered an insufficient reason, a life has been taken: all these are considered to be terrible, and the decisions which brought them about and had to be taken were terrible decisions nevertheless. It is essential to recognise that in moral dilemmas, the discovery of what must be done often involves one in evil, pain and suffering.*

> D. Z. Phillips: 'Some Limits to Moral Endeavour': *Through a Darkening Glass* (1982), p. 38

- A further, and perhaps fatal, issue, consistent with Phillips' argument, is the assumption in situation ethics that right = good. In the examples Phillips gives, we might be doing the *right* thing, but does it follow that it is a *good* one? Temple does not separate the two, arguing in *Christianity in Thought and Practice* (SCM, 1936) that the good is what is right in the circumstances and the right what is good in the circumstances. The same assumption is made by Fletcher. But is this straightforwardly and invariably true? If I give alms to the poor, it might be argued that doing so is both good and right. A moment's thought suggests otherwise. Giving to the poor is surely a *right* act, as an action, but is it *good* even if I do so for unworthy reasons? Would someone say I had performed a *good* act if my motivation were to curry favour with voters rather than for the good of the poor themselves? As Phillips suggests, my actions might be right at times when they seem not good, but merely necessary. If I kill a brutish man as this is the only way to prevent his murder of a child, surely I would argue that the killing is *right* and necessary, but I would not wish to argue that it is a *good* thing, involving as it does the destruction of a man's life. It is unlikely that I would be pleased that I killed him, and I might well have sleepless nights wondering whether I could have found a different way to secure the safety of the child. I hope I would not feel the contentment of a deed well done: it would be a right action causing pain for others.

- Some Evangelicals have argued that the Bible does give firm rules and instructions which must always be followed. Those who accept the Bible as fundamental to their faith, as a complete guide to the Christian life, would argue that the commandment does not say 'Thou shalt not commit adultery (except when …)' or 'Thou shalt not bear false witness (unless of course …)'. Others would point out that the Christian ethic can be difficult, and something people have died to preserve, but that God means what he says and wants heroic virtue. To some, there is something un-Christian in (rightly) picking out the fundamental point of *agape* but treating everything else as negotiable.

5 Conclusions

Perhaps, in his own way, Fletcher shares the view, not uncommon among philosophers, including Bentham and Kant, that the business of living a moral life can be encapsulated in a few simple propositions. It seems however the case that life, as directly and personally experienced, is more complex than that. The business of living goes beyond formulae.

Study advice

Here, as elsewhere in the book, many objections to the theories are listed. Again, as elsewhere, it is unlikely you will remember them all, and you will certainly not have time to explain them all in an examination essay. In constructing your own notes, make a judgement about three or four which seem to you most significant and which you feel confident about explaining. Doing this kind of exercise – making such choices – is an excellent exercise in developing the art of philosophical judgement, because you are having to think through the reasons that led to your selection.

Do not fall into the trap of describing situation ethics as relativist, as it has an absolute principle – of strict love – while relativism denies the possibility of having any absolute principles.

You might find it helpful to think specifically about whether situation ethics offers any more than act utilitarianism and the ways in which it seems to raise the same questions. You might reflect also on whether it is actually loving – indeed, whether by its insistence on a single principle, it pays insufficient attention either to the realities of moral questions or human needs and rights.

Summary diagram: Situation ethics

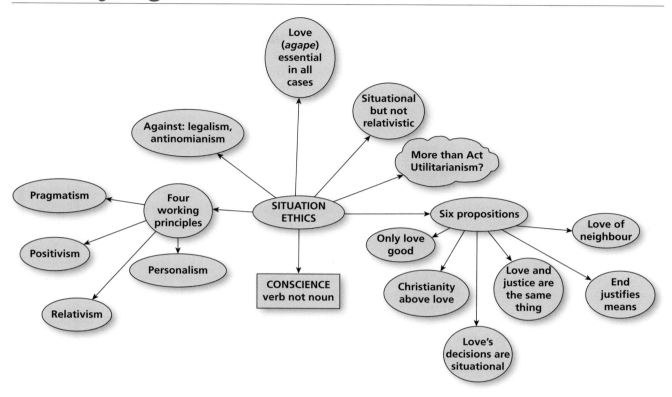

Revision advice

By the end of this chapter you should be in a position to explain the overall principles of situation ethics and how they are meant to reflect agapeistic love. You should be able to reflect on whether situation ethics is religious or whether it is simply a form of act utilitarianism. You should also be able to consider whether no act is definitely right or wrong in every situation.

Can you give brief definitions of:

- agapism
- situation ethics
- legalism
- antinomianism
- personalism?

Can you explain:

- how William Temple influenced Joseph Fletcher
- how the four working principles are used in situation ethics
- how the six propositions develop the ideas of situation ethics
- how the idea of conscience is developed by Fletcher?

Can you give arguments for and against:

- treating situation ethics as a religious theory
- the idea that all moral judgements are situational
- the claim that situation ethics adds anything to act utilitarianism
- the claim that situation ethics is correct to equate the right and the good?

Sample question and guidance

Assess the significance of love in situation ethics.

This question is one which looks simple but could be a trap for the unwary. It asks for more than a simple description of the various ways in which Fletcher refers to love. The question requires you to consider whether love is used consistently or helpfully in understanding the requirements of the ethical life.

A possible way to begin would be to make clear that situation ethics is interested in agapeistic approaches to love, and to show that loving someone does not mean the same as liking that person (see proposition 4). If you are familiar with Aristotle's ethics, it might be helpful to think about a comparison with his notion of civic friendship. Justice is very important in ethics and it would be worth considering how situation ethics relates justice to love.

In developing your ideas, it would be helpful to consider how, in each situation, we should always perform the most loving act. What does this mean? How helpful is this in determining exactly what to do? Suppose in order to perform the most loving actions for some people, I have to create hurt somewhere else. To perform the loving act of saving the child, I must kill the attacker threatening her life. Have I truly shown love towards that man? In what sense is his death a loving action? You might think also about whether I can be sure that the result of an action will certainly maximise love. You might consider either that Fletcher uses the term 'love' too lightly or even that what he describes is not love at all.

In reaching your conclusions, you might choose to consider whether the insistence on love adds anything to situation ethics which is not found in act utilitarianism, or you might, on the other hand, wish to argue that by being so focused on love that this is a true religious ethic. What matters is not the conclusion you reach but whether you have argued for your view in a consistent way.

Further essay questions

'Situation ethics suffers from all the disadvantages of utilitarianism and none of its advantages.' Discuss.

To what extent is it true to say that no action is wrong in every possible circumstance?

'Situation ethics is neither Christian nor believable.' Discuss.

Going further

Situation Ethics is available as a paperback (revised edition, Westminster John Knox Press, 1997) and is not difficult to read, or very long. Perhaps the best introduction to William Temple's situationalism may be found in his 1936 book, *Christianity in Thought and Practice* (SCM, 1936), but this is not widely available. The clearest introduction to Temple is perhaps Stephen Spencer: *William Temple: A Calling to Prophecy* (SPCK, 2001), but his situationalism is dealt with only briefly. For general purposes, the points you need are summarised in this chapter, though it is always worth reading his best-selling *Christianity and Social Order* (Mowbray, 1987), which is also an invaluable resource for the study of business morality. David Mills Daniel: *Briefly: Fletcher's Situation Ethics*, (SCM, 2009) provides a very useful short sketch of Fletcher's book.
Other books discussed in this chapter are:
- Bard B. and Fletcher J. `The Right to Die', *The Atlantic Monthly*, 221 (April 1968).
- Phillips D.Z. `Some Limits to Moral Endeavour': *Through a Darkening Glass* (Blackwell, 1982).
- Ross W.D. *The Right and the Good* (Oxford University Press, 1930).
- Temple W. `A Conditional Justification of War': *Religious Experience and Other Essays and Addresses*, Ed. A. E. Baker (James Clarke & Co, 1958).
- Temple W. *Mens Creatrix* (Macmillan, 1917).
- Temple W. *Nature, Man and God* (Macmillan, 1934).

Chapter 12

Kantian ethics

1 Introduction

Chapter 12 Kantian ethics

> **Chapter checklist**
>
> The chapter begins with a general introduction to Kant's life and thought. It continues by examining his concepts of freedom, reason and autonomy. It examines concepts of good will and duty and explores the differences between the categorical and hypothetical imperatives. It analyses and critiques the three forms of the categorical imperative. Discussion then moves to the moral postulates of God and immortality. The chapter then develops wider objections to Kant's approach, examining issues such as the claim that his theory is impractical, pays insufficient attention to the richness of human nature and can result in cold charity.

'Enlightenment is man's emergence from his self-incurred immaturity.'

This is the opening sentence of Immanuel Kant's essay, 'Answering the Question: What is Enlightenment?', first published in the December 1784 edition of *Berlinische Monatsshrifft* (Berlin Monthly). The essay captures very well the nature of Kant's entire philosophy. For him, the errors of earlier thought were the errors of the lack of courage, of immaturity, in not being willing to use and to trust one's own wisdom, intellect and reason. True enlightenment is about living according to our own unfettered reason – a state of true **autonomy** – and not to live unthinkingly by the dictates of others, whether because we lack courage or because we have not fully cultivated the resources of our own minds. People who live in this condition have 'heteronymous' lives, that is, lives not fully their own. Kant's exhortation to his readers is summarised in the motto, *Sapere aude!* – 'Dare to be wise!'

In these ideas we find the seeds of many later notions, such as the existentialism of Kierkegaard, Heidegger or Sartre, each of whom treats autonomy as central to fully human life.

Kant is generally treated as the supreme exemplar of Enlightenment thought, as he embodied so fully the belief in the power of unaided reason. His philosophical work exemplifies the belief, in an ancestry derived from Newton, that through reason we may not only understand the universe, but govern our own lives fully and rationally. Kant's most famous work was *The Critique of Pure Reason* (1781, revised 1787), but

> **Key terms**
>
> **Autonomy** The belief that we are self-directed beings, the centre of our own worlds, making our own free choices.

his many works include his *Critique of Practical Reason* (1788), *Critique of Judgement* (1790) and *Religion within the Limits of Reason Alone* (1793). His main ethical works were *Groundwork of the Metaphysic of Morals* (1785) and *Metaphysics of Morals* (1797). These works were the product of Kant's later years.

Key person

Immanuel Kant (1724–1804) was born in Königsberg, East Prussia (today's Russian city of Kaliningrad). His mother was fully German, but his father, a harness-maker, had Scottish blood, still spelling his name as 'Cant'. East Prussia was separated from the rest of Germany geographically and socially.

Portraits of Kant show a rather frail man with an unusually developed forehead. His health was never robust. He entered the University of Königsberg at the age of 16, financing himself partly through his ability as a billiards player. His academic life was most obviously concerned with the natural sciences. He developed important theories in astronomy, such as the idea that the Earth and Solar System had evolved from a gaseous nebula, as well as ideas about the Earth's rotation. But the latter half of his life was devoted almost exclusively to his philosophical work. He never married and lived a life of absolutely regular and quiet habits. To a former pupil he wrote:

Any change makes me nervous, even if it offers the greatest promise of improving my state, and I am convinced by my natural instinct that I must pay attention if I want the threads that Fate spins so thinly and weakly for me to be spun to any length. My great thanks … but at the same time, a most humble plea to protect me in my current condition from any disturbance.

'All our knowledge begins with the senses, proceeds then to the understanding, and ends with reason. There is nothing higher than reason.' Immanuel Kant

It is sometimes said that Kant never left Königsberg, but this is not quite true. We know that between 1750 and 1754, he worked briefly as a tutor in Judtschen, 45 kilometres away, and in Gross-Arnsdorf, about 145 kilometres from his home. But the regular habits, including his daily walk over the same route, at the same time, were maintained absolutely over his last fifty years. He was buried in Königsberg cathedral but his bones were moved to a new site, just outside, in 1880. The German-speaking population of the city was expelled by Russia in 1945, the university was named the Kaliningrad State University, but at a ceremony in 2005, it was given the title of Immanuel Kant State University of Russia.

Key term

A priori Knowledge which is not dependent on sense experience, such as 'a circle is round' which is true by definition.

It is beyond dispute that Kant was a truly great philosopher. His attempt to reconcile the different claims of the rationalists, such as Descartes and Leibniz, who believed that some things could be known with certainty *a priori*, with those of the empiricists, notably Locke, Hume and Berkeley, was an astonishing philosophical effort. His exploration of the limits of human knowledge had lasting significance. While a passionate believer in the autonomy of reason, he explored the limits of that reason. He distinguished between what might be the (unknowable) world as it is and the world as it is known to us in the *phenomena* of our minds.

We have seen Kant's arguments against ontological arguments (Chapter 6). It is time to consider his moral teaching.

2 Kant's moral teaching

Central to Kant's moral theorising were his fundamental values of reason, autonomy and freedom.

His argument for our freedom is based on a reasoned consideration of our own mental experience – our ability to set goals for ourselves is something we know by introspection:

> A **goal** is an **object** of free choice, the understanding of which leads it to an action (by which the object is brought about). Every action, therefore, has its goal; and as no one can have a goal without **himself** making the object of his choice into a goal, to have any goal of action whatsoever is an act of **freedom** on the part of the acting subject, not an effect of **nature**.

Immanuel Kant: *Metaphysics of Morals:* Ak.6.384–385

Kant's argument can be summarised by saying that we know we have goals which we make for ourselves. We know ourselves to be the ones who both choose these goals and who decide how to achieve them. To have goals and to be able to choose the actions we take in their pursuit is what makes us freely choosing persons. From this, we can see that we are autonomous, choosing our own ways in life.

As we have seen, for Kant, autonomy was the central condition of rational thought. In the *Groundwork*, he explains his reasons for believing that errors in moral thinking had arisen from **heteronymous** approaches, that is, obedience to moral laws laid down by others, whether rulers or the Church. This was not acceptable to Kant. The only moral law we should follow is that which is knowable by reason. For that reason to flourish it must be absolutely free of coercion. Only in that way can it work as pure reason dictates. Some people are frightened by this, but this is partly because they are swayed by appetites. True reason rises above such temptations.

Key terms

Heteronomy For Kant, the state of being directed by others in our decision-making.
Free will The belief that we are able to make our own uncompelled choices in life.

(a) Duty

Reason enables us to reflect on ourselves. We find in ourselves an awareness of things in life that need to be done, so reason recognises the centrality of duty. By 'duty' Kant means doing what we ought to do. We have a sense of obligation to perform certain actions, such as telling the truth, obeying legitimate instructions, being truthful and doing good for others. We have **free will**, and so we must use our will as well as we can, which means to will the good. Outcomes are never clear, and may be dictated by feeling rather than reason. We do not know whether actions have the effects we intend and we do not know the unexpected ways in which people and things will behave in future. Therefore, Kant argues, what matters in virtue is that the will should be good, regardless of outcome. We should will what is right, and what is right, is duty, the mark of a good will.

Kant argues that only the good will is truly good. He argues:

> There is no possibility at all of thinking of anything in the world – or even outside it – which can be considered good without qualification, except a **good will**. Intelligence, wit, judgment and what talents of mind you may choose to name are in many

Key question

Is Kant right to assume that we all have an innate sense of duty?

respects desirable ... but they can also become most bad and harmful if the will ... is not good. A good will is good not because of what it makes or accomplishes, and not because of its fitness to reach some proposed goal; it is good only through its willing — it is good in itself.

Groundwork of the Metaphysic of Morals: First Section ii, iv

In this extract we see that results are at best incidentally good. What matters is the good will to duty for its own sake — nothing else.

Kant develops this with the example of the shopkeeper. Suppose a shopkeeper is honest in all his dealings, never giving short weight or adulterating his goods. He might do this because it is good for business. Customers, unless very stupid, do not return to shops where they have been treated dishonestly. In this case, the shopkeeper is doing his duty *because* it will lead to good results, achieving the right outcome. He is doing what he should, but is not truly morally praiseworthy. The good man, the good shopkeeper, is honest because it is his duty and for no other reason. He is honest just because it is right and dutiful to be honest.

(i) Deontological or teleological?

It has become normal practice to see Kant's ethical thought as **deontological**: a theory by which the goodness of an act is not dependent on outcome but on its goodness in itself. However, it would be wrong to say that Kant is not concerned with outcomes at all. Clearly, determining duty, requires consideration of outcomes. But, the theory is deontological in this important and central sense: the right-making feature of Kant is whether a person has done her duty for its own sake. Only that is truly good. The consequential aspects of the theory are part of the reasoning rather than what makes an ethical action good in itself.

(b) An absolutist theory

Kant's theory is perhaps the most obviously absolutist of all moral theories. The command to do one's duty is invariable — not to do one's duty is always absolutely wrong. In the same way, as morality, like duty, exists for its own sake, then its commandments always bind us.

> **Key term**
>
> **Deontological ethics** Any ethical system which ignores outcomes, concentrating just on whether the act is good in itself.

3 Hypothetical imperatives

Kant recognises that in life we have various goals, some of which are not shared by all, and are not distinctively moral. For example, someone may have the goal of becoming a doctor, or a lawyer, or a ballet dancer. There is no moral obligation to become any of these things, but I may choose to become — or to try to become — one of these. Suppose I wish to become a lawyer. I would need to take certain steps, such as going to university, to law school, choosing whether to take the examinations and so on required by the Bar or the Law Society. If I wish to follow this career, then there are certain steps I am obliged to take. They are imperatives. I cannot practise as a solicitor if I do not pass the Law Society examinations, nor as a barrister unless admitted to the Bar.

Hypothetical imperative
What we must do to achieve a particular goal. There is no requirement to follow this, but it is how we should act if we wish to achieve something: it has the character of ' ... if ... then ...'.

Categorical imperative That which our reason teaches us must always be done. There are three forms of the imperative.

Notice the grammar of this example:

... *If* ... *then* ...

If I wish to be a barrister, *then* I must follow these steps. The '*if* ... *then* ...' marks the **hypothetical imperative**. This tells me what I must to do achieve certain goals.

But I do not have to be a lawyer, or a doctor, or even a ballet dancer. But I must strive to be good. The moral has an absolute and exceptionless character. Reason insists that I must have a good will, that I must do my duty. It is an absolute demand. It is not dependent on what I might wish, and not different from the demand on anyone else. It is not that I must do my duty and you need not. The requirement is there for both of us as an imperative we must obey. Hence, Kant calls this the **categorical imperative**.

4 The categorical imperative

Key terms

First form of the categorical imperative Act only on that maxim that you can will to be universal law. This means that we should only do what we are willing for everyone to do. If I want to rob a bank, am I willing that everyone should also be a thief? If I cannot will this, then I should not rob banks.

Second form of the categorical imperative So act as to treat persons always as ends and never as means only. Things should be done for the good of people, and people should never just be used for the sake of others or to support some abstract ideal. It would be wrong for a shopkeeper to ignore his customers' good and just use them – and perhaps cheat them – to make a profit.

Third form of the categorical imperative So act as to treat everyone, including yourself, as an end in the kingdom of ends. This connects with the second form of the categorical imperative, and insists upon human dignity. Actions are done for the sake of persons, and we should treat everyone, including ourselves, as the people for whom good must be done.

It is one thing to say that we must always follow the requirements of duty, but that is unhelpful without specifying what our duty is. It is common to describe Kant's understanding of duty in terms of the **first, second and third forms of the categorical imperative**, and this provides a useful shorthand way of describing his theory, and is normal usage in the literature about Kant. It is, however, useful to remember that for Kant himself, the second and third forms are clarifications of the first form. He did not consider them to be something separate.

(a) The first form of the categorical imperative

This is sometimes known as the principle of universalisation or less commonly, and perhaps less clearly, as the 'formula of the law of nature'.

Kant argues that we should act only on that maxim that we are willing to follow as a law (of personal conduct) and, at the same time, have that law apply for everyone. By this he means that we should do only what we are willing that everyone should do.

Suppose that I want to steal from my neighbour. In what sense could this possibly be moral? Would I want my neighbour to steal from me? That would rather spoil the advantage to me of possessing his state-of-the-art TV. Surely, as a rational person, I would not wish everyone to steal from his neighbour, not least as I too am a neighbour. Therefore, I must not steal from my neighbour, however much it might be to my benefit.

Kant argues that by applying this consistently we can see clearly what duty requires.

Interestingly, Kant develops the point through a fairly narrow range of examples:

- deception
- theft
- suicide
- laziness
- charity
- cruelty to animals.

This narrow range of examples perhaps invites philosophers to question whether there are other actions which are moral requirements to be applied universally. Are moral judgements always like that, and where are the limits to be drawn? Some moral judgements seem necessarily particular. I may feel morally compelled to marry Susan, for a host of reasons, including love, commitment, care and so on. But I surely do not wish the whole world to marry Susan. Furthermore, I am not sure that I am even willing that the whole adult world marry. It seems to me that I could morally feel compelled to marry but wish sincerely that George Joseph Smith, hanged in 1915 for murdering three wives in their baths, had not married. It would seem odd to argue that although I believe I should marry, to marry would be immoral because I am not willing to encourage every other person to marry. It seems irrational to argue that therefore my marrying would be an immoral act.

Despite the apparent clarity of Kant's approach, there are other issues.

1   Does being willing to generalise that everyone should do something make it moral? For example, it might be my habit, when putting on a pair of shoes, always to put the left shoe on first. Am I willing that everyone, everywhere puts her left shoe on first? Certainly. But to say that therefore it is a moral duty to put the left shoe on first seems odd. It's fine, but a *moral duty?* Surely this is a just a matter of taste or habit, not a moral duty. Just because I am happy for everyone to do the same thing, this is not by itself a right-making characteristic. Something else seems to be needed to make the action a moral duty.

2   It is not clear that any action can truly be universalised in this way and remain moral. St Thomas Aquinas argued:

> *All people realise that it is right and good to act according to reason ... it follows as an individual conclusion that debts ought to be paid. In most cases this is true, but it could happen in some individual instance that it would be harmful and therefore irrational to repay a debt (if, for example, the money were to be used for a war against one's own country).*

> S.T. I-II, q.94, a. 4c.

This raises a crucial point. It is counter-intuitive at least to suggest that we must *never* break a promise nor tell a lie, irrespective of what harm might follow from our upholding the promise. Kant insists, in his search for a single principle that we must always act on the universalisable maxim, *regardless* of consequences. But this permits actual harm in some cases. In Aquinas' example, could I be said to have behaved morally if the consequence of my paying of the debt is death and destruction in my country? We would perhaps find it difficult not to argue that our honesty in repaying the debt was not only immoral but irrational.

Speech bubble: Does this make me look fat?

Thought bubble: I cannot tell a lie!

Key question

Is Kant unrealistic in thinking that any action could ever be always right, without exception?

(b) The second form of the categorical imperative

This is sometimes referred to as the principle of the priority of ends or occasionally as the 'formula of the end in itself'.

Background

Developments and connections

It is interesting to notice how some later, non-Kantian philosophers have used the idea of treating people always as ends. It directly influenced William Temple's situational ethics and he used it teleologically to show how all our actions should be directed. It also influenced Fletcher's situation ethics. See, for example, his use of personalism in Chapter 11.

It can be summarised as arguing that we should so act as to treat everyone – ourselves as well as others – always as ends, and never as means.

This touches on something very important. Consider a certain type of entrepreneur interested only in the bottom line, the profit his company and himself will make. His workers become tools, to be paid as little as he can get away with, and the customers are considered a bunch of idiots to be treated as means simply to his own accumulation of wealth. In this case, it is easy to see that, for this businessman, people are being used as means to achieve a non-personal end – profit, for its own sake. Most of us would argue that this would be to *use* people, and that this is wrong. (This is not, of course, to argue against profits, because some seek profit as a means to do good for persons.) People are being used, with no concern for their good. In the same way, we might argue that a political leader who sacrificed people for the sake of some political creed would be immorally using them as means to an end – history, and the contemporary world, are filled with such examples of people being sacrificed for an ideology.

This insight of Kant is, arguably, one of the most significant ideas in moral philosophy. Even if we dissent from other aspects of his thought, this prioritising of the personal seems an essential condition of the moral, especially if it is true that something is only ever truly good if it is good for someone. It is difficult to see how something can be held to be good if its goodness cannot be appreciated.

Used without concern for consequences, there are nevertheless difficulties with this form of the categorical imperative. It tells us we should always treat persons as ends, never as means only. If we disregard the realities of living and making decisions in a complex world, the principle seems to work well. Indeed, in the actuality of events and life in the world, generally speaking it is a good and workable principle. But there are always hard cases, some of which cast doubt on the absolutist claim that this principle can and must always be followed.

Consider a real and tragic case. On the night of 14 November 1941, in the largest bombing raid so far carried out, 449 German bombers dropped 30,000 incendiary bombs on Coventry. 568 civilians were killed, 41,500 homes were damaged with 2,306 destroyed. There is evidence that the British authorities had prior knowledge of the raid, because the scientists at Bletchley Park had broken the Enigma codes which contained the orders for the raid. Winston Churchill was left with a decision of appalling difficulty. If he moved the people out of Coventry and the Germans found out, whether through spies or aerial reconnaissance, then they would know that the Enigma codes had been broken. Doing this would have led to untold numbers of deaths and other suffering, because they would devise a new and even more difficult code. If the facts are as they are now believed to be, then the authorities were using the people of Coventry as means for the sake of others as ends. But, if the decision had been taken to move the people out, then the thousands and perhaps millions who might have died would have been used as means to treat the people in Coventry as ends. Apparently Churchill said that the decision not to move the people out of Coventry was the only one from the war to give him continuing nightmares. In warfare not everyone can be saved. There are other circumstances as well when choices have to be made between saving some people at the expense of others. It is not always clear-cut that we should always use people as ends and never as means. To say we should pay no heed to consequences, so long as we do our duty, does not help us to determine what that duty is in these hard cases.

(c) The third form of the categorical imperative

Sometimes known as 'the kingdom of ends', this follows from the other forms. Kant sees it as a clarification of our own duty of acting in accordance with the categorical imperative. This argues that:

■ Every rational being must act as if through his universalised maxim he were always a legislating member in the universal kingdom of ends.

That sounds abstract, but what Kant means is that we must act as if our actions made laws for everyone else, and everyone else acted in the same way. Suppose I want to perform an action, such as giving my aunt a birthday present. This should not be thought of as simply a personal, private act. My choice of action is a commitment to the idea that everyone in the world should always give birthday presents to their aunts. I should think of my action as a rule for everyone, done for the good of persons, and I should treat the actions of all other rational people as rules for me.

This formulation does not add very much to the others except that it is an insistent reminder of our duty and responsibility and emphasises the significance of ends.

(d) Immortality and God

There has been much debate over Kant's religious belief. Some supporters and opponents have seen him as an atheist, given his enthusiasm for unaided human reason. At the same time, his works – the *Groundwork* not least – refer continually to God, to the Holy One, and so on.

His own religious practice is little guide. Even as rector of the university, Kant was inclined to give excuses for religious services he was expected to attend. But Pietist Lutheranism, in which he was brought up, set little store by outward devotion: what mattered was the disposition of his inward nature towards God. Christianity was exhibited in living an active moral life, based on scripture, not church attendance.

Evidence from the ethics is uncertain. The emphasis on reason alone might suggest to some that Kant believed God to be irrelevant. If morality were an internalisation of God's commands, their source would be heteronymous. We might, however, bear in mind that for many Christian philosophers morality is not dependent on God in the way some have argued (see Natural Law in Chapter 10). God, they argue, commands what is right, but its rightness is knowable by reason alone. The natural law tradition believes in 'right reason in accordance with nature'. The moral is rationally determined, and not simply obedience to divine command.

Yet we find in Kant a belief in personal **immortality** and an argument for God.

For Kant, there are three **postulates** of practical reason:

■ that we are free beings.
■ that we are immortal
■ that God exists

Immortality The belief that we will live forever, in afterlife.
Postulate A principle so evident that it needs no further justification: it may be taken as an assumption.

Freedom is connected to Kant's view that we are fully rational beings capable of knowing absolutely what our duty is. When we make a moral decision, we are acknowledging our freedom. In doing this, we are accepting that we are immortal (this seems to Kant necessary for the universe to be the rational entity he thinks it is) and that there is God as guarantor of both the rationality and the immortality.

Of course for him we do our duty *because* it is rational to do so, and not because God has commanded it.

Remember that for Kant, we cannot prove by conventional metaphysics the existence of God, because he lies outside any possible experience. We have seen Kant's rejection of ontological arguments in Chapter 6.

The argument Kant gives is:

- Rationally, perfect virtue ought to be rewarded by perfect happiness.
- The combination of perfect happiness and perfect goodness is the *summum bonum* ('highest good').
- Clearly this is not achieved in this life. Good things happen to bad people and horrid things to the virtuous.
- Therefore, because the *summum bonum* **ought** to be achieved, it **can** be achieved.
- If it is not achievable in this life, it must be achievable in the next, which means we need immortality.
- If the *summum bonum* exists in the next life, there must be someone to provide it.
- This someone is obviously God.

Notice that Kant is arguing that, rationally, immortal reward ought to follow virtuous life. It is important to be clear that he is not saying that we ought to be moral for any reward. Virtue should be rewarded, but we should be virtuous for its own sake, not for reward.

The argument is not convincing. Much debate has concentrated on the assumption that *ought* implies *can*. Kant's notion seems to be that it makes no sense to tell someone that she ought to do something if she cannot possibly do so. Whenever we say *ought*, *can* necessarily follows. If I say, 'You ought to be kind to your mother', it makes sense as far as it is possible for you to do so. If you had no known or no living mother, the instruction would be nonsense. If I said, 'You ought to flap your arms and fly', this would be absurd, because what I am demanding of you is impossible. But in Kant's moral argument there is a different use of *ought*. It is an *ought* of what should exist (the *summum bonum*), not the *ought* of duty. *Ought* has many meanings. Because bad things happen to good people does not mean that *therefore* compensation or justice will be forthcoming. If I say that they *ought* to be recompensed, I am expressing a wish, not saying that they will receive justice or even that it is possible they will do so. Kant seems to assume that the universe is ultimately rational. That is not self-evidently true, and Kant might be accused of thinking it so because he wishes it to be that way. Specific evidence of ultimate justice is difficult to find.

5 Objections to Kant's ethics

Various objections have been made to Kant's theory in addition to those listed when discussing individual points above. Among these, we may note:

- Many argue that we cannot morally ignore the consequences of our actions with the claim that we are doing our duty. In this context, of course, we are talking of our genuinely *moral* duty. We know that in times in history – for example at the Nuremberg trials of leading Nazis after the Second World War – some tried to excuse their crimes by saying that they were 'only doing their duty'. In Kantian terms, they were not, because for him there could be no universalisable duty to be cruel, to torture, to murder, to commit genocide, to kill unarmed prisoners. In Kantian terms, there can be no justification of evil acts under the guise of 'only doing my duty', because no such actions could be true duties.

  But a question remains about those actions which, in Kant's terms, are to be considered truly moral duties, such as honesty or promise-keeping. If a mad-eyed axeman comes to the door of my classroom and asks whether I have any students with names beginning with 'S', my duty requires me to take action. If I always tell the truth, actual harm may come to individuals, and there is a question about whether always telling the truth conflicts with the second form of the categorical imperative, about treating all persons as ends, never as means. If we uphold the duty of truth-telling without exception, in this case we permit actual harm. The difficulty is in determining what we must do in the circumstance in which we find ourselves without giving some thought to actual probable outcomes.

  Teleological theories have difficulties because ultimately they *only* consider outcomes. A theory such as Kant's is difficult if it means we do not consider outcomes *at all*. It is a weakness in Kant's argument that it seems to lack a clear decision procedure for dealing with the problem of principle clash. If we have more than one maxim – and we will, because we are likely on Kant's terms to include things such as always telling the truth, always keeping promises, not committing suicide – then clashes in actual circumstances seem to mean that they cannot be applied 'always' and 'without exception'.

- Kant treats the ethical life as one to be determined by reason alone. We must work according to what we take to be the dictates of reason alone. But is the ethical dimension of our lives a purely rational one? Certainly, life might seem simpler if only we were all coldly rational creatures – but we are not. Our actual decision-making is necessarily affected by feelings such as sympathy and compassion, by affection and the ties of our circumstances. People give to the poor not simply because it is a rational duty but because they feel actual sympathy at the plight of another and feel the need to do something about it. Things are done for others because we feel sorry for them, or because we feel obligations of friendship or family, or because this person is our beloved. Parents look after their children not simply from duty but because of paternal and maternal feelings. They know intellectually that they have duties as parents – but they *feel* responsible.

The bonds that tie us include the rational, but they go beyond the rational. It is not irrational for a mother to love and nurture her child, but the motivation and source of that love and nurture is more than, and other than, simply that her reason tells her what she should do. Qualities such as charity, truthfulness, compassion, concern are reasons perhaps best seen as 'the heart's reasons'. Kant's approach seems to provide reasons rather than motivation for moral action.

■ A connected problem is that if we should do the right thing *because* it is our duty, and for no other reason, and if there is no direct moral merit in enjoyment of our action, for the action must be done purely for its own sake, then the outcome of our duties would seem to be 'cold charity'. The moral giver is not giving with pleasure, for that would not be truly virtuous.

But part of charity is not simply that something is given. *How* it is given, with a generous heart, is surely part of the goodness of the act. Older church collection plates were sometimes adorned with the motto 'God loveth a cheerful giver'. Doing good things gladly is surely part of being truly moral. Aristotle was specific that it is not enough to do the right thing. To be truly moral, it is essential to do so with the right attitude. In religious terms, the right action should be done lovingly, with love both for the receiver and for the action.

■ Kant's attitude to the universe presupposes that it is a rational entity. It might be rational to think that virtue is rewarded, that everyone is capable of rational behaviour, that this is a world in which the rational power of the mind is, ultimately, the highest power and, by implication, the highest value. It is not necessarily or even apparently so. The world might just be a brute fact, just there, without any particular reason. The mind might not be the supremely rational principle, what ought to be might not necessarily be the case.

6 Conclusions

The greatness of Kant as a philosopher cannot be doubted. His moral philosophy remains an important part of the discourse of ethics. While few philosophers have directly adopted all his ideas in ethical philosophy, his discussions of duty and universalisation ask important questions. Simply to think about universalisation is to ask significant questions of our behaviour. Even if Kant is wrong to think that we can universalise to discover every moral duty, to develop a habit of thinking before an action, 'What if everyone did this?' would be invaluable moral advice for anyone. The second form of the categorical imperative, requiring us to make the person central, treating people as ends, is one of the greatest of all moral insights, whether we use it in a Kantian context or treat it more broadly in all our thinking about the good.

Study advice

Kant is not an easy philosopher to read, but the thrust of his argument is relatively straightforward to determine. As you read the points made in the current chapter, and objections put against Kant, it is important to think about these. Are the criticisms we have made fair to Kant? Can you think of better points? Could you make the same arguments more concisely? Also, for each of the major issues, such as the forms of the categorical imperative, or the primacy of duty, can you give strong examples to demonstrate your understanding?

It is important not to concentrate just on the categorical imperative as you study. Take time to think also about the postulates of God, immortality and freedom. You could be questioned on these as they appear on the Specification for the subject.

Be careful to avoid any hint of thinking that the categorical imperative is innate or the voice of God. For Kant it is the conclusion of an entirely autonomous use of pure reason.

Summary diagram: Kantian ethics

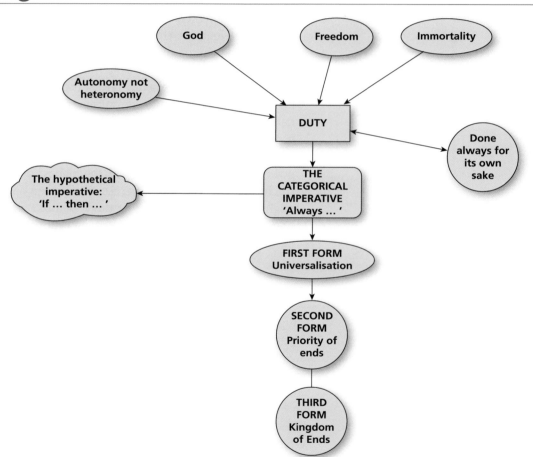

As mentioned above, it is important to be confident in your understanding of duty, autonomy, the categorical imperative and its forms, but also about the postulates of God, immortality and freedom. Look also at the relationship of will and freedom, and the distinction between autonomy and heteronomy.

Can you give brief definitions of:
- autonomy
- duty
- universalisation
- the kingdom of ends
- deontological theories?

Can you explain:
- the difference between the hypothetical and categorical imperatives
- the difference between autonomous and heteronymous thinking
- the first form of the categorical imperative
- the second form of the categorical imperative?

Can you give arguments for and against:
- Kant's argument that duty should be done for its own sake
- the first form of the categorical imperative
- the second form of the categorical imperative
- Kant's postulates of moral reasoning?

Sample question and guidance

> To what extent is it true to say that the only requirement of morality is to do our duty?

Questions of this kind are sometimes asked, and it is worth thinking about how to answer these. A student familiar with Kant should be expected to recognise that this is indeed a question about Kantian ethics. Less perceptive people might be tempted to think this is a question letting them write about every theory they have ever learned. The word 'duty' in a question is always to be understood to direct you to thinking about Kant, the great proponent of the ethics of duty.

It would be a good idea to outline what Kant believes about duty, and your knowledge of the categorical imperative is important here. Doing so might enable you to think about whether the implications of the forms of the categorical imperative might be argued to go beyond just duty. There is no requirement to go into this, if you have nothing you want to say beyond using the forms of the imperative to demonstrate what Kant means by duty.

What is essential is to notice the word 'only' in the title. You are not being asked to write everything you know about Kant, but to think about whether the whole of the requirements can be summarised in the requirement to do our duty. Consider criticisms about how this might lead to 'cold charity' or ignore some of the human aspects of a truly moral life. Does the insistence on duty overlook the questions of virtues we should develop? Is the idea of duty just for duty's sake too narrow?

It is important that you consider these issues and reach a conclusion for which you have supporting arguments. Whether you think doing your duty is or is not the only requirement of morality, it must be clear to the reader the considerations which have led you to your final answer.

Further essay questions

> 'Kant does not properly establish his ethical postulates of God, Immortality and Freedom.' Discuss.

> To what extent is Kant's ethical teaching helpful in resolving all ethical problems?

> 'We cannot universalise our ethical judgements.' Discuss.

The literature on Kant is vast, and it is unlikely that you would find time to do more than dip a toe into the water. Kant is not the easiest philosopher to read. His use of German was sometimes awkward, and translation does not make the process much easier. It would, however, be worthwhile to read a little of the *Groundwork* online. It is an easier work than the *Critique of Pure Reason*, but, more importantly, there is the opportunity to practise reading slowly and carefully. Philosophers develop the habit of reading a little at a time, being patient in teasing out the details of arguments, to see how they develop. Half an hour of intensive work on a couple of paragraphs constitutes admirable training. As background, one of the best expositions of his ethical thought may be found in Dale Jacquette: *Pathways in Philosophy* (Oxford University Press, 2004), pp. 265–317. Roger Scruton: *Kant: A Very Short Introduction* (Oxford University Press, 2001), is not very easy overall, but the chapter on morality is concise and clear.

Chapter 13

Utilitarianism

1 Introduction

> **Chapter checklist**
>
> The chapter begins by outlining the motivation for developing a single-principle theory for determining how to make moral decisions. It examines Jeremy Bentham's hedonist version of utilitarianism, looking at his own formulation of the theory and use of the hedonic calculus. This then leads to discussion of some of the problems of act utilitarianism. The chapter draws a contrast between this and Mill's rule utilitarianism, with discussion of how this is exemplified in his essay *On Liberty*. It identifies problems with Mill's approach. It outlines Peter Singer's philosophy as an example of modern non-hedonist approaches. The final section discusses objections to utility, with particular reference to Kant's second form of the categorical imperative and the absence of any theory of natural rights.

Suppose a friend of yours has been invited to a garden party at Buckingham Palace. You like and care very much for your friend, who is a sensitive soul, easily hurt. She decides that she needs to buy a suitable dress. This worries you, as her sense of what is appropriate can sometimes be mistaken. She buys a dress in the brightest, even garish colours, badly cut, and perhaps appropriate for a dimly-lit nightclub but not for meeting the Queen. And the shoes she has chosen are asking for trouble if the palace lawns are damp.

You have a dilemma. You have been brought up by your parents and others with two principles. They have told you to be truthful. This is easily done, but liable to hurt your friend. But you have also been taught to be kind to people, to spare their feelings whenever you can. What do you do? Saying nothing or saying the dress is lovely spares hurt now, but at the cost of feeling yourself a liar and leading, perhaps, to the future embarrassment of your friend. But saying your friend's choice is horrid would hurt her. Probably you will end with one of those compromises that does no one any good, such as, 'It's an interesting choice' or 'You will certainly stand out!'

In such circumstances, we feel torn. Why is it so? It is because there is a clash of principles, in this case between the two **precepts** of always being truthful and always being kind to people. We are torn because obeying one leads us to fail in the other. We are dissatisfied with ourselves however we handle things.

> **Key term**
>
> **Precept** A general rule designed to regulate behaviour or thought.

191

What would be wonderful would be a life without this type of dilemma. To achieve it, we would need just one principle, a principle which would unfailingly show us what we needed to do. Complex choices would be made simple.

The claim of utilitarianism is to provide this simple and uncomplicated guide, by sticking to one simple principle, the 'principle of utility'.

It is interesting that utilitarianism is a product of the Enlightenment. Remember that Isaac Newton was the presiding genius of Enlightenment thought. Newton seemed to have demonstrated that the universe ran as a kind of giant machine, according to a few fixed and invariable laws. These laws were, in principle, knowable by human reason. This model of thinking gave hope to other thinkers that every problem could be resolved by such simple means.

The first stirrings of utilitarianism may be found in Hume. Hume thought that it was impossible fully to justify morality on rational grounds, but examination of our passions revealed their influence, about which we could reason. We seek our self-interest. Reason can, as it were, advise our moral approach, but ultimately something is only called immoral because it displeases us. Notice that this model is a very simple one. Human behaviour is explained with very few terms.

For more on Isaac Newton, see Chapter 5.

2 Jeremy Bentham and classical utilitarianism

Key term

Utilitarianism The moral doctrine that one should always seek the greatest balance of good over evil.

Jeremy Bentham (1748–1832) is usually considered the father of modern **utilitarianism**, even though his own version of utilitarianism was flawed because he smuggled in a second principle which raises questions, as we shall see. He was an archetypal Enlightenment figure, believing that human nature could be explained by the belief that we are psychological hedonists, so made that we always seek our own pleasure. If this is the way we are, then it makes sense to say that the good for humans would be maximising the pleasure we seek but minimising the pain that we avoid. Bentham applied this insight to his work as a social reformer. He sought to reform society on utilitarian lines. He supported many causes which have continued to be influential. He opposed slavery, the death penalty and corporal punishments such as flogging or caning with a birch (only finally abolished in English prisons in 1967), and mistreatment of animals. He supported equal rights for women, the right to divorce and sought decriminalisation of male homosexual acts. He believed in the separation of Church and State. As a liberal, he supported freedom of expression and economic freedom from regulation. His major work was in legal philosophy, basing his views on strict utilitarian principles. Much of his work in this field has only become available in recent years. His best work in the field, *Of Laws in General*, was not published until the twentieth century.

He believed in the strict application of his principles, not least in regard to his own death.

Jeremy Bentham – the auto-icon

He wished to make that a useful event, leaving his body to be first publicly dissected, for the good of medical science, and then turned into an auto-icon (a reminder of himself made from his own body) as a continual reminder of the principles he taught. This may be seen at University College, London, which he helped to establish.

3 Teleology and relativism

Utilitarianism is a strictly teleological theory in that its goal is the moral good of persons, although, as we shall see, there is no agreement among Utilitarians about precisely what that good is. For some it is pleasure, for most, happiness in some sense. The principle of utility seeks to achieve the good to the greatest possible extent: it is designed to enable us to achieve that goal.

Some forms of utilitarianism – such as Act Utilitarianism, as found in Bentham and others – are very situational, trying to work out in each dilemma what we should do to achieve the good. But it would be wrong to describe this outlook as relativist, because Utilitarianism in whatever form, has two absolute requirements – to work to achieve the good and always to follow the principle of utility to do so.

(a) Bentham's principle of utility

It is important to remember that the claim of utilitarianism is to provide a single principle to resolve the dilemmas of moral life, to be applied without exception. In simple terms, the principle takes some version of the form:

Seek always the greatest balance of good over evil.

Bentham himself wrote of it:

Create all the happiness you are able to create: remove all the misery you are able to remove. Every day will allow you to add something to the pleasure of others, or to diminish something of their pains. And for every grain of enjoyment you sow in the bosom of another, you shall find a harvest in your own bosom; while every sorrow which you pluck out from the thoughts and feelings of a fellow creature shall be replaced by beautiful peace and joy in the sanctuary of your soul.

Jeremy Bentham: 'Advice to a young girl' (22 June 1830)

The principle of utility judges any action to be right by the tendency it appears to have to augment or diminish the happiness of the party whose interests are in question ... if that party be the community, the happiness of the community, if a particular individual, the happiness of that individual.

Jeremy Bentham: *An Introduction to the Principles of Morals and Legislation* (1789 edition)

There are some problems with the principle of utility. It needs to be supplemented by the theory of what the good is.

(b) The hedonic calculus

Bentham took a simple view: he was a strict hedonist, arguing that happiness – and hence the good – is pleasure. It is important to notice that a hedonist is not saying pleasure is a good: he is saying pleasure is the good *and nothing else is the good*. The terms 'pleasure' and 'good' are interchangeable. This is a controversial view. Plato argued against it in *Gorgias* and elsewhere. An obvious issue is that, on this account, it seems impossible for there to be a 'bad pleasure'. Some people take pleasure in hurting others. It seems perfectly possible to call this a 'bad pleasure', but not at all to call it a 'bad good'. The latter phrase contains a contradiction absent from the former. If that is true, 'pleasure' and 'good' are not interchangeable terms. If they were, both phrases would make exactly the same sense in any sentences in which they were used.

But Bentham was insistent on his view of pleasure as the good. It seemed to provide the sort of simple answer he sought. He even attempted to develop a hedonic (or felicific) calculus for determining which act should be performed, using the seven criteria of:

- intensity (how strong is the pleasure?)
- duration (how long will the pleasure last?)
- certainty (how likely is it that the pleasure will truly happen?)
- propinquity (how soon will the pleasure happen?)
- fecundity (how probable is it that pleasant sensations will follow?)
- purity (how unlikely is it that the action will lead to pain rather than pleasure?)
- extent (how many people will be affected?).

Bentham spent years on the calculus, but he could never make a system that worked. His aim, of course, was to reduce life decisions to something which could be precisely calculated. The problem is that there are too many variables.

Suppose someone loves chocolate éclairs, and decides that eating a chocolate éclair equals 10 points of pleasure. In mathematical terms, it would then follow that eating two éclairs would equal 20 points of pleasure, and eating ten would equal 100. But ... even the most dedicated chocolate éclair lover might start to feel a little queasy after only seven or eight éclairs, which makes the assumption that eating ten at a sitting would be ten times as pleasurable as eating one just a little suspect. Then there are other factors to weigh up. Is an éclair as pleasant at breakfast time, or after a hot curry, or with a pint of beer, or after a nasty bout of gastro-enteritis?

Bentham's *Hedonist Utilitarianism* has been challenged from several perspectives. For Bentham, it was a mistake to try to distinguish types of pleasure. All that mattered was the pleasure felt. John Stuart Mill was unhappy about a narrow **hedonism**, concerned that there are higher and lower pleasures: in his essay, *Utilitarianism*, he writes: 'It is better to be a human being dissatisfied than a pig satisfied; better to be Socrates dissatisfied than a fool satisfied.'

(c) Alternatives to hedonism

It should be noted that while Bentham's utilitarianism was hedonist, it need not be so. Utilitarianism seeks the greatest balance of good over

Key persons

Jeremy Bentham (1748–1832): English legal and moral theorist, social reformer and proponent of hedonist utilitarianism. Devoted to social reform, he lived his life according to his principles.

Key term

Hedonism The philosophical view that the good is pleasure, and nothing else is the good.

For a profile of Mill, see Chapter 9.

evil, and the good might be something other than pleasure. Different utilitarians have different ideas of the good. Mill talks of 'happiness' rather than 'pleasure'. Surely, a search for the good should be for what is really good, not just bodily pleasures or what someone – perhaps mistakenly – takes to be preferable outcomes. Ideas on these lines led, following the publication of G. E. Moore's *Principia Ethica*, to the growth of *ideal utilitarianism*, which argues that one should seek always the greatest balance of the ideally good.

(d) The greatest good of the greatest number?

Another issue is what Bentham actually taught as utilitarianism. One of the most famous phrases in philosophy is 'the greatest good for the greatest number'. It is attributed to Bentham, although it was first formulated by Francis Hutcheson in 1725. Some writers have unfortunately taken it to be the belief of utilitarianism as a whole. This is an error to be avoided.

There are two problems with the formulation.

The first, and perhaps more significant, is that it compromises the entire premise of utilitarianism, because it entails a principle of justice – and a very bad one – as well as one of doing good. There are now two principles – do good, and distribute the good in this way. It may be noted, incidentally, that the Christian precept of: 'Love your neighbour as yourself' is also two principles, a principle of love and the other of justice, telling us how to distribute that love. It is understandable how Bentham's formulation came about.

Suppose that I have £100 which I could share among my friends. I could give one friend £100, telling him not to tell my other nine friends. Those nine feel no pain, and he gets 100 points of pleasure. The net result is 100 points of pleasure, and no pain. But the same net result occurs if I give my friends £10 each: 10 points of pleasure each = 100 points, and no pain. So, what should I do? Simply telling me to maximise pleasure is incomplete, and the claim of utilitarianism is to avoid the problem of dilemmas, so that I always know what to do. By letting everyone count for one, and no one for more than one, I know what to do, spreading the good among the greatest number of people. However, there are other issues. Why do I not give 100 people £1 each? Is it appropriate to privilege people just because they are my friends? As we shall see, Peter Singer addresses the issue of privilege.

The second issue with the formulation is that Bentham himself came to repudiate it. In an unpublished manuscript, intended for James Mill, he wrote:

> *Greatest happiness of the greatest number. Some years have now elapsed since, upon a closer scrutiny, reason, altogether incontestable, was found for discarding this appendage. On the surface, additional clearness and correctness given to the idea: at bottom, the opposite qualities.*

Bentham's reason for this repudiation was simple – the dangers of pleasing the majority and ignoring the minority. If the majority hurts the minority, as the 'greatest good of the greatest number' permits, then there is a smaller total amount of pleasure than if the good of the minority were made part of the total outcome.

(e) The rejection of natural rights

This does not deal with what for many is the great difficulty of all forms of utilitarianism: the denial of any notion of natural rights. To assert natural rights would be to produce a second principle which could interfere with utility. It could be argued, with some force, that a right to life and liberty of an individual interferes with the greatest general happiness. To say that the individual right to life is more important than the principle of utility would be a denial of utilitarianism.

Bentham is quite specific about this:

> *That which has no existence cannot be destroyed – that which cannot be destroyed cannot require anything to preserve it from destruction. Natural rights is simple nonsense: natural and imprescriptible rights, rhetorical nonsense – nonsense upon stilts.*

Jeremy Bentham: *Anarchical Fallacies* (1843)

It does not follow that for the utilitarian, rights cannot be enshrined into law as legal rights, if granting that legal right led to the greatest general happiness. It is interesting that John Stuart Mill, Bentham's pupil, in 1859 published *On Liberty*, which argues that in civilised societies, people should have maximum personal liberty. He claims:

> *The object of this Essay is to assert one very simple principle, as entitled to govern absolutely the dealings of society with the individual in the way of compulsion and control, whether the means used be physical force in the form of legal penalties, or the moral coercion of public opinion. That principle is, that the sole end for which mankind are warranted, individually or collectively, in interfering with the liberty of action of any of their number, is self-protection. That the only purpose for which power can be rightfully exercised over any member of a civilized community, against his will, is to prevent harm to others.*

John Stuart Mill: *On Liberty* (1859), Chapter I: Introductory, paragraph 9

That might sound like the assertion of a right to liberty, but he does not apply it to all people. It is not applied to children or people in what he considers backward nations. In the same chapter he is clear that he appeals to the greatest general good. He accepts that maximum personal liberty may permit someone to harm himself. We may know that someone is harming himself through drinking too much, but this, for Mill, would not justify stopping him, though we may advise him to drink less. If we stopped him, we would be interfering with the greater general liberty. Everyone would be less free if we had a state in which people were stopped from doing what they wanted, and, according to Mill, we would all be worse off. He rejects natural rights:

> *It is proper to state that I forego any advantage which could be derived to my argument from the idea of abstract right, as a thing independent of utility. I regard utility as the ultimate appeal on all ethical questions; but it must be utility in the largest sense, grounded on the permanent interests of man as a progressive being.*

John Stuart Mill: *On Liberty* (1859), Chapter I: Introductory, paragraph 11

Although Mill clearly endorses the principle of utilitarianism, there is an important difference between Mill and Bentham.

(f) Act utilitarianism

Bentham's approach is often seen as an example of **act utilitarianism**, the view that for each act we should determine which outcome leads to the greater general good, on a case-by-case basis. This is why he attempted his hedonic calculus to help determine in each instance the best outcome.

One of the problems with such an approach is that often people do not have sufficient time or information to make the necessary calculation. Some do not have the intellectual capacity, even if the information were available. To say to a child, 'Before you put your finger into that electric socket, calculate whether that would lead to the greatest pleasure (be careful to show your working)', would be absurd. It is much better for the parent to say, 'Never do that!' Always following the rule might lead to missing a particular instance of fun, but it would mean the best overall result.

(g) Rule utilitarianism

Rule utilitarianism, as endorsed by Mill, seems a more appropriate response. This argues that we should always follow the rule that will lead to the greatest balance of good over evil. In the case of the parent, she will be able to tell her child not to lie, not to steal and not to play on the railway tracks in the knowledge that if everyone follows these rules, we are all generally better off.

In the case of liberty, Mill argues that his general principle of liberty, if always followed, leads to the greatest general happiness, even though some people will go off the rails and do damage to themselves. The needs of the general good outweigh my individual issues with – for instance – drink or drugs.

The problem with rule utilitarianism is that it seems to place preservation of the rule above individual need. In the case of Mill's theory of liberty, he is reluctant to prevent individual harm, simply because the rule of maximising liberty should be adhered to for the greatest general happiness:

> *... there are questions relating to interference with trade, which are essentially questions of liberty; such as ... the prohibition of the importation of opium into China; the restriction of the sale of poisons; all cases, in short, where the object of the interference is to make it impossible or difficult to obtain a particular commodity. These interferences are objectionable, not as infringements on the liberty of the producer or seller, but on that of the buyer.*

John Stuart Mill: *On Liberty*, Chapter V, paragraph 4

There is no need to look at the history of the Opium Wars of the nineteenth century for some to object to this line of reasoning. Mill's argument is that if we restrict freedom in these matters, then the entire principle of liberty is at risk. Therefore, the fact that some people will kill themselves with drugs or poisons (and, presumably, find themselves unhappy in the process) is insignificant compared with letting individuals be as free as possible. But, for Mill, if I am an intelligent adult in an advanced society, I may use poison to kill myself, or opium to do likewise, because permitting my self-harm is for the greater general good. A critic would argue that this is a case of *instrumentalism* – the rule exists not for my good, but rather my misused liberty is an instrument – a means – of preserving the rule. The question to consider is whether persons exist for the sake of preservation of rules, or whether – as Kant would argue in the second form of the categorical imperative – everything should be done for the sake of persons, never using them as means only.

Another issue is that if it is difficult to calculate the good in an individual case, as we saw in the section on act utilitarianism, how much more difficult will it be to have confidence that adherence to a given general rule will have a better outcome than other possibilities? We know that, along the way, always keeping to the general rule of maximising liberty or always telling the truth will have some unfortunate outcomes for individuals, but it is doubtful that we can ever be certain that following the general rule will always and necessarily lead to the greatest balance of good over evil.

A further problem, and one perhaps fatal for rule utilitarianism, is that it compromises the claim of utilitarianism to resolve dilemmas of what we should do in every case. Rule utilitarianism permits the construction of more than one rule (after all, not all issues would be resolved if the only rule we had were Mill's principle of liberty). The moment we have more than one rule, we raise the possibility – even likelihood – or rule-clash, thus reintroducing the problems which utilitarianism was designed to avoid.

> For further discussion of people as ends, not means, read Kant's moral theory in Chapter 12.

4 Peter Singer and preference utilitarianism

> **Key person**
>
> **Peter Singer** (b. 1946): Probably the most famous contemporary utilitarian. He was born in Melbourne where his Austrian Jewish parents sought refuge from Nazism. His maternal grandmother died in Theresienstadt concentration camp, and his paternal grandparents vanished without trace. He studied in Melbourne and Oxford, and for many years worked principally in Australia. In 1999 he became Professor of Bioethics in Princeton, New Jersey. His best-known works are *Practical Ethics,* first published in 1980 (2011), and *Animal Liberation* (1975, revised edition 1990). Each has been much discussed, and often incompletely understood, despite the remarkable clarity of expression throughout. Like Bentham, he lives his life on strict utilitarian principles.

Much of the most recent debate about Utilitarianism has centred on arguments by Peter Singer, the most famous modern representative of utilitarianism. Knowing his work is invaluable for thinking through many of the issues already discussed, and his concern to explore particular issues attracts much attention in the media.

Singer's position, throughout his works, has been a strictly rational utilitarianism, claiming to think through the issues in a rational way, with no appeal to emotion or sentimentality. In the 1975 Preface to *Animal Liberation,* Singer writes:

> *This book makes no sentimental appeals for sympathy toward 'cute' animals. I am no more outraged by the slaughter of dogs for meat than I am by the slaughter of pigs for this purpose.*

Peter Singer: *Animal Liberation:* Preface to 1975 edition (1995), p. ix

For Singer, we need to apply strictly and unemotionally the principles of utilitarianism. In his view, it is important to recognise that utilitarianism must have a universal quality, weighing the needs and preferences of others as much as my own:

> *In accepting that ethical judgements must be made from a universal point of view, I am accepting that my own needs, wants and desires cannot, simply because they are my preferences, count more than the wants, needs and desires of anyone else.*

Peter Singer: *Practical Ethics* (2011), p. 13

> **Key terms**
>
> **Preference utilitarianism** Holds that we should look to seek as the good that which we would rationally prefer as an outcome, even though it may not be in our own best interests.
>
> **Altruism** Any theory which puts the needs of others first is altruistic.

Classical utilitarianism seemed to favour concern with our own pains and pleasures. Singer rejects classic hedonistic accounts, arguing that we should opt for **preference utilitarianism**. No longer is the aim the maximisation of pleasure over pain, but rather the general satisfaction of preferences. The idea here is that, for various reasons, we may *prefer* outcomes in a rational way even though those outcomes do not directly lead to our own satisfaction. For example, I may prefer the outcomes of **altruism** in terms of a better world even though I am not personally more satisfied as a result of my giving to others. The altruist principle is very significant in Singer's approach. He argues that we should do what on balance furthers the preferences of those affected. In some ways, Singer has recently moved more closely to classical hedonistic positions, but only by interpreting pleasure and pain in a broad sense, connected with the pleasures and pains of achieving or not achieving what is preferred.

(a) Minimising suffering

Central to these arguments is the place of suffering. What matters is the capacity to suffer. This is shared by humans and other higher animals. Humans by tradition have privileged the human being over other animals that are capable of feeling. This is condemned by Singer as *speciesism*. Animals seem to have, in higher species, no less capacity for suffering. Therefore, there should be equality of consideration, with no special privilege for the human. Of course, not all animals have the same capacity for suffering. The amoeba is less capable of experiencing pain than a gorilla or dolphin. Much depends on scientific enquiry to determine the capacity for suffering.

It should be noted that 'animal liberation' is something different from 'animal rights'. Singer makes no claim for animal rights, any more than he accepts human natural rights. The justification for not maltreating animals is the capacity for suffering.

In these arguments, Singer is in the tradition of Bentham. Bentham argued:

> It may one day come to be recognized that the number of legs, the villosity of the skin, or the termination of the *os sacrum* are reasons equally insufficient for abandoning a sensitive being ... What else is it that should trace the insuperable line? Is it the faculty of reason, or perhaps the faculty of discourse? But a full-grown horse or dog is beyond comparison a more rational, as well as a more conversable animal, than an infant of a day or a week or even a month, old. But suppose they were otherwise, what would it avail? The question is not Can they **reason**?, nor Can they **talk**?, but Can they **suffer**?
>
> Jeremy Bentham: *An Introduction to the Principles of Morals and Legislation*, 1823, Chapter 17

Singer's arguments are developed by practical examples, many of which have proved controversial.

An instance of Singer's overall application of principles would be his treatment of the haemophiliac infant. (See *Practical Ethics*: third edition, Cambridge University Press, pp. 162–165.) Haemophilia is a condition carried by the female but inherited by males. This potentially fatal disease means that the blood cannot clot, and the haemophiliac child is in constant danger of death. If a mother carries the gene, there is a 50% chance that a male foetus will have the condition. As medicine stands, the condition cannot be detected before birth. Where the gene is in the mother, abortion is offered when tests show she is carrying a male foetus. Remember that Singer's aim is to reduce overall suffering. He considers the issue of replaceability. If a mother loses a child, he can in principle be replaced. Aborting a fetus because of a 50% chance of haemophilia seems unnecessary: it would be wiser to kill a haemophiliac child after birth, as there would be only half the destruction:

> Self-awareness, which could provide a basis for holding that it is wrong to kill one being and replace it with another, is not to be found in either the fetus or the newborn infant. Neither the fetus nor the newborn infant is an individual capable of regarding itself as a distinct entity with a life of its own to lead, and it is only for newborn infants, or for still earlier stages of human life, that replaceability should be considered to be an ethically acceptable option.
>
> Peter Singer: *Practical Ethics* (2011), pp.164–165

This conclusion is controversial because for many, it contradicts their belief in the sacredness of human life. Believers in natural human rights would reject the entire approach.

5 Objections to utilitarianism

There have been many objections to utilitarianism. The literature generated has been vast. Some doubts have been mentioned above, but other points are included below.

- Some have questioned whether utilitarianism should be considered a genuine moral theory at all. If the purpose of a moral theory is to do good, a theory which includes evil seems hardly a moral theory at all. Utilitarianism permits harm to be done, provided that the evil is outweighed by good. It may be questioned whether this can be called moral.

- The evil permitted may be needlessly great in ways that are counter-intuitive as well as wrong in themselves. Suppose I have two possible courses of action. If I perform one, I achieve 500 points of good, but no harm. In the other instance, I create 1,000 points of harm, but 501 points of good. Remember that utilitarianism demands that I always seek to achieve the greatest balance of good over evil. 501 is a greater balance than 500, so I should perform the second act, even though that is at the cost of great evil, when the first does no one harm. This seems odd, especially if we believe that the aim of the moral person is to do good and to avoid evil. By performing the second act, I have allowed great harm into the world. Intuitively, this seems wrong, as more and more great evils can be permitted for the sake of the greater good. It is helpful to consider this point in relation to Mill's arguments about buying opium or poisons, where to preserve the rule individuals are permitted to do great harm to themselves.

- There is in utilitarianism, as in any **teleological** theory, a fundamental question of how capable we are of calculating outcomes of the decisions we make. To make a sound decision we need all relevant information. This is not always available. Indeed, the nature of some situations means that not all the information *could* be available. We see things always from our perspective, and just as when we look at a landscape, some things are hidden from us because they cannot be seen from where we are standing. And even if we are in an ideal position to gather all possible information, we may be restricted in time. Sometimes – often – we need to decide our actions quickly. If a man is threatening a child, we need to act at once. It is not possible to go through a process of calculation.

- In the same way, we need sufficient intellectual ability to make the appropriate decisions. This is not true at all stages in life or for every person. Is someone not very capable of reasoning through a moral dilemma incapable of being moral?

- In any teleological theory such as utilitarianism, it becomes very difficult to determine whether the agent has performed a good act. If I save someone from drowning, the immediate action may be seen as good. I have reduced harm and maximised good, making me a good agent performing a good act. But the person I have saved might, in future, turn out to be a mass murderer. I could not have known this. Does my act then become a bad act, having been considered a good act when I performed it? The future consequences of apparently good acts are always uncertain. The person I saved might be a good person, but his son, who would not have been born had I not saved his father, might turn out to be the mass-murderer. Given that the future is unknown and there are so often unforeseen consequences, are we ever able to describe a given action as unequivocally good or bad?

- Morality entails more than doing the right thing. Part of morality and the moral life involves such activities as judging the actions of

Key term

Teleological A principle whose goodness or rightness is determined by the outcome.

others, giving counsel and educating the young. As suggested above, it is much more sensible – and liable to bring better results – to tell a child always to obey a particular rule than to tell her always to work out the greatest balance of good over evil. In counselling, if I were a Benthamite hedonist, concerned only with my own pleasure, could I counsel you to act in your best interests, or should I always counsel you with my eye fixed on what would be best for me? Singer recognises that we need to be altruistic in our utilitarianism, so this objection might not appear so effective in his case as with Bentham. But if it is hard to determine my own best interests it is perhaps harder to determine the good outcome from your perspective than from my own. Judgements of any type seem fraught with difficulty.

- The absence of rights is an issue for anyone who believes that there are natural rights. Utilitarianism, in all its forms, seems to exalt the general goal of utilitarianism, whether that is pleasure or a more general happiness, above the person. It seems to make the good of the person secondary. A Kantian, but not only Kantians, would find this unacceptable. The second form of the categorical imperative ('So act as to treat everyone, yourself or another, always as ends, and never as means only') insists on the priority of ends over means, and the good for Kant is ultimately always the good of a person. Kantianism condemns the sacrifice of a person for an abstraction. A good is surely a good only if it is experienced as a good, and such experience can only be felt by someone (however that 'someone' is defined: we might wish our definition to apply also to sentient, suffering animals). If good is always good for a person, that suggests the priority of the person over even general happiness. The denial of natural rights seems to permit actual harm for a person for the sake of the general good.

- A slightly more difficult but ingenious objection has been developed by Sir Bernard Williams. A consequence of a utilitarian outlook is that the conscientious utilitarian will be always on her guard to prevent harm. To do this often entails taking preventative action, doing something in itself unpleasant to prevent something worse. If everyone were to act on utilitarian principles, then there would be these preventative but rather nasty acts taking place everywhere. The result would be a proliferation of acts which are evil in themselves, so the overall picture would be worse than if no one were performing these unpleasant acts. Therefore, on utilitarian grounds, it is better for the majority of people not to be utilitarians. That suggests that the only utilitarians should perhaps be a small elite. But if that were true, utilitarianism is a philosophy that most of us ought not to follow. Williams concludes:

… the world which would satisfy the utilitarian's aspirations would be a world from which belief in utilitarianism as an overall moral doctrine was totally absent …

So, if utilitarianism is true … then it is better that people should not believe in utilitarianism. If, on the other hand, it is false, then it is certainly better that people should not believe in it. So, either way, it is better that people should not believe in it.

Bernard Williams: *Morality: An Introduction to Ethics* (1993), p. 98

Key person

Sir Bernard Williams (1929–2003): British moral philosopher. Taught at Oxford until 1988, then at Berkeley, California until his death. Author of many books and essays, including *Morality: An Introduction to Ethics* (1972), *Moral Luck* (1981), *Ethics and the Limits of Philosophy* (1985).

Religion and ethics

6 Conclusions

As an apparently simple and easily applicable moral theory, utilitarianism has provoked many reactions and many forms, and, as we have seen, many criticisms. Most of these have been about the extent to which it might be thought to diminish the human being. If morality is for the sake of humankind, it seems to many thinkers that utilitarianism promotes a principle above the person. Nevertheless, it must be admitted that in hard decisions, most people do indeed seek to do what will lead to the smallest amount of harm and the most good. Utilitarianism seems to take this reality of human decision-making and apply it to all cases.

The question is whether this is true of every case. Often, we experience no such difficulty. I do not calculate, normally, whether to tell the truth or whether to avoid murdering or raping people. This is not because of calculation, but because I just prefer truth-telling and not being involved in violence, and it seems overall a better world when I do so. But I do not coldly and unemotionally calculate these actions and non-actions. Most of the time, the overall good or harm is not a motive of which I am conscious, which suggests that utilitarianism is not a natural way of thinking.

Consider friendship. I meet people in a variety of contexts, and I find a connection with some of them – and they with me – and we call our relationship 'friendship'. If someone is my friend, she is my friend, we have an affinity. But it would be an odd sort of friendship if it rested on a cold calculation of the utility of the friendship and I broke the friendship because it might bring me distress if she needed me. Aristotle thought friendships based on utility unsatisfactory:

> *Utility is something impermanent as it changes according to circumstances. With the disappearance of the grounds for friendship, the friendship also breaks up, because this [utility] is what kept it alive.*

Aristotle: *Nicomachean Ethics*: Book VIII, iii

If utilitarianism's justification is based, as it seems to be, on the experience of hard cases, then we might think about the lawyers' saying that 'hard cases make bad law'. What the lawyers mean is that to make a general legal requirement from an individual difficulty leads to muddle and unexpected consequences. Perhaps the same is true of the moral theory based on the hard case.

Study advice

Here, as throughout the course, the most important thing is to treat arguments not as bullet-points to be learned but as matters to reflect on and to ponder as you reach your own conclusions. It is important to know the main types of utilitarianism. In preparation, reflect on possible criticisms. We have listed many, so it is valuable to think about this and to select the three or four about which you feel most confident. It is unlikely that you would have time in the examination to spell out every criticism we have indicated, or all the others that you may encounter in your reading.

This is why, in preparing for the examination it is important to think about which criticisms you would use. Selecting before the examination is much wiser than thinking about this in the examination room.

In writing, be careful to use terms and definitions accurately. Incidentally, someone who supports utilitarianism is called a 'utilitarian', not a 'utilitarianist', just to remind you to avoid a mistake often seen in student essays. Do not fall into the trap of describing utilitarianism as concerned with 'the greatest good of the greatest number'.

Summary diagram: Utilitarianism

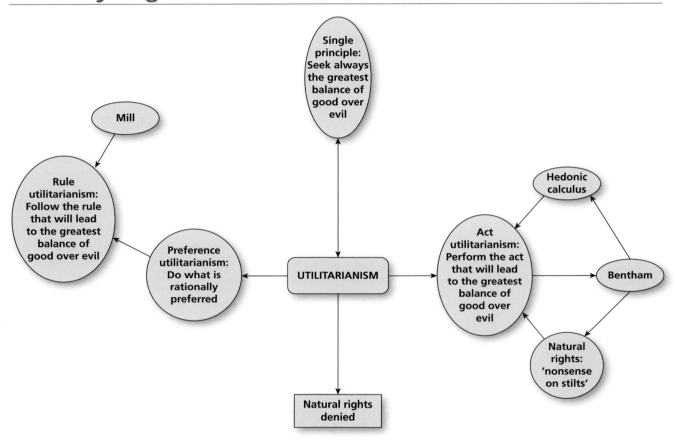

Revision advice

By the end of the chapter you should feel confident about explaining both the general principle of utilitarianism and its different forms in the work of three of its most famous proponents, Jeremy Bentham (act utilitarianism), John Stuart Mill (rule utilitarianism) and the contemporary writer, Peter Singer (preference utilitarianism). You should be able to compare the relative merits and problems of these different forms of utilitarianism and to distinguish hedonic from other types of utilitarianism. You should also be able to reflect on issues of determining outcomes and consider the implications of views which deny the possibility of natural rights.

Can you give brief definitions of:
- the principle of utility
- act utilitarianism
- rule utilitarianism
- preference utilitarianism
- hedonism?

Revision advice (continued)

Can you explain:
- the reasons why utilitarianism seeks to be a single-principle theory
- how Mill's approach to utilitarianism differed from that of his teacher, Jeremy Bentham
- how rule utilitarianism differs from act utilitarianism
- how utilitarianism treats questions of rights?

Can you give arguments for and against:
- hedonist treatments of utilitarianism
- individuals having natural rights even when contrary to the general good
- act utilitarianism
- rule utilitarianism?

Sample question and guidance

'In having no place for rights, utilitarianism fails as a moral theory.' Discuss.

This question asks you to reach a specific conclusion about the success of utilitarianism. Many objections could be brought against the theory, as we have seen, but this title asks you to concentrate on just one area of objection. Good answers would obviously sketch utilitarianism as a theory (though there is perhaps no need to describe every variety as, for this essay, the same points apply to them all), but go on to demonstrate why as a single-principle theory it can have no room for other considerations, especially those of natural rights.

It would be good practice to demonstrate your points with examples of utilitarianism in practice disregarding rights. Giving examples is always good in philosophical writing, both because doing so demonstrates understanding but also because a specific example can sometimes suggest further lines of thought that you can then use later in the essay.

In this essay it is also helpful to consider what natural rights might include. Most natural rights theorists include life and liberty, perhaps developing the list specifically to include ideas such as freedom of religion, speech and assembly. Some include rights to own property and also a right to security. In what ways might utilitarianism infringe on these rights? You might wish also to consider whether Mill's notion of liberty, based not on rights but utility, would sufficiently safeguard those things protected by rights theories.

In reaching your final judgement, take care to justify carefully the points you make.

Further essay questions:

Assess how valuable act utilitarianism is in resolving moral dilemmas.

To what extent is utilitarianism helpful in living a truly moral life?

'Rule utilitarianism works as a moral theory, but act utilitarianism does not.' Discuss.

Going further

The literature on utilitarianism is vast, and there is no easy way to grasp it all. Most textbooks on ethics have at least a chapter on the subject, not least because it has been so influential in the English-speaking world. Bentham's own writings are not always easy to read. John Stuart Mill's style is more approachable, though it can take a little while to become used to his sentence structure. Both his *Utilitarianism* and *On Liberty* are brief texts and may be read for their richness in ideas. Peter Singer is always worth reading as a provocative and consistent thinker. His prose is very clear and it would be helpful to read at least Chapter One of *Practical Ethics*. As always, it is important to read original texts whenever possible.

The final chapter of Bernard Williams: *Morality: An Introduction to Ethics*, (Cambridge University Press, 1993) summarises a range of objections. These are explored in more detail in *Utilitarianism: For and Against*, by J. J. C. Smart and Bernard Williams (Cambridge University Press, 1973). The discussion of utilitarianism in William Frankena: *Ethics* (Pearson, 1988) is concise but admirable, especially in its discussion of different types of utilitarianism. Michael Sandel provides a very clear exposition in his *Justice: What's the Right Thing to Do?* (Penguin, 2009).

Other books discussed in this chapter are:
- Singer P. *Animal Liberation:* Preface to 1975 edition (HarperCollins, 1975, revised edition 1990, Pimlico, 1995).
- Singer P. *Practical Ethics*: (third edition, Cambridge University Press, 2011).
- Williams B. *Ethics and the Limits of Philosophy* (Collins, 1985).
- Williams B. *Moral Luck* (Cambridge University Press, 1981).
- Williams B. *Morality: An Introduction to Ethics* (Cambridge University Press, 1972/1993).

Chapter 14

Euthanasia

1 Introduction

Case study: 'Devoted husband kills wife'

In May 2007, a newspaper headline read 'Devoted husband in 'mercy killing' of depressed wife is found guilty of murder' (*The Daily Telegraph*). Frank Lund had been happily married to his wife for 33 years, but she was severely depressed caused by an acute form of irritable bowel syndrome and had taken a large dose of pills. He bought the tablets for her, but soon after taking them she began to be sick. He was afraid she would not die and because he had promised her that she would not wake up in hospital he put a plastic bag over her head and smothered her with a pillow.

The case is significant because groups campaigning for euthanasia did not give their support to Lund. Why was this? The answer is that Patricia Lund's condition was not life threatening and therefore Frank Lund's action was the direct and immediate cause of her death.

Key question

Euthanasia means literally 'a good death' but is it good to allow a person to choose when they wish to die?

2 A problem of definition

The case raises a basic problem of distinguishing between the right to suicide, assisted suicide, euthanasia, murder and manslaughter (or involuntary homicide). This is not just confusing for those involved in making medical ethics decisions, but also for what it implies about the way we view the value of life and the role of society.

- **Suicide** is when a person dies as a direct result of their own voluntary action.
- **Assisted suicide** is when a person dies as a direct result of their own voluntary action but with the help of another person. This is different from

Persistent vegetative state (PVS) A condition where a patient with severe brain damage is in a state of very limited arousal rather than true awareness or consciousness. The condition is usually regarded as irreversible.

Palliative care The use of drugs and medicine to relieve pain but without directly causing the death of patients.

Key quote

The ability to make complex judgements about benefit requires compassion, experience and an appreciation of the patient's view point.

The British Medical Association (*Medical Ethics Today*, p. 170) about treatment of PVS patients.

voluntary euthanasia only insofar as the person may have many reasons for wanting to die. Their condition does not have to be life threatening.

■ **Physician aided suicide** is when a person dies as a direct result of their own voluntary action but with the help of a doctor or physician.

■ **Physician aid in dying** is when a person's death is hastened but not directly caused by the aid (for example, medication) of a doctor or physician.

■ **Voluntary euthanasia** is when a person's death is directly caused by another person (perhaps a doctor) at their request and with their consent. Most arguments today assume that the person requesting to die is suffering from an incurable or terminal illness and is in great pain.

■ **Passive euthanasia** is when a doctor or physician withdraws life-sustaining treatment which indirectly causes death. Alternatively, the physician allows a patient to die by 'letting nature take its course'.

■ **Non-voluntary euthanasia** is when a person's life is ended without their consent but with the consent of someone representing their interests. For example, a doctor or the courts may decide that a person who is in a persistent vegetative state (PVS) should have his or her life-sustaining treatment removed.

Many of these terms appear to be interchangeable. For example, is passive euthanasia the same as physician aid in dying? Many people who support the view that a doctor may give palliative care which indirectly hastens death nevertheless resist calling this euthanasia. In their own mind this distinguishes between treatment, which is passive (indirect killing) and care which is active (directly reducing pain and killing).

Although the distinction between suicide and euthanasia is the involvement of another person, the fundamental issue is whether it is morally licit or permissible for a person to take their own life.

3 The law and euthanasia

Key question

What reasons should be given to make euthanasia legal?

Until 1961, suicide in the UK was a criminal offence. Although the 1961 Suicide Act decriminalised suicide, it *did not* make it morally licit. As the Suicide Act has direct consequences for euthanasia, it is worth noting its two major clauses.

(a) 1961 Suicide Act

1   The rule of law whereby it is a crime for a person to commit suicide is hereby abrogated.

2   (1) A person who aids, abets, counsels or procures the suicide of another or an attempt by another to commit suicide shall be liable for a term not exceeding fourteen years.

(2) If on the trial of an indictment for murder or manslaughter it is proved that the accused aided, abetted, counselled or procured the suicide of the person in question, the jury may find him guilty of that offence.

Many think that law now supports the principle of autonomy. But, in fact the Act reinforces the principle of the sanctity of life by criminalising any form of assisted suicide. On the other hand, the Act does not hold the **vitalist** position that all life is equally valuable and should be preserved at all costs because there are cases when allowing a person to die is the better course of action.

Key term

Vitalism The view that human life is always sacred because it possesses a God-given soul.

Key question

Does a very sick person have a legal right to assisted suicide or euthanasia?

(b) The right to self-determination

This distinction was famously illustrated in the Diane Pretty case in 2002. Diane Pretty, who was paralysed from the neck down with motor neurone disease, had asked her doctors to assist in her suicide. Her lawyers had presented the case based on the right to self-determination. But her case was not upheld even when taken to the European Court of Human Rights. The reason given was that although the law recognises the right to life, it does not consider its corollary is the right to die. Most importantly, the courts decided that Mrs Pretty was not suffering from a life-threatening condition. If she *had* been, then doctors might have been able to argue that they could assist *in* her dying, even though they could not have helped in the direct *cause* of her death.

On the other hand, the case of Baby Charlotte in 2005 who was born prematurely and with severe brain damage, illustrates that the law does not consider life to be absolutely sacred. Against the wishes of her parents, the High Court ordered the doctors not to resuscitate the baby if she fell into a coma. The principle was that her underlying condition did not justify the medical assistance she was being given just to stay alive.

Diane Pretty (1958–2002) was diagnosed with motor neurone disease and although she argued under the Human Rights Act (1998) that she had a right to assisted suicide this was rejected by the British courts

(c) Physician aid in dying and the slippery slope problem

Many consider that the law has led to considerable confusion and that one way of developing the present situation is to create a new Act which would permit physician aid in dying. The proposal states that there should be a bill to:

> *... enable a competent adult who is suffering unbearably as a result of a terminal illness to receive medical assistance to die at his own considered and persistent request; and to make provision for a person suffering from a terminal illness to receive pain relief medication.*

Assisted Dying for the Terminally Ill Bill, 2004

Key term

Slippery slope An argument that claims that if a rule is weakened, even for good reasons, then what eventually follows if the rule is again weakened for good reasons will be highly undesirable.

One of the major objections to proposals of this kind is the fear that it will suffer from the **slippery slope** whereby what begins as legitimate reasons to assist in a person's death will also permit non-lethal conditions.

In a letter to *The Times* (24 September 2004), a group of eminent academic lawyers and philosophers, including John Haldane and Alasdair MacIntyre, argued that:

■ Supporters of the Bill slide from making the condition one of *actual* unbearable suffering from terminal illness to merely the *fear*, discomfort and loss of dignity which terminal illness might bring.
■ If quality of life is grounds for euthanasia for those who request it, then logically this could be extended to those who do not request it (or who are unable to request it).
■ In the Netherlands where euthanasia is permitted, there is evidence to indicate that many die against their wishes, this shows that the law cannot easily place safeguards against those who simply choose to ignore them.

But Helga Kuhse challenges proponents of the slippery slope argument to provide empirical evidence to support their case. Her conclusion is that the slippery slope argument is used by scaremongers to support their complete ban on all forms of euthanasia. The most frequently cited example of the slippery slope argument is the active non-voluntary euthanasia practised by the Nazis during the holocaust years as a form of **eugenics** where the deaths of millions were justified as part of the 'improvement' of society. Kuhse concludes:

> While the Nazi 'euthanasia' programme is often cited as an example of what can happen when a society acknowledges that some lives are not worthy to be lived, the motivation behind these killings was neither mercy nor respect for autonomy; it was, rather, racial prejudice and the belief that the racial purity of the Volk required the elimination of certain individuals and groups. As already noted, in the Netherlands a 'social experiment' with active voluntary euthanasia is currently in progress. As yet there is no evidence that this has sent Dutch society down a slippery slope.

Helga Kuhse: *Companion to Ethics* Ed. Peter Singer (1993), p. 302

4 Sanctity of life principle

Within Christian traditions, there are many versions of the sanctity of life argument because although the basic proposition is that life is sacred and given to humans by God, modern medical advances have made it increasingly more difficult to determine whether a person has reached a stage where 'life' is still worth living. Some suggest that this weak sanctity of life view is really just another version of the quality of life argument. There is fierce discussion whether this is so, and whether it matters. Those who hold to a **strong sanctity of life** view strongly defend the sanctity of life against all non-religious views which dilute or modify it.

(a) Strong sanctity of life arguments against euthanasia

There are a number of terms used to define the strong sanctity of life principle. In political circles it is often referred to as the pro-life position and in philosophical terms it corresponds to vitalism. Vitalists argue that a human life is always sacred because it possesses a God-given soul and that there are no **ordinary or extraordinary means** which justify the termination of a human life – even from the moment of conception.

The sanctity of life principle is based on Jewish and Christian biblical ideas:

- **Life is set apart by God.** In Christian thought, every human being is created in the image and likeness of God. To be created in God's image implies that humans are set apart and different from all other creatures and that every human being possesses a 'spark' of divinity (Genesis 1:27) within them which sets them apart from other creatures

Key terms

Incarnation The Christian teaching that God became human in the form of Jesus Christ.

Intrinsic value Means that something or someone is of value in itself and independently of whether it is of use or value to someone else.

Key quotes

So God created humankind in his image, in the image of God he created them.

Genesis 1:27

Be fruitful and multiply, and fill the earth and subdue it; and have dominion over… every living thing that moves upon the earth.

Genesis 1:28

And the Word became flesh and lived among us.

John 1:14

Parable of the Good Samaritan see Chapter 19, page 312 for a more detailed explanation.

Key term

Blasphemy Means to dishonour God by setting oneself up to be equal or greater than he is.

(Genesis 1:28). The **incarnation** of the Word of God as man in the person of Jesus (John 1:14) reaffirms the sanctity, holiness and **intrinsic value** of every human life unconditionally in its relationship with God.

- **Life is a gift from God and is on loan to humans.** If God is the author of life, then it follows that he is the one who determines when it should end (Job 1:21). It is not up to the individual whether he or she might add or subtract from his or her life or anyone else's because life is a gift or a loan from God. God is a providential God who through nature or other means is the only being who may directly terminate a person's life.
- **An innocent life is always to be respected.** Taking a life is broader than simply killing and the prohibition in the Ten Commandments (Exodus 20:13) not to murder is part of the social glue which equally shows respect for parents, property, marriage, husband and neighbour. The command in Deuteronomy 30:19–20 to 'choose life' is the believer's response to honour God and respect life.
- **Life is always to be loved and protected.** Love requires the Christian to respect and protect all humans regardless of status, gender and age. This is illustrated in Jesus' Parable of the Good Samaritan (Luke 10:29–37) when a Samaritan overcomes prejudices to help a badly injured man. Love is a central Christian principle. Just as Jesus' life and death is a sign of God's love for the world (John 3:16), so must each person sacrifice his or her own well-being for the lives of others (1 John 3:17–18).

Key quotes

Naked I came from my mother's womb, and naked shall I return there; the LORD gave, and the LORD has taken away; blessed be the name of the LORD.

Job 1:21

You shall not murder.

Exodus 20:13

I call heaven to earth to witness against you today that I have set before you life and death, blessing and curses. Choose life so that you and your descendants may live …

Deuteronomy 30:19

For God so loved the world that he gave his only Son, that everyone who believes in him may not perish but may have eternal life.

John 3:16

Love is patient … It bears all things, believes all things, hopes all things, endures all things.

1 Corinthians 13:4, 6

According to the strong sanctity of life principle euthanasia is always wrong. This is reinforced by the Bible's condemnation of suicide. According to the Bible suicide is **blasphemy** because it is a deliberate rejection of

God's gift of life. It is also blasphemous because it rejects God's redemption through his victory over death through the resurrection of Christ. To deliberately choose death is in effect to deny that redemption is possible. This is why King Saul (1 Samuel 31:4) and Judas (Matthew 27:3–5), who both committed suicide are both strongly condemned by the Bible as those who rejected God's love.

The Roman Catholic Church also rejects euthanasia. Pope St John Paul II in his *Evangelium Vitae* (1995) argues that by accepting euthanasia contemporary society has undermined the sanctity of life and by developing a 'culture of death' devalued the dignity and respect of all humans. This is very dangerous for it marginalises the weak, the ill and the disabled.

> *A person who, because of illness, handicap or, more simply, just by existing, compromises the well-being or life-style of those who are more favoured tends to be looked upon as an enemy to be resisted or eliminated. In this way a kind of 'conspiracy against life' is unleashed.*
>
> *Evangelium Vitae* chapter 1, paragraph 12

Key question

What does the pope mean when he says that rejecting the sanctity of life is a 'conspiracy against life'?

(b) Weak sanctity of life arguments for euthanasia

The Christian **weak sanctity of life** argument does not consider that killing an innocent person out of love is morally equivalent to murder. Murder implies some ulterior motive such as revenge, cruelty, greed or hatred. Suicide, or more particularly euthanasia, as an act of love in exceptional circumstances is not morally wrong.

Key term

Weak sanctity of life principle The belief that although human life is always valuable, there may be situations where it would cause more harm than good to continue with it.

- **No one has a duty to endure a life of extreme pain.** Although Paul calls Christians to be a 'living sacrifice' (Romans 12:1), this does not mean enduring extraordinary pain or suffering.
- **Life is a gift not a burden.** If life is given to us as a gift, it is also given so that we may use it responsibly and dispose of it as we wish. It would not be a gift if the giver still had ownership of it. Therefore, as humans are now owners of God's gift of life, it is up to them as good stewards of this life (Genesis 1:28) to decide when to end it.

5 Quality of life principle

Key terms

Quality of life principle States that human life has to possess certain attributes in order to have value. These attributes might include experience of happiness, having autonomy, being conscious.

Instrumentalism The view that something or someone is of value only if it useful and achieves a desired end or purpose.

The **quality of life principle** takes an **instrumentalist** view of human life; a life is only worthwhile if it can fulfil those things which make life worth living. There is nothing intrinsically good about being alive except as a means of enabling us to experience those things which are desired. In other words, human life has to possess certain attributes in order to have value.

(a) The rejection of the sanctity of life principle

Peter Singer is a prominent philosopher who has strongly argued that it is time now to abandon the sanctity of life principle in favour of the non-religious quality of life argument. Singer's arguments develop John Locke's notion that the value of life depends on a person's ability to have desires and preferences and not on some mystical 'enduring self' or soul which automatically gives priority to humans above all other animals.

Key question

Does the religious concept of sanctity of life have any meaning in twenty-first century medical ethics; should it be replaced with a quality of life principle?

For a profile of Peter Singer, see page 198.

Key person

John Locke (1632–1704): A British philosopher and one of the 'British empiricists' (including Hume and Berkeley). He was one of the first to argue that the human mind and identity are to be viewed in terms of the continuity of consciousness. His book, *An Essay Concerning Human Understanding* (1690), continues to have great influence today in the area of philosophy of mind.

In *Rethinking Life and Death* (1994) Singer sets out his five new rational quality of life commandments to replace those of the traditional sanctity of life position:

- Recognise that the worth of human life varies.
- Take responsibility for the consequences of your decision.
- Respect a person's desire to live or die.
- Bring children into the world only if they are wanted.
- Do not discriminate on the basis of species.

Peter Singer: *Rethinking Life and Death* (1994), pp. 190–202

In 1983, Singer caused controversy with the following comment on the Baby Doe abortion case in the USA:

> *If we compare a severely defective human infant with a nonhuman animal, a dog or a pig, for example, we will often find the non-human to have superior capacities, both actual and potential, for rationality, self-consciousness, communication, and anything else that can plausibly be considered morally significant.*

Peter Singer: *Rethinking Life and Death* (1994), p. 201

However, if the quality of life ethic is adopted, there is still the difficult task of determining the primary principle which permits or restrains a person from taking a life (their own or someone else's). Set out below are various versions of the quality of life arguments each of which offers a rational basis for judging what constitutes a worthwhile life.

(b) Happiness as the basis for the quality of life principle

For many the basic criterion for judging whether life is worthwhile is whether at any given moment a person's happiness outweighs his or her unhappiness. A bad quality of life is a life in which unhappiness or pain outweighs happiness. This is the view held by most utilitarians.

In the case of euthanasia, the utilitarian might make one of the following judgements:

- **Total happiness judgement**. If a person is happy in life then the longer he or she lives, the greater the quality of life they have. But if that person no longer has any quality of life (because they are in pain) because the sum of their happiness cannot be increased, then their life is no longer worth living and can be ended.
- **Average happiness judgement**. If a person's average level of happiness in life can be maintained at a high level, then he or she has a greater quality of life. But if that person no longer has any quality of life when the average of his happiness declines permanently from a previous peak, then their life is no longer worth living and can be ended.
- **Higher qualities judgement**. A person's quality of life is judged by certain minimum standards which are necessary to live a happy life. This might include: memory, ability to form relationships, ability to reason and hope for a future. So, if a person lacks these minimum qualities or the possibility of their development is lacking, then there is no quality of life and life is no longer worth living and can be ended.

Key question

Should a person have complete autonomy over their own life and decisions made about it?

Key term

Liberal principle As developed by Mill and others is that as humans are the best judge of their own happiness they should be given maximum freedom or liberty to live their lives as they consider appropriate.

For a profile of Mill, see page 64.

Key quote

Over himself, over his own body and mind, the individual is sovereign.
John Stuart Mill: *On Liberty* (1859)

Key term

Paternalism Means literally to 'act in a fatherly way' and justifies overriding a person's autonomy if it is for their own good.

Key person

Jonathan Glover (b. 1941): A British philosopher specialising in ethics. His book *Causing Death and Saving Lives* (1977) takes a broadly consequential ethical position on issues such as euthanasia, war and abortion.

From one of these various utilitarian points of view, a person who considers that his or her life lacks value is justified in ending their life through suicide. Those in favour of voluntary euthanasia argue that they should be assisted in doing so in order to make their death as painless as possible.

(c) Autonomy as the basis of quality of life principle

Many argue that the arguments above could be more coherently expressed without necessarily referring to utilitarianism. The value of life comes from the ability to determine one's future, that is 'self-rule' or autonomy. So, although utilitarianism may value autonomy as the means by which preferences can be made, it is not valuable *in itself*. The value of autonomy as an expression of being a human person has a long history but is particularly significant in present day ethical discussions.

John Stuart Mill developed the **liberal principle** in his influential book *On Liberty* (1859). The significance of liberty is that it is the chief means by which a person determines his or her values. A liberal society avoids 'tyrannising' (Mill's phrase) the minority by the majority and aims to maximise personal freedoms wherever possible. Mill's form of liberalism suggests that taking one's own life is a matter of personal autonomy. The only reason for interference would be if doing so would cause harm to others. As Mill argues, causing self-harm is not in itself a reason for interference by others:

> He cannot rightfully be compelled to do or forbear because it will be better for him to do so, because it will make him happier, because, in the opinions of others, to do so would be wise or even right.

John Stuart Mill: *On Liberty*, chapter 1

Mill's argument raises many problems. For example, how is harm to be defined – physically or mentally? Is interference justified if the person is not acting rationally, either because they are too young or because they are temporarily mentally disturbed?

Mill's liberalism can allow for **paternalism** if it is in a person's best interests to over-rule their autonomy. But to do so implies that there is either a standard greater than autonomy which justifies interference or that an individual may not know what is good for them. In many cases, the liberal may just have to leave it to the individual to make their own decisions regardless of whether it causes them harm. It is a matter of dispute whether self-harm which leads to death justifies paternalism or not. This is why the issue of suicide is particularly important.

(d) Consciousness as the basis for quality of life

Jonathan Glover argues that being alive is not itself a sufficient condition for that life being valuable. For a life to be worthwhile it must also be conscious. This means that killing a life is not in itself wrong, it is only wrong if that life is conscious. Glover takes an instrumentalist view of the body; the body is important only in so far as it enables conscious experiences to be possible.

Key quote

Even if we felt confident that we could find a very general account of what makes life valuable for human beings, perhaps by singling out the most important or most frequently occurring features from the lists of what they value of a large cross-section of people, we would have no reason to suppose we had arrived at a satisfactory account.

John Harris:
The Value of Life (1990), pp. 15–16

I have no way of refuting someone who holds that being alive, even though unconscious, is intrinsically valuable. But it is a view that will seem unattractive to those of us who, in our own case, see a life of permanent coma as in no way preferable to death. From a subjective point of view, there is nothing to choose between the two.

Jonathan Glover: *Causing Death and Saving Lives* (1977), p. 45

Glover's argument therefore supports non-voluntary euthanasia for PVS patients. But what about cases where a person is suffering from dementia, Alzheimer's disease, severe brain damage or such severe pain that consciousness is greatly reduced? These examples might suggest that with limited consciousness then the ability to feel happiness and express preferences are so diminished that there is also a case for voluntary euthanasia.

6 Voluntary euthanasia

Key question

Is there a moral difference between medical intervention to end a patient's life and medical non-intervention to end a patient's life?

(a) Allowing to die and cutting short a life

The problem of euthanasia is that it has to straddle both principle and practicalities. Those who consider that there should not be a right to terminate an innocent life nevertheless argue that there are circumstances when some form of assisted dying is permissible. On the other hand. others consider this to be morally confusing and argue that there are circumstances when 'cutting short' a life is not only permissible but good.

Case study: Dr David Moor

His trial concerned the death in 1977 of George Liddell, an 85-year-old former ambulance worker who had recently been discharged from hospital after treatment for bowel cancer. He was bedridden, having suffered a stroke and a heart attack, and was doubly incontinent, deaf, diabetic and anaemic.

The prosecution case hung upon a morphine injection Dr Moor gave to Mr Liddell on the morning of his death. When the investigation began, the doctor had not disclosed the injection to police or NHS officials. He later gave details, saying that he had been panicked by media attention into withholding the information.

Outside the court, Dr Moor repeated his philosophy, saying: 'In caring for a terminally ill patient, a doctor is entitled to give pain-relieving medication which may have the incidental effect of hastening death. All I tried to do in treating Mr Liddell was to relieve his agony, distress and suffering. This has always been my approach in treating my patients with care and compassion. Doctors who treat dying patients to relieve their pain and suffering walk a tightrope to achieve this.' He insisted that the morphine he gave Mr Liddell was to relieve his pain and was in no way a lethal dose.

Detective Superintendent Colin Dobson of Northumbria Police said: 'To a police officer and the criminal justice system, the terms mercy killing and euthanasia are meaningless. If you shorten someone's life by minutes, that's murder, and by law we had to approach our investigation from this viewpoint.'

'Cheers as GP is cleared of murdering patient'

The Times 12 May 12 1999

Dr Moor was acquitted of murder in 1999.

The Moor case illustrates the tension between those such as Dr Moor who argue that allowing to die is not the same as killing and those such as the detective who consider that there is either killing or not killing. The former position is largely supported by deontologists who support the doctrine of double effect and the second view by consequentialists such as utilitarians and situationists.

(b) Consequentialism: end and means

For most consequentialists, all that matters in order to judge a situation is that the outcome is good or bad. Consequentialists reject the distinction made by some deontologists between **acts and omissions**. The acts and omissions principle distinguishes between willing to do x (which is morally culpable or blameworthy) and omitting or refraining to do x (which is not morally culpable if doing x would be to act immorally).

For example, a doctor who refrains from giving a very old and sick person life-prolonging drugs might do so because he reasons that nature should be allowed to take its course. From the deontological point of view, it is not that he has killed his patient but in allowing him to die he has done so out of respect for the life which he is presently living.

For the consequentialists, an omission, such as failing to give a patient some life-preserving drugs and allowing him to die, is morally equivalent to giving a patient drugs which hasten death if both actions result in the death of the patient.

But is the consequentialist position entirely consistent?

If A chooses to shoot B, then we classify this as an intended act. If C sees A and fails to stop A shooting B, then this is an intended omission. Is C at all blameworthy? C could claim that by not acting he was simply complying with another principle (for example, never involve one's self in other people's affairs). Although the consequentialist claims to judge just the outcome, he does nevertheless assume that there are some significant non-consequential factors, such as the duty of the doctor to be responsible for his patients.

(c) Deontology: the doctrine of double effect

A key distinction between consequentialists and deontologists is the place and nature of intention. For deontologists whether an act is intended or not intended is crucial in determining if a person is or is not blameworthy for their action, whereas for the consequentialist what matters is whether the act produces greater or lesser good.

A much-disputed area in this context is the doctrine of double effect which is supported by deontologists but rejected by consequentialists. The doctrine of double effect states that a person may morally perform an act which he or she foresees will produce good *and* evil if:

- The action in itself from the outset is good.
- The good effect and not the evil is intended.
- The good effect is not produced by means of the evil effect.
- There is proportionately good reason to permit the evil effect.

Dr Moor used the double effect argument to defend himself against the charge of murder. He argued that his primary intention was to relieve George Liddell's suffering, but the foreseen but not intended secondary effect was to hasten his death. Deontologists such as Dr Moor do not support euthanasia.

But consequentialists reject the double effect argument. They argue that there is no moral difference between giving a patient drugs which relieve pain and hasten death, and drugs which hasten death, if the result each time is the same. Intention is not morally significant. The deontologist should just accept that he does in fact support euthanasia.

The debate between the consequentialist and deontologist raises some general important medical ethical issues in addition to the morality of euthanasia. Here are some of the central issues:

- **Purity of intention.** Consequentialists are unimpressed by the quality of intention argument. If the deontologist argues that he or she has foreseen a possible outcome then it does not matter how 'good' their intentions are or what kind of person they are. An evil act is an evil act. But the deontologist considers the quality of intention to be very important. There is a significant difference between the grandson who visits his grandmother because he has to and the one who does so because he wants to. In the latter case the outcome is enriched by virtue and likewise deceit can degrade an apparent act of kindness.
- **Arbitrariness.** Consequentialists object to the deontologist's distinction between intended foreseen effects and unintended foreseen effects. For example in the well-known example of the trolley bus, five people are lying on one track and one on another. At the moment the points are switched to the track with five people on it. For the utilitarian consequentialist the choice is simple, change the points and save the five. But the deontologist argues that life is not that simple. For example, if I have one healthy person and five sick people and I could use the organs of the healthy person to cure the five, but do I have a duty to sacrifice the one? The deontologist argues that it is logically possible to have *prior* intentions – I could refrain and allow the trolley bus to kill five people on the grounds that it would be more evil *intentionally* to kill one person. But for consequentialists this defence is irrational and arbitrary.
- **Ordinary and extraordinary means.** Consequentialists consider that the deontologist's rigid refusal ever to use direct killing can lead to more suffering, loss of dignity and confusion over exactly what constitutes 'extraordinary' means. For example, in the natural law tradition a person who refuses food and water in order to die has deliberately committed suicide which is condemned in Roman Catholic theology as a mortal sin. But a person is within their rights to refuse surgery on the grounds that it is over and above what is needed ordinarily for bare existence.
- **Proportionality and quality of life.** The consequentialists point out that the final element of the double effect includes the consequential principle that the evil of the unintended action must not be greater than the intended one. In other words, if prolonging life would bring about disproportionate suffering, then the deontologist should surely permit direct killing. The use of QALYs or 'quality adjusted life years' in some hospitals is thought to be an empirical means of determining the quality of life of a patient in terms of the resources needed to

Key quote

Competent patients have a right to refuse any treatment, including life-prolonging treatment.

The British Medical Association, (*Medical Ethics Today*), p. 149

Key terms

QALY An acronym for 'quality-adjusted life-year'. A QALY takes into account both the quantity and quality of life generated by healthcare interventions. It is judged by making a calculation of life expectancy and a measure of the quality of the remaining life-years.

Empirical Gaining knowledge through observation and experience rather than logic or theory.

maintain a life. Deontologists agree that outcomes are important, but argue that the consequentialist underestimates the importance of means and the very subjective nature of a QALY; namely, who decides what constitutes a worthwhile life?

7 Non-voluntary euthanasia

Tony Bland (1970–1993) was injured in the Hillsborough football stadium disaster, 15 April 1989, He was placed on life-support and in a deep coma. After lengthy legal debate his life-support was turned off 3 March, 1993.

Read page 214 on paternalism.

Read page 214 on paternalism.

Key quote

The ability to make complex judgements about benefit requires compassion, experience and an appreciation of the patient's viewpoint.
The British Medical Association (*Medical Ethics Today*), p. 170 about treatment of PVS patients

Key term

The dead donor rule When there is no brain activity and no body function.

In non-voluntary euthanasia a decision is made on behalf of the patient on the strength of the situation. The landmark case of Tony Bland in the UK was after the Hillsborough football stadium disaster in April 1989. Bland was placed on a life-support and although able to feed and breathe was in a deep coma. Finally after lengthy legal debate, his life-support was turned off. The significance of the case is that it acknowledged that doctors cannot be expected to maintain a life (however defined) at all costs. The moral issue is whether acting paternally and prolonging the life of 'brain dead' patients is necessarily in their best interests.

(a) PVS and the problem of defining death

The Bland case and others like it have set up a precedent which has significantly shifted not only how we understand death but the value of life as well. In the past, death was defined as when the heart ceased pumping blood round the body accompanied with the cessation of other vital bodily functions. Today, a person can be kept 'alive' in this sense for long periods of time even though, as in the Bland case, important parts of the brain have ceased to operate. Being 'pink and supple' does not necessarily equate with being alive. Coma patients in this state can perform a number of involuntary actions and contrary to what many people think the patient is not necessarily lying inert in bed. The new definition of death is when there is no brain activity. So, a patient who is in a persistent vegetative state (PVS) where they have lost part of the brain (that is, the cerebral cortex) would theoretically be deemed dead even if his body was functioning. But recent research has revealed how difficult it is to make such a diagnosis. Not only can it take some time to determine whether the patient is indeed brain dead, but it is now apparent that the brain can function at very low levels, just enough to provide vital hormones for the body.

(b) Deciding on a patient's best interests

In practice, being in a PVS or being declared 'brain dead' is not always taken to mean that the patient is dead (if that were the case then there would be no debate). The issue in broad terms is whether sustaining him or her on life-support is in the best interests of the patient. In other words, 'life' is not just a biological fact but also a moral or evaluative judgement. The same problem of defining death and balancing it against the best interests of a patient also occurs when taking organs from a dead patient. The **dead donor rule** is used by some to define death to be both lack of brain and body function. This rules out any form of euthanasia.

In the end, each case has to be viewed separately on its own merits.

8 Application of natural law and situation ethics to euthanasia

(a) Natural law

The deontological/natural law arguments have already been considered especially their rejection of consequentialism. Natural law's particular criticism is that the consequentialist fails to make the important moral distinction between 'allowing to die' (permitted) and 'cutting short' a life (intrinsically wrong). Without this distinction, the primary precept of self-preservation and protection of innocent life would be a major threat to the well-being of society and undermine a doctor's duty to care for his or her patients. A summary of the natural law views on euthanasia are:

> **Read pages 216–218 on deontology and euthanasia.**

- **Social stability.** Suicide/euthanasia of all kind undermines the social stability of society because it undermines the purpose of the citizen to maintain its laws and it is a sign that society has failed in its duty to care for all its members.
- **Duty to God.** Aquinas states that a primary natural law duty is to worship God, but both he and Augustine argue that suicide (and therefore euthanasia) is a failure of one's duty to protect an innocent life. All active forms of euthanasia or physician aided dying are illicit and intrinsically wrong.
- **No refusal of treatment.** The doctrine of ordinary and extraordinary means does not permit a person to refuse ordinary treatment. In *Evangelium Vitae*, the pope makes a distinction between ordinary and extraordinary treatment. Ordinary treatment is obligatory. Life must be preserved providing that it does not cause extra burdens on the patient. This entails giving a sick person basic care such as food and water which are necessary to sustain life but not necessarily to enhance or even to prolong it. Extraordinary treatment is not obligatory. Extraordinary treatments are those which do not have high expectations of success (such as surgery) or could be dangerous (such as experimental therapies).
- **Duty to protect innocent life.** The natural law argument is that whatever state of consciousness a person is in they cannot cease to be a person. Non-voluntary euthanasia for a PVS, incompetent, seriously disabled people or very sick babies is not permitted on the grounds that death is defined only as the cessation of the heart and brain (dead donor rule). Furthermore, the natural law sanctity of life argument also rejects euthanasia on the grounds that only self-defence is sufficient reason to kill. Therefore, as a doctor has a duty to protect a patient from committing suicide, assisted suicide/euthanasia is murder.

> **Key quote**
>
> Discontinuing medical procedures that are burdensome, dangerous, extraordinary, or disproportionate to the expected outcome can be legitimate.
>
> *Catechism of the Catholic Church*, p. 491

Only the doctrine double effect permits allowing a patient to die in certain rare circumstances as a side effect of pain-relieving treatment, but the intention must never be directly to cause death. Whatever the case, euthanasia is a moral evil. Even passive euthanasia is wrong if the intention is to cause death, this is the position held by the Catholic Church in its *Declaration on Euthanasia* (1980).

Read pages 167–169 on
Joseph Fletcher and situationism.

(b) Situation ethics

Many of the situationist arguments have already been discussed above, when considering the consequential arguments for and against euthanasia. Situation ethics, as developed by Joseph Fletcher, combine consequentialism and the Christian weak sanctity of life principle into what Fletcher hoped would offer a rational means of judging contemporary issues such as sex, abortion, euthanasia and genetic engineering. As a situationist and consequentialist, he rejects the natural law strong sanctity of life position that euthanasia is intrinsically wrong. He believes that there will be some occasions when euthanasia is wrong because it is not the most loving action to take and other times when it will be the most compassionate and just thing to do. The moral issue, Fletcher argues, can be summarised as follows:

> In a few words, it is whether we can morally justify taking it into our own hands, as human beings, to hasten death for ourselves (suicide) or for others (mercy killing) out of reasons of compassion. The answer in my view is clearly yes, on both sides of it. Indeed, **to justify one, suicide or mercy killing, is to justify the other.**

Joseph Fletcher: *Humanhood: Essays in Biomedical Ethics* (1979), p. 155

Fletcher's four working principles might be applied to active and passive euthanasia as follows:

- **Pragmatism.** Each case has to be judged according to its merits, as there are no intrinsic laws which prohibit the use of euthanasia. In the case of a PVS with little quality of life, then passive euthanasia is justified as being the most compassionate action and also the best use of resources. Using limited resources to keep a terminally ill patient alive at all costs at the expense of other patients' welfare is unjustifiable.
- **Relativism.** Killing innocent people cannot be an absolute wrong, as each case has to be judged according to love and compassion. The weak sanctity of life principle means life is given to us to use wisely and this might mean sacrificing one's life for someone else, or helping someone to die who is in considerable pain.
- **Positivism.** There is no law which states that a life must be preserved at all costs. Laws and rules are invented by humans to assist in the humane treatment of each other and this might mean allowing someone to die (passive euthanasia) or helping them to cut short their life (voluntary active euthanasia).
- **Personalism.** At the heart of situationism is respect for a person's autonomy and their human integrity. The principle of love means acknowledging that a person's life might cease to be instrumentally of value to them. It also recognises that their humanity is more significant than mere biological existence.

In conclusion, the debate over euthanasia relies on one basic question according to Fletcher. For the situationist the issue is whether:

> It is harder to justify letting somebody die a slow and ugly death, dehumanised than it is to justify helping him escape from such misery.

Joseph Fletcher: *Humanhood: Essays in Biomedical Ethics* (1979), p. 149

Key quote

The fair allocation of scarce resources is as profound an ethical obligation as any we can level when triage officers make their decisions at the expense of some patients' needs in favor of others'.

Joseph Fletcher: *Humanhood: Essays in Biomedical Ethics* (1979), p. 155

Religion and ethics

Summary diagram: Euthanasia

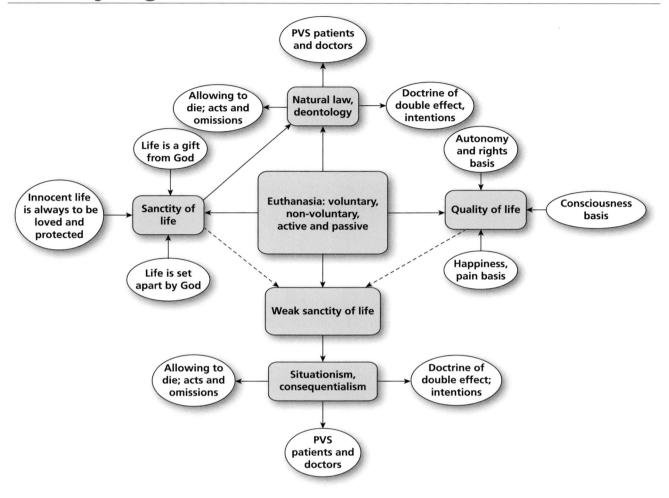

Revision advice

By the end of this chapter you should have considered the problems of trying to define the moral and legal distinctions between different types of euthanasia. You should be clear about the differences between passive and active euthanasia and the significance of these distinctions for doctors and their patients. Finally, you should be aware of the debate between the consequentialists and the deontologists about ends and means, intentions, ordinary and extraordinary means, the doctrine of double effect and the acts and omissions distinction.

Can you give brief definitions of:
- physician aided suicide
- palliative care
- voluntary euthanasia
- passive euthanasia
- vitalism
- non-voluntary euthanasia?

Can you explain:

- the principles of the 1961 Suicide Act
- the biblical basis of the strong sanctity of life principle
- the basis for the quality of life principle
- the slippery slope problem and euthanasia?

Can you give arguments for and against:

- whether euthanasia is blasphemous
- whether doctors are obliged to use extraordinary means to keep a patient alive
- whether non-voluntary euthanasia is always morally wrong
- whether the use of doctrine of double effect justifies the indirect death of patients?

Sample question and guidance

'Situationism is the best method of assessing whether euthanasia is morally acceptable.' Discuss.

The essay might begin by briefly defining situationism as a consequential ethical system which judges each case according to the principle of love and compassion. Fletcher's views on euthanasia might be summarised according to his four working principles. The essay might then go on to show why situationists as consequentialists are critical of deontologists and the strong sanctity of life principle because they make rules and duties more important than humans. Situationists also consider that natural law deontology is irrational, arbitrary and likely to cause more suffering. The situationist considers that if the key principle is love, then respect for a person's autonomy should be the basis on which euthanasia should be considered.

The essay might then evaluate situationism. It might consider that it is very hard to know when a life ceases to be worthwhile and whether a person who is very ill is rationally capable of making decisions about whether to die. A contrast might be made with the sanctity of life principle which respects a person's life not death and in denying the right to die avoids problems such as the slippery slope.

Further essay questions

Assess the view that the sanctity of life no longer has any place in twenty-first century medical ethics.

'Voluntary euthanasia is morally acceptable; non-voluntary euthanasia is always wrong.' Discuss.

To what extent is the quality of life principle useful when debating the issues of euthanasia?

Going further

Nigel Biggar: *Aiming to Kill* (Darton, Longman and Todd, 2004) Chapter 4 on the problem of slippery slopes.

Jonathan Glover: *Causing Death and Saving Lives* (Penguin Books, 1977), contains a useful consequentialist discussion of all life/death ethics.

Helga Kuhse in Peter Singer (Ed.) *A Companion to Ethics* (Blackwell, 1993) Chapter 25 on euthanasia is a very good summary of the philosophical issues.

Peter Singer: *Rethinking Life and Death* (Oxford University Press, 1994) Chapter 4 considers the failure of the sanctity of life principle in light of the Tony Bland case.

Other books discussed in this chapter are:

- Fletcher H. *Humanhood: Essays in Biomedical Ethics* (Prometheus Books, 1979).
- Harris J. *The Value of Life* (Routledge, 1990).

Chapter 15

Business ethics

1 Introduction

Chapter checklist

The chapter begins with some reflections on how questions of business ethics have become more central in the last 150 years, although they have always been part of philosophical and religious discourse. Some background is given on principles enunciated in the Christian discussion of business and their application to practice. Particular mention is made of Catholic and Anglican approaches to these questions. There is then wider and specific consideration of the specified areas of corporate social responsibility, whistle-blowing, good ethics as good business and globalisation. The chapter discusses these in terms of the major ethical traditions studied. The chapter gives guidance on the importance of illustrating arguments with real examples.

Key persons

Milton Friedman (1912–2006): Nobel prizewinner (1976) for economics. Chicago-based economist and passionate advocate of free market economics and monetarist policy.

Robert C. Solomon (1942–2007): American philosopher, theorist of the emotions and other aspects of philosophy. From 1972 until his death, he was Professor of Philosophy and Business at the University of Texas at Austin.

*So the question is, do **corporate executives**, provided they stay within the law, have responsibilities in their business activities other than to make as much money for their stockholders as possible? And my answer to that is, no they do not.*

Interview 'Milton Friedman Responds' in *Chemtech* (February 1974), p. 72

… as I watch our more ambitious students and talk with more and more semi-successful but 'trapped' middle managers and executives, I become more and more convinced that the tunnel vision of business life encouraged by the too-narrow business curriculum and the daily rhetoric of the corporate community is damaging and counter-productive. Good employees are good people, and to pretend that the virtues of business stand isolated from the virtues of the rest of our lives - and this is not for a moment to deny the particularity of either our business roles or our lives — is to set up that familiar tragedy in which a pressured employee violates his or her personal values because, from a purely business point of view, he or she 'didn't really have any choice'.

Robert C. Solomon: *Ethics and Excellence: Co-operation and Integrity in Business* (1993), p. 130

It sometimes is said that the economic events of the past ten years – bank crashes, rogue traders, fraud, insider dealing, bribery, blackmail – with all their consequences of human misery, unemployment, poverty and other evils, have made it more urgent to develop an appropriate ethical framework for business. But there is nothing new in the awareness of ethical issues in the world of business (interpreted widely to include any type of organisation that employs people, sells or provides services). In scripture, whether the Vedas of India, Jewish Scriptures, the New Testament, the Qur'an, or Buddhist writings, we find condemnation of the sin of usury. Usury involves the making of immoral loans to borrowers. An immoral loan is interpreted by some as one on which interest is charged, while others take into account things such as the rate of the interest or the penalties which might be inflicted. Throughout history there have been dishonest shopkeepers. In ancient and medieval times, through to our own day, states have found it necessary to legislate against dishonesty, regulating weights and measures and preventing adulteration of goods sold.

> **Key term**
>
> **Usury** The practice of lending money at unreasonably high rates of interest.

(a) The development of business ethics in Britain

There is more to business ethics than simply not cheating customers or creating unreal desires. Consider the state of Britain in the nineteenth century. The Industrial Revolution, unchecked, led to the employment of millions in unhygienic conditions, with dangerous machinery, long hours, no holidays, pollution and very low wages. Workers were without rights. Over a period of 200 years, efforts were made to improve things, by trade unions, by parliamentary action, by brave groups and individuals – such as the Earl of Shaftesbury – who sought to improve general working conditions, especially in the area of child labour. Progress was often slow. Only in 1970 was there an Equal Pay Act, ensuring equal pay and treatment for men and women doing equivalent work. Until 1971, there was virtually no protection of a worker in Britain against unfair dismissal. Women could be dismissed for becoming pregnant. Some organisations dismissed women if they married. In the years before the Second World War, one major group of shops employed no 'coloured' people, no men with beards and no one with red hair. They wanted no employees who drew attention to themselves by their appearance. That we find such an outlook bizarre as well as unacceptable perhaps says something about our growing concern for ethical ways of living.

In 1889, the dockers at the Port of London went on strike, an action that would become known as The Great Dock Strike. Until the strike, not only were dockers very poorly paid, but they had no guarantee of work. The practice was that each day, dockers would gather at the gates of the dock companies. The foremen would select those who would be given work, just for that day. The rest would be sent away, unpaid and hungry.

Dockers waiting for the call to work

The general manager at Millwall Docks, in evidence to Parliament, said of the dockers:

The poor fellows are miserably clad, scarcely with a boot on their foot, in a most miserable state ... These are men who come to work in our docks who come on without having a bit of food in their stomachs, perhaps since the previous day; they have worked for an hour and have earned 5d. [2p.]; their hunger will not allow them to continue: they take the 5d. in order that they may get food, perhaps the first food they have had for twenty-four hours.

An effective trade union was created, but no less significant was the way the dockers conducted themselves. Their dignified processions through London, with many wearing fish-heads around their necks to demonstrate the poverty in which they lived, brought home the extent of the social problem. Parliament became involved and issues of the morality of employment were widely discussed. The Anglican Bishop of London, Frederick Temple, and the Roman Catholic Archbishop of Westminster, Cardinal Henry Manning, did all in their power (Manning perhaps more effectively) to create pressure for a just settlement.

On the Catholic side, the significance of these events was profound. In 1891, Pope Leo XI published an encyclical letter, *Rerum Novarum*, often known as 'The Workers' Charter', condemning both the excesses of unbridled capitalism and materialist communism, setting out the conditions of the dignity of all workers, a theory of the just wage, calling for the setting up of wage boards and reminding people of the social responsibilities of governments, employers and workers. This papal initiative has been followed by popes through to the present day, working within the **natural law** tradition.

> **Key term**
>
> **Natural law** 'Right reason in accordance with human nature'. This can be worked out by considering what is good for human flourishing.

For more detail on St Thomas Aquinas, see Chapters 5 and 10.

For a profile of William Temple, see Chapter 9.

Key persons

Henry Manning (1808–92): Archbishop of Westminster 1865–92. Created Cardinal 1875. Former Archdeacon of Chichester, he converted to Catholicism in 1851. Deeply concerned about the social issues affecting the poor of his diocese and beyond.

Pope Leo XIII (1810–1903): Reigned as pope 1878–1903. In his encyclical *Aeterni Patris* 1878 he promoted the thought of Thomas Aquinas. His encyclical *Rerum Novarum* ('The Workers' Charter') was a major development in Catholic social thought and very influential. The first pope whose voice was preserved on record and the first to appear on film.

In the Church of England, Bishop (later Archbishop) Frederick Temple's intervention was part of a tradition calling for appropriate moral treatment of workers. In the 1840s, the Christian Socialist movement began, led by Frederick Denison Maurice, John Malcolm Ludlow, Charles Kingsley and others. It looked not only to alleviate the lot of the worker but to find better and more just arrangements of business. It encouraged and created co-operative enterprises. In the twentieth century, Frederick Temple's son, Archbishop William Temple, became a major figure in social reform. Although an Anglican, he paid close attention to papal teaching, to the natural law tradition and to practical social reform. It was he who coined the term 'Welfare State', and his *Christianity and Social Order*, published in 1942, was a major contribution to post-war reconstruction of industry and welfare. It was a huge bestseller (and still very worth reading), influencing all the major political parties.

Despite all these interventions, there are still those who argue that 'the business of business is business' seeing business in the terms outlined by Milton Friedman in the quotation above. According to this view, all that matters is the bottom line – making profits for shareholders. Critics might argue that shareholders are people, but, so too, are customers and the workers in the company. Shareholders have interests but others have also. Are the needs of workers restricted simply to earning a fair wage? What are the limits of duties to customers?

Think also about how a business enters contracts. If a company needs a new warehouse, it needs architects, builders and so on, and these companies in their turn depend on suppliers, scaffolders and their own workforce. The building of the warehouse entails a series of contracts. The company needing the warehouse signs contracts with the builders, they with their subcontractors. Specialist workers are employed on short-term contracts. A contract involves both duties and responsibilities as well as penalties. If I am to have the warehouse built in time, I expect the builder to guarantee a completion date, with penalties if he is late. He in his turn expects, in return for his work, to be paid the promised fees at the promised time. If he has duties to me, so have I to him. He entered the contract with expectations that I would take my own responsibility seriously. His right to be paid entails my duty to pay him. It is an ethical commonplace to argue that rights entail duties and vice versa. This is sometimes overlooked. It was fashionable for a while for managers to talk about 'management's right to manage'. This slogan needs supplementing – a right to manage surely entails a duty to manage well.

Looking at contracts takes us to several considerations. The obvious one is that business decisions are not self-contained. Business does not operate in a vacuum. The lives of many are affected, and not just those involved in building the warehouse. We might need a loan from the bank or we may need to hold back some profits from shareholders. Or current workers might be affected while the construction work is being done, new workers might be employed, suppliers are needed, and there could be wider environmental and social concerns. We see when a mining village has lost its mine how the entire community has suffered. Lives will be affected and perhaps permanently changed.

Notice something else. Consider the grammar of what we have said. We have spoken about duties, responsibilities, rights, what ought to be done, needs and expectations and the good of persons. The law might be invoked in listing our duties and responsibilities, but the language we have used is also very much the language of morality. Something is implied beyond merely what the law requires. Discussion about the morality of business is now not merely part of the academic discussion but a live topic among theologians and philosophers: it is also a concern among business people and within and beyond companies.

2 Corporate social responsibility

If it is true that no man is an island, the same is true of an organisation, whether it is a business or another enterprise such as a school or a university, or a public service such as the police or fire service. As individuals we are always part of a wider community. We may live in a family. We have friends, superiors and perhaps people answerable to us. If I work for a company, I am at the same time a citizen of my country, perhaps the parent of a family, a taxpayer, a consumer of government services and so on. No matter how devoted I might be to my work, my role is inescapably wider than that, and, as we have seen in the Introduction, the same is true for a business. Businesses have responsibilities to governments, to tax authorities and, it would seem, to the wider community.

In the last 30 years, much work has been done on the broad concept of *stakeholding*. A **stakeholder** is anyone who has an interest in an organisation. The interests of shareholders, workers and customers are evident, but others are concerned. If I lose my job, my family is affected. If many lose their jobs, the whole local economy will be touched. If an organisation closes its canteen, then staff lose work, but so too do the bakers who provide the bread, butchers who provide the meat, and so many others. Stakeholding theory looks at the broader range of people affected by organisations, as you can see in the diagram on the next page.

Aristotle in his ethical writings always insisted on the communal aspects of the ethics. For him, the good of an individual was splendid, that of the community as a whole even greater. The community for Aristotle was the *polis*, essentially the small state of ancient Greece, bound together by notions of civic friendship and mutual dependency and service. In the modern world, for many, and for much of the time, the workplace is a major

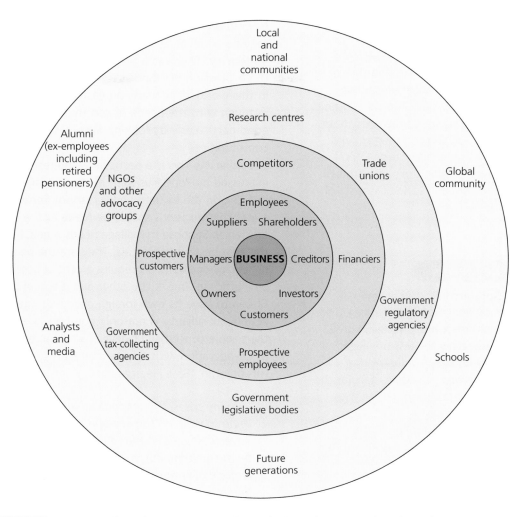

Local and national communities

Research centres

Alumni (ex-employees including retired pensioners)

NGOs and other advocacy groups

Competitors

Trade unions

Global community

Employees

Suppliers   Shareholders

Prospective customers   Managers   **BUSINESS**   Creditors   Financiers

Owners   Investors

Customers

Prospective employees

Government regulatory agencies

Schools

Analysts and media

Government tax-collecting agencies

Government legislative bodies

Future generations

For more detail on Aristotle, see Chapter 3.

Key question

What ought to be the moral values embodied by an organisation?

Key terms

Human dignity People are valuable by virtue of their being human, not because of their usefulness.

Common good A state of affairs in which everyone can flourish most effectively.

part of our lives. We not only work there, but meet friends and partners, and form other bonds. Many people's sense of self-worth is intimately tied up with how they define themselves in relation to their work. It is sometimes said that in the United States, on first meeting, people are asked first, 'Where are you from?', whereas in Britain the first question is, 'What do you do?' For many, to lose a job is to lose part of who they are.

If the place of work is to be treated as our *polis,* as Solomon thinks it should be, interacting with other organisations, each with its own culture and needs, then what are the values that should sustain that organisation?

In an important address in 2012, 'A Blueprint for Better Business?', Cardinal Vincent Nichols, Archbishop of Westminster, drew on natural law and the tradition of Catholic social teaching to commend seven principles for good business:

■ **Human dignity.** This notion is part of the idea that we are all made in the image of God, but in secular terms it emphasises, as the Cardinal said, that 'each person can never be merely an instrument valued just for their usefulness'. To say this is to invoke Kant's second form of the categorical imperative. William Temple had also insisted in his work that good is always personal. Things are done for the sake of persons (See Chapter 11).

■ The **common good.** Nichols defines this as 'the set of social conditions which allow people more easily to develop, individually and communally'. Like Temple, he examines the challenges of moving

Key person

Pope Pius XI (1857–39): (Reigned 1922–39). Author of major encyclicals, including *Quadragesimo Anno* (1931) on social issues, condemning both fascism and communism and *Mit brennender Sorge* (1937) condemning the paganism of Nazism and various aspects of its activity.

Key terms

Solidarity People are inter-dependent, needing each other and responsible for each other, especially the less privileged.

Subsidiarity The belief that decisions should be made at the lowest level compatible with efficiency.

Fraternity Literally 'brotherhood' – the belief that we should treat everyone as our brothers and sisters.

Reciprocity Giving to everyone what is due and being willing to do more than strict justice requires.

Sustainability The belief that we are responsible for maintaining Earth and its resources for ourselves and future generations.

Key person

Vincent Nichols (b. 1945): Appointed Archbishop of Westminster in 2009, and a Cardinal in 2014. Very concerned with social and ethical issues. He has been the driving force behind the organisation, Blueprint for Business involving people from various backgrounds, religious and non-religious.

beyond profit as an end to the actual good of persons (for which profit may be an invaluable means).

- **Solidarity.** This was a major concern of Pope St John Paul II. It is the expression of Donne's idea that 'no man is an island'. We are all in this world, dependent on each other; for Nichols, it 'means being in touch with the needs of communities, striving for the common good particularly by looking for ways of helping underprivileged communities.'

- **Subsidiarity.** This is a particularly interesting notion. It was formally expressed by Pope Pius XI in his encyclical *Quadragesimo Anno*, published in 1931, on the fortieth anniversary of *Rerum Novarum*. This principle states that decisions should be made at the lowest level compatible with efficiency. Suppose my village needs a new bench. The people who know the area best are the locals. They are the people best placed to make the necessary decisions. To require a central body in London to decide would be inefficient. But at the other end it would be absurd for every village in Britain to have its own foreign policy: that requires a central government action. Subsidiarity is not only good business practice but it is good for the people concerned. It develops character and self-confidence as well as co-operation with others. Interestingly, John Stuart Mill had made just this point in 1859. He argued:

> In many cases, though individuals may not do the particular thing so well, on the average, as the officers of government, it is nevertheless desirable that it should be done by them, rather than by the government, as a means to their own mental education – a mode of strengthening their active faculties, exercising their judgment, and giving them a familiar knowledge of the subjects with which they are thus left to deal.

John Stuart Mill: *On Liberty*: Chapter Six, p. 19

As a political principle, subsidiarity has been a central concern of the European Union when determining which decisions should be made nationally, locally or internationally.

- **Fraternity.** For Nichols, this entails fellowship towards those of different cultures. It is central to building relationships, to values such as trust and honesty. In his writings, William Temple developed the idea of 'fellowship' as the social glue – Aristotle's idea of civic friendship, which is something deeper than whether we like someone.

- **Reciprocity.** The Cardinal says: 'Catholic Social Teaching identifies two levels of reciprocity. The lowest is at the level of justice: giving what is due, including truth and honesty and not misusing knowledge and power. But it also extends to what we call "fraternity" or "gratuity", something that goes beyond duty, something that is part of charity, properly understood. There is a basic level of justice in which we give what people have a right to, but no more. Charity asks more of people than that. When we care for others, we do not just give them what we *must* give them, but go further in our generosity. True reciprocity is a call to generosity.'

- **Sustainability.** This stresses our duties to future generations, care for resources and the environment.

Taken together, these seven points provide a very good summary of what is entailed in corporate social responsibility. What matters is something more than simply performing our duties, whether legal or moral. The call is to be *certain types of people* in our business dealings, being not merely honest but genuinely concerned about other people, and being generous in ourselves. Cardinal Nichols is clear about the need for the Aristotelian virtues of developing good habits:

*... simply knowing the moral law ... no more makes someone a better person than knowing the rules of football makes them a better player. What matter is practice and the cultivation of habits – skills – which over time form character and make acting well easier and more habitual ... It matters then that the prevailing *ethos* in a company clearly brings together, consciously and consistently, corporate purpose and personal values, and that business should be seen to prize the development of both competence and character.*

Some might argue that business takes place in a harsh and demanding world, and that there is no place for sentiment. But is it sentimental to be ethical? Some thinkers argue that a business is better in every way by making the ethical central to its purpose. Robert C. Solomon argues, within the Aristotelian tradition, that:

The purpose of business is to provide the 'things that make ordinary life easier'. Business is not an isolated game, which the public may play if it will, and the point is not just to win, for the impact on the non-players is typically greater than the rewards for the participants ... the values of our society – for better or worse – are essentially business values, the values of 'free enterprise', the values of necessity and novelty and innovation and personal initiative. But this does not mean that our society is or should be a 'free-for-all', an unhampered, unregulated scramble for wealth and profits. Neither does it mean that it is 'everyone for himself or herself', a 'dog-eat-dog' world, or a world in which 'anything goes'. To the contrary, it is a world defined by tacit understandings and implicit rules, a practice defined, like all practices, by mutual understandings and underlying trust, and justified not by its profits but by the general prosperity it brings about. Productivity and serving the public and taking care of one's own employees are neither mere means or an afterthought of business but rather its very essence. Then, as every smart entrepreneur knows well enough, the profits will come as a consequence.

Robert C. Solomon: *Ethics and Excellence: Co-operation and Integrity in Business* (1993), pp. 123–124

His claim is that there is no contradiction between exhibiting good values in business behaviour and being successful. After all, in our daily lives we learn to trust individuals, to seek their company, to return to them for mutual help if they behave honestly, kindly and with concern for general good. Many people make a point of buying what they perceive as ethically sourced goods and will not buy from companies which use what they see as unethical practices, such as child-exploitation or deforestation. Few people return to companies they feel have treated them dishonestly or disrespectfully.

Key term

Ethos The characteristic spirit of a culture, era, or community that can be observed in its attitudes and aspirations.

Key question

What do we really want from business organisations?

231

3 Applying ethical theories to business ethics

Key term

Utilitarianism The moral
doctrine that one should always
seek the greatest balance of
good over evil.

For an explanation of
utilitarianism and the thought of
John Stuart Mill, see Chapter 13.
For a profile of Mill, see
Chapter 9.
For a profile of Jeremy Bentham,
see Chapter 13.

Key term

Free market economy An
economy in which prices, wages
and so on are determined by
the laws of supply and demand,
with minimal government
interference: the role of
government is simply to uphold
honest dealing, enforcing
contracts. A view held by
classical liberals such as Jeremy
Bentham and Adam Smith. It
claims that the unregulated
market ultimately is best for
achieving the greatest general
happiness.

For more biographical
information on Kant, see
Chapter 12.

Key question

Does utilitarianism provide
a good basis for the range of
ethical issues found in business?

(a) Utilitarianism

The position outlined here about good business is one rooted very much in the natural law/virtue ethics tradition. How might a utilitarian approach the same issue?

There are many varieties of utilitarianism as we have seen, and different versions might lead to different consequences for business ethics. Classical utilitarians such as Mill and Bentham were committed to free market economics with minimal state intervention, to be used only to uphold contracts and to regulate weights and measures. A free market economy should be left to resolve its own issues on the grounds that this would be conducive to the greatest general good. As we saw in Chapter 13, Mill believed that maximising liberty of speech and action led to greatest good overall.

Much depends on what a given utilitarian defines as the good. He might believe in the free market but not identify the good of the market as maximum profit for shareholders. Other goods might seem to him more significant, such as general welfare or – as in Mill's case – the freedoms which come from non-interference. If the good is the good of persons overall, then the good of all stakeholders would seem to be an appropriate goal.

Critics of utilitarianism might argue that the absence of concern about rights limits the usefulness of utilitarian theories. If the greater good (cheap but good-quality goods, produced for the benefit of many) is best achieved at the expense of a limited number of child-labourers in poorly paid sweat-shops in developing countries, would that be justifiable? A Kantian might argue that those labourers are being used as means only. A believer in human rights might argue that such exploitation could never be justified, no matter what good (however defined) might result from it.

A particular strength of the utilitarian position is that, unlike Kantianism, it does pay attention to the consequences of actions; the effects of what business does are part of the calculation.

(b) Kantianism

As we saw in Chapter 12, Immanuel Kant, considering the example of the shopkeeper, developed an ethic of 'duty for duty's sake', doing the right thing because it is the right thing. The good shopkeeper is honest not because it is good for business but just because it is the right thing to do.

A critic might argue that duty cannot and should not be so divorced from outcomes. The shopkeeper should be honest but he should surely consider outcomes for his family and dependents. A shop that is not successful does not serve its customers well, because in the end, it cannot serve them at all. The good of customers and of staff needs to be part of the business of ethics.

However, Kantian ethics has an important contribution to make to discussion about business. The emphasis on duties well done is a reminder that duty consists of more than doing the minimum required to stay within the law. Duty ties very closely to the sense of responsibility for others as a habit to be nurtured and developed.

No less significant to business practices is the **second form of the categorical imperative**. William Temple, both in *Christianity and Social Order* and elsewhere, develops the second form of the categorical imperative teleologically. This requires us to prioritise the good of persons over the non-human and to act always for the good of persons. He reminds us that the purpose of production is consumption. To manipulate the market by creating shortages to maximise prices is immoral. To use buyers just as a means for profit regardless of their own true good is to treat them as less than persons, to deny fellowship and human dignity. This is also, as Aristotle well knew, bad for the bonds that hold society together. If we prioritise the good of persons, then economic institutions such as slavery would seem to have no place in the world. Aristotle did not draw this conclusion, but Kant himself opposed slavery, on the slightly roundabout basis that a contract requires the consent of autonomous parties but the slave cannot enter such an agreement as his autonomy would be denied. A slave has neither rights nor autonomy.

4 Whistle-blowing

Suppose that you are working for a local authority, in the planning department. A local developer wishes to build a new block of flats in an area of low-rise, residential housing with limited parking. The design he proposes is an ugly one and residents are worried that it will spoil the area and lead to a poorer quality of life for themselves. When the planning application is published, many letters of opposition are received. Permission must be granted by the Planning Committee of the authority. Normal procedure is for a planning officer to write a report making recommendations for the councillors on the committee. If he recommends that the development goes ahead, the councillors are more likely to approve the application. You are not the relevant planning officer, but you are a keen golfer. While in the bar of the golf club, you see across the room the developer and the planning officer in conversation. They too are keen golfers. You see the developer pass a thick brown envelope to the planning officer. The next week you see his report to the Planning Committee. The report pays little attention to the letters in opposition to the development, over-stresses the benefits and strongly recommends granting permission for the flats to be built.

What ought you to do? Should you report the episode, and to whom? Here there is evidence of corruption. In Kantian terms, the planning officer has failed in his duty of honesty and integrity. In legal terms, he is guilty of a crime in relation to public office. In utilitarian terms, he has not acted in a way that maximises the good over evil.

If you report the actions you have witnessed, your action is called 'whistle-blowing', a throwback to the days when a policeman on the beat would use his whistle to summon help if he witnessed a crime in progress.

It might seem obvious that in the case of the planning officer, his actions should be reported. But, often, employees do not report such things even though – at least in the public sector, not always in the private – there are procedures by which such misconduct can be brought to the attention of the right people. Why then are such corrupt activities not more widely reported? In many cases it is the consequence of fear, whether of reprisal for pointing something out or a more generalised one in the sense of feeling that 'it is not my place' to do anything. But there are also other considerations. Many people are brought up 'not to tell tales', and telling someone about wrongdoing by a fellow employee feels very like 'teling tales to teacher' — and we remember how classmates reacted to those who tell tales! It also can feel like a question of loyalty. No one likes to be thought disloyal.

It is helpful to remember some recent problems in sport. In cricket, some players, through mistaken loyalty to 'the team', have failed to report illegal approaches by book-makers to 'throw' games. Problems have come to light in relation to the national teams of New Zealand, South Africa and Pakistan. Members of Lance Armstrong's team knew about the cyclist's immoral practices in pursuit of victory and fame, but most did nothing.

It is worth considering whether loyalty is a virtue. In ordinary discourse, we think of loyalty as a virtue. Companies and organisations in general seek to foster loyalty, and with good reason. An army without loyal troops becomes a rabble. A company that pays no attention to the goodwill and loyalty of its employees will find itself quickly in trouble. Loyalty is essential to preventing abuses, avoiding absenteeism and for building teams. Loyalty matters for building trust and the good relationships that are the social glue of functioning organisations — part of Aristotle's civic friendship.

But in this dilemma, it would seem that we have a misplaced loyalty if our 'loyalty' to the wrongdoing colleague is allowed to take precedence over other loyalties. This would seem to be where clear, rational ethical reflection is required.

(a) Whistleblowing and the contract between employer and employee

A question to consider in the issue of the planning officer is one of our responsibility. To whom are we responsible? When we join a business, we sign a contract with our employer. This contract sets out certain duties and responsibilities that employer and employee have towards each other. Things like rates of pay, holiday pay, hours of work, notice periods are all set out. There may be other requirements such as uniforms, discipline procedures and the requirements of proper confidentiality or relations with the media. But in addition to what is set out, there are ideas that are implied. Few contracts would say specifically that if you turn up to work drunk, get into physical fights with other employees or steal that you would be in breach of contract, yet each of these is treated in employment law as proper reasons for an employer to dismiss you.

Beyond the actual words of the contract there are these implied terms. There is an assumption that you will behave honestly and truthfully. It is difficult to see how you might perform your duties properly if you lack the necessary integrity.

Your first duty in relation to the case of the planning officer is surely not to your colleagues, but surely to your employer, in this case the local authority you work for, and ultimately with the people of the area whose servant you are. The contract is with the employer to whom you have promised service.

Where things become more difficult is the circumstance in which the wrongdoer is not the fellow employee, but the employer himself. Suppose you discover that the employer has taken money from the company's pension scheme in order to use it for his own purposes, or that the company wishes you to act in an illegal or immoral way, perhaps giving you money to bribe people to obtain contracts.

In these cases, we return to the issue of loyalty. We may feel uncomfortable about reporting the employer to outside bodies, such as the police or one of the financial authorities. But, at the same time, there are wider loyalties. We do not, when we join a company, lose responsibility for our wider loyalties, to our own moral values or to the community at large. We have more than one loyalty. Honesty seems to require us to take action as citizens. But saying that does not make doing so any easier. Knowing what we should do, and having the courage to do that, are two very different things.

(b) The application of ethical theories to whistle-blowing

A Kantian might say we must do our duty, and our duty includes loyalty. However, she would also have to ask whether we were willing that our covering up for a corrupt colleague is an action we would be willing that everyone, everywhere, carried out. It seems unlikely we would be willing to universalise either corruption or its cover-up.

A utilitarian would ask whether the greater good is served by allowing this kind of corruption. Cover-up would (normally) lead to greater actual harm for those whom planning officers are supposed to be protecting.

Against the narrow Kantian approach, we might argue that thought has to be given to consequences, but that a dutiful employee must nevertheless prevent wrongdoing. For the ethically minded, there are issues here of right and wrong loyalties and – by implication – of right and wrong duties. Should first loyalty be to the company – with whom the employee has a formal, contractual relationship – or to the colleague who could make life difficult if I tell the truth? If I say the loyalty should be to the organisation, should that be the first loyalty? Generally speaking, members of the Mafia are loyal to their organisation above the individual, and members of the SS were often fanatically loyal to Nazism. But this higher loyalty is not a good if it is a loyalty to a bad purpose. In the case of the planning officer, the loyalty owed is a loyalty to the public at large, not to his friend the developer nor his own bank balance.

(c) The difficulties of whistle-blowing

It is important to remember that whistle-blowing is far from easy. We may consider some spectacular modern examples. There have been individuals who have denounced their entire organisation for systemic wrongdoing. There have been cases of accusations against tobacco giants, or various military people and federal agents denouncing the US Army, the FBI, the CIA, and others. In organisational structures like the military, the entire culture is influenced by a code of conduct in which superiors are never questioned. The political thinker, Hannah Arendt (1906–1975) has pointed out how in totalitarian countries such as Nazi Germany or Soviet Russia, individuals think they can make no difference, so just concentrate on doing their own work well and say nothing about the evils around them. This phenomenon is sometimes called 'group think'. Things can go very wrong. When the Enron organisation collapsed in the United States in 1999, in perhaps the biggest ever example of financial misconduct, hundreds of people were involved in fraud, even to the extent of people being brought in to pretend to work hard, to give the impression that the corporation was an outstanding investment. The accounting company, Arthur Andersen, was punished for covering up and destroying inconvenient documents during their audits of Enron. Such military/corporate cultures make people afraid to speak out.

In the United Kingdom, recent exposure of scandals, such as the sexual and child abuse by Jimmy Savile and others, especially at the BBC, has revealed instances of people being either afraid of reporting what had happened or actively discouraged from doing so because of the fame of those involved.

Whistle-blowing is a useful reminder that choosing to do the right thing is ethical and proper – but not always easy. There are ways in which our emotions are pulled in various ways. If we are fond of the wrongdoer we are pulled by the bonds of our affections. We may err in other ways if we take malicious joy in someone we dislike getting his come-uppance.

Key question

To what extent are individuals to be blamed for not reporting corporate wrongdoing?

5 Good ethics is good business

In the section on Corporate social responsibility, we read Robert C. Solomon's argument that an ethical company is more likely to prosper. It is worth thinking about examples from the world of sports to explore this in a little more depth.

At the time of writing this chapter, there has been considerable coverage of events at FIFA, the world governing body for football. Offices in Switzerland have been raided and very senior figures arrested on charges of corruption and especially financial impropriety and bribery in relation to the awarding of major international tournaments. The IAAF, the international organisation responsible for athletics, has been accused of covering up doping scandals, and similar accusations have been made against international cycling authorities. International cricketers have been imprisoned or been given lifelong bans for match-fixing.

Think about the consequences. Sportspeople compete, and honest sportsmen and women want to compete fairly. Professionals do not want to be beaten, but they know that winning and losing matter in the context of sport. It is one thing to be beaten honestly, another to be beaten by a cheat. Sportspeople depend on honesty from each other, or trust disappears. Professional sport is not a matter of theatre, in which I might be intrigued, but not personally changed, by the outcome. In sport, I want my team to win, but I want them to win well – that is, because they have played as well as they could, not because someone has been paid to cheat. Even if my side lose, it matters that the result is honestly reached, that, if possible, the best team on the day won.

If I thought cricket matches were all fixed, I would not pay to go. The income stream to the game would be reduced, players would not trust each other, sponsors would withdraw their sponsorship (this has happened in world football, athletics and cycling), parents would discourage their children from becoming professional players, and the honest players would have their reputations tarnished. No one would benefit and many suffer actual harm. Just as customers shun dishonest shopkeepers, so many would shun dodgy sports.

Key question

Why is cheating so wrong?

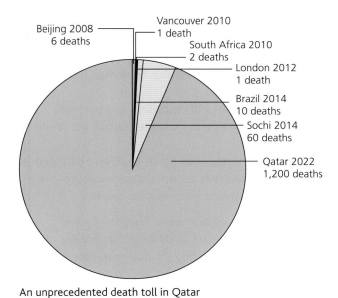

Beijing 2008
6 deaths

Vancouver 2010
1 death

South Africa 2010
2 deaths

London 2012
1 death

Brazil 2014
10 deaths

Sochi 2014
60 deaths

Qatar 2022
1,200 deaths

An unprecedented death toll in Qatar

In this case we notice several things. It is a reminder that organisations such as FIFA have many stakeholders – players, paying customers, workers who build the stadiums, those who maintain them, those whose careers are bound up with the teams as transport managers, physiotherapists and so on. Major sports generate major revenue. Major events create issues of their own, with wide consequences.

If we take Brazil as an example, we may think about the 2014 World Cup and the 2016 Olympics. There is much prestige around these events. They act as advertisements for the nation as a whole. But the money used to gain this prestige might have been better spent on social assistance to the local populations. According to the charity, *Terre des Hommes*, 170,000 poor people lost their homes to make room for new stadia, approach roads and other infrastructure, and thousands of families were rehomed in basic huts without electricity or water. There is clear evidence that the award of the 2022 World Cup to Qatar has, among other things, led to the mass exploitation – including deaths – of imported labourers who work in unprotected and unconsidered conditions.

If all this is true of the sports business, it remains true across business. If banking is corrupt there are major problems, because banking affects the lives of everyone and ultimately rests on people trusting banks to take good and proper care of their money. If confidence in banks goes, results are dire, not just for customers and banks themselves, but for the economy at large.

(a) Is business ethics just hypocritical window dressing?

In one sense, this is a difficult question for a philosopher, as it is at one level a sociological question about how organisations do in practice behave, rather than about how they *ought* to behave. Just as individuals have a variety of motives, some of which clash with others, so too do organisations. In our own behaviour we may genuinely want to be honest, we may even think of ourselves as honest, and yet find ourselves concocting some lie to get out of trouble or to avoid some unpleasant task. Organisational behaviour is not that much different. It would perhaps be as foolish to say all businesses are dishonest as to say all politicians are dishonest.

A special difficulty with business is that it is hard to separate businesses being ethical for its own sake with the fact that being ethical might well be good for their business. It is worth considering whether we can disentangle in the way that Kant thought the difference between the shopkeeper being honest just because it is the right thing to do, from the shopkeeper who is honest as it is good for business. Human motivation is very mixed. We may wish to be honest for its own sake, but if we then find that being honest helps us to prosper, our motivation is supported by its results. Reward encourages good habits, even if the initial motivation was the good in itself and not the reward.

At one level it seems that honesty is good for business. Behaving honestly builds trust with customers, who will be more likely to return. A company acting ethically can lead to positive outcomes:

- A company known for its integrity might be able to charge higher prices for its products or services.
- An organisation honest in its dealings with suppliers and partners, for example, paying bills promptly, can negotiate better terms, get credit more easily.
- Honesty and fair treatment with employees builds trust and confidence. Good business requires a stable and reliable workforce, willing to share the goals of the organisation and taking pride in their work.

Companies can behave ethically in various ways. They might see honesty not simply in terms of being honest in dealings but honest in the quality of the goods they produce, avoiding shoddy materials or using Fairtrade and other ethically sourced goods as part of demonstrating their global responsibilities. In their relations with employees they may commit to fair pay by guaranteeing everyone at least the living wage. Honest dealing makes relations with trade unions much better, leading to industrial peace, without damaging strikes and walkouts.

If we follow recent events, we become very aware how dishonest dealings have affected business. Publishing false data about emissions damaged Volkswagen and other car companies, both in terms of share price and sales, because customers lost confidence in a previously well-regarded organisation. Some customers will not buy goods from Nike because of reports of their use of child labour in Asian workshops.

But, of course, being ethical does not guarantee success. Companies such as Primark have been accused of being able to sell cheap goods because so many of their clothes come from foreign workshops with bad conditions. Sports Direct have been argued to have poor employment practices and paying less than the minimum wage. Ryanair have faced claims of taking any legal steps to make profits and to use inappropriate employment practices. Some shoppers have found the lure of cheap prices overriding any ethical concerns they might have, while many simply cannot afford to pay more for their goods.

What is not so clear is whether such organisations truly prosper in the long term. If by 'prosper' we mean simply that they make money, then we might think that they do. But if we think of prosperity as involving flourishing in the wider sense of creating happiness, enabling people to become better citizens, to take care of their families, to live well and generously, to care for the world and all who are in it, to grow as persons, we might argue then that in the wide sense dishonest organisations do not truly prosper.

6 Globalisation

Once, businesses were relatively or actually local. A shopkeeper ran a shop, a farmer a farm, an inn-keeper an inn. These businessmen would work in their shops, mills or inns, with local customers, supplied largely by local suppliers. Those around them knew who they were, where they worked, whether their business was honest or otherwise, whether they paid their debts, their taxes, their other dues. But even in ancient times, some businesses went much further, to other nations. Greek and Roman merchants would travel beyond their borders to trade goods. The Phoenicians were a great merchant people and trade routes opened up. Some trade was done by barter, some by payment in coin. But in many ways this global reach had its limitations. Merchants were limited by the amounts of gold they could physically carry. There were issues of security. Bandits and robbers preyed on caravans in search of money and other goods.

One of the most significant of the many important inventions of the Middle Ages, was a development often overlooked: the invention of double-entry bookkeeping. From about 624AD Muslim civilisations had a form of double-entry bookkeeping.

This simple invention, taken for granted in business today, had a revolutionary effect. No longer would merchants need to travel with large amounts of cash. They could deposit money in a bank in one country and draw against that deposit at a branch of the bank in another. Banks such as those of the Fuggers or the Medicis became international. Not only did they provide service to trade but also lent money to ruling authorities. This was to mean that often governments were limited by their credit with bankers who were not necessarily their own citizens. Banks thus became global powers with a reach which went beyond their boundaries, as they were sources of capital and of loans.

The term 'globalisation' has in modern times been much discussed, though many do not fully think through the implications. Companies were once simply local affairs selling to people who could reach their goods. Food, apart from dried items like tea, could not be sent around the world because much of it would quickly become rotten. Transport was often poor and risky, and a letter from a distant branch somewhere in the British Empire could take months to arrive at London headquarters.

These concerns no longer necessarily apply. Refrigerated containers, the internet, good transport links make global links possible. Enterprising businesses which see a market they can get to will see it as an opportunity. National boundaries become less significant. Countries need investment and will welcome firms who offer to open factories which will provide jobs and investment in the economy.

The power of governments is more constrained – a government cannot in the same way step outside its own nation or its own sphere of influence. Whitehall could not decamp to Paris or Kuala Lumpur in search of cheaper running costs. A fundamental concern is how governments can ensure that a company pays its taxes and obeys national laws, especially when it could simply relocate to a more amenable jurisdiction. Some businesses are bigger than governments of smaller nations.

If there is a major catastrophe in one country, the stock markets of the world all suffer. Electronic investment means that investors can trade instantly all over the world. Big banks, oil companies, insurance companies, retailers become global in scope. Names such as Kentucky Fried Chicken, Adidas and General Motors are known worldwide. Their fortunes affect whole economies. The effect is not simply in questions of investment but use of local suppliers and labour. Should a major company pay its taxes in the way that individual citizens do? If so, to whom? A multi-national company earns money in different countries. It has tax liabilities, but different countries have different regulations on the filing and publication of accounts.

To maximise profits an organisation may locate its headquarters in countries where they will have only light-touch regulation. In shipping, since the 1920s, many companies have chosen to sail under 'flags of convenience', registering their ships as belonging to nations such as Liberia or Panama or even Mongolia – a landlocked nation. By doing so, they are subject to the regulations of that nation, which may be lax in employment rules or other conditions. The arguments for doing so are generally matters of convenience and profit. The consequences may include sailors being exploited, lax safety and other forms of abuse. Accusations are also made that multi-national companies are guilty of treating suppliers in developing countries unfavourably to get goods at minimal prices. Various companies, such as some in sportswear, have been accused of permitting the use of child labour in poor countries.

Another issue in globalisation has been the cultural effects on indigenous peoples as they are affected by businesses whose values are not their own. Deforestation by international companies has been an issue in the Amazon and elsewhere. On the other hand, increased and rapid communications have brought increased awareness of these issues.

(a) Globalisation and ethics

The questions for the ethicist are vast. Modern technology makes ethical judgement more, not less, complex. Papal social documents, such of those of Popes Leo XIII and Pius XI tended to concentrate on issues of the organisation of business and labour within nations. In 1961, Pope St John XXIII published his encyclical, *Mater et Magister*, reinforcing the principles expressed by his predecessors but also developing them in relation to globalisation:

> 157. Probably the most difficult problem today concerns the relationship between political communities that are economically advanced and those in the process of development. Whereas the standard of living is high in the former, the latter are subject to extreme poverty. The solidarity which binds all men together as members of a common family makes it impossible for wealthy nations to look with indifference upon the hunger, misery and poverty of other nations whose citizens are unable to enjoy even elementary human rights. The nations of the world are becoming more and more dependent on one another and it will not be possible to preserve a lasting peace so long as glaring economic and social imbalances persist …

> 171. There is also a further temptation which the economically developed nations must resist: that of giving technical and financial aid with a view to gaining control over the political situation in the poorer countries, and furthering their own plans for world domination.

> 172. Let us be quite clear on this point. A nation that acted from these motives would in fact be introducing a new form of colonialism – cleverly disguised, no doubt, but actually reflecting that older, outdated type from which many nations have recently emerged. Such action would, moreover, have harmful impact on international relations, and constitute a menace to world peace.

Pope St John XXIII: *Mater et Magister*

Religion and ethics

Stating the issues does not make resolution much easier. Nevertheless, John XXIII identified very clearly the issues that needed to be addressed, broadening the principles of natural law and the ideas of Catholic social teaching. Notice also his reference to solidarity and his identification of neo-colonialism as an issue.

(b) Neo-colonialism

This neo-colonialism can be of different types. There is the colonialism of one nation so dominating another through its manner of providing aid and assistance that the developing country becomes at best a client state, subordinate to and dependent on its donors, and at worst is treated almost as a resource for the major power. But today the neo-colonialism can be an economic one. Global companies are often richer and better-resourced than many nations, and their reach across the world becomes an economic weapon. It is possible to colonialise without armies.

The moral question is whether such companies are using the natural resources for their own good or for the good of the nation involved. It needs to be said that a global company is not necessarily an immoral one, concerned only with its own good. There is often awareness of ethical dimensions and responsibilities in company policies. Some shareholders will not invest in companies they believe to be exploitative and there are organisations which campaign for ethical investment.

(c) The application of ethical theories to issues raised by globalisation

Businesses exploiting the natural resources or labour force of developing countries raises moral concerns. If the company is acting just for its own good, then in Kantian terms it is treating the people (and resources) of the poorer nation as means, not as ends. A Kantian might argue also that no one could universalise exploiting every nation and every person, everywhere, so it cannot be right to do so in this case. For a Kantian, such exploitation shows no good will, for its end is not dutiful, nor does it reveal good will to all others.

The case with utilitarianism (and, to an extent, situation ethics) is especially interesting. A critic might argue that the absence of a belief in natural rights provides scant protection for those exploited. All depends on how utilitarianism is to be understood. If we argue that utilitarianism is to be understood in terms of 'the greatest good of the greatest number' then someone might construct a case that the suffering of a few workers in a far-off place can be off-set by the greater good created for the majority of stakeholders. But, as we saw, this crude view of the principle of utility came to be rejected even by Bentham. Other utilitarian thinkers such as Peter Singer would point to the ability of persons to suffer as a crucial factor in making the right decision. A poor person in a poor land is as capable of suffering as I am and therefore is worthy of equal consideration. I cannot privilege my pleasure in profit and cheap goods over the suffering he feels. I am not intrinsically more valuable than he is. Whether this is sufficient defence of the poor compared with a theory that endorses natural rights is an interesting idea to consider.

For a profile of Peter Singer, see Chapter 13.

A feature common to many of these theories – perhaps all – is a growing interest in issues of the environment. Peter Singer has been passionate in his concern for the environment. It is not enough for him to consider just our needs now. The concern has to be with all people, whether now or in the future. Pope Benedict XVI and Pope Francis have both moved issues of the environment to the centre of moral discussion. In 2015, Francis argued in an encyclical:

> *95. The natural environment is a collective good, the patrimony of all humanity and the responsibility of everyone. If we make something our own, it is only to administer it for the good of all. If we do not, we burden our consciences with the weight of having denied the existence of others. That is why the New Zealand bishops asked what the commandment 'Thou shall not kill' means when 'twenty percent of the world's population consumes resources at a rate that robs the poor nations and future generations of what they need to survive'.*

Pope Francis: *Laudato Si'*, 2015

Sustainability is a concern. It seems not unreasonable to argue that if moral duty is a duty for others, it seems that any calculation must not merely be horizontal, that is, concerned with those in our current world, but vertical, concerned with the heritage we have received from the past, but also with those who live in the future. If ethics is for people, the unborn generations are people too.

7 Conclusion

The assumption made by Milton Friedman that the only responsibility of business is to its shareholders seems, at best, an improbable conclusion to draw. A business is not an abstract entity. It is sometimes tempting to treat the term 'company' or 'organisation' as being somehow separate from all those elements that make it up. An enterprise involves material things, offices and factories, supplies and equipment, but these material things are given direction by human minds, goods are consumed by persons, services are used by people, supplies are provided by people and profits are enjoyed by people. None of these people is an abstract. If a public servant is corrupt, it is people who suffer. A shopkeeper who cheats his customers and an entrepreneur who uses slave labour both act in ways bad for people. All business is ultimately about people, their moral worth and their value and needs. Business exists for the good of humankind, not humankind for the good of business. Morality exists for people, not the other way round, and if good is always personal, then the goodness or otherwise of business is at the centre of proper business ethics.

Study advice

As with all philosophical topics, the importance of careful consideration of both issues and philosophical approaches should not be underestimated. In business, decisions are rarely absolutely simple and many factors are involved. In this chapter, we have outlined some of the pressures that are involved but also some of the values to think about and to balance against each other. A business that thought only of profits for shareholders could well be treating other people in ways we would find immoral, but a business that paid no heed to profits would fail, causing suffering for many. Balances have to be found and it is important when considering the issues to be aware of different dimensions of issues.

It is helpful in thinking to use actual examples. Throughout this book there has been a stress on the use of examples. This is especially true in business ethics. In business ethics, the best examples are often those drawn from contemporary events. One of the difficulties of writing a textbook is that there is a time gap between when this chapter was written and when you are doing your work. What is contemporary at the time of writing will not be contemporary when you do your examination. Pay attention to news items about the conduct of organisations. An essay demonstrating lively awareness of current issues that builds arguments on the basis of specific instances will be particularly impressive.

Karl Popper hated it when people said, 'It's fine in theory, but it won't work in practice.' The only test of a theory is practice. If a theory doesn't work in practice, it is a bad theory. Thinking about issues in business ethics might give you useful ideas on the adequacy of a given theory. Does a strictly utilitarian theory work here? Thinking about such issues can be useful in more general questions. Good students use material learned in one topic as illuminating for their ideas about others. For example, you might find ideas from your study of liberation theology relevant here.

See Chapter 20 for a discussion of liberation theology.

Key person

Karl Popper (1902–94): Viennese-born philosopher of science and politics, generally considered one of the greatest twentieth-century philosophers. Taught at London School of Economics 1946–69. Knighted in 1965. Famous works include *The Logic of Scientific Discovery* (1959), *The Open Society and Its Enemies* (1950), and *The Poverty of Historicism* (1957). Famous for the clarity of his thought and writing.

Summary diagram: Business ethics

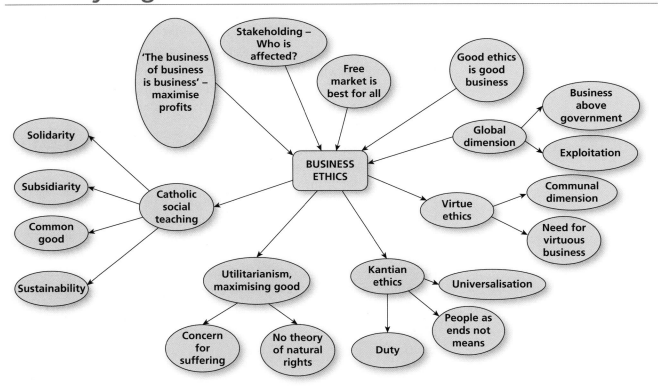

Here, as elsewhere, it is important to be clear about definitions of terms. It is important to remember that the examination could focus on one of the specified aspects of the theme, so you will want to be able to write with some insight about the major themes, such as whistle-blowing or globalisation. As always, think of supporting examples, preferably from actual business practice, and reflect on the issues.

Can you give brief definitions of:
- whistle-blowing
- subsidiarity
- globalisation
- bribery
- usury?

Can you explain:
- the issues of globalisation
- Kantian approaches to honesty in business
- solidarity
- stakeholder theory?

Can you give arguments for and against:
- the belief that the only concern of business should be to maximise profits
- the concept of corporate responsibility
- use of cheap labour from developing countries
- utilitarian approaches to business ethics?

Sample question and guidance

To what extent is utilitarianism helpful in deciding whether whistle-blowing is a correct action to take?

This is an interesting question calling for reflection. It is important to define what whistle-blowing is and to say something about the considerations of whistle-blowing. Utilitarianism, as a teleological theory, judges the goodness of an action by its outcome, in terms of the general balance of good over evil.

If you consider act utilitarianism, you might consider for each instance of wrongdoing whether the greater good is served by informing authorities about the wrongdoing. But there is then a question about what the general good is. Whose good should be considered in making the decision? Is a company's general good better served by being open about wrongdoing or attempting to preserve the reputation of the firm by cover-up? However, if an individual wrong-doing is covered up, does this create a bad culture and set a bad example? Rule-utilitarian approaches might suggest that we should always act in a particular way — that overall the greatest general good is ultimately best served by honesty.

In answering this question you might choose to argue that other ethical theories, such as Kantianism, provide a better and more effective answer to the issues. You might even want to consider whether the ability of a theory to work in this situation is good evidence for the adequacy or inadequacy of the theory overall.

However you argue, it is important to justify the choices you make, with good reasons.

Further essay questions

'The only concern of business should be to make a profit.' Discuss.

Consider whether Natural Law is useful in dealing with the issues of business in a global context.

'Human dignity should be the main value of any good business.' Discuss.

Going further

There are many current books on business ethics, many of which are geared to higher-level courses such as the MBA. For studying business at any level a superb collection of resource material may be found in *On Moral Business: Classical and Contemporary Resources for Ethics in Economic Life*, Eds. Max L. Stackhouse, Dennis P. McCann, Shirley J. Roels and Preston N. Williams (Eerdmans, 1995). Both Robert C. Solomon: *Ethics and Excellence: Co-operation and Integrity in Business* (Oxford University Press, 1993) and Peter Singer: *Practical Ethics* especially chapters 8, 9 and 10 (third edition, Cambridge University Press, 2011) give much food for productive reflection. Michael Sandel: *Justice: What's the Right Thing To Do?* (Penguin, 2010) touches on many issues of business ethics, and is very readable. Although in some ways dated, William Temple: *Christianity and Social Order*, (new edition, Shepheard-Walwyn, 1984) remains a very readable and thought-provoking (brief) introduction to a range of issues. The papal encyclicals referred to in this chapter may be studied online at the Holy See website: http://w2.vatican.va/content/vatican/en.html. Click on the portrait of the pope whose encyclical you wish to see.

Cardinal Nichols' speech may be read at: http://rcdow.org.uk/cardinal/news/address-to-business-leaders/. It is also very useful to explore the website: www.blueprintforbusiness.org for further and thoughtful discussion of the points he raises.

Other books discussed in this chapter are:

- Popper K. *The Open Society and Its Enemies* (Princeton University Press, 1950).
- Popper K. *The Poverty of Historicism* (Routledge and Kegan Paul, 1957).
- Popper K. *The Logic of Scientific Discovery* (Hutchinson, 1959).
- Solomon R.C. *Ethics and Excellence: Co-operation and Integrity in Business* (Oxford University Press, 1993).

3

Developments in Christian thought

Chapter 16

Augustine on human nature

1 Introduction

2 The human potential

Anders Breivik

Anders Breivik shocked the world when he carried out a series of attacks and mass murders in 2011. On 22 July 2011 he killed eight people by setting off a van bomb in Oslo followed by the shooting and murder of 69 young people at the left-wing Workers' Youth Club League at their summer camp on the island of Utoya, Norway. His motives were to cleanse Europe of non-European elements such as Islam, cultural Marxism and multiculturalism. He was diagnosed as having a narcissistic personality disorder. He was convicted in 2012 of mass murder and imprisoned for life.

In July 1941, three inmates escaped from Auschwitz concentration camp. The deputy camp commander selected ten men to be starved to death in an underground bunker as a deterrent. One of the men cried out that he had a wife and children and Maximillian Kolbe offered himself in exchange for the man's life. Kolbe supported the nine men to the last over two weeks while they starved to death until only he was alive. Finally, the prison guards killed him using a lethal injection.

Key person

Maximillian Kolbe (1894–1941): was a Polish Catholic priest and Franciscan friar. He was imprisoned in a Nazi concentration camp during the Second World War because the monastery where he lived was publishing anti-Nazi literature. He was transferred to Auschwitz 28 May 1941 where he died. He was canonised by the Catholic Church 10 October 1982.

Maximillian Kolbe

To what extent are humans in control of their lives?

Jean-Jacques Rousseau
(1712–78): French philosopher
and writer. He set out his
political philosophy in *The
Social Contract* (1762) where he
distinguishes between humans
originally living in a 'state of
nature' and the need for a social
contract.

Thomas Hobbes (1588–1679):
Educated at Oxford and later
began writing political pieces
of which *Leviathan* (1651) is his
most developed work.

The life of man, solitary, poor,
nasty, brutish, and short.
  Thomas Hobbes: *Leviathan* XIII.9

These two examples illustrate the polar opposites of human nature.
Breivik's nature is of a self-obsessed narcissist, cold-blooded and life-
denying, whereas Kolbe's nature is selfless, generous, courageous and
life-affirming. It seems that human beings have the potential to act in
diametrically opposed ways. Rousseau and Hobbes give two very different
philosophical explanations why this should be so.

■ The French philosopher Jean-Jacques Rousseau argued that humans
  are essentially generous and only act otherwise when situation and
  circumstance cause them to act otherwise. He famously said that,
  'Man is born free, and everywhere he is in chains'. The metaphor of the
  chains describes how the human competition for land, resources and
  power had resulted in loss of freedom. For Rousseau, the purpose of
  life is to cut free from these chains and rediscover the 'state of nature'
  by learning to be more co-operative and appreciative of each other.

Man is born free, and everywhere he is in chains. Many a man
believes himself to be the master of others who is, no less than they,
a slave.

Jean-Jacques Rousseau: *The Social Contract* Book 1.1

■ The English philosopher Thomas Hobbes' starting point was very
  different from Rousseau. He thought that in a 'state of nature' humans
  are not naturally co-operative but selfish and brutish (animal-like).
  Humans are, however, in one vital respect different from animals; the
  human power of reason is enough to realise that if they co-operate
  with each other, life becomes more tolerable. The purpose of life is to
  conquer the brutish animal side of human nature and create just and
  fair societies.

Describing and understanding human nature must be the starting point
for ethics, politics, sociology and philosophy. However, it is less obviously
the starting point for theology. Theology is after all the 'study of God',
whereas the 'study of humans' is the domain of anthropology. But there
need not be a sharp distinction because in understanding what it means
to be human we are also asking what the purpose of human life is and
that is as much a theological question as it is philosophical, psychological
or biological.

3 Augustine on human nature

Augustine's influence on Western Christianity is fundamental both for
Catholics and Protestants. Even today, in the light of modern science,
history and psychology, his judgements and insights continue to be the
source of fruitful reflection. It is largely because he is so honest about his
own inner experiences that his theological and philosophical reflections
on human nature have considerable influence. The main source for his
early life up to his conversion to Christianity is in his book the *Confessions*
(written between 397 and 400AD).

(a) Augustine's life

Augustine was born in Thagaste, North Africa in 354AD. His mother Monica was a devout though uneducated Catholic Christian and his father, Patrick, a merchant. Although they were not well off, his father realised his son's genius and gave him the best education he could. Augustine did not share his mother's faith, but he grew up knowing about Christianity and probably attended festivals with his mother.

In 370AD at the age of 16, Augustine went to Carthage to study law but changed courses to study rhetoric (a mixture of philosophy, literature and public speaking). He quickly rose to the top of his class and impressed his professors. But his experience of Carthage was not favourable and he described it as a 'hissing cauldron of lust'; the students were rowdy and constantly disrupted classes. Although Augustine never formally joined the 'Wreckers', a club for fashionable students, he mixed with its members and enjoyed their riotous company.

During this time two important things occurred:

■ The first was when he read Cicero's *Hortensius* as part of his rhetoric course. It was the first time he had read a serious philosophy book and it stirred up in him a strong desire to pursue wisdom. By comparison he found the Bible full of contradictions and unable to deal with the questions raised by Cicero.
■ The second was his encounter with a group of extremely **esoteric** Christians called the Manicheans. The Manicheans offered Augustine the answers to the questions he was seeking replies to and he 'gulped down' (*Confessions* 3.6) everything they taught. They thought that only they knew the truth and they despised Catholic Christians. His mother, Monica, was appalled and refused to let Augustine home, but she was advised by her bishop not to do so because he knew that as an intelligent young man Augustine would soon grow tired with the Manicheans, and eventually he did.

Augustine of Hippo (354–430AD)

> **Key term**
>
> **Esoteric** Teachings which are only intended to be understood by only a small number of people with specialised knowledge.

> **Key question**
>
> Why did Augustine find the Manichean belief that the world is evil convincing?

> **Key term**
>
> **Manicheism** A form of esoteric Christianity which believed that suffering and evil in the world are not caused by God but by a lower power (Satan). Humans have two souls: the higher soul desires God and the lower soul desires evil.

> **Key person**
>
> **Cicero** (107–43BC): Marcus Tullius Cicero was a Roman consul, philosopher, politician, lawyer, orator and political theorist. *Hortensius* or *On Philosophy* was written around 45BC and is a philosophical dialogue on the pursuit of happiness.

(i) Manicheism

In studying Cicero, Augustine became increasingly more interested in the problem of evil and suffering. He wanted to know what caused it and what we could do about it. If philosophy is about the quest for wisdom and happiness, how can we know which philosophical or religious path will lead there? **Manicheism** appeared to offer Augustine the rational view of the world which gave him the answers he was looking for.

The Manicheans were dualists and believed that suffering and evil in the world are not caused by God, but by a lower evil power:

■ the world is a battlefield between the forces of light and darkness
■ the higher human soul is a particle of light which has become trapped in the material body

- the human task is to liberate the higher soul so it can return to the Greater Light
- the lower human soul craves the delights of the material world
- release can be accomplished by prayer, abstinence from all the enjoyments of evil such as riches, lust, wine, meat, or luxurious houses.

It was during this time that Augustine took on a mistress and by her had a son, Adeodatus. He never names her but it is clear that he loved her and even though she was not his wife, they lived together as husband and wife. In this he was different from other young men of his class who often had several mistresses. But the experience was a formative one for Augustine and his later writings often make reference to the powerful psychological effects of sex.

(ii) Platonism

As a gifted young man of 19, Augustine was offered a post at Carthage to teach rhetoric in 374AD. But he found many of the students badly behaved and he gladly accepted a teaching position in Rome in 383AD. He had many admirers in high places and although he hadn't been in Rome long he was offered the position of orator at the imperial court in Milan in 384AD. Now that his career was moving towards a role in government, he did the 'respectable thing' and sent his mistress back to Carthage and became engaged to a girl from a high-ranking Milan family.

Increasingly Augustine had become dissatisfied with the inability of Manicheism to give satisfactory explanations for the universe based on the latest mathematics and astronomical observations. He was coming to the conclusion that despite its appeal to reason, Manicheism was in many ways no better than superstition. This was confirmed after his meeting with the Manichean bishop, Faustus – a kind but intellectually weak man.

During this time Augustine had become increasingly involved with a group of intellectuals called the Platonists. Although the Platonists were great admirers of Plato, their **Platonism** (or Neoplatonism as it is now called) differed in some important ways:

- Firstly, under the influence of Plotinus they believed that some human minds are able to contemplate the One (i.e. God) by ascending up different levels of reality from this material world to the One. The soul and body ought to work in harmony but in practice the soul cannot control the body in the material world and this is the cause of evil and suffering. Truth, wisdom and happiness can only be achieved once the soul has separated itself from all material influences through contemplation and merges with the One.
- Secondly, they combined Plato and certain passages from the New Testament. The Platonists of Augustine's day developed a form of Christianity which did not believe that Christ had died for the sins of the world but saw him as an enlightened being or *logos* (as referred to in the opening of John's Gospel) who had pure knowledge of the One.

Neoplatonism played an extremely important role in Augustine's theology. His view of the soul and its relationship to the body is strongly Platonic and his early writings share the Platonic optimism that the soul can find wisdom and happiness through its own efforts.

> **Key term**
>
> **Platonism** Usually referred to as Neoplatonism is the term scholars use to refer to the followers of Plato in the third century AD, notably Plotinus (205–270AD). They believed that the soul can ascend to merge with the One (or God) where it encounters truth, wisdom and happiness.

251

Above all it solved the problem of evil: evil is not a separate power (as the Manicheans believed) but the absence of good. But Augustine did not find Platonism emotionally or spiritually satisfying: he still experienced an inner conflict which intellect alone could not solve.

(iii) Conversion to Christianity

However, despite his career prospects, hope of marriage and new-found intellectual stimulation with the Platonists, Augustine was still struggling to make sense of his emotions, sense of guilt and lack of inner happiness. It was during this time that he managed to arrange a meeting with Ambrose, the Catholic Christian bishop of Milan. Ambrose was a man of great learning and was much sought after for his wisdom. What Augustine learnt from him was how to read the Old Testament at a symbolic level. This suddenly removed many of the objections Augustine had struggled with and resolved the problem of conflicting passages.

Then in 386AD, when he was 32, he relates in the *Confessions* how he had spent an emotional day in the garden of the house he shared with his friend Alypius. His body was in turmoil; he recorded in the *Confessions* that he tore his hair, hammered his forehead with his fists and was weeping. Embarrassed he left Alypius and then, sitting under a fig tree, he heard a voice of a boy or girl (he wasn't sure) say, 'Take it and read, take it and read.' He took it as God's command and returning to his study he picked up the copy of St Paul's letters he had been reading earlier and read:

> *... not in revelling and drunkenness, not in debauchery and licentiousness, not in quarrelling and jealousy. Instead put on the Lord Jesus Christ, and make no provision for the flesh, to gratify its desires.*

Romans 13:13–14

It appeared the passage provided the last part of the intellectual and emotional jig-saw he had been looking for; wisdom cannot be provided by the pursuit of intellect alone but through God's grace in Jesus Christ. Augustine and his son Adeodatus were baptised by Ambrose in 387AD much to his mother's delight. After Monica and Adeodatus' deaths two years later, Augustine returned to North Africa on his own.

(iv) Life as a Christian bishop

On his return Augustine joined a monastic community at Thagaste and was ordained priest in 391AD. In 396AD (when he was 41) he was consecrated bishop of Hippo where he remained until his death in 430AD. During this time, he completed his *City of God* (410AD). His last few years were dominated by his two great theological struggles with the Donatists and Pelagians. Of these two the Pelagian controversy had the greatest effect on altering his theology.

(v) Dispute with the Pelagians

His life was marked by conflict but it was his dispute with the Pelagians from 411AD onwards, which marked the biggest shift in his theology. Pelagius was a Christian monk who did not believe that Original Sin

Key quote

For in an instant, as I came to the end of the sentence, it was as though the light of confidence flooded into my heart and all darkness of doubt was dispelled.

Augustine: *Confessions* Book 8. 2

caused universal guilt which only God could remove. The Pelagians argued that humans have sufficient free will to overcome personal sin. Pelagius taught:

- Even if Adam had not sinned he would have died.
- Adam's sin harmed only himself not the human race.
- Children are born in the same state as Adam before his Fall.
- The whole human race neither dies through Adam's sin or death nor rises again through the resurrection of Christ.
- Even before the coming of Christ there were men who lived without sinning.

Augustine opposed Pelagius, stating that human nature, after the Fall of Adam and Eve, is entirely corrupt and that Adam's Original Sin and guilt is passed on from generation to generation. Therefore, because all humans are born in sin they are incapable of choosing to do good or to follow God, that is only possible because of God's grace. But in refuting Pelagius, Augustine took an increasingly hard-line view that God's grace would only extend to a select few, the elect. Although he had officially rejected Manicheism this aspect of his theology was strongly reminiscent of Manichean teaching.

(b) The human will before the Fall

Augustine's starting point is Genesis 1–3. Here we are given accounts of the creation of man and woman, their time in the Garden of Eden (paradise), their relationship with each other, the natural world and God. Until **the Fall** humans enjoyed a time of harmony. Harmony is expressed in the complete obedience of Adam and Eve to God and in their duties to other living creatures. It is also, according to Augustine, a time when the human body, will and reason are in complete co-operation with each other.

(i) The will as love

The will is God-given, created along with humans *ex nihilo* (from nothing) and can choose to do good or evil, to believe in God or to reject him. The will determines the kind of person we are. Above all, the will is synonymous with love – a kind of force or weight pulling us in various directions. Therefore, the will is driven by *cupiditas* (self-love) and *caritas* (generous love). *Cupiditas* and *caritas* are both necessary elements of the will, for in order for a person to love his neighbour he must also love himself; this in turn leads to the love of God.

(ii) Sex and friendship

Augustine wrote extensively on friendship. In his ground-breaking commentary on *Genesis*, Augustine argued that in paradise Adam and Eve were not only married, (other theologians of the time argued that marriage only occurred after the Fall to control lust), but married as friends, where they equally and mutually participated in the friendliness of God. Augustine argued that as God had commanded Adam and Eve to be 'fruitful and multiply, and fill the earth' (Genesis 1:28) then friendship between men and women also included reproduction as well as the pleasure of sex. Nevertheless, sex is always secondary to friendship; friendship being the highest expression of human existence.

Key person

Pelagius (354–440AD): He was born either in Britain or France, became a monk and taught in Rome. After the sack of Rome in 410AD, he fled to Carthage where he briefly met Augustine before settling in Palestine. His unorthodox teaching on free will meant that he was regarded as a heretic.

Key term

The Fall The moment described in Genesis 3 when Adam and Eve rebelled against God and were punished by being expelled from Eden (paradise). After the Fall humans are in disharmony with God and nature.

Key question

Why is obedience a virtue?

Key terms

Cupiditas and *caritas* Two Latin key words used by Augustine meaning love. The will is driven by *cupiditas*, self-love and *caritas*, generous love. Before the Fall they operate in harmony but after the Fall they work contrary to each other.

Therefore, sex when required would occur without lust and Adam could summon an erection at will; the will was in complete harmony and in control of the body.

Even after the Fall, friendship continues to express *caritas* as *amor Dei* (love of God). But in a fallen world friendship is far more complicated and fraught with anguish. Even so, as Augustine wrote in one of his letters, 'There is nothing truly enjoyable without a friend'. The solution is that true friendship (as experienced before the Fall) is only possible for those who love Christ first. Love for neighbour is then generous, forgiving and non-judgemental – it is removed from *cupiditas*. Christ, Augustine famously said, did not choose his friends because they were senators but because they were fishermen - people without pride or arrogance.

(c) The human will after the Fall

And the Lord God commanded the man, 'You may freely eat of every tree of the garden; but of the tree of the knowledge of good and evil you shall not eat, for in the day that you eat of it you shall die.'

Genesis 3:16–17

(i) Pride and disobedience

Augustine discusses the Fall (from Genesis 3) at length in his *City of God*. The key problem which faced Augustine was what caused humans to reject their perfect relationship with the world and with God. The answer is pride. Augustine interpreted Adam and Eve's decision to eat from the forbidden tree of knowledge in Eden to be a sign of their desire to be like God, knowing good and evil and having its powers. Pride means that they can never again enjoy the harmonious relationship with God and with each other because *cupiditas* has now been separated from *caritas*.

Nevertheless, there still remained the question of how the idea of wanting to have God's knowledge and disobeying God's command could have entered the minds of Adam and Eve in the first place. Augustine's answer is based on the tradition that Satan was originally an angel who through pride fell from grace and tried to rule the Earth. In Eden he takes on the form of the serpent and out of envy he plants the idea of disobedience into Eve's mind. Augustine describes the Satan's intention as the serpent in this way:

After his fall, his ambition was to worm his way, by seductive craftiness, into the consciousness of man, whose unfallen condition he envied, now that he himself had fallen.

Augustine: *City of God* Book XIV, Chapter 11

Satan's idea of disobedience is not the cause of the Fall but it provides the stimulus for the will to disobey God's commands. God may have foreseen that Adam and Eve would disobey him, but Augustine stresses that the act of rebellion is entirely the result of human free will. As he says more than once, 'the evil will precedes the evil act'. So, Augustine argues, as obedience is the 'mother and guardian of all the other virtues', pride (disobedience) is the cause of all other vices.

For they would not have arrived at the evil act if an evil will had not preceded it. Now, could anything but pride have been the start of the evil will? For 'pride is the start of every kind of sin'. And what is pride except a longing for a perverse kind of exaltation?

Augustine: *City of God* Book XIV, Chapter 13

Importantly, if the evil will precedes the evil act, then it is not the body which is corrupt but the will; Augustine resisted the Manichean idea that the body (along with the rest of the material) was evil and corrupt. But now that the will is weakened it is unable to control bodily desires and the natural desires for food and sex – especially sex – are no longer in harmony with the will but dominate it.

(ii) The divided will

Augustine argued that the distorted soul or will had now become divided. Although it was still rational enough to know what is morally good, the damage done to it in the Fall meant that despite willing to do good it is weakened by desires and does the opposite. This is the paradoxical state of the will which St Paul describes in his Letter to the Romans:

I do not understand my own actions. For I do not do what I want, but I do the very thing I hate … For I do not do the good I want, but the evil I do not want is what I do. Now if I do what I do not want, it is no longer I that do it, but sin that dwells within me.

Romans 7:15, 19–20

Ancient philosophers called this problem weakness of will or **akrasia**. Plato and Aristotle doubted whether there really is such a state as weakness of will. For example, when I lie in bed for another ten minutes in the morning when I should be getting up, it is not that I lack moral will power, it is simply that I have given preference to one choice over another. Or it could be that I have unconsciously reasoned that I need more sleep so although it may *feel* as if I have weakened, in fact I am only doing what I intended to do. But the explanation for Augustine (as it is for St Paul) is that the will is weakened because of the sin caused by Adam at the Fall.

Augustine presents his commentary on Romans 7 in his *Confessions* Book 8. Here he describes this will as 'half wounded' and divided, ingrained out of habit, like trying to leave a comfortable bed but failing to do so. The will is at war with itself and unable to obey its own orders. Augustine realises that he cannot put behind him his past relationships with women and embrace celibacy. Even the vision of '**Lady Continence**' calling him to the pure, serene and chaste life is not enough to overcome his desires:

But by now the voice of habit was very faint. I had turned my eyes elsewhere, and while I stood trembling at the barrier, in the barrier, on the other side I could see the chaste beauty of Continence in all her serene, unsullied joy, as she modestly beckoned me to cross and hesitate no more … I was overcome with shame, because I was still listening to the futile mutterings of my lower self.

Augustine: *Confessions* 8.11

Key question

Why do people do the things they don't want to do?

Key terms

Akrasia (weakness of will) Aristotle describes four stages of the moral life: wickedness (*akolosia*); weakness (*akrasia*); self-control (*enkrateia*); and temperance, life without struggle (*sophrosyne*).

Continence Self-restraint especially to abstain from sexual pleasures. Augustine describes continence using the metaphor of a beautiful chaste woman.

255

Key term

Concupiscence Sexual lust but can also refer to uncontrolled desires of all kinds such as craving food, power, and money.

Key quote

Human nature then is, without any doubt, ashamed about lust, and rightly ashamed.

Augustine: *City of God* Book XIV, Chapter 20

See pages 250–252 on Manicheism.

Key quote

The snare of concupiscence awaits me in the very process of passing from the discomfort of hunger to the contentment which comes when it is satisfied.

Augustine: *Confessions* 10.31

Key question

Should Original Sin be understood symbolically or as a reality?

Key term

Post-Lapsarian The world after the Fall of Adam and Eve, or simply the fallen world.

Augustine believed that it was because of Adam's disobedience that it has from that time onwards made it impossible for humans to be truly good.

(iii) Concupiscence

In his fallen state man is no longer able to control his libido and the appetitive or desiring aspect of his soul is completely dominated by concupiscence. Augustine was careful not to accept either the Manichaean argument that the body is evil and sinful or the Neoplatonic notion that because it belongs to the realm of flesh the body is necessarily imperfect. The body cannot be sinful because it was created to be good by God. But now that the will is weak and divided, concupiscence dominates human existence. Unmoderated, the body craves power, food, money and above all sexual intercourse.

Concupiscence	
In morality	*In theology*
The bodily appetites or tendencies, or simply passions.	The proneness of sin in humankind's nature due to the fall of Adam and Eve.

Concupiscence is most clearly and painfully experienced in friendships. Augustine shared with his philosophical friends the idea that nothing could be better than a community of friends as equals. But in reality even with the closest friends jealousy, betrayal, even death all conspire to cause pain and undermine true friendship. We also invest so heavily in friendships that we are distracted from loving God. Friendship illustrates Augustine's deep ambivalence about human nature. For example, although he had many women amongst his friends he would never meet them alone. Peter Brown comments:

> He would never visit a woman unchaperoned, and he did not allow even his own female relatives to enter the bishop's palace. He expelled a young clergyman who had been found speaking with a nun 'at an inappropriate hour of the day'.

Peter Brown: *The Body and Society* (1988), p. 396

(iv) Original Sin

In the post-Lapsarian world the effects of Adam's sin can be seen in the continued rebellious state of the will. Everywhere one looks the effects of the Fall on human nature can be seen. Man has spontaneous erections, wet dreams and loss of rational control during sexual orgasm. The presence of concupiscence illustrates the lack of control that the rational soul has over sin. Even impotence or lack of libido is a sign that the uncontrolled body mocks the weak and divided will.

Original Sin The Christian notion that despite being created in the image of God, all humans fail to fulfil this potential and live in disharmony. This is the human condition. Original Sin is different from actual sins which are committed by individuals.

Ontology The study of how something exists and the nature of its properties.

Key quote

Hence from the misuse of free will there started a chain of disasters: mankind is led from that original perversion, a kind of corruption at the root, right up to the disaster of the second death.

Augustine: *City of God* Book XIII, Chapter 14

Key question

Does Augustine's teaching on predestination suggest he has a pessimistic view of human nature?

See pages 279–281 on predestination.

Augustine had now forged a very distinctive view of **Original Sin**. Whereas other theologians took the phrase from St Paul that 'sin came into the world through one man' (Romans 5:12) to describe the inadequacies that all humans are prone to, Augustine made this sin an **ontological** condition of human existence, not just a description of our behaviour on occasions. No one is truly good however virtuous they might appear to be.

The chief characteristic of Original Sin is that it is passed on from the first or original moment to all generations. Augustine describes Original Sin in the following ways:

■ **Double death.** The first 'death' is caused by Adam's rebellious will which kills the relationship of friendship between humans and God; it is symbolised by Adam and Eve's embarrassment of their nakedness in front of God (Genesis 3:8–10). The second death is the mortal state of every human and is God's punishment for the first disobedience (Genesis 3:19).

■ **Transmission of sin.** The original act of disobedience is transmitted by a 'chain of disasters'. Just as a bad tree bears rotten fruit, so Adam's children also bear his rebellious nature. Every act of sexual intercourse is tainted by concupiscence, so that every human is 'born in sin'. Therefore, with the exception of Mary, who conceived Jesus without lust, all other humans are tainted with the Original Sin of Adam.

Hence from the misuse of free will there started a chain of disasters: mankind is led from that original perversion, a kind of corruption at the root, right up to the disaster of the second death, which has no end. Only those who are set free through God's grace escape from this calamitous sequence.

Augustine: *City of God* Book XIII, Chapter 14

(v) Free will and predestination

Augustine's view of free will changed over time. As a young scholar, Augustine believed that humans do have free will. He argued along Platonist lines that living the virtuous is possible; sin and evil are merely the failure to do good. Later he radically revised his book *On Free Will*; he no longer accepted that the Platonist view that reason is sufficient to live a good life and he now concluded that the sex drive, ignorance and death were punishments for human rebellion which no amount of human reasoning could ever overcome. His important Christian insight was that human beings do not voluntarily choose to sin but are inevitably prone to sin whether they will it or not. Humans prefer falsehoods to truth because their souls are 'fettered' and chained down by sin.

Augustine's sense of sin is so powerful that even those living a chaste life as a monk or nun, will never be free or strong enough to resist concupiscence – particularly the desire for sex. For that reason he encouraged married couples to abstain from sex after having children.

But the implications of this reasoning and his strong rejection of any view which undermined God's grace (in particular Pelagianism) led him to a hard-line view of predestination which even he found worrying. As only God knows who is deserving of his grace (the elect) to be rewarded with heaven then all humans can do is to persevere in hope and faith. From this point of view Augustine is not a pessimist but an optimist – for without God's grace no one would be saved from the effects of Original Sin. Augustine was much criticised by his contemporaries (as he is now) for a view which undermines the Christian belief in the God of love and the sacrifice of Christ for all the 'sins of the world' not for the sins of a few.

(d) Grace

Key question

Is Augustine right that sin means that humans can never be morally good?

Key term

Grace God's generous, undeserved and free act of love for the world expressed supremely in the giving of his son Jesus Christ in order that humans might overcome their sinful natures.

Human nature offers a tantalising possibility that with just a bit more effort we could achieve the harmonious relationship with God which would lead to the *summum bonum* – the greatest good. Augustine's experience of life, his memories of past pleasures which continued to haunt his dreams, led him frequently to ask the question posed by St Paul, 'who will rescue me from this body of death?' (Romans 7:24). There is only one answer and that is God. It is through God's generous love that the damaged will can be healed and the human relationship with God restored. The wound is healed through God's **grace** alone as expressed in God's gift of his son Jesus Christ in which the guilt and punishment of the Original Sin committed by Adam and Eve are removed. If this were not so, then there would be no possibility of redemption for humankind.

Augustine concludes that although he admires the philosophy of the Platonists and Stoics, he does not accept their belief that humans have sufficient reason to live the good life. Just as he rejected Aristotle's interpretation of the weakness of will (*akrasia*), he also dismissed the idea that through self-control humans can live life without struggle (*sophrosyne*). The purpose of faith is to recognise the failings of human nature and to place one's trust in God's love and grace.

4 Interpreting Augustine today

(a) The Fall and Original Sin

(i) The Fall as symbol of a person's spiritual journey

Key question

Should the Fall and Original Sin be understood in historical or in symbolic terms?

For many, the symbols of the Fall, renewal (dying to sin rising to new life) and redemption are positive symbols of the spiritual and psychological life.

Many Christians today consider creation, Fall and redemption not as separate events in world history but the history of each person's individual life. The Fall as described in Genesis 3, might be interpreted generally as an imaginative story about humans and their relationship with the world and specifically as the moment when each of us loses our innocence and have to engage with the harsh realities of life. In other words, the Fall is not a one-off moment in the mists of time, but a crucial moment when each person rebels against God and acts selfishly for their own ends.

This interpretation is much closer to the Jewish interpretation of Genesis 3. For in Judaism there are no doctrines of Original Sin and Fall. Genesis 3 is read as an example of the human journey towards perfection made possible through the subsequent giving of the Torah. Whereas for

Christians it is Christ not the Torah which is the example of perfection, many Christian theologians today consider that Augustine's idea of the 'Fall' does not leave enough room for human moral and spiritual development.

While contemporary science and philosophy may have challenged some aspects of the Augustinian tradition, the value of Augustine's assessment of the human condition is that he highlights the significance of the *spiritual* dimension of being human. Even so, some modification of Augustine is needed. For example, some scholars have pointed out that Augustine has misinterpreted what Paul meant when he spoke of our 'body of death' (Romans 7:24). What Paul meant by 'body' is not a Platonic separation between the corrupted body on the one hand and soul or spirit on the other, but the whole human personality which has fallen short of perfection. The spirit is not a disembodied power but the aspect of an individual's personality which is open to God and desires **redemption**. The Fall is the symbolic moment when a person first realises his situation and begins his spiritual journey.

So, if the Fall is a moment in the Christian human narrative describing the beginning of every individual's spiritual life, then the end of the narrative concludes as each person achieves a state of wholeness in Christ. In other words each person's life is not merely a biological journey from birth to death but a spiritual journey of body *and* spirit. This Christian view believes that human existence is not defined by death but the hope that the spiritual journey will continue on until each person is united with God after death. It is not an easy journey, as Augustine's evocative examples of human behaviour illustrate, for even the greatest of human achievements are counterbalanced by acts of human horror.

(ii) Belief in Original Sin is irrational and dangerous

Richard Dawkins finds the whole Christian notion of Fall and Original Sin not only entirely contrary to evolutionary biology but also absurd and dangerous. He blames a very great deal of human suffering and conflict on the 'Original Sin' tradition which Augustine created. Dawkins argues that:

- It is absurd to imagine the corruption of all humans rests on two individuals. As evolutionary biology considers that humans (as *Homo sapiens*) emerged from less sophisticated animal forms who did not have the kind of consciousness which enabled them to make an active decision to rebel, then a literal belief in Adam and Eve makes no sense.
- Even a symbolic account of the Fall does not rid Christianity of its unhealthy obsession with sin, guilt, violence and repressed sexuality.
- The idea that God should wish to restore human nature by killing Jesus on the cross is sadomasochistic and irrational.

> **Key person**
>
> **Richard Dawkins:** An evolutionary biologist and outspoken atheist critic of religion. He was professor of the Public Understanding of Science at Oxford University and has published widely. His many books include *The Selfish Gene* (1976), *The Blind Watchmaker* (1986) and *The God Delusion* (2006).

> **Key term**
>
> **Redemption** When humans are freed from sin, suffering and death. In Christian thought redemption of the world is through Jesus Christ.

> **Key question**
>
> Does Augustine's teaching on the Fall actually cause emotional harm?

> **Key quote**
>
> What kind of ethical philosophy is it that condemns every child, even before it is born, to inherit the sin of a remote ancestor? ... But now, the sadomasochism. God incarnated himself as a man, Jesus, in order that he should be tortured and executed in *atonement* for the hereditary sin of Adam.
>
> Richard Dawkins: *The God Delusion* (2006), pp. 251–252

Key question

Do humans become less violent as society becomes more rational and less religious?

Key terms

Post-Enlightenment Refers primarily to the eighteenth-century thinkers such as Hume, Rousseau and Kant who argued that knowledge could only be obtained through human reason and observation and not through divine revelation or other authorities.

Humanitarian principle Proposes that humans get on better when each person takes into account the interests of others.

Key person

Steven Pinker (b. 1954): The Johnstone Family Professor of Psychology at Harvard University whose research interests include language and cognition.

Key question

Would public leaders achieve more if they believed in the reality of sin?

(iii) The challenge of the humanitarian principle

Dawkins' views are shared and developed by the psychologist Steven Pinker. Pinker's argument is that religion in general, and Christianity in particular, has been responsible for violence, suffering and the debasement of humanity until **Post-Enlightenment** when the irrational superstitions of Christianity such as the Fall, Original Sin and grace were replaced by the **humanitarian principle**. The humanitarian principle makes the simple but significant proposal that humans get on better when each person takes into account the interests of others. This works because as each person is a rational being then each respects the interests of others as rational beings. This doesn't require God's grace as it can be done through autonomous rational negotiation.

> *You and I ought to reach this moral understanding not just so we can have a logically consistent conversation but because mutual unselfishness is the only way we can simultaneously pursue our interests. You and I are better off if we share our surpluses, rescue each other's children when they get into trouble, and refrain from knifing each other than we would be if we hoarded our surpluses while they rotted, let each other's children drown, and feuded incessantly.*

Steven Pinker: *The Better Angels of Our Nature* (2011), p. 182

Pinker argues that for the past two hundred years since the humanitarian principle has become established as self-evidently right, the West has seen the rapid decline of capital punishment, everyday use of torture in the judicial system, wars of religion, abuse of women, tyrants and despotic leaders.

(b) Sin and collective moral responsibility

Reinhold Niebuhr argued that although the post-Enlightenment thinkers such as Hume, Kant, Bentham and Mill (the tradition which Pinker associates with) have made it unfashionable to talk about sin, failure to understand sin leads to colossal mistakes being made by society and especially by those in power.

Key person

Reinhold Niebuhr (1892–1971): An American theologian and influential writer on ethics and politics. As a young man he embraced a liberal form of Christianity but in the 1930s he transferred to neo-orthodoxy because of its realistic understanding of sin and the human condition. For most of his career he was professor of Christian Ethics at the Union Theological Seminary, New York. His books include *Moral Man and Immoral Society* (1932) and *The Nature and Destiny of Man* (1941).

Niebuhr's argument is quite simply that the rationalism of Western philosophy and politics has failed. The optimistic vision of the post-Enlightenment thinker has not only failed (war, poverty and cruelty abound) but more worryingly the idea has corrupted the human sense of responsibility. By rationalising and rejecting the traditional notion of sin, humans at every level fail to realise that no action can ever be entirely good and this causes greater injustices and more suffering. This may not be so apparent at the individual level, but collectively when people act in groups then their faults become greatly exaggerated.

> **Key quote**
>
> The perennial tragedy of human history is that those who cultivate the spiritual elements usually do so by divorcing themselves from or misunderstanding the problems of collective man, where the brutal elements are most obvious ... To the end of history the peace of the world, as Augustine observed, must be gained by strife. It will not be perfect peace.
>
> Reinhold Niebuhr: *Moral Man and Immoral Society* (1932), p. 256

In Augustine's terms the inner spiritual will is defeated by egoism and self-interest. In particular, Niebuhr accuses both religious and non-religious leaders of ignorance if they think that the power of reason and belief in moral goodness is enough to bring about just and fair societies. This ill-founded idea must be rejected.

But Niebuhr is no fatalist; he does not think, as some Augustinians have, that there is nothing we can do to remedy the human condition as this would remove all responsibility; the solution is for the human ego to understand its own nature fully by coming into a proper relationship with God. Once the ego comes into contact with God it is able to realise both its limitations and its possibilities.

Niebuhr has had enormous influence on a wide range of theologians. His illustrations of the paradoxes of human behaviour have reminded theologians that human nature cannot be easily defined as either good or evil. Three such paradoxes are that:

- Original Sin is both 'inevitable but not necessary'.
- Sin is apparent in evil as well as good acts. Evil people can do kind things; good people still selfishly desire self-affirmation.
- At an individual level good people may do good things but when acting as part of a group they do not.

Niebuhr's teaching on sin shares similarities with Augustine's sense of its power and pervasiveness while avoiding linking it to sex and the body. But it is in his challenge to moral and political philosophy and theology where his impact has been most felt.

(c) Sex and human nature

> **Key quote**
>
> Has Christianity focused too much on sex and sin?

Just how significant is the sex drive for understanding human nature? Many have argued that it is largely Augustine's fault that for hundreds of years, Western societies have felt guilt about sex. During this time the Church has seen its role as controlling sexual behaviour through marriage and teaching people to repress and banish all sexual impulses. Sigmund Freud's considerable contribution to the Western view of sex and human

Summary diagram: Augustine on human nature

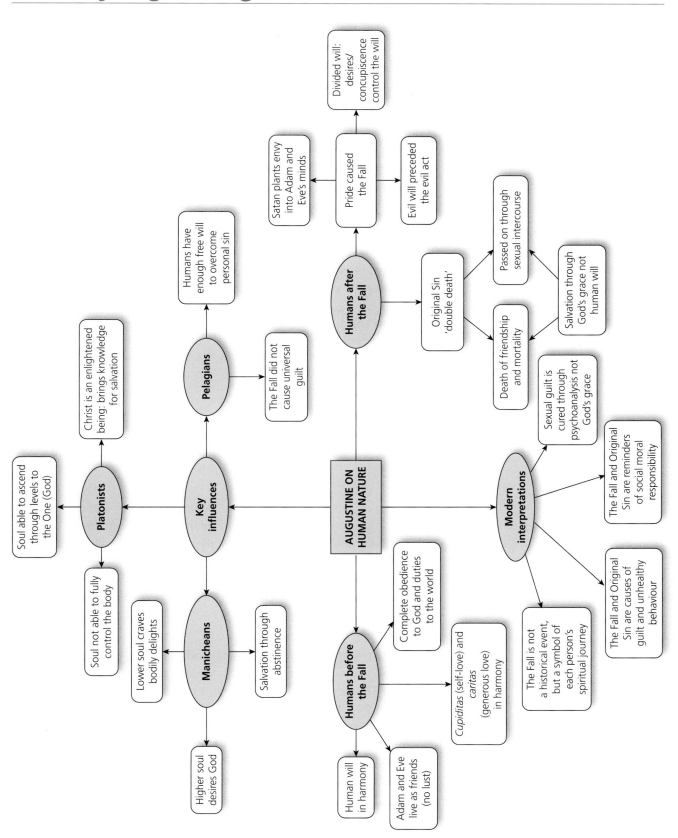

AUGUSTINE ON HUMAN NATURE

Key influences

Platonists
- Christ is an enlightened being: brings knowledge for salvation
- Soul able to ascend through levels to the One (God)
- Soul not able to fully control the body

Manicheans
- Lower soul craves bodily delights
- Salvation through abstinence
- Higher soul desires God

Pelagians
- Humans have enough free will to overcome personal sin
- The Fall did not cause universal guilt

Humans after the Fall
- Pride caused the Fall
  - Satan plants envy into Adam and Eve's minds
  - Divided will: desires/concupiscence control the will
  - Evil will preceded the evil act
- Original Sin 'double death'
  - Passed on through sexual intercourse
  - Death of friendship and mortality
  - Salvation through God's grace not human will

Humans before the Fall
- Complete obedience to God and duties to the world
- Cupiditas (self-love) and caritas (generous love) in harmony
- Human will in harmony
- Adam and Eve live as friends (no lust)

Modern interpretations
- Sexual guilt is cured through psychoanalysis not God's grace
- The Fall and Original Sin are reminders of social moral responsibility
- The Fall and Original Sin are causes of guilt and unhealthy behaviour
- The Fall is not a historical event, but a symbol of each person's spiritual journey

Sample question and guidance

Assess the view that Augustine's teaching on human nature is too pessimistic.

The essay might begin by setting out Augustine's main ideas such as his explanation of men and women's relationship before the Fall and the notion that in this state of harmony the body and will were one and Adam and Eve enjoyed perfect friendship. It might then go on to explain that the Fall was caused by the rebellious will and that the disharmony which followed can be seen in the failure of the will to control the natural drives of the body and in the failure of society to live according to God's laws.

The essay might then consider whether Augustine's view of life and human nature is pessimistic. On the one hand, as the Fall has destroyed human free will, then there is nothing humans can do to overcome Original Sin – Augustine's notion of predestination and human depravity is pessimistic especially when compared to other Christian interpretations of human nature. On the other hand, it might be argued that his teaching is realistic and society should take into account the effects of sin (as Niebuhr suggests).

Further essay questions

'If the Fall did not actually happen, then Christian teaching on human nature makes no sense.' Discuss.

Critically assess Augustine's analysis of human sexual nature.

To what extent has Augustine's teaching on human nature caused more harm than good?

Going further

Augustine: *The City of God* (Penguin, 1972). Book XIV deals with the Fall and its effects.

Peter Brown: *Augustine of Hippo* (new edition, University of California Press, 2013). This is the classic biography which was first published in 1967; read chapter 16 on the *Confessions*.

Henry Chadwick: *Augustine: A Very Short Introduction* (Oxford University Press, 1986). A very accessible introduction; read it all but chapter 10 is specifically on human nature.

Reinhold Niebuhr: *Moral Man and Immoral Society* (Charles Scribner's Sons, 1932). A highly influential book which deals with the effects of collective sin and its impact on society.

Steven Pinker: *The Better Angels of Our Nature* (Penguin, 2012). Chapter 4 describes society before and after the emergence of the humanitarian principle.

Rowan Williams: *On Augustine* (Bloomsbury, 2016). Chapter 5 on evil provides a useful way of combining Augustine's analysis of human nature and the study of evil in the philosophy of religion section of this course.

Other books we've talked about in this chapter are:
- Brown P. *The Body and Society* (Columbia University Press, 1988).
- Dawkins R. *The Blind Watchmaker* (Norton, 1986).
- Dawkins R. *The God Delusion* (Bantam Books, 2006).
- Dawkins R. *The Selfish Gene* (Oxford University Press, 1976).
- Niebuhr R. *The Nature and Destiny of Man* (Prentice-Hall, 1941).

Chapter 17

Death and the afterlife

1 Introduction

Chapter checklist

This chapter begins by considering the origins of Christian ideas of purgatory, heaven and hell in the New Testament and several problems which these ideas have posed for Christian theology. It then looks at Jesus' parable of judgement, the Sheep and the Goats where heaven, hell and judgement are considered and their moral implications are discussed. The chapter then investigates how purgatory, heaven and hell have been interpreted by various theologians, thinkers and philosophers over time to the present day.

2 New Testament foundations

Key terms

Eschatology Means literally 'discussion (description) of the last things' at the end of time such as: the battle between good and evil; the judgement of the world by God; the transformation of the world to its final perfect state. Some forms of eschatology consider the process of transformation to have already started and will only be completed at the end of time.

Pharisees Were emerging at the time of Jesus as a distinctive and influential group of religious teachers. Their aim was to achieve ritual cleanliness and fulfil the commandments of the law. Unlike many traditional Jews in the first century (such as the Sadducees) they believed in the existence of angels and resurrection of the body after death.

(a) Jesus' resurrection and its implications

As important as Jesus' resurrection is for the writers of the New Testament, there is no systematic explanation of resurrection and the afterlife. Nevertheless, there is broad agreement that for those early writers:

- Jesus' death and resurrection did not mark the end of the world but the beginning of the Jesus movement and the foundation of Christianity.
- Jesus' resurrection was a moment of hope over despair.
- Jesus' resurrection was a moment in which God acted in a mysterious and spectacular way.

As time went on the early Christians reflected on these ideas and began to give them greater theological and philosophical emphasis.

(b) The ambiguities of Jesus resurrection

Jesus' teaching on life after death and the coming of the Kingdom of God was deeply rooted in the Jewish **eschatology** of his day – especially in the teaching of the **Pharisees**. Pharisaic Judaism had, to a certain extent, absorbed Greek philosophical ideas about the soul and immortality. But Jesus' teaching on death and its significance is not just about immortality but the establishment of a new world order. He taught that:

- His life was a sacrifice for sin.
- His death would prompt God to establish a new world order/kingdom.

■ He would be raised up with the saints and **martyrs** who had died before him and his followers would have a place in the new kingdom.

However, Jesus' own teaching must have been sufficiently ambiguous for a variety of different views to have developed about when and how the kingdom would be established.

Consider the following sayings of Jesus:

The time is fulfilled, and the kingdom of God has come near.

Mark 1:14

Truly I tell you, there are some standing here who will not taste death until they see that the kingdom of God has come with power.

Mark 9:1

But if it is by the finger of God that I cast out the demons, then the kingdom of God has come to you.

Luke 11:20

Some passages in the New Testament suggest that many early Christians thought they were living on the threshold of a new era. They seem to have expected the resurrected Jesus to return shortly and herald in the new glorious state. The word in Greek used to describe the arrival of Jesus is **parousia** and it became a technical expression for the arrival of Christ after his resurrection when he would usher in the Kingdom of God. The role of the parousia is to judge the world and select those who have lived a good life to live eternally in the world, now restored and renewed by God.

Jesus' parables variously describe the restored world using metaphors of weddings, feasts and harvest time, but the fullest descriptions are to be found in the **Book of Revelation** where the author depicts the age to come as a time when there would be no more suffering and a new heavenly Jerusalem would descend to Earth as a symbol of the renewed world.

Then I saw a new heaven and a new earth; for the first heaven and first earth had passed away, and the sea was no more. And I saw the holy city, new Jerusalem, coming down out of heaven from God, prepared as a bride adorned for her husband. And I heard a loud voice from the throne saying,

'See, the home of God is among mortals.
He will dwell with them;
they will be his peoples,
and God himself will be with them;
he will wipe away every tear from their eyes.
Death shall be no more;
mourning and crying and pain will be no more,
for the first things have passed away.'

Book of Revelation 21:1–4

For Jesus' moral example and teaching read pages 307–309.

(c) The Kingdom of God

Jesus' teaching on the age to come served several purposes depending on how we interpret what he meant by the Kingdom of God. There are three possible interpretations of what the Kingdom of God might be. It could be:

- an actual place
- a spiritual state
- a symbol of the moral life.

Depending on which of these interpretations seems most likely will determine whether we think heaven, hell and purgatory are actual places, spiritual states, or symbols of the moral life. We shall be constantly considering these possible interpretations in this chapter.

(i) The Kingdom as present moral and spiritual state

Jesus' own teaching on the Kingdom of God as presented in the Gospels was a call for moral and spiritual reform now. In many of Jesus' teachings he presents the Kingdom of God as if it has already started. Scholars refer to this as 'inaugurated eschatology'. Jesus' healing miracles where he cures the lame, gives sight to the blind and hearing to the deaf are the signs of the age to come as promised by the Old Testament prophets such as Isaiah.

Jesus' parables and moral example frequently emphasise the 'nowness' of the Kingdom as a time to overcome racial prejudice, discrimination against the poor and marginalised, and the failings of established religious practices.

(ii) The Kingdom as future redeemed state

But in other respects Jesus' eschatology is traditional and he preaches that the future Kingdom is a state where the righteous live in perfect harmony with God in a redeemed world. St Paul argues that Jesus' resurrection is the first sign that the fallen world is restored and that humans can at last 'see' and 'know' God face to face (1 Corinthians 13:12). St Paul says that before Christ humans were only able to see the future heavenly state dimly or through a 'dark glass' but now it is possible to glimpse what the future will be like 'clearly'. John the Divine, the author of the Book of Revelation, says that Jesus' sacrificial death has washed away sin so that the righteous may live in the New Jerusalem and experience the joy of God's presence (Revelation 21:1–4).

Other writers of the New Testament use a wide range of images to express the future state as a time of perfection and completion of the God–human relationship.

(iii) Punishment and justice

In answer to the question often posed in the Old Testament, notably by the prophet Jeremiah, why is it that the wicked prosper and the good suffer, the response is that whereas the good will be rewarded, the wicked will be punished. As Jesus says, the wicked have enjoyed their 'reward' and so as a matter of justice the wicked will be excluded from the future Kingdom.

And if your eye causes you to stumble, tear it out and throw it away; it is better for you to enter life with one eye than to have two eyes and to be thrown into the hell (Gehenna) of fire.

Matthew 18:9

Key terms

Gospel of Matthew Probably written around 75AD. Scholars generally consider the author to have revised Mark's Gospel and arranged the material in five teaching blocks. The author is especially interested in Jewish Law and its relationship with Jesus' new law.

Hades and **Gehenna** Hades is the place of departed spirits awaiting judgement. Gehenna originally referred to as the Valley of Hinnom as it was associated with death and pollution. In later Jewish thought it became a symbol of punishment for the wicked.

Sheol Old Testament equivalent to Hades, the underworld of departed spirits.

The Story of the Richman and Lazarus Also known as Dives and Lazarus (dives being the Latin word for rich man) is only found in Luke 16:19–31.

Sadducees A political party at the time of Jesus representing the interests of high-ranking aristocratic priests. Unlike the Pharisees they rejected ideas of the afterlife and the resurrection of the body.

The **Gospel of Matthew** in particular refers to the state as **Hades** and sometimes as **Gehenna** often translated as hell. Hades, in Greek thought, was a shadowy half existence of human spirits after death awaiting judgement whereas Gehenna, in later Jewish thought, was a place of torment and suffering for the wicked. The Old Testament equivalent to Hades is **Sheol**, the underworld of departed spirits. Matthew combines all these ideas to warn the unrighteous that the state of hell is fire, torment, wailing and lament. The Book of Revelation similarly describes hell as a lake of fire.

Then Death and Hades were thrown into the lake of fire. This is the second death, the lake of fire; and anyone whose name was not found written in the book of life was thrown into the lake of fire.

Revelation 20:14–15

One of the most influential passages for later Christian theologians is the story told by Jesus of **The Richman and Lazarus**. The story relates how a rich man steadfastly ignored Lazarus, a poor and ill man who lay at his gate, while he 'feasted sumptuously' and dressed in the finest clothes. It so happened that both died on the same day and in a great reversal of fortunes Lazarus found himself in heaven with the righteous (described as being far away in 'Abraham's bosom') and the rich man in Hades. In Hades, the rich man is in torment and desperate for a drink because of the flames. From hell the rich man can see Lazarus in heaven and requests that he comes and 'dip the tip of his finger in water and cool' his tongue. Even though pictorially heaven and hell are presented as being close to each other, spiritually and morally they are utterly different. The rich man's unreformed attitude to Lazarus reinforces why he has been punished. To his request Abraham answers with a stern warning:

Child, remember that during your lifetime you received your good things, and Lazarus in the like manner evil things; but now he is comforted here, and you are in agony. Besides all this, between you and us a great chasm has been fixed, so that those who might want to pass from here to you cannot do so, and no one can cross from there to us.

Luke 16:25–26

No account is given of Lazarus' moral character, so it is assumed that he lived the best life that he could, given his circumstances. But the real purpose of the story is to challenge the common belief that being rich on Earth was a sign of God's blessing. Some scholars suggest that rich man may have been a wealthy **Sadducee**. The Sadducees were priests who maintained the Temple in Jerusalem and did not believe in the afterlife. The story therefore challenges a number of well held beliefs, but above all answers Jeremiah's question: the wicked will receive their just deserts if not now, then in the next life.

(d) Four problems

(i) The delay of the parousia

It seems that the first generations earnestly hoped for Jesus' return and the arrival of the Kingdom for one of the earliest prayers recorded in the

Key term

Maran atha An Aramaic term which is often translated as, 'O Lord, come!' or 'Come, O Lord!' The Aramaic language is related to Hebrew and was spoken by Jesus and the very early Christians. The fact that the word is recorded in Aramaic indicates its importance although the New Testament is written in Greek.

Key quote

Therefore you also must be ready; for the Son of Man is coming at an unexpected hour.
Matthew 24:44

Key question

Is God's judgement to take place immediately after death or at the end of time?

New Testament uses the Aramaic term *maran atha* meaning 'O Lord, come!'.

> Let anyone be accursed who has no love for the Lord. Our Lord, come!

1 Corinthians 16:22

But a generation later Jesus had not returned and so a new eschatology emerged to deal with this problem, what contemporary scholars call the delay of the parousia issue. That is:

- On reflection many recalled that Jesus himself had warned against making exact calculations when the present age would end and judgement day take place. Referring to himself as the Son of Man, Jesus says: 'But about that day and hour no one knows, neither the angels of heaven, nor the Son, but only the Father.' (Matthew 24:36).
- Reviewing Jesus' parables some emphasised that the theme of delay and sudden return of a master 'like a thief at night' (1 Thessalonians 5:3). With this came a warning that despite the delay of the Kingdom, there was every reason to be morally vigilant because the end when it arrives will be without warning.

(ii) Place

Another problem which has already been touched on is where the new kingdom would be located and would this be the same as heaven? John the Divine's vision in the Book of Revelation, suggests that heaven is not a disembodied state but a continuation of the conditions of this world. He describes this in two ways. In the first, the saints who have undergone the 'first resurrection' (Revelation 20:4–5), rule in some form of heavenly state in this world for a thousand years. In the second, after the final vanquishing of Satan, the world is replaced by a 'the new earth and new heaven'.

(iii) Time and judgement

Even though the exact moment of judgement day at the 'end' of time is uncertain, many of the New Testament writers suggest that 'final' judgement may be less important than personal judgement. We have already seen in the story of The Rich Man and Lazarus, that judgement is immediate after death. And in Luke's Gospel, Jesus says to the penitent robber who was crucified alongside him, 'today you will be with me in Paradise' (Luke 23:43).

In Matthew's Gospel, the writer describes how the righteous, who have died before Jesus, are resurrected at the moment when Jesus dies and his death establishes the new covenant with God (Matthew 27:51–53).

The author of John's Gospel offers the most radical interpretation of judgement. For him, what matters is the way in which individuals respond to Christ: judgement is personal and continual. Those who reject Christ's teaching effectively condemn themselves, as this passage suggests:

> For God so loved the world that he gave his only Son, that everyone who believes in him may not perish but may have eternal life. Indeed, God did not send the Son into the world to

condemn the world, but in order that the world might be saved through him. Those who believe in him are not condemned; but those who do not believe are condemned already.

John 3:16–18

Nevertheless, even though John's Gospel largely marginalises the idea of last judgement, it does not dismiss it completely. For example, in the following passage Jesus is presented as acting on God's behalf as the judge of the good and the evil. It is ambiguous whether this judgement takes place at Jesus' own resurrection or at the moment of an individual's death or a collective event, at an unspecified time in the future.

Do not be astonished at this; for the hour is coming when all who are in their graves will hear his voice and will come out – those who have done good, to the resurrection of life, and those who have done evil, to the resurrection of condemnation.

John 5:28–29

It is for these reasons that the Catholic Church teaches that judgement is particular and general. At death each person's soul will receive its 'eternal retribution' with a *particular* judgement depending on how they have lived their life in relation to Christ. Each soul is rewarded with the blessed state (heaven), purification (purgatory) or everlasting damnation (hell). But the world is yet to find completion and this can only happen when at the last judgement *all* people will be judged, 'in the presence of Christ, who is Truth itself, the truth of each man's relationship with God will be laid bare' (*Catechism* para. 1039).

Finally, based on Revelation 20:2–6, there is the problem of **millenarianism**, the belief that when Christ returns he will rule for a thousand years with the saints on Earth and at the end judgement would follow for the rest of humanity. Millenarianism has always been popular at times when the world appears to be on the brink of political and natural disaster as these are the signs that the present age is about to come to an end. Some millenarianists have positively encouraged environmental and nuclear destruction as a means of hastening the end for God to establish his kingdom.

However, since the time of Augustine, the more generally accepted interpretation of Revelation 20 is that it is referring to the rule of the Church in preparation for Christ's return. The role of the Church is to administer God's judgement on Earth until the last day when God will visibly judge the world.

(iv) Purgatory

Although the New Testament doesn't use the term **purgatory**, there is a widespread view that after death those who have died in a state of grace may continue to seek forgiveness for their sins and receive due punishment until final judgement.

In later Christian teaching, the idea that there is an intermediate state between death and everlasting life in heaven evolved for two reasons: firstly as a matter of fairness by allowing a person who had not fully prepared themselves for God's final judgement to do so and secondly

Key question

How should Revelation 20:2–6 be interpreted?

Key terms

Millenarianism (also known as the Chiliastic Doctrine): Is based on Revelation 20:2–5. It is the idea that Christ will return and rule on Earth for a thousand years followed by the last judgement.

Purgatory The state after death where those who have died in a state of grace may continue to seek forgiveness for their sins and receive due punishment until final judgement. Some Christians prefer to think of the soul continuing its journey through an intermediate state to heaven.

Key question

Is the idea of purgatory or intermediate state after death supported by the New Testament?

because of the ambiguity between personal and final judgement. A frequently cited passage in support of purgatory is the following verse from St Paul's letter to the Corinthians.

> *If what has been built on the foundation survives, the builder will receive a reward. If the work is burned, the builder will suffer loss; the builder will be saved, but only as through fire.*
>
> 1 Corinthians 3:14–15

For some, the phrase 'only as through fire' is interpreted to be the process of purging or cleansing required when at his personal judgement his work's or deeds on Earth were found to be inadequate or 'burned up'. However, many theologians don't find this interpretation at all convincing.

3 The parable of the Sheep and the Goats

Key term

Parable A short story or simple saying which illustrates a moral, spiritual or religious idea.

Key quote

Immediately after the suffering of those days, the sun will be darkened and the moon will not give its light.

Matthew 24:29

Key question

Read Matthew 25:31–46. What do you think the main purpose of the parable is?

See pages 281–282 where the idea of universalism is considered in more detail.

Matthew 25 forms part of the fifth section or discourse in the Gospel. In the previous chapter he describes the signs which will herald the end of the world and the coming of Jesus, as the Son of Man. So it is perhaps natural that this chapter should focus on God's judgement of the world prior to the arrival of the Kingdom.

The setting of this parable is drawn from farming life. The practice at that time was for goats and sheep to graze together during the day but to be separated out into different pens at night time. As sheep are worth more than goats the farmer usually places them in more secure accommodation. So, the parable suggests that even though in this life there appears to be no particular advantage to living morally, there is when judgement day arrives as the reward of eternal life is offered to those who have lived righteously.

The main teaching points of the parable are:

- For the members of Matthew's community the theme of reversal of expectation is particularly prominent in this parable. The 'righteous' would have been understood to refer to those who have kept the commandments of the Torah and have assumed that this was sufficient to earn themselves a place in heaven. It therefore comes as a great shock to learn that being righteous or religiously observant is not enough to be rewarded with eternal life. It is those who have pursued justice for the marginalised, oppressed and poor without thinking of heavenly reward who are given eternal life.
- Another surprise is that those who are rewarded are not necessarily Christians but *all* those who have pursued justice. This point is particularly emphasised by theologians today when considering the question of whether non-Christians can be saved or receive God's grace. The answer based on this parable is that the God of love rewards all people of good will.
- The list of good works reflects Jesus' own ministry of attending to the poor, the sick and even those in prison.
- The phrase 'just as you did it to one of the least of these who are members of my family, you did it to me' challenges the traditional teaching that one is only obliged to help those who belong to the same social and religious group as oneself. Surprisingly for the

so-called righteous, Christ's image or presence is to be found in the least attractive members of humanity.

4 Developments in Christian eschatological teaching

According to J. N. D. Kelly, in the early Christian period Christian eschatology focused on the four things: parousia, resurrection, judgement, the end of the present order. But as Kelly comments, these were not well thought-out systematised ideas.

> *In the primitive period they were held together in a naïve, unreflective fashion, with little or no attempt to work out their implications or solve the problems they raised.*

J. N. D. Kelly *Early Christian Doctrines* (1958) p. 462

The problems have not gone away. As each generation deals with these difficult ideas in its own historical and cultural context, it has to re-think life and death and the 'art of dying well'. The art of dying well depends on what the Christian thinks this life means and what happens next. In addition to considering whether heaven, hell and purgatory are places or spiritual states, Christian theologians over the years have also debated the following key questions:

- Are hell and heaven eternal?
- Is heaven the transformation and perfection of the whole of creation?
- Is purgatory a state that everyone goes through?
- Does God's judgement take place immediately after death or at the end of time?

(a) Hell

Of all Christian doctrines the notion of hell in recent times has been the least acceptable. This is due in part to the rejection of the over literal interpretation of hell as a place and the reinterpretation of it in psychological terms but more significantly its contrary purpose to God's love and desire for the redemption of the world. Concerns such as these have occupied the minds of Christian theologians from the earliest of times.

- **Spiritual state.** Origen regarded hell as a spiritual state where 'each sinner kindles his own fire ... and our own vices from its fuel'. Punishment is not inflicted by God through Satan but is rather each person's own 'interior anguish' at being separated from God. Origen did not think hell was a permanent state; it too will pass away when the world is finally redeemed.
- **Conscience.** Gregory of Nyssa argued that judgement and the torture of hell are the result of a guilty conscience when a person is placed in front of Christ.

Traditionally, though, final judgement is universal and the punishment eternal. For those who support this notion of hell, its purpose illustrates the necessity of belief in Christ and the need for repentance. Far from diminishing God's love, hell illustrates God's love and justice; if the wicked are not punished then God is diminished and his goodness questionable.

See Dante *Divine Comedy* 'Inferno' canto 28.

Key question

What do you think is the most heinous sin or crime in today's society?

Key person

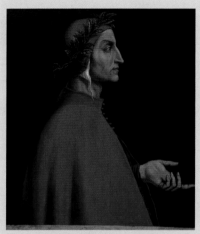

Dante Alighieri (1265–1321): Born in Florence, Italy and was a statesman and poet. His *Divine Comedy* describes his journey through hell (*Inferno*), purgatory (*Purgatorio*) and heaven (*Paradiso*) guided by the ancient Roman poet Virgil and then Beatrice – the object of his love. The *Comedy* is an imaginative and richly poetic work which is also deeply theological. His theology is greatly indebted to Thomas Aquinas.

Key term

Lucifer Means 'light-bearer' who, according to tradition, was a fallen angel.

(i) Dante's vision of hell

Perhaps the most influential, powerful and imaginative account of hell, purgatory and heaven is that given by Dante in his *Divine Comedy* (1308). Hell is in all respects, physical, mentally and spiritually, an utterly dysfunctional state. It was created at the moment of Jesus' death when, according to Matthew's Gospel (27:51–53), an earthquake caused the dead to awaken from their tombs. It is the antithesis to heaven – here reason is abandoned to irrationality, its inmates lack faith in God and live without hope. Dante records the terrifying sign over the gate to hell:

> *Through me the way into the woeful city,*
>
> *Through me the way to the eternal pain,*
>
> *Through me the way among the lost people.*
>
> *Justice moved my maker on high,*
>
> *Divine power made me and supreme wisdom and primal love;*
>
> *Before me nothing was created but eternal things and I endure eternally.*
>
> *Abandon every hope, ye that enter.*

Dante *Divine Comedy* 'Inferno' canto 3:1–9

Hell is characterised by the Aristotelian and Christian vices each of which occupies one of the nine circles of hell. In some graphic descriptions every sin is matched with an appropriate punishment – he sees a man carrying his head and swinging it like a lantern because in life he had taught lies and caused rebellions.

From *Dante's Inferno* by Gustave Doré

Finally, Dante is led by his guide to the ninth circle which is populated by the most heinous of vices, the sin of fraud through treachery. Betrayal of this kind is condemned because it is the ultimate misuse of reason and the cause of social and religious discord. This is the deepest and darkest part of hell where **Lucifer** has his throne. In Luke 10:18 Lucifer is equated with Satan (or the devil). and whose giant wings fan the freezing cold air over the traitors who are condemned there. It is so cold that they are unable to move or weep, incapable in other words to reason or repent and utterly unable even to glimpse either purgatory or heaven.

> *I was already – and with fear I set it down in verse – where the shades were wholly covered and showed through like straws in glass; some were lying, some erect, this with the head, that with the soles uppermost, another like a bow, bent face to feet.*

Dante *Divine Comedy* 'Inferno' canto 34

Dante singles out two examples of treachery: Judas Iscariot, who betrayed Christ, and Brutus and Cassius who murdered Caesar; together they represent those who have deliberately destabilised the God-given moral/spiritual order as well as the political order.

(ii) Hell as a symbol of alienation

For many theologians the power of Dante's terrifying descriptions of hell is that they force us not only to think about the consequences of our actions but also the kind of people we become through our actions. In Dante's hell, there is no escape and no redemption because all have alienated themselves from God's love. We might think his hell is unduly harsh on those who are there because they have never had the opportunity to know Christ, but hell in a sense is of our own making. His vivid descriptions were not intended to be taken literally but nor were they merely symbolic.

In our contemporary cosmology, we know that hell is not situated at the core of the Earth and heaven above – even though we may use the language of above and below. So, the question is whether hell-type language has any meaning or should be abandoned altogether as outmoded.

The existentialist theologian argues that there is a place for hell-type language if the traditional metaphors are reinterpreted as psychological and spiritual descriptions of human alienation. Paul Tillich follows the argument going back to Origen that if out of love God reconciles all things to himself, then it would be contradictory and immoral to exclude some of his creatures. So for Tillich, 'heaven and hell must be taken seriously as metaphors for the polar ultimates in the experience of the divine' (*Systematic Theology* III, 1964, p. 446). Hell maintains its psychological power as life alienated from God.

So, what might it mean to be alienated from the divine? Existentially it means to find no purpose in life, to lie to one's self, to escape from reality into trivia, to find no joy in music, art, nature and so on. Hell is not a place but a state of being.

A dramatic example of existential hell of this kind is not given by a theologian but the atheist playwright and philosopher Jean-Paul Sartre In his play *Huis Clos* ('No Exit') his hell is occupied by three people who have just died and think they are in a room waiting for the conventional religious hell of fire, brimstone and torture. But as time goes on they realise that there is no hell of this kind, the hell they discover is living with the lies, deceits, false relationships, cowardices and murders each has committed on Earth. They torment each other about the other's failings until it dawns on them that they have each become psychologically the torturer they were expecting of traditional hell. This is an acute example

Key person

Judas Iscariot: One of Jesus' twelve disciples who betrayed him for money to the Romans. In addition to his treachery, he committed suicide.

Key question

Is Tillich right? Is hell just an idea or a symbol of life alienated from God?

Key person

Paul Tillich (1886–1965): German-American Lutheran theologian and philosopher. Professor of philosophy at Frankfurt University and then moved to the USA in 1933 where he taught at first at the Union Theological Seminary in New York, then Harvard Divinity School and finally at the University of Chicago. His theology was strongly influenced by existentialism as can be seen in his influential three-volume *Systematic Theology* (1951–64).

Jean-Paul Sartre (1905–1980): Was a French philosopher, novelist, playwright and political activist. He developed the ideas of Heidegger into what was popularly called existentialism. His major philosophical work is *Being and Nothingness* (1943).

Mortal sin Sin which is morally gravely deficient, deliberately willed and in defiance of God's law. Venial sins by contrast, are errors of judgement and lack of moral knowledge which can be absolved through repentance.

of what Sartre calls 'bad faith' or the alienated and imprisoned human state. As the play draws to an end the terrible realisation is that there is 'no exit' because there is no freedom to be a truly individual person. In the final words of the play, 'hell is other people'.

(iii) Hell as eternal separation

The Catholic Church's teaches that hell is eternal for those who have committed **mortal sins**. Mortal sin includes hating one's neighbour and not meeting the needs of the poor and the weak (Matthew 25:31–46). To die in the state of mortal sin without repentance and 'accepting God's merciful love means remaining separated from him for ever' (*Catechism* para. 1033). Hell is not something which God actively chooses for humanity, rather it is the result of free choice and is self-imposed; hell is 'self-exclusion'.

Hell is not merely an idea it is a real eternal state; its chief punishment is the 'eternal separation from God, in whom alone man can possess the life and happiness for which he was created and for which he longs' (*Catechism* para. 1035). The notion of hell is to urge people to use their freedom wisely and to do good. It is the reason ultimately why the Church has an 'urgent call' or mission to convert people to Christianity. Hell is not something God wills for his creation but it is reserved for those who persistently reject goodness until final judgement.

(b) Purgatory and intermediate states

There is no clear idea of purgatory in the New Testament but it is part of both the Catholic and Protestant traditions as a way of extending the chance of repentance beyond this life.

- **Foretaste of heaven and hell**. Ambrose (340–397AD) considered purgatory to be a place where souls wait for judgement and have a foretaste of what is in store for them – either heaven or hell.
- **Probationary school.** Origen argued that purgatory was like a probationary school when the soul is given the opportunity over 'many worlds' of experience, to develop and perfect itself.
- **Redemption of the whole of creation.** Gregory of Nyssa held a similar view to Origen and emphasised the purifying purpose of purgatory is so that all people, both wicked and good, can be cleansed of their sins and enter heaven. In this way God, completes his purpose to redeem and restore the whole of creation.

(i) Dante's vision of purgatory

Purgatory, according to Dante, is for those souls who believe in Christ and have repented before death. They now have the opportunity to purge themselves of all wrongful desires and actions. As they are now unable to sin, the process is entirely positive and is totally unlike hell where punishment perpetuates the initial sin. Dante poetically describes how the soul ascends various 'terraces of the mountain' whose summit or goal is the beatific vision. At the end of the journey the mountain shakes and the soul ascends to heaven. Each of the terraces represents one of the seven deadly sins and is overseen by angels. The soul's driving force is love and increasingly towards the end of the ascent, reason. But the vision of

Engraving by Gustave Doré from Dante Alighieri's *Divine Comedy* 'Purgatory and Paradise'; Dante and Virgil meet the Avaricious

purgatory is not merely a description of what lies in store after death, but an allegory of how life should be lived now. Earth, like the mountain, provides various temptations which the soul has to conquer in its journey to achieve salvation in heaven.

(ii) Catholic teaching on purgatory

All who die in God's grace and friendship, but still imperfectly purified, are indeed assured of their eternal salvation; but after death they undergo purification, so as to achieve the holiness necessary to enter the joy of heaven.

Catechism of the Catholic Church para. 1030

Although the Catholic Church acknowledges that there is no specific teaching on purgatory in the New Testament, it reasons that ideas such as 'cleansing by fire' suggest that some sins can be forgiven in this age and some in the age to come. If this is so, then purgatory as a post mortem and interim state is just another stage in the soul's journey to redemption.

Purgatory also explains why the Church prays for the souls of the departed. This practice predates Christianity. The *Catechism* refers to the example of Judas Maccabeus (who lived in the second century BC), who prayed that the souls of the dead should be freed from sin.

(iii) John Hick on the intermediate state

Although purgatory has a significant place in Catholic theology, its lack of biblical support has meant that many Protestants have rejected it, preferring instead to focus on judgement, hell and heaven. However, many recent Protestant theologians have increasingly seen the value of purgatory, inspired by the arguments of Origen and Gregory of Nyssa, as it makes sense morally and philosophically to consider the state after death as a continued dynamic journey of soul or self. John Hick argues that the need for an intermediate state makes a great deal of logical sense as the 'gap between the individual's imperfection at the end of this life and the perfect heavenly state in which he is to participate has to be bridged' (*Death and Eternal Life,* 1976, p. 202). He rejects the Roman Catholic teaching that God judges who enters heaven, hell or purgatory at death and then makes his final judgement at the end of time. Hick argues that it makes more sense to think of the afterlife as a continuation of the 'person-making process' started on Earth where there are many intermediate states which people pass through on their journey to being finally united with God.

(c) Heaven

Heaven is the ultimate state in which humans come to see God 'face to face' (1 Corinthians 13:12). It is the state of pure knowledge when sin has been purged and the soul experiences the fullness of joy (John 15:11). As we have seen earlier in this chapter, heaven is not just the restoration of the God–human relationship, but of the *whole* of creation. This raises some important contemporary questions: is 'heaven' a state of life after death or just this world restored; can non-human animals enter heaven; are all humans capable of achieving the 'beatific vision'?

(i) Dante's vision of heaven

Heaven or paradise is beyond description, as Dante says, 'To go beyond the human cannot be put into words' ('Paradiso' canto 1:70–71). Whereas those who enter hell lack faith and reason, in paradise the rational soul yearns for the ultimate good and harmony with God's love. The end of the journey is Empyrean, from which God's light – the source of knowledge and illumination – descends. Just as there are nine spheres of hell, there are ten heavens or mobiles of paradise, each representing a different intellectual level of truth. Each soul, therefore, finds its own intellectual resting place and different degree of bliss. As Dante and Beatrice (his guide) rise up the spheres they are surrounded by the brightness of the souls; the light increases as the souls' bliss intensifies. They arrive in heaven illuminated by Christ's light and Beatrice takes her place amongst the saints. St Bernard now takes on the role of guide. He prays to the Virgin Mary on Dante's behalf and Dante finally ascends to the vision of God. The overwhelming experiencing is that God is the source of love which governs the universe.

(ii) Catholic teaching on the beatific vision

Dante's beautiful vision of heaven depends on a cosmology which thought that the world was at the centre of the cosmos and the planetary spheres. Beyond the final sphere, God rules in his heavenly court. Today, our cosmology is very different and while Dante's vision presents a psychologically evocative expression of the final human–God relationship, it would be wrong to think of heaven as occupying actual space and time.

The Catholic Church today teaches that the 'perfect life with the Most Holy Trinity – this communion of life and love with the Trinity, with the Virgin Mary, the angels and all the blessed – is called heaven' (*Catechism* para 1024). It is a 'state of supreme, definitive happiness', where God reveals himself and gives people the capacity to know and contemplate him in a new glorious way. This is the **beatific vision** or blessed state of everlasting bliss. The Catholic Church today teaches that heaven is a community of immortal souls who continue to be obedient to God's will as they reign with Christ for ever (Revelation 22:5) in this world and the world to come.

Key quotes

Paradise is the most beautiful and demanding of the three parts of the poem.

Peter Hainsworth and David Robey *Dante: A Very Short Introduction* (2015), p. 99

All powers of high imagining here failed. But now my will and my desire were turned, as wheels that move in equilibrium, by love that moves the sun and other stars.

Dante *Divine Comedy* 'Paradiso' canto 33:142–143

Key question

Is it wrong to think of heaven occupying space and time?

Key term

Beatific vision The final and perfect human state of everlasting happiness and knowledge of God. For the righteous it is achieved after death in heaven.

5 Election

Then he will send out the angels, and gather his elect from the four winds, from the ends of the earth to the ends of heaven.

Mark 13:27

God has not rejected his people whom he foreknew.

Romans 11:2

Key question

Who are the elect? On what grounds are they chosen? When are they chosen?

Key term

Predestination The Christian teaching that God choses and guides some people (the 'elect') to eternal salvation.

The word 'elect' (*ekloge* in Greek) is used by the New Testament writers and means 'choice' and refers to those who have been chosen or called by God for eternal life. But who are the elect? On what grounds are they chosen? When are they chosen?

(a) Limited and unlimited election

To complicate matters further, election is often associated with the closely related idea of **predestination**; whilst for some theologians the ideas are distinct for others election and predestination are interchangeable terms. But in simple terms both election and predestination are attempts to explain why it is that some people will be granted eternal life and others will not. But there is more to election than this. Election is about the nature of God and his relationship with his creation and particularly his just and gracious nature. These two ideas do not necessarily fit easily together and the two broad versions of election which emerge are incompatible for reasons which will become clear. The two versions are:

- **Limited election**. Salvation and reward of heaven in the afterlife is only for those whom God, out of his graciousness, chooses and judges to be righteous. From this some theologians have developed the idea of 'limited atonement': that is, that Christ died only for the sins of the elect.
- **Unlimited election**. The God of love calls all people to salvation and to achieve perfection; the promise of heaven in the afterlife is possible for all. Unlimited election leads to the doctrine of 'unlimited atonement': that is, that Christ died only for the sins of the whole world.

Alister E. McGrath *Christian Theology* (1994), p. 365.

Both views lead to considerable speculation; as Alister McGrath comments, election and predestination are 'often regarded as one of the most enigmatic and puzzling aspects of Christian theology.'

(b) Election and predestination

Key question

If God 'desires all men to be saved' then why haven't all theologians developed the doctrine of unlimited election?

It is from Augustine that the idea of predestination develops as a doctrine and which whom subsequent theologians take their lead. As we have seen Augustine's analysis of human nature led him to conclude that even faith in Christ's redemption was insufficient to overcome sin and concupiscence. This is so because the will has been so weakened by the Fall that it lacks any capacity to achieve sufficient merit for eternal life; salvation is only possible because of God's mercy and grace.

See pages 257–258 on Augustine and predestination.

God's grace is key to Augustine's doctrine of predestination. Grace is not prompted by the human condition or as a reward for human moral behaviour or human merit, because in each case God would be obliged to act. As God is the only completely free agent, his grace is freely given, uncoerced and unprompted.

Key term

Perdition Refers variously to: eternal punishment, hell, purgatory and damnation.

Therefore, even though God has called all people to salvation, he knows from the beginning that only some are eligible for a place in heaven; these are the elect. There are also those who are not capable of receiving grace and are therefore predestined to **perdition**. This was Augustine's interpretation of a much-discussed passage from one of St Paul's letters to Timothy:

This is good, and is acceptable in the sight of God our Saviour, who desires all men to be saved and come to the knowledge of truth.

1 Timothy 2:4

Key term

Divine decree: God's judgement or ruling.

Double predestination

(c) Single and double predestination

The scholars who reflected Augustine's teaching developed two forms of predestination:

- **Single predestination.** God elects only those whom he ordains to enter heaven and eternal life.
- **Double predestination.** God elects only those whom he ordains to enter heaven and eternal life and also decrees that the reprobate or sinners are destined for hell and damnation.

Within these two versions, scholars propose a further division as to when God issues his '**divine decree**':

- **Antelapsarian decree.** God decreed who were the elect (and reprobate) at the moment of creation before the Fall.
- **Postlapsarian decree.** God decreed who were the elect (and reprobate) after the Fall.

(i) John Calvin and Calvinism

The doctrine of predestination in the popular mind is mostly closely associated with Calvin. While it is true that Calvin developed his distinctive version of the 'eternal decree' from Augustine, it was his followers who pushed his ideas further and developed a strong version of limited election.

Key terms

Double predestination God elects or predestines the righteous for heaven and eternal life and also condemns sinners to hell.

Westminster Confession of Faith The Confesion was drawn up in 1646 at the command of the English government. It sets out the principle beliefs of Reformed (largely Calvinist) Christianity. It has been adopted and adapted by many Protestant churches.

Key quote

By the decree of God, for the manifestation of His glory, some men and angels are predestinated unto everlasting life; and others foreordained to everlasting death.

Westminster Confession of Faith 3:3

Calvinism is associated with **double predestination**, as set out in the **Westminster Confession of Faith** is as follows: .

However, Calvin's own position was more subtle than Calvinism. Whilst he is in broad agreement with Augustine's interpretation of 1 Timothy 2:4, Calvin argues that:

- God's will is hidden (*voluntas abscondita*) and we shouldn't presume to know what he has in store, even though God foreknows all that will happen.

- What God reveals to humans takes into account their limited knowledge.
- When St Paul says that God chooses all people he is not referring to individuals but all kinds of people; God wills his mercy and grace for all.
- Christians have a duty to preach the Gospel to all kinds of people. Christians must treat this as 'unlimited election', even if (unknown to us) God has chosen particular individuals.
- Both elect and non-elect have a duty to act morally. The elect must do so, so that they become more aware of their sinful state. By rejecting gospel values the non-elect are therefore without excuse when it comes to judgement and punishment in hell.

We can now understand that when Calvin said of double predestination that it is the most 'dreadful decree' he meant that even though it is too difficult for human reason fully to comprehend, it does not undermine the moral life but encourages it.

Calvin's criticism is in part aimed at the medieval scholars, such as Thomas Aquinas, whom Calvin accused of of leaping 'over high roofs' by wanting to over intellectualize and systematize the doctrine of predestination.

(ii) Thomas Aquinas and Catholicism

Aquinas' interpretation of Augustine led the Catholic Church in a very different direction. Whereas Calvinism tends to stress the utter sinfulness of humanity and God's active abundant grace but at the loss of human free will, Aquinas' did not consider the Fall to have wiped out human freedom. The Catholic Church today teaches **single predestination**. This is the view that God elects the righteous for heaven but the wicked select themselves for hell by deliberately committing mortal sins. When God judges the wicked it is to reward them with their just desserts, which is their place in hell. The Church's teaching is that:

> *God predestines no one to go to hell; for this, a wilful turning away from God (a mortal sin) is necessary, and persistence in it until the end.*

> *Catechism of the Catholic Church* para. 1037

The elect are chosen not because God foreknows every action they will make, but because he knows they will accomplish the good end for which they are called. But the problem of the relationship between God's foreknowledge and human freedom is one which challenges all aspects of predestination and limited election because it appears to diminish human moral responsibility and the validity of trying to live the good life.

(d) Election and universalism

The basic notion of universalism or *apokatastasis* is that hell is not eternal and that the eschatological goal of the cosmos is perfection and restoration of the world to its pre-Fall state. But there are other considerations as well:

- God's goodness and love requires that all humans achieve salvation.
- If humans have free will, then every person must eventually be able to achieve perfection.

The attraction of universalism is that it includes those who have no religious faith or belong to another religious faith tradition. For many Christians (especially in plural and multi-faith societies), it is reasonable to suppose that for geographical, cultural and political reasons people follow different belief systems but this should not exclude them from eventual reconciliation with God.

(i) John Hick

Universalism is attractive to liberal Christian theologians such as John Hick because he does not think that the God whom Jesus preached is the God of judgement and exclusion which hell requires. The overwhelming emphasis of the New Testament, he argues, is reconciliation with God. For example one of John's Gospel's great themes is abundant life; Jesus' resurrection is the triumph of life over death not eternal damnation. Furthermore, what purpose does it serve to punish someone eternally? If earthly existence is a journey of moral and spiritual education, then it makes more sense to see hell existentially as continuation of that journey from which a person learns to amend their ways and strive for perfection.

(ii) Karl Barth

Although Karl Barth is a Calvinist theologian and not strictly a universalist, his original theology of election also contributes a distinctive way of understanding universalism.

Barth argued against the simplistic idea that election is choosing a few for heaven and condemning the rest to hell. Election describes every revelatory action of God where God always acts freely from the general to the particular. We can know this because in the incarnation Jesus Christ reveals that he is both the *subject* of election as God and the *object* of election as a human being. He is elector and elected.

- **As subject and elector.** God in Christ elects to redeem all fallen humanity by dying and overcoming death on its behalf.

- **As object and elected.** God in the person of Jesus Christ reveals his friendliness towards humanity by entering fully into its fallen state and even dying on the cross.

Just as Calvin had left the question of whom God elects open, so Barth also argues that it is not for humans to speculate on the mystery of salvation and the fate of individuals. As elector and elected God reveals in Christ his 'friendliness' towards all of humanity that through his grace it might be restored.

Some scholars, therefore, argue that whilst Barth might have rejected universalism as a *principle* of salvation nevertheless his own version of universalism was to be inclusive of all those who, through the incarnation, are 'in Christ'; election to heaven or hell can only be truly known at the end time. So, as Barth once said:

> *I don't believe in universalism, but I do believe in Christ, the reconciler of all.*

Summary diagram: Death and the afterlife

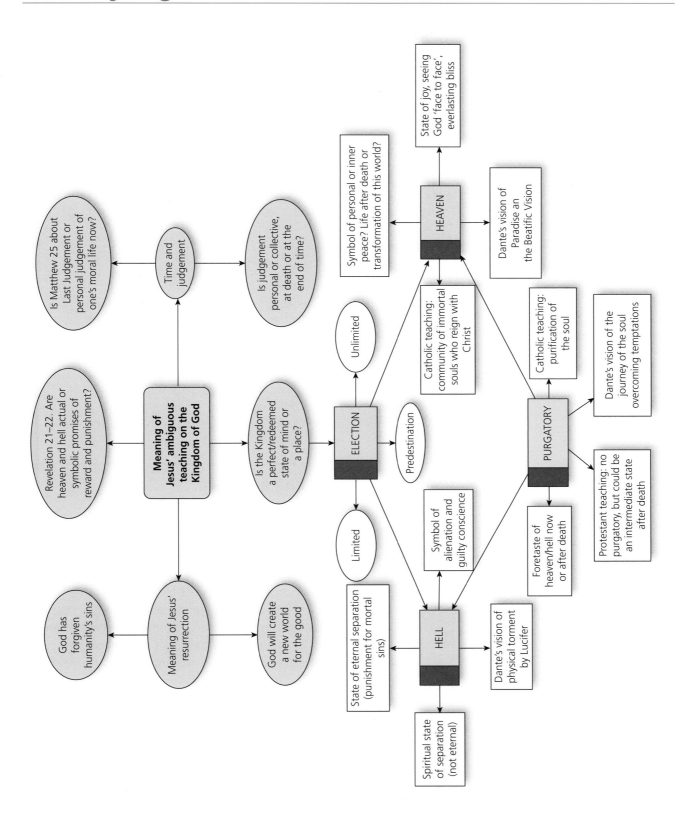

Further essay questions

To what extent is the Parable of the Sheep and the Goats in Matthew 25 only about heaven and hell?

Assess the view that there is no last judgement; each person is judged by God at the moment of their death.

'Purgatory is the most important Christian teaching about the afterlife.' Discuss.

Going further

Geoffrey Chapman: *Catechism of the Catholic Church* (1994) Chapter 3 Article 12 'I Believe in Life Everlasting'. Clearly sets out Catholic teaching on heaven, purgatory, hell, last judgement and the hope of a new heaven and new Earth.

John Hick: *Death and Eternal Life* (Fount, 1979). Section III surveys Christian teaching, but chapter 13 on universalism reveals Hick's own views. This is a classic and although it is a little dated, it is still worth reading.

Alister McGrath: *Christian Theology* (fifth edition, Wiley–Blackwell, 2011). Chapter 18 is an excellent and comprehensive survey of all the key ideas.

Other books we've talked about in this chapter are:

- Hainsworth P. and Robey D. *Dante: A Very Short Introduction* (Oxford University Press, 2015).
- Kelly J. N. D. *Early Christian Doctrines* (Adam and Charles Black, 1958).
- Tillich P. *Systematic Theology,* volumes I–III (University of Chicago Press, 1951-1964).

Chapter 18

Knowledge of God's existence

1 Introduction

Chapter checklist

This chapter begins by considering what is meant by true knowledge. It then looks at the Christian claim that true knowledge is knowledge of God and distinguishes between those who argue that God can be known through reason and experience of the natural world, and those who argue that God can only truly be known through revelation. The two views of knowledge of God are reviewed by comparing the teachings of Calvin and the Roman Catholic Church. The chapter concludes by considering contemporary discussion of natural and revealed theology.

2 Natural and revealed theology

(a) Knowing

In day-to-day life we use the word 'know' in several different ways. Consider the difference of usage in the following:

(a) I know that 2 + 2 = 4.
(b) I know that Paris is the capital of France.
(c) I know of Peter Smith.
(d) I know Peter Smith.

Very briefly we might argue that: a) is logical knowledge based on the definition of what 2 means and what addition entails; b) is factual knowledge either based on very well-established report or first-hand experience; c) is very similar to the previous example and establishes Peter Smith's existence and maybe some of his characteristics; d) suggests a personal relationship which is more intimate and complete than the previous example based on first-hand experience or knowledge of Peter Smith which only he has given me.

(i) God of the philosophers

Given the ambiguities of knowing in these ordinary circumstances, what does it mean to say 'I know God'? For many it means that God's existence is logically true or that God's existence is a widely held fact.

Key question

Is natural knowledge of God the same as revealed knowledge of God?

Demonstrating God's existence has long been of interest to philosophers of **natural theology**. But the problem with this approach is that this kind of knowledge is often far removed from the kind of knowledge which religious traditions talk about when they speak of God as a God of love or a God of mercy.

(ii) God of Abraham, Jesus Christ and Muhammad (pbuh)

For most religious believers, knowledge of God is much closer to knowledge of Peter Smith in example d) than the other examples. It is also at this stage that different religions speak in specific ways. Judaism knows God as the giver of Torah and the one who establishes his covenant with Abraham, Isaac and Jacob; Christianity knows God in the person of Jesus Christ; Islam knows God from the Qur'an and in the example of the Prophet Muhammad (pbuh). According to **revealed theology**, these statements are possible only because each religion claims that God has let himself be known in a special way.

(iii) Justification

But the fundamental problem for both natural and revealed theology is that unlike all other forms of knowledge, the object, God, is uniquely different from any other object (in fact, he is no object at all). Therefore, while the attractiveness of natural theology is that it offers a rational and reasonable *justification* for the existence of God, it also has to acknowledge that by definition God as an infinite being lies beyond reason. On the other hand, although revealed theology argues that what can be known of God is only that which he reveals of himself, it is much harder for it to offer any rational justification why one should believe that this knowledge is true. For many, this suggests that revealed theology, on its own, is irrational.

(b) True knowledge

At the heart of this debate is an ancient argument about what constitutes 'true knowledge'. True knowledge could mean hard, **incorrigible facts** about the world. Some associate this with scientific knowledge. But is this really true knowledge? It might be considered true insofar as it describes the physical properties of matter, but it is not knowledge in terms of understanding life and what makes it worthwhile.

In the ancient world, this second kind of knowledge is called 'wisdom' and considered to be 'true knowledge'. The source for wisdom was oneself because to 'know oneself' meant understanding one's place in society and in the world and how to live well. For a very long time that was the aim of philosophy – the love (Greek – *philos*) of wisdom (Greek – *sophos*).

But there is a third possibility which is that true knowledge is knowledge of God. If God is the source of life, then knowledge of God leads to a profound understanding of one's own life and purpose. Here is how the Catholic Church puts it:

> For if man exists it is because God has created him through love, and through love continues to hold him in existence. He cannot live fully according to truth unless he freely acknowledges that love and entrusts himself to his creator.

Catechism of the Catholic Church para. 27

287

Key terms

Natural theology Considers that God can be known through reason and observation of the natural world.

Revealed theology Considers that God can only be known when he lets himself be known. Revelation might occur through a prophet, scripture, prayer and so on.

Key term

Incorrigible facts Facts which are unshakably or unalterably the case.

Key question

Is true knowledge scientific, philosophical or religious?

3 Natural knowledge of God's existence

Key term

Point of contact God's revelation in the world which provides humans with the first step to knowing him as redeemer.

Key person

John Calvin (1509–64): Born in France and trained initially as a lawyer. In 1533, he converted to the Protestantism of Martin Luther but later joined the Swiss Reformed Protestants. Calvin developed his Reformed Protestant theology in Geneva where he produced his most influential book, *Institutes of the Christian Religion* (final edition 1559).

Key term

Sensus divinitatis The Latin phrase used by Calvin meaning a 'sense of God' or 'sense of the divine'.

Natural theology supposes that as God is the creator of the universe and humans are conscious elements of that universe, then they have a natural predisposition to know God as their creator. To use a phrase which has become much debated, natural theology claims that the natural world provides a **point of contact** between ourselves and God, which tells us something of his nature.

Natural theology is supported by all branches of the Christian Church and is the official teaching of the Roman Catholic Church today. However, there is considerable debate amongst Protestants about the validity of natural theology. This is highlighted in the way in which it is presented by the great Protestant reformer John Calvin.

The views of both the Catholic Church and Calvin will be considered below.

(a) The innate human sense of God

Both Calvin's *Institutes of the Christian Religion* (1559) and the *Catechism of the Catholic Church* (1994) begin in very similar ways. Both state that the knowledge of God is innate or imprinted in human consciousness:

> *The desire for God is written in the human heart, because man is created by God and for God; and God never ceases to draw man to himself. Only in God will he find the truth and happiness he never stops searching for.*
>
> Catechism of the Catholic Church para. 27

Calvin's thesis is explicitly set out in the opening chapter heading of the *Institutes*, 'Without knowledge of the self there is no knowledge of God'. This is how he explains it:

> *Nearly all the wisdom we possess, that is to say, true and sound wisdom, consists of two parts: the knowledge of God and of ourselves. But, while joined by many bonds, which one precedes and brings forth the other is not easy to discern. In the first place, no one can look upon himself without immediately turning his thoughts to the contemplation of God, in whom he 'lives and moves' (Acts 17:28).*
>
> John Calvin: *Institutes* I.I.1

Calvin called this inbuilt or innate sense of the divine, the **sensus divinitatis**; sometimes he referred to a *semen religionis*, a 'seed of religion', the natural human inclination to carry out religious practices such as rituals and prayer.

(i) Innate knowledge

How can the claim that the knowledge of God is innate or part of 'natural instinct' be supported or justified? One argument is that as every human society has some form of religious practice and worship then humans must be naturally disposed to know God.

■ **The unknown god.** The speech of Paul to the Athenians recorded in Acts 17:16–34 is often referred to as biblical support for the *sensus* *divinitatis* or innate knowledge of God. In this passage, Paul has to convince the Athenians that they are actually worshipping the true God because although they don't know this explicitly, amongst their large number of altars to the gods Paul has seen, one altar is dedicated to 'the unknown god'. Paul argues that the desire to know who the 'unknown god' is has been the constant quest of their Greek philosophers, even if they haven't been fully aware that this is so.

- **Universal consent argument**. A well-known argument suggested by the philosopher Cicero, whom Calvin refers to, is that as so many people believe in the gods or God, then the gods or God must exist – or even if this doesn't prove their existence it does, at the very least, suggest that it is reasonable to believe in the gods or God.
- **Humans are religious beings.** The *Catechism* also concludes that so widespread are the practices of prayer, sacrifice, ritual and meditation that, 'despite the ambiguities', they are 'so universal that one may well call man a *religious being*' (*Catechism* para. 28).

(ii) Human sense of beauty and moral goodness

For what can be known about God is plain to them, because God has shown it to them. Ever since the creation of the world, his eternal power and divine nature, invisible though they are, have been understood and seen through the things he has made.

St Paul: *Letter to the Romans* 1:19–20

The human sense of the beauty of the world caused by listening to a sublime piece of music, reading an inspiring book, admiring a natural landscape or by a person's skill at playing the piano all indicate that humans have an 'openness to truth and beauty' (*Catechism* para. 33) which leads to an apprehension of God's existence. In both Catholic and Protestant Christianity, the human sense of beauty and moral goodness are the foundations of knowledge of God.

- **Natural law**. Catholicism in particular regards natural law to be an indication of human innate knowledge of God. Natural law rests on the supposition that all humans have an innate sense of goodness, fairness and justice however ill-formed those views might be. Small children, for example, quickly develop a strong sense of fairness and justice.
- **Conscience**. Calvin considered conscience to be particularly important in our knowledge of God and moral goodness. He argued that conscience is our God-given faculty as creatures made in the image of God. As such, it is part of our moral choice-making processes which responds to God's will of what is right and wrong. Conscience literally means 'joint knowledge' between ourselves and God; it is God's presence which gives us our sense of moral judgement.

(iii) Human intellectual ability to reflect on and recognise God's existence

An important aspect of natural theology for some considerable time has been the so-called arguments for the existence of God. Some of these were gathered together by Aquinas in his Five Ways in which he reflects

For a detailed discussion on the arguments for the existence of God based on reason, see Chapter 6.

on the nature of causes and their effects in the material world. His conclusion is that the finite material world could not continue to exist unless there was an uncaused causer who set up the initial conditions of the world (otherwise it would not exist), sustains all material causes (or else the world would cease to be) and orders these causes to be purposeful (otherwise there would be chaos). The inference from reason is that this uncaused causer is what Christians call God.

As many scholars point out, all these arguments for God's existence do not prove his existence but rather provide strong *reasons* to believe. The *Catechism* says of these arguments that they are 'converging and convincing'.

But what kind of knowledge do they give us about God? The knowledge gained is probably closest to the first of the three kinds of knowledge we considered at the start of this chapter: that is, that God exists in a different way from other beings; that he is a being greater than can be conceived by finite minds; that he is a unique cause. This might be considered useful knowledge, but is it sufficient to know God other than in some abstract and theoretical way? It also begs the question: is the God of these philosophical arguments really God?

(b) The order of creation

In the *Institutes,* Calvin makes a distinction between knowledge of God as Creator and God as Redeemer, it is known as the *duplex cognitio Domini* or 'the two-fold knowledge of God'. As God the Creator, the most powerful indications of his existence and presence in the world are in the ordering and design of nature. The idea is ancient and often referred to in the Bible. For example, when contemplating the stars the Psalmist declares:

> The heavens are telling the glory of God;
> and the firmament proclaims his handiwork.

Psalm 19:1

(i) Order and design

> Yet, in the first place, wherever you cast your eyes, there is no spot in the universe wherein you cannot discern at least some sparks of his glory. You cannot in one glance survey this most vast and beautiful system of the universe, its wide expanse, without being completely overwhelmed by the boundless force of its brightness. The reason why the author of the Letter to the Hebrews elegantly calls the universe the appearance of things invisible is that this skilful ordering of the universe is for us a sort of mirror in which we can contemplate God, who is otherwise invisible.

John Calvin: *Institutes* I.V.1

This quotation from Calvin is not so much an **argument from design** about God's existence as it is an expression of what can be known about God from the beauty and awesome nature of the creation.

The argument also includes Calvin's important **principle of accommodation**. This is the principle which states that because human

Key terms

Duplex cognitio Domini A Latin phrase meaning 'the two-fold knowledge of God'. This is Calvin's distinction of knowing God as Creator and God as Redeemer.

Argument from design Claim that as the world and the universe show clear signs of organisation and purpose that it is reasonable to infer that it must have a designer. As this designer must be greater than the universe then the designer must be what is usually referred to as God.

Principle of accommodation The principle that God manifests himself through creation in ways that human finite minds can best understand.

The beauty of nature

minds are finite and God is infinite then humans will never be able to know God through their own powers of reason. However, God manifests himself through creation in ways that human finite minds can best understand. This he does by adapting himself to human needs. For example, a teacher giving a lesson to group of five-year-olds will adapt her language and examples to suit their understanding. If she were to give a similar lesson to a group of sixteen-year-olds then her examples and range of language would be appropriate for their stage of life. In each case, the teacher has practised accommodation.

Using the principle of accommodation Calvin explains how God reveals himself in nature. Calvin argues that what we know of God in nature is a 'sort of mirror' or reflection of his invisible nature. What we observe of God in nature is not his *essence* but his *appearance* – the aspects of himself which mean something to us. By contemplating and reflecting on these aspects, what Calvin refers to as the 'sparks of glory', it is then possible to form some idea of God's essential being such as his love, power, justice and mercy.

(ii) Purpose

In more recent times William Paley's argument from design has become widely known as powerful and rational argument for God's existence. Paley's argument rests on an inference from an analogy with a watch. When we look at a watch we see that all the various parts of it are designed and purposeful for it to function as a watch. We know that this did not happen by chance because the watch has been created by a watch-maker. In a similar way when we observe the world we also see signs of design and order and so by analogy we can infer it too must have a maker, but an infinitely powerful one which is what we mean by God.

There are many objections to the design arguments. One of the most powerful is that as nature is more brutal than it is beautiful, then this would mean that God is also cruel, which is contrary to the God of faith. But more problematic is that since Darwin's notion of evolution by natural selection, it is no longer widely accepted that the world or the universe is purposeful; nature has no final cause, but develops merely to survive but even then, there is no guarantee that this will happen and eventually it may just cease to exist. Nature without a purpose makes God redundant.

(iii) Process

In response to these objections, the latest version of 'design' natural theology has been developed by a group of theologians influenced by quantum physics and the principle of quantum uncertainty. This is called **process theology**.

Process theologians argue that God and the world act in tandem; God is not independent from the natural processes but works with them to maximise their greatest potentials at *any moment of time*. In other words, there is no grand end point to which nature is moving, for every moment is an end in itself. Process theologians refer to this process as God's 'persuasion'. One of them, Ian Barbour, comments:

> *Both experience and history point to a God who acts not by coercing but by evoking the response of his creatures.*

Ian G. Barbour: *Issues in Science and Religion* (1966), p. 463

Read pages 60–62 for a detailed discussion of William Paley's design argument.

Key term

Process theology Developed from the mathematical and philosophical ideas of A. N. Whitehead and in particular his book *Process and Reality* (1929). Other influential process theologians include Charles Hartshorne, John Cobb and Ian Barbour.

Therefore, God is not the totally different and unknowable God of classical theology, but a God who loves his creation, suffers with it and desires every creature to achieve its potential. Process theologians, therefore, don't make a sharp distinction between natural and revealed theology as every moment in creation is a revelation of God's participation in nature.

4 Revealed knowledge of God's existence

(a) Faith and God's grace

(i) The Fall and human finiteness

Key question

Has the Fall completely removed all natural human knowledge of God?

In theory, knowledge of God could, through the *sensus divinitatis*, conscience, creation and even allowing for finite human minds, bring humans into relationship with God. However, this 'simple knowledge' (Calvin) completely overlooks one key factor: the corruption of humanity due to the Fall. If, Calvin argues, Adam had remained upright, *si integer stetisset Adam*, then everyone would have known God and achieved a state of perfect happiness or blessedness. But, that was not the case.

> *... I speak only of the primal and simple knowledge to which the very order of nature would have led us if Adam had remained upright (si integer stetisset Adam). In this ruin of mankind no one now experiences God either as Father or as Author of salvation, or favourable in any way, until Christ the Mediator comes forward to reconcile him to us. Nevertheless, it is one thing to feel that God as our Maker supports us by his power, governs us by his providence, nourishes us by his goodness, and attends us with all sorts of blessings – and another thing to embrace the grace of reconciliation offered to us in Christ.*
>
> John Calvin: *Institutes* I. II.1

Key terms

Si integer stetisset Adam The Latin phrase used by Calvin meaning 'if Adam had remained upright' and refers to the Fall when Adam and Eve sinned and fell from grace.

Regeneration In Christian terms, the process of renewal, restoration and recreation associated with baptism and other sacraments of the Church.

See page 287 on 'true knowledge'.

This passage clearly states the second aspect of Calvin's *duplex cognitio Domini* the distinctive Christian knowledge of God the Redeemer as mediated by Christ. It is only this knowledge of God which brings humans into full and complete relationship with God. Knowing God in this way is, to use Calvin's language, to be **regenerated** – renewed, restored, recreated. True knowledge is salvation in Christ.

The Catholic position is that the Fall did not cut humans off from knowing God, but it did confuse and distract their desire for him. The effects of Original Sin are seen through: 'religious ignorance or indifference; the cares and riches of this world; the scandal of bad example on the part of believers; currents of thought hostile to religion; finally, that attitude of sinful man which makes him hide from God out of fear and flee his call' (*Catechism* para. 29). To overcome this state, the *Catechism* states that:

> *There is another order of knowledge, which man cannot possibly arrive at by his own powers: the order of divine Revelation.*
>
> *Catechism* para. 50

God reveals his plan 'freely' through his prophets and in Jesus Christ.

(ii) Faith

Belief that God has revealed himself in his prophets and in Jesus Christ is not something which can be worked out by reason alone; it requires faith. However, even faith requires some form of reason otherwise faith would be random and meaningless. That is certainly the conclusion of critics such as Richard Dawkins, who considers faith as a 'cop-out' and as a way of not having to give reasons for religious belief.

But in Catholic teaching, faith is not independent from reason, but is a willed assent to a set of propositions. In other words, it is one thing to demonstrate through reason the existence of God but quite another to allow oneself to believe it is true. Aquinas, for example, made the distinction between unformed and formed faith:

- **Unformed faith.** This is faith which may find intellectual reasons why, for example, a person may believe that the afterlife is possible but cannot accept it is true. Aquinas says that even the devils believed in God but they did not trust him to save them.
- **Formed faith.** This is faith which wills to accept or 'assent' what it can believe through the intellect. For example, faith is willing to believe that the evidence of those who witnessed Jesus' resurrection is trustworthy. Formed faith takes time and effort and requires the discipline of prayer and worship to know and accept that which is good and perfect.

In Calvin's Protestant teaching, faith is:

- **Firm and certain knowledge.** Calvin defines faith along similar lines to Aquinas as the 'firm and certain knowledge of God's benevolence towards us'. But Calvin criticises Aquinas because he has not made Christ the direct object of faith. Calvin argues that firm knowledge is only possible as revealed by Christ and sealed by the Holy Spirit.
- **Willingness to believe.** Faith 'is given to anyone who is willing to accept it'. It is, according to Calvin, a cognitive process when a person is willing to believe in the certain knowledge of redemption and salvation in Christ. It is not just a cerebral moment but an emotional and spiritual experience of assurance, 'sealed upon our hearts'.

(iii) Grace

But both in Catholic and in Calvin's protestant theology, faith alone is not sufficient to know God. Although faith may be an assent of the mind and spirit, it requires God's gracious act to complete the relationship. Aquinas argues that faith can ultimately only be justified by grace through the Holy Spirit (the creative presence of God). The *Catechism* describes this as the moment when a person enters into real intimacy with God and 'the grace of being able to welcome this revelation in faith'.

For Calvin the gift of the Holy Spirit is to aid in the creation of a person's faith by repairing the damage caused by original sin.

(b) Revealed knowledge of God in Jesus Christ

Calvin doesn't make a sharp distinction between general and special revelation. Scripture, as special revelation, offers knowledge of God as creator, but it is only the final and complete revelation in Christ contained

---

Key question

Is faith sufficient reason for belief in God's existence?

Key quote

Faith is the great cop-out, the great excuse to evade the need to think and evaluate experience.

Richard Dawkins (Edinburgh International Science Festival, April 1992)

Key quote

Faith is 'a firm and certain knowledge of God's benevolence toward us, founded upon the truth of the freely given promise in Christ, both revealed to our minds and sealed upon our hearts through the Holy Spirit.

John Calvin: *Institutes of the Christian Religion* III.ii.7

Key question

Is true knowledge of God only revealed in Jesus Christ?

Trinitarian view of God Central to the Christian teaching that God is one but reveals himself as three 'persons': Father, Son and Holy Spirit.

Key quote

In their case the god of this world has blinded the minds of the unbelievers, to keep them from seeing the light of the gospel of the glory of Christ, who is the image of God.

St Paul: *Second Letter to the Corinthians* 4:4

Key question

Is the Bible a source of God's revelation or human experience of God?

in the New Testament which resolves any of the possible contradictions of the Old Testament.

This is one reason why the Bible should be read from a **Trinitarian** perspective:

- through God as Father, the prophets and writers bear witness to his revelation
- through Christ as mediator, clarity is given to God's promises
- through the Holy Spirit, Christians are inspired, sustained and led in the process of interpretation.

However, even the knowledge of God mediated in Christ cannot tell us what God is in essence. The principle of accommodation means that Christ is the *image* or likeness of the invisible God (2 Corinthians 4:4) and he appears to us in a way that finite minds can understand.

God becomes a human being in the person of Jesus Christ because he accommodates himself to our actual physical and mental condition. This is why Calvin describes Christ as the mirror and mediator of the divine. As a 'mirror' he reflects those qualities (such as love, forgiveness and mercy) of God which would otherwise be hidden from us and as mediator he is the means by which sinful humans are reconciled and brought into the knowledge and love of God.

The Catholic position agrees with this view but it adds that although Christ is the full and final revelation of God, the significance of this revelation does not end here. It is the role of faith (for individuals as well as the Church) to re-think it for every generation:

> Yet even if Revelation is already complete, it has not been completely explicit; it remains for Christian faith gradually to grasp its full significance over the course of the centuries.
>
> *Catechism* para. 66

There is considerable debate as to whether Christ can be known by non-Christians (the anonymous Christian argument) or indeed whether knowledge of God is exclusive to Christians.

(i) The Bible and life of the Church

Christian revealed theology considers the Bible to be more than a historical collection of religious experiences but a witness to God's active and specific action in the world. This knowledge cannot be gained merely through experience. For traditional Catholics and Protestants 'God is the author of Sacred Scripture' (*Catechism* para. 105) and its words are the 'speech of God as it is put down in writing under the breath of the Holy Spirit'.

But, as the *Catechism* warns, Christianity must not be reduced to the Bible (a tendency of a very limited form of fundamentalism) because 'the Christian faith is not a "religion of the book"', but the religion of the 'eternal Word of the living God' (*Catechism* para. 108). So, even in Catholicism which takes natural theology seriously, the Bible provides the 'soul of sacred theology' and takes 'pride of place' in sermons, teaching and life of the Church.

Ultimately, as Calvin argued, knowledge of God the Redeemer is revealed specifically in the person of Jesus Christ; the Bible read from this perspective prepares for him in the Old Testament and culminates in the New Testament with the decisive events of his life, death and resurrection.

Even those Christian scholars who take a natural theology position recognise the importance of the Bible as a significant source for knowledge of God, but for rather different reasons than those just outlined. From a natural theological point of view the Bible is an extraordinarily diverse collection of experiences of God from the early days of the Hebrew people through to the formation of early Christian communities. Although it is possible to rationalise God's qualities from these experiences, the important knowledge of God gained is the personal and collective encounter with God. The Psalms, for example, cover every kind of existential experience from the knowledge of God who judges one's inner thoughts to the God of love who is a refuge and friend.

5 The natural–revealed theology debate

Key question

How much does the natural world provide a point of contact with God?

Key term

Immanence Means 'being part of' and so when applied to God it refers to the way he participates in all aspects of world and universe.

At the heart of Calvin's theology there is ambiguity. Did he have a natural theology or is his theology entirely based on explaining revelation? Linked with this is whether he presented two quite different Gods: the God who as creator is a transcendent grand cause detached from the world and God the redeemer who is a personal loving being, closely involved **immanently** in the world. The tension between these ambiguities has been the source of great debate amongst modern theologians.

Catholicism on the other hand is less ambiguous and embraces natural theology as it allows humans to know God in a general way for, 'Without this capacity, man would not be able to welcome God's revelation' (*Catechism* para. 36). But many argue that this position does not go far enough; natural theology is not just preparation for general knowledge *about* God, but true knowledge *of* God in itself.

(a) The Barth–Brunner debate

The questions Calvin raises became the focus of a celebrated debate between two Reformed theologians Emil Brunner and Karl Barth in 1934.

Key persons

Karl Barth

Karl Barth (1886–1968): A Swiss Reformed minister and theologian. Early on he rejected liberal Protestantism and developed what has sometimes been called neo-orthodoxy – a rejection of natural theology and a revival of Reformed theology. His greatest work is the multi-volume *Church Dogmatics* (1932–1967).

Emil Brunner (1889–1966): A Swiss Reformed minister and theologian. He supported Barth's neo-orthodoxy but was also influenced by Aquinas' teaching that God can be partially known through the creation. Brunner's use of Aquinas was fiercely rejected by Barth and led him to write his strongly worded essay *Nein!* or No! in 1938. Brunner's and Barth's essays were published together as *Natural Theology* in 1946.

(i) Tensions in Calvin's theology

Barth and Brunner's debate illustrates some of the tensions and ambiguities in Calvin's theology of knowledge, namely that if humans are in a state of sin, how can they know and be prompted to be open to God's grace unless God reveals himself generally in nature? On the other hand, God's grace is not something we can ask for and we can only know God because he chooses to let himself be known. Brunner considered that Calvin's argument that God's 'sparks of glory' in nature provided 'a point of contact with God' which enable humans to have some knowledge of God's existence however vague. Barth completely disagreed. He considered that Calvin's teaching on the Fall had so distorted human nature that there was absolutely no point of contact between God and humans. So, how can there be such different interpretations of Calvin?

(ii) Brunner's proposal

Brunner's argument follows Calvin's notion that God's general revelation in nature (as experienced through conscience and *sensus divinitatis*) as a point of contact enables humans to become aware of God's commands and consequently their sinful state. But, Brunner argued, this is not sufficient to achieve redemption which is revealed in the person of Jesus Christ. The limited purpose of natural theology is to offer 'the possibility of a discussion pointing toward such evidence of the existence of God as we have'. Brunner's views are as follows:

- **Imago Dei**. The image of God in humans after the Fall has been destroyed but only at the *material* physical and emotional level. At the *formal* or spiritual level the human image of God exists uncorrupted (otherwise humans would not be unique and different from animals). The formal image allows humans to be addressed by God. But the material image is almost completely but not totally sinful and corrupt.
- **General revelation.** God communicates through nature which reflects his nature. But owing to sin humans are blinded and almost incapable of receiving this communication of grace; all they can know is that God exists. Nature provides a point of contact with God, but no more.
- **Conscience.** Conscience and the experience of guilt make humans aware of God's law.
- **True knowledge.** Through grace and renewal of the material self, true knowledge of God is available only to the person who has faith in Christ. The revelation of Christ, Brunner argues, 'far surpasses' general knowledge of God's revelation in nature.

(iii) Barth's reply

Barth's decisive No! (or *Nein!*) to Brunner is uncompromising. Barth's view is that human nature is completely corrupted by the Fall and that there are no points of contact in nature of any kind which would allow humans to know. Only God can chose to reveal himself to sinful man. Barth disagrees with Brunner's interpretation of Calvin in three ways.

- **The formal self cannot inform the material self of God's existence**. Barth argues that humans may be uniquely different from animals, but the Fall has so utterly blotted out the material self's ability to know anything about God that it is impossible for the spiritual formal self to inform the material self of God in any way. Barth accuses Brunner of not taking sufficiently into account the corruption of the material self; the formal self is utterly unable to inform the corrupted material self of God's existence by itself.

- **No points of contact.** Barth argues that nature, conscience and guilt do not provide any points of contact with God. Barth argues that conscience and guilt are only experienced *after* a person has experienced God's grace, not before or independently of it. Brunner has wrongly considered these to be natural points of contact when in fact they are the result of God's mercy and grace.

- **Order of creation**. Barth argues that although we are able to perceive order in nature it is not the basis for morality or salvation. This is because God's moral commands, revealed in the Bible are entirely different from any natural laws which humans think they can perceive. The order we see in creation is only *after* it has been revealed to us through faith and in the Bible. Barth considers that Brunner has given too much importance to human reason and undermined the uniqueness of faith.

Many argue that Barth's emphatic 'no' to Brunner was due to the rise of Nazism which liberal Christianity had failed to reject. The Nazi appeal to the natural order of society resulting in mass exterminations explains why Barth was so suspicious of reason and natural law. With this in mind we can understand why Barth was so suspicious of all human philosophies which elevate human reason to the status of a god or ideology, but it doesn't mean that his interpretation of Calvin is necessarily right. Many argue that Brunner's account of the relationship of faith and reason is much closer to the biblical tradition and to Calvin.

(b) Alvin Plantinga

The accusation is that natural theology offers sound reasons to believe in God whereas revealed theology does not. However, the Reformed theologian Alvin Plantinga considers that in fact it is the other way round. It is revealed theology which is reasonable and that, to use his particular phrase, Christian beliefs are 'warranted' or justified whereas natural theology can never offer sufficient reason to believe in God and certainly no knowledge of the God of love and grace. Plantinga's argument is rooted in Calvin's argument and this way of thinking is generally referred to as **reformed epistemology**.

> Read page 342 on Barth and Bonhoeffer and the creation of the Barmen Declaration.

> **Key term**
>
> **Reformed epistemology** The view held by some modern theologians and philosophers in the Reformed or Calvinist tradition such as Alvin Plantinga, Nicholas Wolterstorff and Michael Rea, who believe that knowledge of God is a 'properly basic belief'.

> **Key person**
>
> **Alvin Plantinga** (b. 1932): The retired professor of philosophy at the University of Notre Dame, USA. He argues that Christian belief can be subject to the same rigorous philosophical analysis as any other belief system. As a Calvinist he begins with the notion that God can be held as a 'basic belief' along with other basic beliefs. He has written many books on this including *Warranted Christian Belief* (2000).

Key question

Is there anything you can know for certain which you can prove to be so?

See page 289 on the universal consent argument.

Key term

Atheological objector Plantinga's term referring to those who reject all theological claims.

(i) Basic knowledge

The dream of scientists and philosophers alike is to begin with a piece of knowledge which is so completely certain that it cannot be doubted. Once this is established then all other claims can be based on this foundational idea. For scientists this foundation might be a basic law of physics; for philosophers such as Descartes it is an irreducible fact that I am a thinking being. However, such foundational epistemological claims are very hard to establish. Scientific knowledge changes; what is thought of as being a hard fact today may turn out to be not entirely so tomorrow. Scientists nowadays often prefer to talk in terms of probabilities rather than certainties. In other words it is unlikely that there can ever be a totally convincing foundation of knowledge, but it is still possible to have broad agreement (what Plantinga calls 'warrant') as to what can reasonably to be considered 'true'.

Basic knowledge is a belief which is held to be true because it just is so and it makes sense of many other experiences. The onus is on others to show that these basic beliefs would be better explained by other more reasonable (and therefore basic) beliefs about the world. Plantinga's argument is that certain Christian revealed truths are basic.

(ii) *Sensus divinitatis*

Plantinga argues that there is no separate independent natural theology for the knowledge of God but there is a general religious sense which makes it reasonable for Christians to make basic religious claims. These claims are not the product of reason through philosophical arguments or the evidence of science – Plantinga fiercely rejects natural theology – but the *sensus divinitatis*, the God-given faculty which enables humans to be able to know God. So, Plantinga argues (along similar lines to Calvin), if there were no God then there would be no claims to know him; but as many people claim to believe in God then knowledge of God can be counted as basic knowledge.

However, basic knowledge is only available to the Christian because only Christ can remove sin which distorts or corrupts the *sensus divinitatis* and the Holy Spirit continues to help the believer to respond to the defect much like a pair of spectacles is necessary for defective eyes.

(iii) Responding to the atheological objector

A typical Christian might claim to know that God exists, that God speaks to him and that God forgives him. But according to the **atheological objector** there are many good reasons to suggest that these theological beliefs are no more than wish fulfilment or conditioning of some kind. For example, they may be held to be contradictory (the existence of evil is incompatible with a good God). Religious experience may be explained as a neurosis or hallucination. Finally, religious claims, such as miracles, may merely lack sound evidence. Together these objections justify considering theistic knowledge as irrational. The conclusion of the objector is that God does not exist.

In response, Plantinga argues that although there can be no incorrigible proof of one's belief, there can nevertheless be good reasons to maintain it. In response to the atheological objector's arguments against God's existence, the Christian theologian may have to sift a whole range of strong and weak arguments for and against God's existence. But it becomes quickly apparent that there is no one totally convincing argument which proves, or at the very least provides a strong *probability,* that God does not exist.

But this doesn't mean that the Christian theologian has to come up with a more substantial reason to defeat the atheological objector. As Plantinga says, 'All I need to do is refute this argument; I am not obliged to go further and produce an argument for the denial of its conclusion'. In conclusion Plantinga argues that belief in God's existence is no more or less rational than the atheist's non-belief in God.

(iv) Criticisms of Plantinga

Reformed epistemology has generated a great deal of criticism within and outside revealed theology. The following are just a few of the points being made:

- Plantinga's knowledge of God argument is not really basic. His claim is that millions of people have for thousands of years claimed to have a sense of God. But this could just be that many people have interpreted this experience incorrectly, but more significantly many have not had this experience. The evidence is not strong enough to support a properly basic belief in God's existence.
- Plantinga assumes that Christian beliefs, such as the incarnation and the Holy Spirit, are true. A warrant for belief is only possible if they are true but he has given no reason to explain why they are so. Appealing to faith and to the Bible is not enough.
- Plantinga's argument supports any firmly held beliefs believers consider to be basic. These basic beliefs could be equally those of Christians, non-Christians and atheists. They could also be bizarre beliefs such the existence of the tooth fairy and goblins.

(c) Natural theology

(i) Fideism and revealed theology

Despite the best efforts of reformed epistemology there are many who consider that it falls into the error of **fideism**. The accusation is that by ruling out reason there is no means of testing true or false religious beliefs. The Roman Catholic position stated at the First Vatican Council (1869–70) in the 'Dogmatic Constitution of Faith', outlawed fideism preferring instead a midpoint between the rationalism of natural theology and the faith position of revealed theology. The great strength of natural theology is that knowledge of God is reasonable and can be held consistently with other non-Christian religions as well as non-religious scientific and philosophical views of the world.

(ii) Is natural theology Christian theology?

But the challenge to natural theology is whether it justifies particularly Christian claims such as the divinity of Christ, the resurrection, the existence of heaven and hell and so on. Critics of natural theology argue

Key question

What response would you make to defend Plantinga against each of these criticisms?

Key term

Fideism The requirement that revelation is essential for the human mind to know anything about God's existence or nature with certainty.

Key question

Does natural theology undermine traditional Christian beliefs?

Each of these ideas are discussed later: Jesus as teacher and prophet, pages 307–309; resurrection as experience of hope, pages 316–318; heaven as political goal, pages 268–272.

Key question

Why might the use of the imagination lead to a true understanding of the world?

See Douglas Hedley's article in *The Oxford Handbook of Natural Theology*, pages 539–550. For more about the Simile of the Cave, see pages 22–23.

Key thought

Thought experiment Similar to a scientific experiment but done without instruments and as series of experimental thoughts in the mind. The intention is to discover, through reasoned reflection, truths about the real world.

Read the sections in Chapter 17 on Dante's descriptions of hell, heaven and purgatory.

that as natural theology's tendency is to reduce these claims to the human rational level then:

- Jesus was no more than an inspired teacher and prophet.
- The resurrection is no more an experience of hope over despair.
- Heaven is just a political goal of this world transformed.

(iii) Natural theology and the imagination

One response to the criticism that natural theology undermines Christian belief is that natural theology does not rest exclusively on the place of reason to test and interpret religious claims. Douglas Hedley, for example, argues that while reason has its place in philosophy, the imagination is also an essential aspect of philosophical investigation. Consider how Plato at various points in his arguments provides imaginative stories or analogies to illustrate ideas which reason alone is unable to discern. Plato's famous Simile of the Cave in *The Republic* continues to fascinate and prompt discussion about the purpose of philosophy, the nature of the soul, different kinds of knowledge and the nature of the good, because it engages with the imagination as well as reason.

The imagination, therefore, shares many of the characteristics of faith: it is intentional and conscious. While imagination can simply refer to fantasy, we also use the imagination in understanding other people's states of mind, when planning the future and when working out problems. Philosophers often use **thought experiments** to deal with complex issues in a world which cannot easily be explained in solely rational terms.

Key quote

Drama, prose and poetry can be considered as both creative and truthful.

Douglas Hedley: *The Oxford Handbook of Natural Theology*, p. 547

For example, Dante's extraordinary poetic descriptions of hell, heaven and purgatory are not intended to be factual, but they are poetically true. Likewise, the writers of the New Testament were consciously aware that the deep mysteries they were attempting to convey could often only be achieved through the power of symbol, analogy, allegory and story. What is required from the reader is the use of his imagination to engage properly with these narratives. Failure to do so results in lack of true knowledge.

The author of John's Gospel is very much aware of what happens when the imagination is not used and symbols are treated at face value. For example, he recounts a story of how Nicodemus entirely misunderstands Jesus' analogy of 'being born anew' when he thinks it means literally entering back into his mother's womb. There is intentionally no simple explanation of what it means to 'be born anew' because the reader must use his imagination to reflect on the mysterious truth.

Key question

Read John 3:1–10 (the story of Jesus and Nicodemus). What does 'being born anew' mean?

Summary diagram: Knowledge of God's existence

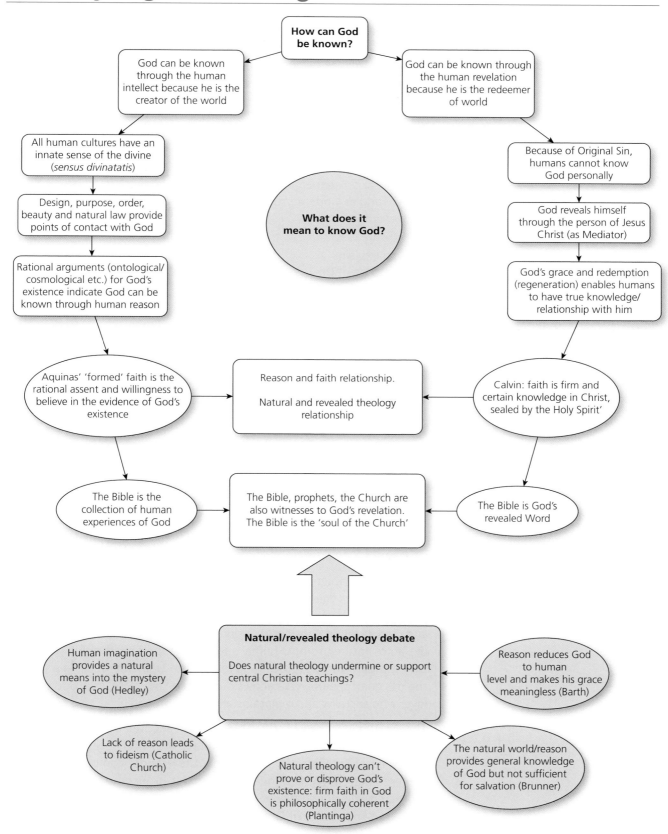

How can God be known?

God can be known through the human intellect because he is the creator of the world

God can be known through the human revelation because he is the redeemer of world

All human cultures have an innate sense of the divine (*sensus divinatatis*)

Because of Original Sin, humans cannot know God personally

Design, purpose, order, beauty and natural law provide points of contact with God

What does it mean to know God?

God reveals himself through the person of Jesus Christ (as Mediator)

Rational arguments (ontological/cosmological etc.) for God's existence indicate God can be known through human reason

God's grace and redemption (regeneration) enables humans to have true knowledge/relationship with him

Aquinas' 'formed' faith is the rational assent and willingness to believe in the evidence of God's existence

Reason and faith relationship.

Natural and revealed theology relationship

Calvin: faith is firm and certain knowledge in Christ, sealed by the Holy Spirit'

The Bible is the collection of human experiences of God

The Bible, prophets, the Church are also witnesses to God's revelation. The Bible is the 'soul of the Church'

The Bible is God's revealed Word

Natural/revealed theology debate

Does natural theology undermine or support central Christian teachings?

Human imagination provides a natural means into the mystery of God (Hedley)

Reason reduces God to human level and makes his grace meaningless (Barth)

Lack of reason leads to fideism (Catholic Church)

Natural theology can't prove or disprove God's existence: firm faith in God is philosophically coherent (Plantinga)

The natural world/reason provides general knowledge of God but not sufficient for salvation (Brunner)

Revision advice

By the end of this chapter you should be able to discuss what true knowledge is and whether this can only really be applied to God. You should be able to discuss critically why some argue that humans may acquire knowledge of God from the natural world and why others consider that this is not true knowledge of God unless given by God as revealed in Jesus Christ. You should have some knowledge of modern scholars (such as Barth, Brunner, Plantinga, Hedley and Barbour) to develop your own views of natural and revealed theology.

Can you give brief definitions of:
- the *sensus divinitatis*
- universal consent argument
- the world as God's mirror
- regeneration
- fideism?

Can you explain:
- knowledge of the natural world as 'point of contact' with God
- the principle of accommodation
- the significance of the Fall
- formed and unformed faith?

Can you give arguments for and against:
- whether knowing about the existence of God is the same as knowing God
- whether revealed theology is irrational
- whether true knowledge of God is only revealed in Jesus Christ
- the use of the Bible in Christian theology?

Sample question and guidance

'God can be known because the world is so well designed.' Discuss.

The argument might begin by referring to the argument from design which supports the idea that as the world is so well organised, it does provide a 'point of contact' between humans as rational finite beings and God. It might consider that human experience of the beauty and design of nature prompts humans to explore their relationship with God through worship, prayer and music. The essay might explain that the design of the universe allows humans to know God as a God of love, who sustains and maintains all natural process.

The essay might then consider the position adopted by Barth that the natural world provides no point of contact with God because human minds are so corrupted by the Fall that they cannot comprehend God. The argument might continue that even if it is the case that the world is ordered, it is not sufficient for sinful human minds to truly know God. True knowledge of God, as the God of love, is only possible for those who have faith in Jesus Christ.

The argument might then go on to compare and analyse these two positions and to offer a conclusion whether knowledge of God is revealed, natural or a combination of both.

Further essay questions

Critically assess the view that the Bible is the only way of knowing God.

'Everyone has an innate knowledge of God's existence.' Discuss.

To what extent is faith in God rational?

Going further

Emil Brunner: *Nature and Grace* (in *Natural Theology*, Geoffrey Bles, 1946). Contains the two famous essays which debate whether the natural world provides a point of contact between humans and God.
Geoffrey Chapman: *Catechism of the Catholic Church* (Geoffrey Chapman, 1994). Section One covers both natural and revealed theology and considers the relationship between them.
Russell R. E. Manning (editor) *The Oxford Handbook of Natural Theology* (Oxford University Press, 2013). A comprehensive set of articles on natural theology. Chapters 11 and 12 cover the Catholic and Protestant perspectives.
Alister McGrath: *Christian Theology* (fifth edition, Wiley–Blackwell, 2011). Chapter 7. An excellent survey of all the issues.
Other books we've talked about in this chapter are:
- Barbour I.G. *Issues in Science and Religion* (Prentice-Hall, 1966).
- Plantinga A. *Warranted Christian Belief* (Oxford University Press, 2000).
- Whitehead A. N. *Process and Reality* (Cambridge University Press, 1929).

Chapter 19

Jesus Christ

1 Introduction

> **Chapter checklist**
>
> The chapter considers three ways in which Jesus Christ has authority: as a moral teacher of wisdom, as liberator of the oppressed and as Son of God. It considers: Jesus' role as liberator of the marginalised and his challenge to secular and religious authority; his teaching on repentance, inner purity and forgiveness; his divinity as expressed in his relationship to God, miracles and resurrection. The chapter concludes by discussing whether his authority is unique.

2 Jesus Christ's authority

Key question

What does it mean for someone to have authority?

Jesus Christ has authority for Christians because of his teaching, his example and relationship to God – many non-Christians admire him and consider that he has authority, especially in his moral teaching. But even amongst Christians there is no single factor as to why he has especial authority and this is due in part to the elusive nature of authority.

(a) What is authority?

Why do parents have authority over their children?

What authority does a soldier have to fight?

What does it mean when we say a person or an institution has authority? Recognition of authority means that we recognise them as having special powers which we acknowledge and defer to. How and why we acknowledge these powers is by no means clear. Here are three different ways in which authority works.

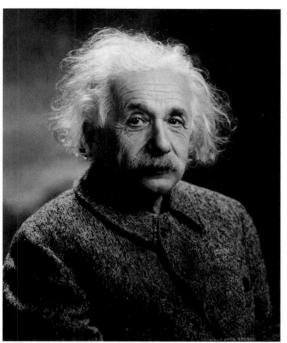

Why is Einstein considered to be an authority in physics?

- Authority sometimes refers to those who are more experienced and have a greater understanding of life and the world. For example, a child recognises the authority of his parents to punish him because they are responsible for looking after him and he accepts their greater knowledge and moral wisdom so that when he is disobedient he accepts he will be punished.
- Authority is ascribed to someone who is highly knowledgeable or skilled in their field. It is by their authority that others can act and change the world. For example, Albert Einstein is an authority on physics; Emile Durkheim is an authority on sociology; Immanuel Kant is an authority on philosophy.
- Authority can also be transferred by proxy from one person to another. For example, when a soldier fights and kills the enemy in battle, he does so by acting on the authority of the state. As he acts on the authority of the state, it is the state which takes on the ultimate responsibility of his actions. But as soon as he acts outside this authority then his actions are not recognised as being lawful; he therefore becomes a murderer not a legitimate combatant.

The chief characteristic of authority is recognition. Without recognition of others, those who may have had authority become nothing.

(b) Jesus' authority

For Christians, Jesus Christ is recognised as a fundamental source of authority. But it is by no means clear how and in what way his authority is recognised. Even from the earliest days, Jesus' authority was discussed and disputed. All the Gospels record how his authority was constantly being questioned and how he, in return, questioned the authority of his Jewish and Roman accusers.

This chapter will review three areas in which Jesus Christ is considered to have authority:

- **Jesus as teacher of wisdom and morality**. Jesus' moral example and teaching is authoritative because he developed Jewish ethics in ways which people found enlightening as a means of living morally and spiritually fulfilled lives.
- **Jesus the liberator**. Jesus' actions challenged the political and religious authorities. He took on the mantle of the great prophets before him (such as Amos and Isaiah) and used his skills as a reformer to tackle the social issues of his day.
- **Son of God**. Jesus' intimate relationship with God gave him the authority to carry out God's will on Earth and ultimately to bring salvation.

3 Jesus the teacher of wisdom

(a) Jesus' affirmation of life

It was during First World War that the Austrian philosopher Ludwig Wittgenstein, a soldier in the Austrian army, began to read Leo Tolstoy's *Gospel in Brief* and was completely won over by his presentation of Christ. For the first time he felt that he was spiritually alive and with a clarity of vision. He wrote in his diary, 'I am on the path to a great discovery. But will I reach it?'

For Wittgenstein the truth and authority of Christianity lay not in God's promise of redemption and the reward of an afterlife but in living life as honestly as possible. What gave Jesus authority was his role as a teacher of wisdom.

Wittgenstein admired Jesus because he affirmed authentic human living. This is all the more striking when we know that Wittgenstein was at the time working on his first great philosophical book, *The Tractatus,* whose aim was to test language against basic propositions about the world. But increasingly Wittgenstein was dissatisfied with this notion because there are very few propositions which can be held to be true – and the ones we are left with don't tell us much about life as we actually experience it. Wittgenstein argued that unless an idea can be *lived*, practised and experienced then it has no value. It has been suggested that it was Wittgenstein's admiration of the person of Jesus Christ which was largely responsible for this shift in his philosophical outlook.

For Wittgenstein (as for countless others), what impressed him about Jesus was his commitment to the truth, his courage to speak against hypocrisy, his simple unadorned lifestyle and ultimately his acceptance of death. By the time Wittgenstein came to write the *Philosophical Investigations*, his older notion of philosophy had made way to the idea that the function of language is not merely to make logically true or false propositions about the world, but to be a '**form of life**' as a way of living. The purpose of philosophy, therefore, is to clarify words and meanings and strip away confusion so as to *practise* the authentic life. Thus, for Wittgenstein, Jesus is not an abstract idea but the 'living word', the embodiment of the external moral and inner spiritual life.

(b) Jesus' moral teaching

Just how different was Jesus' moral teaching from the Judaism of his day and what made his teaching authoritative? There is considerable debate amongst scholars as to whether Jesus was a moral reformer or revolutionary as regards the practice of the **Torah** was concerned. In the collection of his teaching material known as the **Sermon on the Mount**, where the gospel deliberately presents Jesus as the new Moses going up a mountain to receive and deliver the Law, Jesus says:

> Do not think that I have come to abolish the law or the prophets; I have come not to abolish them but to fulfil. For truly, I tell you, until heaven and earth pass away, not one letter, not one stroke of a letter, will pass from the law until all is accomplished. Therefore, whoever then breaks one of the least of these commandments, and teaches others to do the same so, will be called least in the kingdom of heaven.
>
> Matthew 5:17–19

The ambiguity of this statement is the meaning of 'fulfil'. Did Jesus think the essence of the Torah (or law) was not being practised by the religious leaders and teachers so that as a reformer he was returning it to its original purpose? Or did he think that with the arrival of the Kingdom of God the Torah would be replaced, so that his teaching was a preparation for the new order and a radical departure from the old moral order?

Key terms

Form of life (or *Lebensform* in German) In Wittgenstein's philosophy of language refers to the historical, sociological, moral and psychological conditions in which ordinary language operates and has meaning.

Torah Refers to the Jewish body of law and teaching traditionally believed to have been given to Moses at Mount Sinai around 1250BC. It is contained in the first five books of the Bible.

Sermon on the Mount Found in Matthew 5–7 and is Jesus' longest discourse on ethics. It begins with the qualities or virtues a Christian requires to lead the good life and then discusses a range of moral and religious issues, from the use of force to the practice of prayer and worship.

Key quote

What is this? A new teaching – with authority! He commands even the unclean spirits, and they obey him.

Mark 1:27

Besides the Sermon on the Mount, Jesus does not appear to have given long discourses but preferred to teach in a variety of ways, through parables, short sayings, everyday examples and actions (such as healings). His moral teaching covers a wide range of issues but here are four examples.

(i) Forgiveness and repentance

At the heart of Jesus' announcement of the coming of the Kingdom of God was the call to repentance. The word repentance in Greek is *metanoia* and means a radical change of mind-set or heart; it is more than merely saying sorry, but a desire to change a whole way of life. Jesus gave many illustrations of repentance, including the tax collector Zacchaeus who offered to pay back all those he had cheated. But perhaps the most famous of Jesus' parables which dramatically describes the spiritual and psychological effort required for true *metanoia* is the **Parable of the Lost Son**.

Having squandered his inheritance on a frivolous and selfish lifestyle, the son realises that his only hope is to return to his father's house and beg forgiveness. The parable also describes how hard it is to forgive, for whereas the son's father generously welcomes his son home with joy, his older brother is unable to forgive. It is easy to condemn the older son, but Jesus' parable recognises that true forgiveness is hard. When asked how many times a sin should be forgiven Jesus answered 'seventy times seven' (Matthew 18:22): that is, for as many times as it takes. Forgiving others is also at the heart of Jesus' prayer, the 'Our Father' or 'Lord's Prayer' where it is also associated with cancellation of debts, literal and metaphorical, meaning that once forgiven a person is set free mentally and materially to start afresh.

(ii) Motive and inner purity

Although Jesus was critical of the Pharisees, he admired those of them who were trying to achieve spiritual holiness or 'righteousness'. He taught his followers that their aim was to exceed the righteousness of the Jewish lawyers and Pharisees (Matthew 5:20). He taught that morality is therefore about developing one's character and that requires rigorous analysis of motive. The Sermon on the Mount provides numerous examples of what he has in mind. For example, by checking anger, a person is not led to commit murder; by resisting lust, a person is not led to commit adultery; by resisting using oaths, then one's language and intentions are pure. The Sermon on the Mount sets a very high standard, for the aim of the moral life is perfection. Jesus says:

> Be perfect, therefore, as your heavenly Father is perfect.
>
> Matthew 5:48

(iii) Personal responsibility

Keeping the sabbath day holy is a central religious and social law because not only is it commanded in the fourth of the Ten Commandments (Exodus 20:1–17) but it is the basis for social justice – everyone in society is entitled to a day free from labour. Jesus argued, however, that all too often people were using the sabbath laws as a means of avoiding social

Read Luke 19:1–10 for the story about Zacchaeus.

Key terms

Metanoia The Greek word usually translated as repentance. But it also means a radical change of mind-set and heart.

Parable of the Lost Son or the Prodigal Son (Luke 15:11–32) One of several parables Luke collects together in his Gospel on the theme of 'lost and found'. The 'lost' are probably those who have strayed from their Jewish faith.

Key quotes

And forgive us our debts, as we also have forgiven our debtors.
The Lord's Prayer, Matthew 6:12

You have heard that it was said, 'You shall not commit adultery.' But I say to you that everyone who looks at a woman with lust has already committed adultery with her in his heart.
Matthew 5:27–28

Let your word be 'Yes, Yes' or 'No, No'; anything more than this comes from the evil one.
Matthew 5:37

responsibility. The rabbis had developed a list of 39 definitions and examples of work as a means of honouring the sabbath and keeping it holy, but in practice the Pharisees and Jewish lawyers were hiding behind their religious duties and failing in their duty to humans.

One of his memorable short sayings was: 'The sabbath was made for humankind and not humankind for the sabbath' (Mark 2:27). He pointed out the hypocrisy of the teachers of the law who allow an ox to be fed on the Sabbath but at the same time forbid treating a sick human being (Luke 13:10–17). Jesus therefore cured the sick on the sabbath when the occasion required it. Jesus knew the risks of deliberately breaking the sabbath rules which, if proved, might have resulted in the death penalty (the punishment for blasphemy).

Jesus focused on the sabbath rules because he wanted to show that:

- Morality requires personal responsibility, not blind obedience to the rules (he called the Pharisees 'blind guides').
- Religious practices are there to serve human needs.
- Being holy is not achieved simply by carrying out external rituals but by purity of mind.

(iv) Is Jesus just a teacher of wisdom?

For many scholars presenting Jesus as a teacher of wisdom is compatible with a belief in his resurrection (as a sign of his special relationship with God). But for other scholars all supernatural elements of Jesus' life are to be rejected as unscientific inventions of the early Christian Church to explain his divinity. Once these elements, such as Jesus' encounters with demons and performance of miracles, are stripped away we are left with the authentic Jesus, the teacher of wisdom.

For these scholars presenting Jesus as the teacher of wisdom and morality is particularly attractive as it means that Christianity is not in competition with other religions in claiming Jesus as the only means to truth because it recognises that there are other great teachers of wisdom such as the Buddha, Muhammad (pbuh), Moses, Laozi and Vivekananda.

John Hick describes such teachers of wisdom as 'gifts to the world' and argues that it is only once the supernatural elements of Jesus' life are reinterpreted as symbols of his close relationship with God that Christianity will be able to enter into full and healthy dialogue with other world religions.

Presenting Jesus as a teacher of wisdom and morality is clearly attractive for those who find the idea of his divinity hard to accept and for those Christians working on interfaith dialogue. For others such as Tolstoy, Wittgenstein and even Nietzsche, the power and authority of Jesus' moral teaching is that it does not rely on abstraction but rather a real engagement with and affirmation of life.

However, if scholars such as Hick are right, then it is not clear what gives Jesus' teaching any especial authority even for those who admire him. For if Jesus' teaching and wisdom is also to be found on the lips of other important teachers there is no especial novelty in it and no apparent reason for adopting it more than any other moral teaching.

Key question

How different was Jesus' moral teaching from that of other teachers of wisdom?

Key persons

The following teachers of wisdom are considered to have a key place with the following religious traditions: The **Buddha** or Siddhartha Gautama (563–483bc) with Buddhism; **Muhammad** (pbuh) (570–632ce) with Islam; **Moses** (thirteenth century bc) with Judaism; **Laozi** (d. 531bc) with Taoism; **Vivekananda** (1863–1902) with Hinduism.

Key person

John Hick (1922–2012): Professor of theology at Birmingham University and philosophy of religion at Claremont Graduate University.

4 Jesus the liberator

Just how politically motivated was Jesus and the Jesus movement which continued after his death? Much of Jesus' adult life, as presented in the Gospels, was spent in conflict with the Jewish authorities over the application of the law and then finally with the Roman authorities who put him to death on the grounds of rebellion and treason. The question is of more than merely historical interest because it implies that if Jesus was politically motivated then Christians are justified in being fully involved in the political world today. Many scholars agree that Jesus' teaching on the Kingdom of God was not just spiritual preparation for the age to come, but a call to change the social structures of society now. But there is far less agreement as to whether Jesus belonged to a particular political movement or party and what methods of political activism he advocated.

(a) Liberator of the poor

In S. G. F Brandon's influential though controversial study of Jesus, *Jesus and the Zealots* (1967), he argued that the historical Jesus was a politically driven freedom fighter but that later presentations of him in the Gospels toned this down and re-wrote passages to make him a pacifist.

Although Brandon's argument has been severely criticised by scholars, the idea that Jesus was a political activist is particularly attractive in parts of the world where there has been considerable class antagonism and exploitation. During the time of civil war and massive exploitation of the poor in Latin America in the 1970s to 1990s, liberation theologians found inspiration in the **Zealot**-type presentation of Jesus. For too long the Jesus presented by the Church was as a politically neutral character who preached spiritual values without wanting to make changes to the unjust economic social structures. The liberation theologians saw in Jesus' actions a bias towards the poor and exploited. These are the people the liberation theologians described as occupying the '**underside of history**'. By thinking of Jesus as the liberator the Church ensures that the Christ of faith is fully engaged with the affairs of the world. If this doesn't happen then, as Gustavo Gutiérrez argued, all the characters in the Gospels become merely fictional stereotypes rather than actual people engaged with the same kind of issues we deal with today.

The liberation theologians describe Jesus' bias towards the marginalised as a **preferential option for the poor**; his historical example therefore sets the agenda for Christians in every historical age. As Leonardo Boff says:

> A Christology that proclaims Jesus Christ as the Liberator seeks to be committed to the economic, social and political liberation of those groups that are oppressed and dominated. It purports to see the theological relevance of the historic liberation of the vast majority of people in our continent.
>
> Leonardo Boff: *Jesus Christ Liberator* (1972), p. 266

Some priests really saw Jesus as a type of Zealot. Camilo Torres Restrepo, for example, was a Roman Catholic priest who joined the communist people's army as a soldier in the guerrilla war against the government troops. As he said, 'If Jesus were alive today, He would be a guerrillero.'

Key quote

The duty of every Catholic is to be a revolutionary. The duty of every revolutionary is to make the revolution.

Camilo Torres Restrepo
(speech, 1965)

Key persons

Leonardo Boff (b. 1938): A Catholic priest. He was professor of systematic theology at the Institute for Philosophy and Theology at Petropolis, Brazil. In 1992, he left his priestly ministry and Franciscan religious order because he felt the Church was 'fossilised' and too stuck in its ways. He was awarded the alternative Nobel Prize in Stockholm (2001).

Camilo Torres Restrepo (1929–66): A famous Colombian Catholic priest who joined the communist guerrilla group ELN (The National Liberation Army of Colombia) in their active resistance against the government. Although by the time he came to fight he was no longer a priest, he still regarded his actions in a priestly way. He was killed in his first combat experience, when the ELN ambushed a Colombian military patrol.

Camilo Torres Restrepo

Gutiérrez argues that although Jesus may be seen as a Zealot he was much more than that. Jesus did not set himself up to be a national leader and it is frequently recorded in the Gospels that he told people not to think of him in political messianic terms. Furthermore, Jesus' mission was not just the restoration of Israel but all human societies. As Gutiérrez concludes:

> *The liberation which Jesus offers is universal and integral; it transcends national boundaries, attacks the foundation of injustice and exploitation and eliminates politico-religious confusions, without therefore being limited to a purely 'spiritual' plane.*

Gustavo Gutiérrez: *A Theology of Liberation* (2001), p. 213

(b) Liberator of the marginalised

Some of Jesus' most memorable parables deal with those who were considered to be on the fringes of society – often referred to by the religious leaders as the 'sinners' (or *hamartoloi* in Greek; literally 'those who miss the mark'). Sinners included despised trades such as tax collectors and dung collectors; the sexually impure such as prostitutes and bastards; religious heretics such as the **Samaritans**. These sinners

Key term

Samaritans A group of Jews living in Samaria midway between Judaea in the south and Galilee in the north of Israel. They were regarded by Judean Jews as being racially and religiously impure because they had married foreigners and built their own temple. Most Jews travelling north to Galilee would have avoided passing through Samaria.

were considered unclean and any contact with them would necessitate undergoing washing ceremonies to remove contamination. The other group Jesus frequently mixed with were simply known as the 'people of the land' (or 'am ha'aretz' in Hebrew) – the uneducated who were largely ignorant of the finer points of the Torah. These included: farmers, fishermen, servants and labourers. Jesus' teaching was revolutionary in so far as it frequently used sinners and people of the land as examples of the moral life rather than the religious leaders or members of the religious groups.

So, it is the despised Samaritan, for example, who in Jesus' parable, The Good Samaritan (Luke 10:25–37), illustrates true love of neighbour, mercy and generosity. In the parable a man is beaten up and left for dead. On their way to the Temple in Jerusalem two Jewish officials (a priest and Levite) fail to attend to the man perhaps fearing that if they touched his body they would become unclean. But it is the Samaritan man who dismisses these religious rules and carries out the central commandment of the law, to love God 'with all your heart, and with all your soul, and with all your strength, and with all your mind; and your neighbour as yourself' (Luke 10:28). Not only does the Samaritan treat the man's wounds but he pays for him to be looked after at a local inn. By using the Samaritan as an example of exemplary moral behaviour, Jesus touches on the consciences and prejudices of his audience; liberation is not necessarily about political revolution but in shifting consciousness.

Another example (Mark 5:24–34) is where Jesus touches a woman who has been bleeding for twelve years. According to the Torah (Leviticus 15:19–28) touching a woman who is having her period would automatically make him unclean and yet he chooses to see her action as one of faith and in accepting her, Jesus challenges some of deep-seated body prejudices and attitudes to women of his day.

Finally, Jesus frequently keeps table-fellowship with tax-collectors, prostitutes and thieves. Amongst the Pharisees table-fellowship meant maintaining very precise standards of religious rituals (keeping to the food laws, maintaining the sabbath rules and washing rituals, and so on), so Jesus' deliberate rejection of the table-fellowship rituals was a symbol of his frequently uttered phrase that 'the last shall be first, and the first last' in his vision of a transformed society, the Kingdom of God.

(c) Is Jesus just a liberator?

Many scholars find the depiction of Jesus as liberator powerful because it provides a model of how to challenge an unjust world. Others, though, consider that Jesus' authority was not political but spiritual. At his trial when Pilate asks him if he is the king of the Jews, Jesus replied:

My kingdom is not from this world. If my kingdom were from this world, my followers would be fighting to keep me from being handed across to the Jews. But as it is, my kingdom is not from here.

John 18:36

Key quote

When the scribes of the Pharisees saw that he was eating with sinners and tax-collectors, they said to his disciples, 'Why does he eat with tax-collectors and sinners?'

Mark 2:16

Key question

Was Jesus more than a political liberator?

There is more Gospel evidence to suggest that Jesus never advocated political revolution supported by violent struggle. For example:

- At the Garden at Gethsemane when Jesus was arrested, he scolded one of his disciples for drawing his sword (Matthew 26:47–56).
- The authorities did not consider Jesus to be a revolutionary leader otherwise they would have arrested the disciples as well as Jesus.
- Jesus resists being called messiah or king. At the feeding of the multitude (John 6), when Jesus sees that they wanted to make him a king, the Gospel writer records that Jesus 'withdrew again to the mountain by himself' (John 6:15).

5 Son of God

For many Christians Jesus' authority is of the third kind which we considered earlier (see page 304). For some, his authority comes from carrying out God's will in a special way and acting on God's behalf, whereas for others he was God or rather God embodied in human form. Philosophically and theologically these are immensely complex issues and the early Christians found them just as difficult to explain as we do today.

Jesus was given many titles, but one summarised all the others and that was the term **Son of God**. It was not a term Jesus used himself but his followers used it to describe his special relationship with God.

In Jewish terms, the phrase Son of God was often used to refer to the king, as someone chosen by God to carry out his will on Earth. As the king was anointed as a sign of his responsibility, there also developed a hope that a specially anointed person would arrive and free Israel politically, morally and spiritually. The Hebrew for 'anointed one' is messiah or *Christos* (in Greek). In other words, Son of God and Christ are equivalent terms.

But in the non-Jewish Greek world of the first century, Son of God referred to a human who had been elevated to become a divine being. That is probably what the centurion meant when he saw how Jesus died on the cross and said:

Truly this man was God's Son!

Mark 15:39

Key terms

Son of God The term used by Jesus' followers to describe his special relationship with God.

Council of Chalcedon The city of Chalcedon (in modern Turkey) was chosen as being close to Constantinople (modern Istanbul) which was the centre of the Roman Empire and Church. The meeting in 451AD was attended by 600 bishops with the primary purpose of re-affirming the central Christian beliefs, in particular the divinity and humanity of Christ.

Whether the centurion meant Jesus was *the* Son of God, or *a* son of God, it is clear that he considered that Jesus was more than a mere mortal. In time, the Church combined the Jewish and Greek meanings of the term Son of God and the official view was that Jesus Christ was both fully God as well as being truly human. In 451AD a council of church leaders at **Chalcedon** defined Jesus Christ as:

... one and same Son, the same perfect in Godhead and the same perfect in manhood, truly God and truly man ... one and the same Son, only-begotten, divine Word, the Lord Jesus Christ.

Chalcedonian Definition of Faith

Chalcedon did not and has not finalised exactly what Christians mean when they called Jesus Christ the Son of God.

(a) Christology

Key term

Christology The area of Christian theology concerned with the nature of Jesus Christ's relationship with God.

The nature of Jesus' relationship with God is called **Christology**. There are broadly two kinds of Christology – from above (also called high Christology) and from below (also called low Christology). The kind of Christology Christians believe in changes what they think is meant by salvation, the relationship of humans with God.

- **Christology from above** focuses on Jesus' divinity and God's act of bringing humanity back into relationship with him. High Christology is not something which can be proved for it relies on faith.
- **Christology from below** focuses on Jesus' message, example and teaching. Salvation focuses on how people respond to Jesus the way this helps to develop their relationship to God and the world.

(b) Knowledge of God

Key question

Did Jesus think he was the divine Son of God?

Even Christians who hold a high Christology position realise the difficulty of claiming that Jesus knew he was the Son of God if at the same time it is also thought that he was fully human. For example, in John's Gospel, Jesus makes a number of great statements, beginning with 'I am ...'. 'I am' is especially powerful because it is reminiscent of God's description of himself to Moses when he reveals his name as 'I am' (Exodus 3:14).

Jesus says,

> *I am the way, and the truth, and the life. No one comes to the Father except through me.*
>
> John 14:6

Key quote

God said to Moses, 'I AM WHO I AM.

Exodus 3:14

In some ways this couldn't be clearer. Jesus expresses that his unique relationship with God the Father is the only means to salvation because, as he says elsewhere in John's Gospel, 'The Father and I are one' (John 10:30) and, 'Whoever has seen me has seen the Father' (John 14:9).

Yet, for some theologians what these sayings really illustrate is not so much that Jesus was God, but that he was fully consciousness of God's will and entirely desired to fulfil it. Again in John's Gospel, Jesus says 'the Father is greater than I' (John 14:28) because as a human being he could not have been all-knowing and all-powerful as God is.

(c) Miracles

> *Who then is this, that even the wind and sea obey him?*
>
> Mark 4:41

Key question

Do Jesus' miracles prove he was the Son of God?

> *Jesus accompanies his words with many 'mighty works and wonders and signs' which manifest that the kingdom is present in him and attest that he was the promised Messiah.*
>
> Catechism of the Catholic Church para. 547

What is the answer to the question posed by Jesus' disciples in Mark's Gospel? Jesus had just ordered a great storm on the Sea of Galilee to be calm and brought the disciples to safety, but it is not immediately apparent to them what kind of person has the power to do this. The disciples would have known that in the Old Testament prophets such as Moses and Elijah performed mighty wonders, signs or miracles but these were occasional and not attributed to the prophet themselves but to God working for them. By contrast, Jesus' frequently performs miracles and every stage of his earthly life is marked by wonders and signs. In traditional Christianity, the disciples' question is one of awe; they have grasped that 'the mighty works' which Jesus performs are the result of his own commands and are therefore confirmation of his divinity and status as the Son of God. The *Catechism of the Catholic Church* follows the same line of reasoning when it says:

> So miracles strengthen faith in the One who does his Father's works; they bear witness that he is the Son of God.
>
> *Catechism of the Catholic Church* para. 548

But for many other theologians, miracles are not so much indicators of Jesus' divinity as special moments of insight into his teaching on the nature of the Kingdom of God. They argue that the New Testament does not have a single word for miracle but uses terms such as 'mighty works', 'wonders' and 'signs'. These are not terms describing how the laws of nature have been suspended but rather moments of deep insight and awe about the nature of God and reality. Those who hold a low Christology interpret Jesus, 'miracles' as they would parables; that is as dramatic signs to illustrate his teaching and understanding of God.

(i) Birth and incarnation

Traditionally Jesus' birth to Mary is a miracle. She is a virgin and the conception and pregnancy is the result of the Holy Spirit (Luke 1:35). While this may be a unique occasion, its significance is more than just a biologically unusual moment. As the Chalcedonian Definition states, this is the **incarnation**, the moment when God becomes fully human; Mary doesn't conceive just another human being but God in human form. This is why she is described as *theotokos*, or God-bearer. For God to restore humans to the state of perfection before the Fall, he had to become human.

However, from early times Christian theologians have been deeply divided over exactly what the incarnation means. The following are all examples of those whose views were all rejected as heresies by the Church (at Chalcedon) even though their views were influential.

- **Nestorius** (d. *c.*451) argued that the two natures of Christ, the divine and the human, were completely separate, and only became one when the human Jesus will become one with God's will.
- **Apollinarius** (*c.*310–390) argued that in the incarnation the divine will replaced Jesus' ordinary human reason. Jesus was still a complete person as he possessed body and soul and as such he would have experienced suffering in the flesh, but he could not have sinned because,

Key terms

Incarnation Literally means 'in flesh' and is one of the central Christian teachings that God became flesh as a human being in the person of Jesus Christ.

Theotokos The Greek term translated variously as 'God-bearer' or 'God-producer' when referring to Mary, the mother of Jesus, and is widely used today in the Eastern churches. Other Christians prefer to refer to Mary as the Mother of God rather than theotokos.

Key question

Why have the Christologies of Nestorius, Apollinarius and the docetics all been regarded as heresies by the Church?

as his human rational soul had been replaced by the divine *logos*, he would have never experienced any form of inner conflict on how to act.

- **Docetic** Christians taught that at the incarnation God only appeared to take on human form but Jesus could not have been fully human. As the Son of God he was fully divine and brought salvation through his special knowledge of God.

Nestorius' theology still finds particular favour from those today whose Christology is 'from below' as it gives a psychological rather than a scientific explanation of Jesus' human and divine nature. It is much more convincing to think of Jesus' relationship to God being one of the obedient son rather than having part of him which was God.

(ii) Miracles as signs of salvation

Both high and low Christologies agree that Jesus' miracles are signs of salvation. As signs (the preferred term in John's Gospel) they indicate what it would be like to live in a world restored. His healing miracles in particular illustrate Isaiah's vision of a renewed society where seeing, hearing and walking are also symbols of new insight, understanding and acting in the world.

> *Then the eyes of the blind shall be opened;*
> *and the ears of the deaf unstopped;*
> *then the lame shall leap like deer,*
> *and the tongue of the speechless sing for joy.*

> Isaiah 35:5–6

So, for example, in the story of the healing of a man born blind (John 9:1–41), the focus of the story is not so much on how he receives his sight but the contrast between the man's gradual faith as 'seeing' and understanding of Jesus as the bringer of salvation and the inability of those who have physical sight but are blind to the truth of his teaching.

Sometimes a contrast is made between Jesus' healing miracles and his 'nature' miracles. But salvation does not just apply to the human–God relationship but to the whole of the nature. So, for example, Jesus' walking on the water (Mark 6:47–52) is a reminder of how God's Spirit hovered over the waters of chaos in the creation of the world (Genesis 1:2) to bring order and beauty out of chaos.

Even the Gospels themselves do not regard Jesus' mighty works as conclusive proofs that he was the Son of God. They record moments when even in his own time miracles were seen to be works of magic which were no different from those performed by local 'wonder makers'.

(d) Resurrection

If Jesus' death on the cross had marked the end of his life as a teacher, then perhaps the notion that he was the divine Son of God may never have been considered, but of all events in the Christian story, Jesus' resurrection was the most important.

However, there was clearly something different about Jesus' resurrection as resurrection was a Jewish idea taught by the Pharisees of Jesus' time that the righteous would be resurrected to live in God's kingdom at the end of time. What appears to have made the difference was firstly, that Jesus' resurrection was experienced by hundreds of different people over a long period of time and not just immediately after his death and secondly, the overwhelming experience of the early followers was that something decisive had changed in their relationship with God; Jesus' resurrection marked the start of a new era.

(i) Confirmation of divinity

When St Paul describes Jesus' resurrection as the 'first fruits' of the harvest (1 Corinthians 15:20) his metaphor expresses a theoretical possibility that is now a reality for all humanity and all creation (Romans 8:29), that God brings everything to completion.

But even those scholars, who see Jesus as no more than an ordinary human being during his lifetime, the resurrection is the decisive moment which reveals him as the divine Son of God. Wolfhart Pannenberg, for example, argues that as Jesus' resurrection is uniquely a sign of God's completion and perfection of creation at the end of time, then it 'visibly and unambiguously' reveals him as God.

> *Only because the end of the world is already present in Jesus' resurrection is God revealed in him.*
>
> Wolfhart Pannenberg: *Jesus – God and Man* (1968), p. 69

(ii) Authority to worship and proclaim

The Incredulity of Saint Thomas, 1603 by Caravaggio

> *Then he said to Thomas, 'Put your finger here and see my hands. Reach out your hand and put it in my side. Do not doubt but believe.' Thomas answered him, 'My Lord and my God!'*
>
> John 20:27–28

Key question

Does Jesus' resurrection reveal him as the divine Son of God?

Key quote

But in fact Christ has been raised from the dead, the first fruits of those who have died. For since death came through a human being, the resurrection of the dead has also come through a human being; for as all die in Adam, so all will be made alive in Christ.

1 Corinthians 15:20–22

Key person

Wolfhart Pannenberg (1928–2014): A German theologian. In his influential book, *Jesus – God and Man* (1968), he argued that Jesus' resurrection, not his life, was a decisive moment in history which revealed him as God's Son.

Key question

Why do Christians worship Jesus Christ?

And Jesus came and said to them, 'All authority in heaven and on earth has been given to me. Go therefore and make disciples of all nations.'

Matthew 28:19

The story of doubting Thomas (John 20:24–29) is a powerful example of how the resurrection was more than the transformation of Jesus' body into its spiritual state, but was also the experience of God's presence. It is a religious experience which confirms Jesus Christ as Lord who can be worshipped as God without committing blasphemy. But the story goes on to commend those who believe in the resurrection without having first-hand experience of the resurrected Jesus. This is crucially important as Christians take it on trust that the resurrection is the deciding event which gives them authority to proclaim the truth that Christ is the Son of God.

6 Uniqueness

Key question

Was Jesus' relationship with God very special or truly unique?

For many Christians, it matters very much whether Jesus Christ is unique or not. If Jesus is just one of many teachers of wisdom, political liberators or visionaries, then it undermines the significance of the Christian message.

On the other hand, the very idea of uniqueness is meaningless as no one is identical with another and we are in that sense all unique. For many Christians, Jesus' 'uniqueness' is just a way of explaining their personal belief and commitment in Christ as the one who defines their existence.

(a) History and faith

The New Testament scholar E. P. Sanders, in his investigation of the historical Jesus, commented that there is no way that the Christian claims about the uniqueness of Jesus Christ as Son of God can ever be substantiated from the evidence of history alone. This is because history and faith are separate categories.

*History, in fact, has difficulty with the category 'unique'. Adequate comparative information is never available to permit such judgments as 'uniquely good', 'uniquely compassionate' and the like. It is, rather, a fault of New Testament scholarship that so many do not see that the use of such words as 'unique' and 'unprecedented' shows that they have shifted their perspective from that of critical history and **exegesis** to that of faith. We can accept with argument Jesus' greatness as a man, but we must stop well short of explaining his impact by appeal to absolutely unique personal qualities.*

E. P. Sanders: *Jesus and Judaism* (1985), p. 320

Key term

Exegesis The close analysis and interpretation of a text.

Key person

E. P. Sanders (b. 1937): Professor of New Testament at Oxford University and then Duke University. His influential books, which include *Jesus and Judaism* (SCM, 1985) and *The Historical Figure of Jesus* (1993), investigate the relationship of Paul and Jesus to Judaism.

Sanders argues that Jesus' miracles, teaching on non-violence, hope for outcasts, and eschatological hope or teaching of God's grace make him substantially different from others at the time, but these are not sufficient to make him unique.

On the other hand, Sanders does not take into account the significance of the resurrection because for him it cannot be objectively and historically analysed as it belongs to the subjective category of faith. But for other scholars, whose Christology is from below even, the resurrection is the decisive moment and reveals Christ's divinity in an entirely new way.

But does this make Jesus unique? Some Christians consider that it does, for Jesus' teaching, his death and resurrection establish a new relationship with God as 'the way, and the truth, and the life' (John 14:6) and not *a* way or *a* truth. For others (such as John Hick) though the resurrection is a powerful metaphor of Christian hope – the triumph of hope over despair, it is not a unique idea or claim and nor should it be.

(b) The Christ-event

As the question of uniqueness is ambiguous, then perhaps it is unhelpful and should be abandoned. That is John Macquarrie's conclusion. Macquarrie's argument is that *every* life is in some respects unique, as everyone lives their own particular historical existence in a different way. Jesus' life was no different in that respect. Unlike Pannenberg, Macquarrie rejects the claim that any one moment in Jesus' life makes him uniquely the Son of God. What makes Jesus especially significant is his place in history; in the events which led up to his life, the effects of his life and on human history afterwards.

> **Key question**
>
> What does it mean to say that Jesus Christ was a defining moment in history?

> **Key quote**
>
> I would have to say that the word 'unique is not helpful in discussing this question.
>
> John Macquarrie: *Principles of Christian Theology* (1977), p. 304

> **Key term**
>
> **Christ-event** Refers to Jesus' birth, ministry, death and resurrection. It is used by scholars to suggest that the significance of Christ lies in no one particular historical moment but the whole of his life and its relationship with history before and after.

> **Key person**
>
> **John Macquarrie** (1919–2007): Lady Margaret Professor of Divinity, Oxford University. His philosophical theology was strongly influenced by Martin Heidegger's existentialism. Of his many books, the most popular titles are *Existentialism* (1972) and *Principles of Christian Theology* (1966).

Viewing the whole of Jesus' life and its place in history is called the **Christ-event**. The meaning of his life is not to be found in any *one* particular moment of his existence (such as his birth, his miracles or resurrection) but the part the whole of it plays in understanding human existence. Macquarrie prefers to think of Jesus' life as being a *defining* moment in the human relationship with God (or Being as he prefers to call God) but not exclusively so. This is unique in so far as it is a 'focus of Being ... in this particular person, Jesus Christ', but other non-Christian religious figures have also been defining moments of human existence in world history. However, for Christians, Jesus Christ is significant because of the effect the Christ-event has on their lives and in:

> *... the deepest level of conscience, where conscience is understood as man's fundamental self-awareness as one is summoned to an authentic personal and communal existence.*
>
> John Macquarrie: *Principles of Christian Theology*, (1977), p. 305

In summary, although Macquarrie rejects any presentation of Jesus Christ which claims he is unique, he does not think that Christ is just another prophet, political leader or teacher because for many people Christ defines what it means to live an authentic human existence. It is in that existential sense that Christ becomes, but only for each particular individual, 'the way and the truth and the life'.

Summary diagram: Jesus Christ

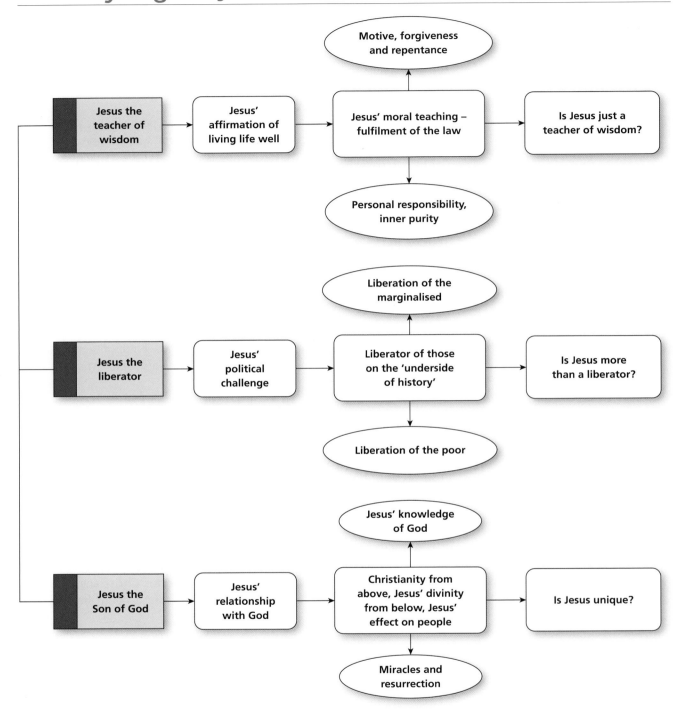

Revision advice

By the end of this chapter you should be able to explain the different ways in which Christians understand and present Jesus Christ as having authority. You should be able to explain the ways in which scholars have presented Jesus as a teacher of wisdom and morality, especially his message of hope to the marginalised in his role as liberator. Finally, you should understand the ambiguity of the phrase Son of God and the different ways in which Christians have explained Jesus' relationship with God.

Can you give brief definitions of:
- authority
- *metanoia*
- preferential option for the poor
- Son of God
- Christology?

Can you explain:
- why Ludwig Wittgenstein was inspired by Jesus as a moral teacher
- Jesus' teaching on inner purity
- how Jesus challenged the place of the marginalised in society
- why Christians worship Jesus Christ
- the meaning of the term 'Christ-event'?

Can you give arguments for and against:
- presenting Jesus as a political revolutionary
- Jesus as just a teacher of wisdom
- the miracles as proof of Jesus' divinity
- Christ as the unique means of truth?

Sample question and guidance

'Jesus' role was just to liberate the poor and weak against oppression.' Discuss.

The essay might begin by setting out some examples of the way in which Jesus sided with the poor and the weak, especially those who were termed 'sinners' (tax collectors, prostitutes, Samaritans and so on). It might consider the shocking impact his parable of the Good Samaritan would have had on the religious leaders and the fact that he ate and kept table-fellowship with the marginalised. The essay might consider how liberation theologians in South and North America have been inspired by Jesus' political challenge to authority to do the same.

The essay might then question whether Jesus' role was only as a political liberator. It might argue that he was just as much concerned with inner purity, forgiveness and repentance of ordinary people as the marginalised. The essay might consider that his teaching as focused on liberation from personal sin, not political activism, as he saw his role as helping people achieve spiritual perfection.

Further essay questions

Assess the view that the miracles prove Jesus was the Son of God.

'Jesus Christ is not unique.' Discuss.

To what extent was Jesus just a teacher of morality?

Going further

Geoffrey Chapman: *Catechism of the Catholic Church* (1994) chapter 2, 'I Believe in Jesus Christ, the Only Son of God'. A very clear summary of Catholic Christology and useful when considering radical alternative views.

John Hick: *The Metaphor of God Incarnate* (1993, second edition, SCM, 2012) Chapter 2. A good example of liberal protestant theology which sees Jesus' birth, incarnation and resurrection as symbols of his relationship with God but not signs that he was God.

Alastair MacGrath: *Christian Theology* fifth edition (Wiley–Blackwell, 2011) Chapters 11 and 12 on the person of Christ and Christology. A mine of useful ideas.

Wolfhart Pannenberg: *Jesus – God and Man* (Westminster Press, 1968) Chapter 3 on Jesus' resurrection. Although this is a demanding book, it is a classic and worth making the effort to read.

Other books we've talked about in this chapter are:

- Boff L. *Jesus Christ Liberator* (Orbis, 1972).
- Brandon S. G. F. *Zealots* (Manchester University Press, 1967).
- Gutiérrez G. *A Theology of Liberation* (SCM, 2001).
- Macquarrie J. *Existentialism* (Westminster Press, 1972).
- Macquarrie J. *Principles of Christian Theology* (revised SCM, 1977).
- Pannenberg W. *Jesus – God and Man* (Westminster Press, 1968).
- Sanders E. P. *Jesus and Judaism* (SCM, 1985).
- Sanders E. P. *The Historical Figure of Jesus* (Penguin, 1993).
- Wittgenstein L. *Philosophical Investigations* (1953, English edition, Macmillan, 1957).
- Wittgenstein L. *Tractatus Logico-Philosophicus* (1921, English edition, Kegan Paul).

Chapter 20

Christian moral principles

1 Introduction

Chapter checklist

This chapter considers the various ways in which Christian moral principles are formed and why there is such a variety of different views about what Christian ethics are. The chapter considers three approaches: Christian ethics are revealed by God almost entirely through the Bible; Christian ethics are formed through a combination of biblical revelation, reason, tradition, conscience and Christian community/church; Christian ethics are not distinctive from other forms of ethics, as they are just the Christian principle of love being used to inform moral reasoning.

Key question

Why are there such differing views about what Christian ethics are?

We have already considered Jesus as the moral teacher in Chapter 19 and whether his teaching was distinctive and what its relationship was with Jewish ethical teaching. Chapter 18 discussed whether moral knowledge is natural or revealed or a combination of both. These issues alone indicate that there is a considerable variety of views as to what Christian ethics are and how they should be practised.

2 Theonomous Christian ethics and practices

Key term

Theonomous Christian ethics
Means that ethics are governed by God's law or commands. Theonomous derives from two Greek words: *theos* meaning God and *nomos* meaning law or rule.

For many Christians it is self-evident, as St Paul and St Augustine so clearly described, that as all humans are by nature sinful and ignorant, they are incapable of living good lives based on their own powers of reason. As this is the case the only source for living the good life must be revealed by God himself. This is called **theonomous Christian ethics** and for many Christians the only source for God's moral commands is the Bible.

(a) The Bible as the only authority for Christian ethical practices

Key question

How comprehensive a guide is the Bible for making moral decisions?

All scripture is inspired by God, and is useful for teaching, for reproof, for correction, for training in righteousness.

2 Timothy 3:16

David and Bathsheba

On Inner law or purity, see pages 307–309 on Jesus, the moral teacher.

This passage from the Second Letter to Timothy, in the New Testament, is often quoted by those who hold a **biblicist** or fundamentalist view of the Bible and supports the view that as all scripture (Old and New Testaments) is inspired by God then the Bible alone must be used for moral instruction.

In other words, the Bible alone is the source of moral authority because God is its author. He is the one who spoke to his prophets and writers and inspired them to compose the various parts of the Bible. From this point of view, the Bible is infallible and if there are problems with understanding a biblical text, the problem lies with us not the text.

One of the glories of the Bible and a great strength of theonomous Christian ethics is that ethics are not always spelled out as separate commandments but illustrated through real life situations. For example, the story of King David's adulterous relationship with Bathsheba in which he not only makes her pregnant but also misuses his kingly powers and causes the death of her husband, powerfully illustrates what it means, or rather does *not* mean, to live a moral life. The story also demonstrates that David is not merely judged on whether he has broken the commandments but the kind of person he is. By contrast, Uriah (Bathsheba's husband) is everything which David is not – law-abiding, loyal, faithful, honest and courageous.

Although God is not mentioned until the very end of the story, the whole incident must be understood in the general theological context of life lived as a **covenant** with God, a covenant which is expressed in the New Testament in terms of Jesus' life, death and resurrection.

- In the Old Testament, the covenant establishes the notion that ethics are both social and personal. The **Ten Commandments** (Exodus 20:1–17) are a summary of these two ideas. The prophets, such as Amos and Isaiah, focus in particular on social justice and the treatment of the poor as examples of the proper response to God's covenant.
- In the New Testament, Jesus' **Sermon on the Mount** (Matthew 5–7) is often considered the focal point of his moral teaching. Jesus teaches that the new covenant is not only about keeping the law as set out in the Old Testament but the inner law of love, righteousness, peace and faith. Christians are to be 'perfect, as your heavenly Father is perfect' (Matthew 5:48). As Jesus' own life based on these principles led to his crucifixion and sacrifice, St Paul describes the Christian covenantal life as a 'living sacrifice' (Romans 12:1); a life which places devotion to God and love of neighbour before self-centred desires.

(b) Literalism and interpretation

No intelligent reading of the Bible can take every word literally and at face value. For example, Jesus says, 'If your right eye causes you to sin, tear it out and throw it away' (Matthew 5:29). Even very conservative biblicist Christians would not actually do this because they understand that the command to 'pluck out' in its context is really a metaphor for seeing things in the wrong way and is a call for repentance and change.

This example illustrates the dangers of a limited understanding of how to interpret the Bible. Despite the high status he gave to the Bible, the great Protestant theologian Karl Barth (1886–1968) also warned of the dangers of literalism because it falsely gives the Bible a divine status which may only be attributed to God. He called this 'bibliolatry': that is, the false worship of the Bible. Barth's view was that God's Word, his revelation in the world, has worked *through* the different writers of the Bible over a long period of time. The Bible's words, therefore, are a *witness* to the Word, but not the Word itself. While the Bible is a supreme source of Christian moral truth it is not the truth, itself and must be read critically as a source of inspiration.

In other words, even Christian theonomous ethics has to take into account the place of human reason to decide what kind of literature a text belongs to, how it fits into the larger biblical themes such as covenant and justice and whether it is symbolic, metaphorical or literal.

(c) Dealing with contradictions

One of the most problematic challenges for theonomous Christian biblical ethics is how to reconcile apparently contradictory commands or rules. For example, does the Bible command the use of violence for just means in cases of capital punishment or war?

- **Old Testament**. Many contrast the shift in attitude to the use of violence between Old and New Testaments. The Old Testament permits war and retributive justice, summarised as an 'eye for an eye, tooth for a tooth' (Exodus 21:24). Capital punishment is seen to be part of God's judgement on those who blaspheme by destroying human life made in the image of God (Genesis 9:6). The death penalty is for all those who undermine social and divine order: adultery (Deuteronomy 22:22), dishonour to parents (Exodus 21:15) and the stranger who enters the Temple (Numbers 1:51). In Deuteronomy 20:10–20, which sets out the rules of war, the Israelites are permitted to kill foreign women and children.
- **New Testament**. But in the New Testament, Jesus' Sermon on the Mount (Matthew 5–7) consciously appears to revise the old law. Retribution is replaced by reconciliation (Matthew 5:38–42) and love of one's enemies (Matthew 5:44). The shift is not just a problem for biblicists. Some argue that Jesus' teaching stresses the future ideal state of Kingdom of God, just as the prophets in the Old Testament had done (Micah 4:1–4) and that meanwhile in an imperfect world, the use of war and violence is a necessary evil. This is the view of many, such as Augustine, Luther and conservative interpreters today. Yet, even those who are not biblicists, such as Martin Luther King, argue

Key question

How should the following biblical command be interpreted?

If your right eye causes you to sin, tear it out and throw it away.

Matthew 5:29

Key question

Does the Bible consistently command Christians to be pacifists?

that the biblical vision of pacifism and non-violence is the one which Christians have a duty to follow because it is at the heart of Jesus' teaching on love.

Although there appears to be a problem for theonomous Christian ethics, this is only so if the Bible is treated in a very narrow sense as a rule book. For many, apparent contradictions are necessary if Christians are to fully engage with the problems of ethical decision-making and work out for themselves how the biblical principles are to be applied to life today. However, this suggests that Christian ethics necessarily involves more than merely following the Bible – that is the conclusion of those who hold a heteronomous view of Christian ethics.

3 Heteronomous Christian ethics and practices

The Bible is part of the Christian tradition in which humans from very different periods of history have been inspired by God to reflect and write down their thoughts. But it would be very odd to think that this process should end with the last book of the Bible. The process has continued to develop through the inspiration of leaders, theologians, Church councils and debates. The Bible is a significant source of authority of Christian ethics, but our understanding of the world is very different from the biblical writers, and the ethical issues raised by modern science and technology are so different from biblical times that modern Christians have to use reason to reflect and consider how to apply Christian principles in new situations.

This is why some Christians consider that ethics must be a combination of biblical teaching, Church teaching and human reason. This is a **heteronomous** view of Christian ethics because it considers there are several sources of Christian moral authority.

(a) Roman Catholic ethical heteronomy

In the Roman Catholic tradition, Christian ethics are not confined to the Bible but are accessible through the natural world, reason, conscience and Church authority. Collectively these elements are known as natural law. Natural law has biblical precedence in St Paul's *Letter to the Romans* where he states that even Gentiles (non-Jews) can behave morally when they act according to conscience and the 'law written on their hearts' (Romans 2:15).

(i) Natural law: revelation and reason

Natural law is based on the *theological* notion that as God is the creator of the world and gives it order and purpose then all things have a good or natural purpose. This is God's eternal law or plan for the universe. Beings which achieve their God-given purpose are said to be in a state of flourishing.

Although there are many presentations of natural law, it is Thomas Aquinas' version which still has considerable influence in the Church today. For Aquinas what distinguishes humans from all other creatures is their ability to know God's eternal law through the power of reason. This knowledge gives humans a richer and more creative existence than any

For further discussion on Aquinas and natural law, see Chapter 10.

other being. The human experience of God's eternal law is natural law and it is based on a simple self-evident principle that good is to be done and evil is to be avoided. Good is the state or goal of human flourishing.

- **Eternal Law** refers to the underlying principles of the universe which only God fully knows.
- **Divine Law** refers to God's laws revealed in the Bible (particularly in the Ten Commandments and the Sermon on the Mount).
- **Natural Law** contains the primary precepts or premises. The primary precepts are the goals humans share with all beings: that is the desire to live and survive. The second precepts are the goals humans share with animals: that is, to reproduce and bring up the young. The third set of precepts is purely human: that is, to develop reason, to know and worship God and to live in an ordered society.
- **Human Laws** or secondary precepts are detailed rules deduced by reason from primary precepts. These include the protection of innocent human life; the goodness of marriage and wrongness of adultery (in establishing an ordered society); respect for property. Although these are practised in all human societies they are not in themselves self-evident. Importantly, human laws indicate that secondary precepts are not themselves fixed but can change according to circumstance.

(ii) The Magisterium

But in addition to divine and natural law, morality is also informed by the traditions and practices of the Church. From time to time the collective wisdom of Church leaders and teachers is published in a **Papal encyclical** on contemporary moral issues. These encyclicals express the **Magisterium** or official teaching of the Church. As the Magisterium has authority it is expected that in all ordinary circumstances it will be followed. The *Catechism* states:

> The Church, the 'pillar and bulwark of the truth', 'has received this solemn command of Christ from the apostles to announce the saving truth.' 'To the Church belongs the right always and everywhere to announce moral principles, including those pertaining to the social order, and to make judgements on any human affairs to the extent that they are required by the fundamental rights of the human person or the salvation of souls.'

Catechism of the Catholic Church para. 2032

One particularly important recent encyclical on moral theology is *Veritatis Splendor*, issued by Pope St John Paul II in 1996. *Veritatis Splendor* reasserts the centrality of reason, conscience, natural law and the Magisterium in Catholic moral theology.

In *Veritatis Splendor*, the pope argues that moral law is knowable to all people — all people in all cultures have some sense of good and evil. Moral law may be known through human reason in the form of natural law and through conscience which awakens a person's awareness of divine law. Nevertheless, because they are weak and sinful, humans cannot rely on reason and conscience alone. The Church's role is to guide individuals in their moral decisions. *Veritatis Splendor* reasserts that some moral acts

Key terms

Papal encyclical Letter issued by the pope to his senior clergy on some significant topic or teaching. An encyclical is considered to have doctrinal authority.

Magisterium or more fully 'the Magisterium of the Pastors of the Church': The official and authentic teaching of the Church vested in the pope and his bishops.

Key term

Intrinsic Means in itself or essential. In ethics, a moral duty which is considered to be intrinsically good is so because it is an aspect of nature or because God has commanded it so.

Read pages 310–313 on Jesus' role as liberator.

are **intrinsically** wrong and that it is never right to do something which contradicts the moral order.

(iii) Liberation theology

Finally, since the 1960s, a radical strand of Catholic ethics has developed called liberation theology. Two elements mark it out as controversial. Firstly, it has placed the Bible at the centre of ethics and secondly, it has often questioned or been suspicious of 'top-down' traditional Church teaching. Liberation theologians are inspired by the biblical theme of liberation from Moses' escape from Egypt to Jesus' role as liberator. Liberative ethics is 'ethics from below': it begins with the economic, social and political conditions which have exploited and marginalised people.

Some liberation theologians have argued for the use of Marx as a means of analysing the economic conditions which have led to exploitation. Marxism is particularly good at questioning who has power and is using it to benefit themselves financially. However, as Marxism is an atheist system and considers religion as a major source of exploitation, even minor use of it by liberation theologians has been strongly criticised by the Church's Magisterium.

(b) Protestant ethical heteronomy

(i) Bible, reason, conscience and Church tradition

Although there are many Protestant natural law theologians, notably the Anglican Richard Hooker (1554–1600) and the Dutch Protestant Hugo Grotius (1583–1645), the Protestant tradition has tended to begin with the Bible as a primary source of authority. Modern Anglicans, for example, consider that as the Bible did not appear as a single document but evolved over time and developed out of the reflections and needs of communities, then ethics should continue to develop in the worshipping community and be guided by reason, conscience and Church tradition. In this respect it is similar to Roman Catholics but without investing the Church authorities with Magisterium.

(ii) Stanley Hauerwas

Stanley Hauerwas is an example of a highly influential but controversial contemporary theologian who has argued that Christian ethics can *only* be done within the Christian worshipping community. He argues that Christian ethics are part of a narrative which develops out of the Bible and continues on through Christian history and tradition. Jesus' Sermon on the Mount, for example, was part of a tradition rooted in Judaism, but its purpose was to adapt old values to a new kind of community. The tradition does not end in the New Testament but continues to adapt according to situation.

Key question

Is the Christian community the most importance source of Christian ethics?

Key person

Stanley Hauerwas (b. 1940): Until recently professor of ethics and theology at Duke University, USA. Brought up as a Methodist, his theology is broad ranging and is strongly influenced by the virtue ethical tradition and Karl Barth. He is a prolific writer but his most widely known and influential book, co-written with William Willimon, is *Resident Aliens: Life in the Christian Colony* (2014).

But this does not mean that Christian ethics are subjective and individual because the Sermon on the Mount was not aimed at individuals or Christian leaders, as some have claimed, but at all members of a Christian community. This must the case, Hauerwas argues, because the moral demands Jesus makes in the Sermon are all examples of the kind of values *Christians* must develop in their own communities in response to the God who: sides with the poor, comforts those who mourn, generously feeds the hungry, shows mercy to the merciful (Matthew 5:1–12). These are the God-given virtues which Christians are to adopt when dealing with issues in the community such as: legal disputes, sexual attitudes, marriage and divorce, oaths and promises, revenge and treatment of enemies. (Matthew 5:21–48)

Although many of these virtues might have meaning outside Christianity they are not the same as the ones Christians understand as expressed in the life and example of Christ and the life of the Church. The role of Christian communities (as 'resident aliens') is to question society's values, not through superficial political campaigns but by living and practising the Christian social virtues. So, what does this mean in practice? Here is Hauerwas' example of a pregnant teenager considering an abortion:

> So our response to an issue like abortion is something communal, social, and political, but utterly ecclesial – something like baptism. Whenever a person is baptized, be that person a child or an adult, the church adopts that person. The new Christian is engrafted into a family. Therefore, we cannot say to the pregnant fifteen-year-old, 'Abortion is a sin. It is your problem.' Rather, it is *our* problem. We ask ourselves what sort of church we would need to be to enable an ordinary person like her to be the sort of disciple Jesus calls her to be. More important, her presence in our community offers the church the wonderful opportunity to be the church, honestly to examine our own convictions and see whether or not we are living true to those convictions. She is seen by us not as some pressing social problem to be solved in such a way as to relieve our own responsibility for her and the necessity of our sacrificing on her behalf (for our story teaches us to seek such responsibility and sacrifice, not to avoid it through governmental aid). Rather, we are graciously given the eyes to see her as a gift of God sent to help ordinary people like us to discover the church as the Body of Christ.

Stanley Hauerwas and William H. Willimon:
Resident Aliens (2014), pp. 81–82

It is for these reasons that Hauerwas is particularly suspicious of Western society's over-emphasis on human rights language, individualism and autonomy.

(c) Problem of sources

Christian heteronomous ethics raise several problems about the range and authority of appropriate sources. Two questions stand out:

- What are the legitimate sources for Christian ethics? Are some sources, such as the use of Marxism or reason, alien to Christian thinking?

■ Do some sources have greater authority than others? If so, what principle determines the hierarchy of these sources?

4 Autonomous Christian ethics and practices

For some Christians, there are no separate *Christian* ethics but rather simply ethics as done by those who have Christian beliefs about the world. This view is called **autonomous Christian ethics**.

In this view, the Bible is not a specially revealed document but a Christian 'classic', much in the same way as Shakespeare's plays are considered to be great classics of English literature, and the source of study and inspiration.

(a) Love as the only Christian ethical principle that governs Christian practices

Although there are many different versions of the autonomy interpretation of Christian ethics, most consider that there is one guiding principle which shapes the mind-set of the Christian and that is Jesus' command to love. Love or *agape* in its distinctive Christian form is summarised in Jesus' own life sacrificed for others and his teaching on 'other-centredness' and not 'self-centredness'.

Jesus says:

> *This is my commandment, that you love one another as I have loved you. No one has greater love than this, to lay down one's life for one's friends.*
>
> John 15:12–13

St Paul says that:

> *Love is patient; love is kind; love is not envious or boastful or arrogant or rude. It does not insist on its own way; it is not irritable or resentful; it does not rejoice in wrongdoing, but rejoices in the truth. It bears all things, believes all things, hopes all things, endures all things.*
>
> 1 Corinthians 13:4–7

Love is therefore the *motivating* factor which human reason has to decide how best to apply to other moral principles and situations.

(b) Roman Catholic ethical autonomy

Hans Küng is an influential example of a liberal Catholic who advocates much greater autonomy in ethical decision-making. Küng also argues that there is nothing in the content of Christian ethics which could not be found elsewhere by *any person of good will*. Küng has long been a champion of the necessity for what he calls a 'global ethic' if the world is to tackle global environmental issues and save humanity from destroying itself. He defines a global ethic as the 'minimal consensus concerning binding values, irrevocable standards and fundamental moral attitudes'. What make the global ethic a Christian concern is the Christian motivation to love one's neighbour as someone created in the image of God and part of the global community.

So, for example, Küng argues that although euthanasia is contrary to official Catholic moral teaching, it is not contrary to the principles of Catholic reasoning and conscience to conclude that keeping someone alive at all costs cannot be morally right. The model for autonomous moral reasoning is that Jesus specifically challenged rule based ethics and encouraged his disciples to make their own judgements and take on personal responsibility for their actions. The question of euthanasia is not whether it is intrinsically good or bad but whether its use is respectful of a person's life. Küng writes:

> So what about active help in dying? Where some call this 'killing', others refer to 'compassion', 'mercy', 'grace', 'helping love'. What is the case? For a Christian who is a disciple of the merciful Jesus, at any rate there must not be just an ethic of prohibitions and sanctions. What then? With discipleship of Jesus goes an ethic of the responsible shaping of life – from beginning to end.

Hans Küng and Walter Jens: *A Dignified Dying* (1995), pp. 28–29

Ethical autonomy of the kind developed by liberal Catholicism is strongly rejected by 'faith-ethic' Roman Catholic theologians such as Joseph Ratzinger (b. 1927, subsequently Pope Benedict XVI) and Hans Urs von Balthasar (1905–88) as undermining the Magisterium of the Church.

(c) Protestant ethical autonomy

For radical Protestant Christians, such as Joseph Fletcher and James Gustafson (b. 1925) goodness is not revealed by God nor is it intrinsic and part of natural law, but simply a condition of being human. What Christianity does is to highlight it explicitly as the principle of love (*agape*). In all other respects ethics are essentially autonomous and teleological – they aim for the most loving situation.

Fletcher is probably the most well-known figure and best represents the autonomy school with his influential book *Situation Ethics* (1966). His situational approach considered that every situation is judged relatively to the principle of love (*agape*) and guided by four 'working principles':

- **Pragmatism** considers what should be done to make the situation most loving. This is at the heart of the Christian life. No moral issue is intrinsically right or wrong but must be judged against the command to love.
- **Relativism** ensures that there are no absolute duties which make people less important than rules. But for relativism to mean anything it must 'be relative to something' (*Situation Ethics* p. 44) and that is love.
- **Positivism** is the view that religious laws (such as the Ten Commandments) are not God-given or natural but human.
- **Personalism** considers that all humans should be treated as persons because as God is personal and humans are made in his image, then 'personality is the first order concern in ethical choices' (*Situation Ethics* p. 50). People should be treated as people and never as means to an end.

For more details on Joseph Fletcher (1905–91) and situation ethics, see pages 167–169.

(d) Sufficiency of love

As attractive as autonomy ethics are for Christians living in Western secular culture, many Christian critics think that there is more to Jesus' teaching than love. For example, Jesus' teaching in the Sermon on the Mount does not dispense with law but looked at ways to 'fulfil' it (Matthew 5:17) by considering how to develop it inwardly in relationship with God and in overcoming sin. In short, it is not sufficient to summarise the Christian ethics just by the word 'love' because Christian values have to be grounded in the Christian narrative which deals with such fundamental issues as: human nature, forgiveness, redemption, the afterlife and community. Belief in these ideas does make a difference to a person's values and moral actions. Christian ethics are distinctive and they are sometimes at odds with society's values.

The issue of what makes Christian values distinctive and how they should operate in a non-religious society has been of major concern to theologians over the past century. But this is not merely an academic exercise – as the life and martyrdom of Dietrich Bonhoeffer illustrate in the next chapter.

Summary diagram: Christian moral principles

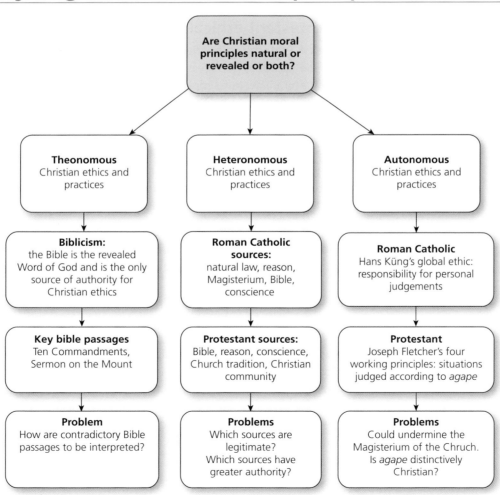

Revision advice

By the end of this chapter you should be able to explain why Christians form their moral principles in such a variety of different ways. You should be able to explain the three broad approaches (theonomous, heteronomous, autonomous) and the way in which each treat the Bible, reason, tradition and the Church/community in the formation of Christian ethics.

Can you give brief definitions of:
- biblicism
- the covenant
- the Magisterium
- *agape*
- pragmatism?

Can you explain:
- the main difference between theonomous and heteronomous Christian ethics
- why Catholic natural law ethics is a theological idea
- why some Christians argue that the Christian community is the most important source of Christian ethics
- the significance of the Sermon on the Mount for Christian ethics?

Can you give arguments for and against:
- love (*agape*) as the only basis for Christian ethical practices
- whether natural law is especially Christian
- whether Bible passages which appear to be contradictory undermine its moral authority
- whether Christian ethics are personal or communal?

Sample question and guidance

'The Church should decide what is morally good.' Discuss.

The essay might begin by considering why the Church is significant in the formation of Christian ethics. From a Roman Catholic perspective, the Church represents the continuation of Christ's authority on Earth to make judgements through the collective wisdom of the pope and his bishops. From some Protestant perspectives the Church or community is the means by which morality is worked out collectively as exemplified in Jesus' Sermon on the Mount.

The essay might argue in favour of this view that Christian ethics are not about how individuals behave because Christian ethics are about 'loving one's neighbour' as well as oneself. However, it might be thought that giving the Church the power to decide on what is morally good removes personal autonomy and responsibility and for that reason the authority of the Church or Christian community should always be subservient to the Christian principle of love or *agape*.

Further essay questions

Assess the view that the Bible is a comprehensive moral guide for Christians.

To what extent do Christians actually disagree about what Christian ethics are?

'Christian moral principles are not self-evident.' Discuss.

Going further

Geoffrey Chapman: *Catechism of the Catholic Church* (English version, 1994). Part Three, section one, 'Man's Vocation: Life in the Spirit'. Although this is long and reasonably detailed, reading it through will illustrate how Catholic ethics are integrated into the life of the Church.
Stanley Hauerwas and William H. Willimon: *Resident Aliens* (expanded version, Abingdon Press, 2014), Chapter 4. Written in a non-technical, but thought-provoking way. Hauerwas is critical of both liberal Christians and the Christian right-wing in the USA.
Neil Messer: *SCM Study Guide to Christian Ethics* (SCM Press, 2006). An excellent, clear and comprehensive survey with many useful examples and discussions of Christian and non-Christian ethics.
Other books we've talked about in this chapter are:
- Fletcher J. *Situation Ethics* (Westminster John Knox Press, 1966).
  Küng H. and Jens W. *A Dignified Dying* (SCM, 1995).

Chapter 21

Christian moral action: Dietrich Bonhoeffer

1 Introduction

> ### Chapter checklist
>
> This chapter considers how Dietrich Bonhoeffer developed Christian moral and theological teaching in the time of Hitler and Nazi rule in Germany. The chapter first outlines his life and then considers three important aspects of his teaching: duty to God and to the state; the role of the Church as community and his religious community at Finkenwalde; discipleship and moral action. Finally, it considers the extent to which Bonhoeffer's teaching can be applied to the world today.

2 Bonhoeffer's life

Not only was Dietrich Bonhoeffer one of the outstanding academic theologians of the twentieth century, but he lived a life which attempted to embody the principles of the Christian moral and spiritual life. He has had a profound effect on both Protestant and Catholic theology and he epitomises what it actually means to put Christian moral principles into practice.

(a) Early life

Dietrich Bonhoeffer

Dietrich Bonhoeffer was born on 4 February 1906 in Breslau, Germany (now part of Poland) to Karl and Paula Bonhoeffer. In 1912, the family moved to Berlin where his father became professor of psychiatry and neurology. He had an idyllic childhood and loved outdoor sports especially tennis. But it was cut short in 1918 by the war and the traumatic death of his elder brother Walter, who was killed in action. This event was probably responsible for persuading Dietrich to study theology. His family were not keen, for although his mother ensured that the family kept to the traditions of Lutheran Christianity, they were not a church-going family. But even at the age of 13, Dietrich had a vision of how the Church should be transformed and this was sufficient for him to persuade his parents to let him study theology.

(b) University

In 1923, he went to Tübingen University and then a year later to Berlin. In 1930, he completed his doctoral thesis *Act and Being* and became a lecturer at the University of Berlin. During this time he was working on his idea of a radical form of Christianity. He argued that rather than allow the state to make important decisions, the Church should be much more active in challenging it to achieve justice. For centuries, since the Reformation, German society had developed its own understanding of Luther's argument that Church and state should be seen as two sides of the same coin. To disobey the state therefore would be to disobey God. Bonhoeffer not only thought that this idea gave too much power and authority to the state and its rulers but undermined the true purpose of Christianity. It was also a false understanding of Luther's theology; a great deal of Bonhoeffer's subsequent academic theology was dedicated to a radical reinterpretation of Luther.

Tübingen University

(c) America

In September 1930, Bonhoeffer travelled to New York and studied with some of the USA's most influential theologians. He was impressed by their teaching on Christian social responsibility yet felt that it underestimated the goodness of human nature. But more significantly he was introduced to members of the black churches. His experience of their vibrant Christianity (very different from his own Lutheran Church tradition) helped him to realise how Christianity needed to build relationships between its different Churches without racial or geographical boundaries. So, even before Hitler came to power, Bonhoeffer's theology had set out a radical challenge to Church and state.

New York in the 1930s

(d) Resistance to Nazism

The opportunity came on 30 January 1933, when Hitler was made Chancellor and Führer of Germany. On 1 February 1933, Bonhoeffer began to deliver a radio broadcast called, 'The Younger Generation's Altered View of the Concept of the Führer'. As he began his talk it became apparent that he was deeply critical of the 'leadership principle' which Hitler represented and the effect that this was having on the Church. But the authorities very quickly realised what he was saying, for just as he was about to say that if people give power to an earthly leader (or *Führer* in German) they turn him into an idol and 'misleader', the microphone was turned off.

Bonhoeffer had placed himself against the state and from now on he worked actively for its demise in two ways:

- First, he became a member of the Confessing Church, a group of clergy who refused to accept that only Aryan Germans could become members of the Church and who accepted only one authority that of Christ.
- Second, he joined the Resistance (*Widerstand*). This was the most momentous decision of his life. At the time of his decision he was

Key quote

If we took the precept of non-resistance as an ethical blueprint for general application, we should indeed be indulging in idealistic dreams: we should be dreaming of a **utopia** with laws which the world would never obey.

Dietrich Bonhoeffer: *The Cost of Discipleship* (2001), p. 93

Key terms

Utopia Literally means 'no place' or 'good place'. It refers to an ideal state where everything is perfect and is therefore often used to describe a unrealistic view of the world.

Secular pacifism Secular means 'of this world': pacifism is the belief that the use of violence and especially war is morally wrong. Bonhoeffer invented the phrase 'secular pacifism' to mean a false non-religious belief that society can achieve a state of non-violence.

For more on Reinhold Niebuhr, see pages 260–261.

staying in New York having endured several years of investigation by the Gestapo because of his role training clergy in the Confessing Church.

In June 1939, Bonhoeffer returned to America for a second brief visit. The visit was prompted partly because he knew that he was about to be called up to serve in Hitler's army and if he refused this would damage the reputation of the Confessing Church as he would be condemned as a pacifist. So, a return to the USA as a theology lecturer in New York was a short-term solution to the dilemma.

But he quickly realised that if he was to be true to everything he had taught and believed in then the test was to return to Germany and attempt to overthrow the evil Nazi regime. Up to this point he had thought of himself as a pacifist, but now he realised that this kind of pacifism was not based on a Christian view of the world but a secular one which fails to prepare the Christian for the coming of the Kingdom of God. Bonhoeffer called **secular pacifism** a 'scandal' because it fails to acknowledge that true justice and peace are not aspects of this world; without this vision secular pacifism is not sufficient to tackle evil and perpetuates lies and injustice. His choice to join in the resistance against Nazism was not one which one could call intrinsically good, for in the world of harsh realities or 'terrible alternatives' as he called it, all choices inevitably have bad consequences.

Here is part of a letter he wrote in July 1939 to his American friend and theologian Reinhold Niebuhr explaining why he felt that his duty was to return to Germany and be part of 'the terrible alternative':

> *I have come to the conclusion that I have made a mistake in coming to America. I must live through this difficult period of our national history with the Christian people of Germany. I will have no right to participate in the reconstruction of Christian life in Germany after the war if I do not share the trials of this time with my people ... Christians in Germany will face the terrible alternative of either willing the defeat of their nation in order that Christian civilisation may survive, or willing the victory of their nation and therefore destroying our civilisation. I know which of these alternatives I must choose; but I cannot make that choice in security.*

Dietrich Bonhoeffer: *The Way to Freedom* (1966), p. 246

On his return to Germany in 1940, he joined the Counter Intelligence Section of the Armed Forces, the *Abwehr*, which included his brother-in-law, Hans Dohnanyi. Unofficially both men also worked for the Resistance and for the overthrow of Hitler's regime. Together they were able to find out information to aid the Resistance and support the victims of Nazism, in particular the Jews.

Tegel Military Prison

(e) Arrest and execution

On 5 April 1943, the Gestapo arrested and imprisoned Bonhoeffer and his brother-in-law Hans Dohnanyi on the grounds that they had helped Jewish immigrants escape to Switzerland. He then spent eighteen months in Berlin's Tegel Military Prison where he wrote many letters, a play and a novel. On 24 July 1944, the failed Resistance attempt to kill Hitler implicated Bonhoeffer and Dohnanyi and they were moved to several prisons including Buchenwald concentration camp. Then in 1945 Hitler ordered that all resisters should be annihilated. The Gestapo tracked Bonhoeffer down and on 9 April 1945 in Flossenbürg concentration camp, shortly before the American Army liberated the area, he was given a mock trial and hanged. A few weeks later on 23 April his brother, Klaus, and Hans Dohnanyi were also executed.

3 Duty to God and duty to the state

Key question

When, if ever, is it morally justifiable for Christians to disobey the state?

Bonhoeffer never completed his famous book, *Ethics*, which was put together after his death, but in it he set out to explain how Christian ethics are very different from human ethics. With Nazism clearly in mind Bonhoeffer warned against all forms of ethics which claim to be based on an ideology. Ideologies are dangerous because they are simply extensions of human ideas to justify the use of power over others.

Christian ethics, on the other hand, begin with the view that humans are finite and sinful; no human decision can be absolutely right or wrong. Influenced by the existential theology of Søren Kierkegaard (1813–1855), Bonhoeffer argued that in some extreme situations we can do nothing but act out of despair, but in faith and hope. As Luther famously said, 'Here I stand; I can do no other.' Bonhoeffer knew that the assassination of Hitler was the only option for the Church – even though killing is wrong and killing a powerful leader could undermine the stability of the country.

But the decision to overthrow Hitler and act against the state was not an easy one. Bonhoeffer was broadly in agreement with Luther and others that it was the duty of a Christian to be obedient to the government because a government's aim to is to impose law and order on the sinful human tendency towards disorder. But the problem has been that in practice either the state gains too much power and makes justice subordinate to its policies or the state thinks that it is the embodiment of justice and uses this to justify any of its actions. In either case the state inflates its own sense of self-importance because it fails to acknowledge its obedience to God's will. But Bonhoeffer's point is that the state can never represent God's will and so can never assume any ultimate form of power. The role of the Church is not to be part of the state but rather to keep it in check.

However, at what point may a Christian decide that the state is acting in such an unjust way, that it his duty to disobey it to avoid more suffering and disorder?

(a) Obedience to God's will

Key question

How can one know whether one is carrying out God's will?

In traditional Christian teaching, two passages from the New Testament reinforce the view that Christians have a duty to obey the state because, as Luther taught, there are two kingdoms ordained by God: the spiritual kingdom of Christ which is governed by the Church and the political kingdom of the world which is governed by the state.

- Jesus said, 'Give to the emperor the things that are the emperor's, and to God the things that are God's.' (Mark 12:17)
- St Paul wrote, 'Let every person be subject to the governing authorities; for there is not authority except from God, and those authorities that exist have been instituted by God.' (Romans 13:1).

But the question which Bonhoeffer posed was not whether it is *good* or *bad* to obey the state but whether it is the will of God.

> *Whoever wishes to take up the problem of a Christian ethic must be confronted at once with a demand that is quite without parallel. He must from the outset discard as irrelevant the two questions which allow him to concern himself with the problem of ethics, 'How can I be good?' and 'How can I do good?' and instead of these he must ask the utterly and totally different question 'What is the will of God?'.*

Dietrich Bonhoeffer: *Ethics* (1955/2005), p. 161

And how does one know what is the will of God? Bonhoeffer's reply is that it will 'only be clear in the moment of action' (*No Rusty Swords* p. 43). That action requires ridding oneself of personal ambition and submitting afresh every day to what God wills. It is an act of faith:

> *The nature of this will of God can only be clear in the moment of action; it is only important to be clear that every man's own will must be brought to be God's will, that his own will must be surrendered if God's will is to be realised, and therefore insofar as complete renunciation of personal claims is necessary in action before the face of God, the Christian's ethical action can be described as love.*

Dietrich Bonhoeffer: *No Rusty Swords* (1965), p. 43

See pages 330–332 on autonomy view of Christian ethics.

So while Bonhoeffer agrees that there is nothing novel about the Christian principle of love, he is very critical of the autonomy Christian school of thought which considers that this is the only moral principle by which to live the moral life. That is because if love were knowable as a self-evident principle, then morality would be purely human and this would reduce God to a human idea. Human based principles don't free

Jesus' inner law or purity:
See pages 307–309 on Jesus,
the moral teacher.

Key question

Was Bonhoeffer's involvement in
the plot to kill Hitler justified in
Christian terms?

Key quote

But when men are confined to
the limits of duty, they never
risk a daring deed on their own
responsibility, which is the only
way to score a bull's eye against
evil and defeat it. The man of
duty will in the end be forced to
give the devil his due.

Dietrich Bonhoeffer: *Letters and
Papers from Prison* (1959), p. 136

Key terms

Tyrannicide The deliberate killing
of tyrant for the common good.
A tyrant is a ruthless ruler who
governs without restraint.
Consequential ethics Any form
of ethical systems which judges
the rightness or wrongness
of an act by its outcomes.
Based on this principle many
consequentialists believe that
the 'end justifies the means'.

humans but make them slaves to the ideas; whereas responding every day
to the will of God is truly liberating. This, Bonhoeffer argues, is the
essence of Jesus' teaching on the inner law achieved through prayer,
conscience, and reflecting on the example of Christ and life in the
Christian community.

(b) Leadership

The notion of leadership is different from the idea of being a leader. Whereas
the former is grounded in the community, the idea of the leader is specific
to a particular person. Whereas leadership can be rationally justified,
Bonhoeffer argued that by contrast, 'it is virtually impossible to give a
rational basis for the nature of the Leader' (*No Rusty Swords* pp. 195–196).

Leadership focuses on matters beyond the leader (such as society or
God) not the leader himself; but now, Bonhoeffer argued, Germany has
invented a new category of Leader which is divorced from society. It is
one which replaces the imperfect father and teacher with the strong and
perfect father and teacher. This is extraordinary, Bonhoeffer said, because
the group has chosen to give up its freedoms and identity in obedience to
a tryant.

(c) Justification of civil disobedience

*For the sake and purpose of Christ there is and ought to be
worldly order in state, family and economy. For the sake of Christ
the worldly order is subject to the commandment of God. It is to
be noted that there is no question here of a 'Christian state' or a
'Christian economy', but only of the rightful state and the rightful
economy as a secular institution for the sake of Christ. There
exists, therefore, a Christian responsibility for secular institutions,
and within a Christian ethic there exists propositions which relate
to this responsibility.*

Dietrich Bonhoeffer: *Ethics* (1955/2005), p.289

The key to understanding Bonhoeffer's eventual justification for civil
disobedience is that Christians have a 'responsibility to the state'; this
does not entail turning it into a Christian state but to ensure that it acts
in accordance with God's will. If it is the case that the state is making
'reasonable people face unreasonable situations', then a Christian has a
duty to disobey it. In the case of Germany under Hitler, Bonhoeffer
considered that the Church was being seduced by the power of Nazism.
What the Church thought that Nazism was doing was imposing order
over a disordered nation whereas its marginalisation of minorities and
blatant disregard for life were gross distortions of the God-given order.

Bonhoeffer concluded that **tyrannicide** may be a Christian duty if
it means establishing social order. Reinterpreting Luther, he called this
'suffering disobedience'. But disobedience is not easy to justify as it is
not self-evident or morally clear ultimately whether any of our actions
are good or not. Bonhoeffer was deeply critical of those who justify
their actions simply because they feel they are doing their duty but in so
doing allow evil to prevail; he was equally dismissive of **consequential
ethics** where the ends justify the means as we are never in a position

to calculate all possible outcomes. So, there can be no ultimate rational justification for civil disobedience even if that appears to be the best option; all a Christian can do is to act in faith and in hope.

> Now, day by day, hour by hour, we are confronted with unparalleled situations in which we must make a decision, and in which we make again and again the surprising and terrifying discovery that the will of God does not reveal itself before our eyes as clearly as we hoped.

Dietrich Bonhoeffer: *No Rusty Swords* (1965), p. 46

In prison Bonhoeffer concluded, in one of his papers, that the attempt to kill Hitler and disobey the state is not justified in ordinary ethical terms but by 'bold action as the free response of faith'. But killing is killing and there is no amount of human reason that can make it morally justifiable, the only possible consolation is that God promises to forgive the 'man who becomes a sinner in the process' (*Letters and Papers from Prison* p. 138).

4 The role of the Church as community

Read pages 179–180 on Kant's idea of duty.

Key terms

Liberal societies Societies which develop their laws based on the principle that humans flourish when given maximum freedoms and minimum control by governments.

World come of age Used by Bonhoeffer to describe how the Western culture has grown up and in embracing a rational view of the world has discarded a superstitious view of religion.

The Western void Bonhoeffer's description of the state of the Western secular world without Christianity filled with all kinds of dangerous beliefs and ideas.

Religionless Christianity The phrase Bonhoeffer used to describe Christianity without the baggage of the past and contamination by the ideological beliefs of the present.

No Christian can act morally in isolation. Bonhoeffer agreed with Kant that when a person acts out of duty he knows that he does so because he is acting in solidarity with all humankind. For the Christian the role of the Church is to provide a moral and spiritual community which equips each person with the tools and attitudes to live morally in the world. For this to happen, Bonhoeffer argued that a Christian community or Church cannot be the middle-class institution it has become over the centuries but should be stripped of false pretence at being religious. The Church must grow up and embrace a religionless world and fully engage with it.

(a) Religionless Christianity

Although Bonhoeffer was deeply critical of certain aspects of **liberal societies**, he didn't for one moment think that democracy was wrong and that personal autonomy was essential for choosing the life best suited to one's own happiness. He described modern Western culture as a **world come of age**, which having grown up and matured was embracing a rational view of the world and rightly discarding its childish superstitious practice of religion. But Bonhoeffer also felt that this had come at a cost. Liberalism may have thrown out many Christian values as being irrational but in doing so it had created what he called '**the Western void**': that is, a moral and spiritual vacuum which was open to all kinds of dangerous beliefs seeking to fill the gap which Christianity used to occupy. Some of these beliefs might appear fairly innocent such as human progress and competition but there was nothing to stop these becoming a new 'religion'. National Socialism under the Nazis was an example of one of these new religions filling the gap. This is why, paradoxically, Bonhoeffer argued for a **religionless Christianity** – Christianity without the baggage of the past and contamination by the ideological beliefs of the present.

Key term

No rusty swords Bonhoeffer's metaphor to describe the outworn ethical attitudes which the Church has used and which now have no use today.

Key question

By the loss of unity which it possessed through the form of Jesus Christ, the western world is brought to the brink of the void.

Dietrich Bonhoeffer: *Ethics* (1955/2005), p. 85

Karl Barth, see page 282.

Key term

Barmen Declaration (1934) Set out the basic belief of the Confessing Church in opposition to the German Christian movement (*Deutsche Christen*) which was strongly influenced by Nazism. It was largely composed by Karl Barth.

Key quote

The Church is her true self when she exists for humanity.

Dietrich Bonhoeffer: *Letters and Papers from Prison* (1959), p. 166

Another phrase that Bonhoeffer used was that there should be '**no rusty swords**'.

Rusty swords are the outworn ethical attitudes which the Church has used effectively in the past but which have no use today. That is why, Bonhoeffer provocatively argued, 'Christianity and ethics do indeed have nothing to do with another' (*No Rusty Swords* p. 41). The challenge is for Christians to rethink ethics *theologically* and embrace the contemporary world.

(b) The Confessing Church

The birth of the Confessing Church (*Bekennende Kirche*) was a reaction against the Nazified faction of the Protestant clergy in the German Christian movement (*Deutsche Christen*) who had blended Christianity and National Socialism. The German Christian movement achieved its goals when Hitler created the German Evangelical Church (*Deutsche Evangelische Kirche*) which in 1934 issued the 'Aryan Paragraph' removing all clergy from the Church who were not of Aryan descent. Bonhoeffer and Martin Niemoeller organised a group of clergy who disagreed with this requirement; the group became the foundation of what became known as the Confessing Church. In 1934, the Confessing Church held a meeting at Barmen and from this meeting Karl Barth produced the foundations of the **Barmen Declaration**.

The Declaration states categorically that a Christian's primary duty is to Christ; the Church should reject any teaching which is not revealed in Jesus Christ. It was theologically a firm denial of Nazi National Socialism but as some have commented, only presented 'limited disobedience' against the state. Politically it could have gone further especially with regard to the Jews and other minorities – Bonhoeffer thought so, and his subsequent life was spent developing a wider more inclusive role of the Confessing Church. To this end, he developed what he called his 'ecumenical theology' in direct dispute with the German Christian movement. In the spirit of religionless Christianity the Confessing Church was not to become a national Church because Christian communities must have no national, political and racial boundaries.

In his final days in prison he became increasingly disillusioned with the Confessing Church. He felt it had become too defensive, too concerned with itself and less engaged with the world. 'The Church is her true self when she exists for humanity', he wrote from prison. For just as Christ was the man for others so must the Confessing Church be in its involvement with the world, but it had failed to topple Hitler, so it was not a Church 'come of age'.

(c) The religious community at Finkenwalde

Immediately after his return from the USA in 1935, Bonhoeffer was responsible for setting up a community at Finkenwalde for the training of ministers or pastors for the Confessing Church. The creation of the community was partly in response to the lack of pastors. Since the Nazis took control of the German Church and appointed a 'Reich Bishop', the number of suitable clergy had greatly declined. In August 1937, the Nazi regime announced the Himmler Decree which declared the training of

Confessing Church ministers illegal. Finkenwalde was closed down by the Third Reich in September 1937.

But the real purpose of the community at Finkenwalde was to develop practical Christian living as a community of disciples and to exercise the most practical of all Christian virtues, the virtue of discipline. The central practices at Finkenwalde included:

- **Discipline**. Discipline of oneself in relationship with others is the foundation of the Church. Discipline leads to action. Life at Finkenwalde was very basic and almost monastic. Bonhoeffer insisted that the body just as much as the spirit had to be disciplined and exercised. Often the whole community would go on long bicycle rides.
- **Meditation**. Discipline is developed through meditation as the foundation for prayer.
- **Bible**. Frequent reading and discussion of the Bible is at the heart of Christian daily life. Debate and discussion along with evening lectures encourage intelligent understanding and development of Christian teaching.
- **Brotherhood**. The community is bound together by love of and for Christ, sustained by the Holy Spirit. In practical terms Bonhoeffer insisted that the director should change frequently so that the community should not become stuck in its ways. To extend the brotherhood beyond Finkenwalde, Bonhoeffer ensured that former students were to be informed by regular reports/letters of life in the community.
- **Community for others**. Bonhoeffer insisted that the Church is a community of the forgiven not of the righteous because no one is perfect. Furthermore, as Christ died for all human beings (not just Christians), the Church as community must be outward looking and engage with the world.

5 The cost of discipleship

Bonhoeffer's distinctive ethical contribution was to focus attention on obeying the will of God rather than being side-tracked into issues of good and evil. How do we discern the will of God? There is no easy answer to this and to form a series of ethical commands on the basis of this would be to miss the point. Christianity, as Bonhoeffer frequently stated, is not an otherworldly institution but is grounded in the everyday world. In becoming human God reaffirms what it means to live in the world. Thus, the questions Christians should be asking are not abstract questions such as the nature of Christ's divinity but, 'who is Christ for us today?' Christology, ethics and discipleship are inseparable for Bonhoeffer.

(a) Ethics as action

Bonhoeffer's most important intellectual encounter in the Finkenwalde years (1935–37) was with the Swiss Calvinist theologian Karl Barth. Barth taught Bonhoeffer that if Christianity is to mean anything it cannot simply be an abstract system of human thought. Barth's notion of God is that it is not we who know God but God who chooses to reveal himself to us. God's revelation is not general but always a special act – as in the supreme example of the person and life of Jesus Christ.

Key question

Look up Luke 10:38–42. How do you think Bonhoeffer would have interpreted it?

Bonhoeffer agreed with Barth but argued that Barth had not gone far enough. The danger is that we can conclude that if only God can truly act in the world then we can be no more than passive recipients of his revelation. Bonhoeffer likened this to the Pharisees who were very good at hearing God's commands but did nothing to act on his behalf. In his book *Ethics* he argues that hearing the law must entail being a doer of the law; in the story of Mary and Martha (Luke 10:38–42), Jesus' criticism of Martha is that she acts but she doesn't hear or listen to Jesus' teaching. In summary:

- Ethics is action and action is liberating.
- Action is prompted by conscience, conscience is the experience of disunity in oneself, with God and with others. Conscience is therefore a moment of self-knowledge – just as Bonhoeffer experienced in America when he decided to engage in the 'terrible alternative'.
- Ethical decisions are always ones of conflict and action; the conflict is between knowing good and evil and the action is distinguishing between them.
- Love overcomes disunity. Love (*agape*) is not a human attitude but is revealed in God's love for humanity as expressed in Jesus Christ. 'Only in Jesus Christ do we know what love is, namely, in His deed for us.' (*Ethics* p. 34).

(b) Costly grace

But how can Christianity be religionless? Taking his lead from Luther, Calvin and the Reformers, Bonhoeffer argued that authentic Christianity has to be based on the three fundamentals: 'only Christ, only scripture and only faith' – anything else is human invention. Therefore, it follows that religion as an institution is simply a human invention, just as politics and political parties are human inventions. So, in order for Christianity not to be used for political and personal ends, Bonhoeffer argued that it was essential for it to be separate and free from the state. This can come at a cost. The cost as Bonhoeffer knew was that in taking on the world, especially an unjust society, the Christian disciple is placed in a dangerous and precarious situation. God's grace cannot be bought as if it is a commodity merely by going through the Christian rituals; this is 'cheap grace' as he calls it. 'Costly grace', on the other hand, is 'costly because it costs man his life, and it is grace because it gives man the only true life … Above all, it is *costly* because it cost God the life of his Son' (*The Cost of Discipleship* p. 5).

(c) Sacrifice and suffering

'It is good for me that I was afflicted, that I might learn thy statutes' (Psalm 119:71). One of my favourite verses from my favourite psalm.

Dietrich Bonhoeffer: *The Way to Freedom* (1966), p. 247

The experience of suffering is Christianity's engagement with the world as reflected in the cross. In the world come of age, God is not the supreme leader but, as he is revealed in Christ, weak and powerless

Key quote

In shame man is reminded of his disunion with God and with other men; conscience is the sign of man's disunion with himself.

Dietrich Bonhoeffer: *Ethics* (1955/2005), p. 9

Key quote

Cheap grace is the preaching of forgiveness without requiring repentance, baptism without Church discipline, Communion without confession.

Dietrich Bonhoeffer: *The Cost of Discipleship* (2001), p. 4

Key question

Do Bonhoeffer's ethics focus too much on suffering?

in his struggle against the world. He is the suffering God who acts in solidarity with his creatures. To describe this Bonhoeffer adopted Barth's use of the New Testament Greek word '*krisis*' – meaning both 'dispute' and 'judgement'. The great Christian paradox is that it is because of the crisis of the world (its sinfulness, disputes, waywardness and lack of belief) that God reveals his 'crisis', his judgement on sin and gift of grace and redemption in Jesus Christ. This is sometimes called a **theology of crisis**.

Costly grace underpins Bonhoeffer's realisation that he would in all probability have to pay the ultimate sacrifice of death, but he did not seek to suffer and he never saw himself as a martyr. During his time in prison, as his *Letters from Prison* demonstrate, he did not dwell on suffering but rather affirmed the Christian life in his continuing stand against wickedness. As Klemens von Klemperer concludes:

> He was distinctly a Christian martyr despite the lingering disclaimers of the German Churches. Bonhoeffer's resistance was essentially an expression of his theology.

Klemens von Klemperer: *The Terrible Alternative* Ed. Andrew Chandler (1988), pp. 96–97

(d) Solidarity

One of Bonhoeffer's favourite descriptions of Jesus was that he was 'the man for others'. As the Church represents Jesus as the 'body of Christ', it follows that it must be the 'Church for others'. The Church as Bonhoeffer viewed it had singularly failed in this role; it had not acted in solidarity with humanity especially those whom Jesus made it his mission to value – the weak, the vulnerable and oppressed. In particular, he was dismayed by the German Church's attitude to the Jews and although he considered Christianity to be the true path to salvation, he did not consider that it was the Church's role to make judgements about people's beliefs for only God can make those kinds of judgements.

(i) Solidarity against injustice

Bonhoeffer was explicit about the Church's obligations to fight political injustice. In his essay, 'The Church and the Jewish Question', he wrote that the Church must fight the evil of Jewish discrimination in three ways:

- First, the Church must question whether the state's actions are legitimate; it can call on the state to be fully responsible for its decisions.
- Second, the Church must help all victims of injustice of whatever faith or belief.
- Third, it must be fully engaged in resistance to reverse the machinery of injustice. The Church must take direct action, 'not just to bandage the victims under the wheel, but to put a spoke in the wheel itself.'

But the Church has failed and must confess that:

> … she has witnessed the lawless application of brutal force, the physical and spiritual suffering of countless innocent people, oppression, hatred and murder, and she has not raised her voice on behalf of the victims and has not found ways to hasten to their aid.

Dietrich Bonhoeffer: *Ethics* (1955/2005), p. 93

Key term

Theology of crisis Teaches that the crisis of human sinfulness can only be overcome by God's judgement (*krisis* in Greek) and faith in his grace and redemption through Jesus Christ.

Key quote

I am afraid that Christians who dare to stand with only one leg on earth stand with only one leg in heaven.
Dietrich Bonhoeffer letter to Maria von Wedemeyer, as quoted in *The Terrible Alternative* Ed. Andrew Chandler, 1988, p. 87

'The Church and the Jewish Question' can be found in *No Rusty Swords* (1965), pp. 221–237.

Key quote

The third possibility is not just to bandage the victims under the wheel, but to put a spoke in the wheel itself.
Dietrich Bonhoeffer: *No Rusty Swords* (1965), p. 225.

(ii) Solidarity with the Jews

Bonhoeffer was as good as his word. In April 1933, following the boycott of Jewish businesses, he wrote 'The Church and the Jewish Question' which explicitly criticised the Nazi regime and called for solidarity to all those persecuted by Nazism. During the same week he and his brother Klaus met the American theologian Paul Lehmann and drafted a message to the US Jewish leader Rabbi Stephen Wise. Then after *Kristallnacht* or the 'Night of Broken Glass' (9–10 November 1938), when German synagogues and Jewish businesses were burned and destroyed, he publically rejected the common view that this was God's just punishment of the Jews for their rejection of Jesus Christ and called it an act of a godless and violent regime. Later he and his brother-in-law collected large sums of money to aid Jewish immigrants – it was this action which ultimately ended in his arrest and execution.

6 Bonhoeffer's relevance today

Key term

Post-Christian society A society which still employs Christians moral values as part of its culture but does not practise or believe in Christianity as a belief system.

Key question

Does Bonhoeffer's theology have relevance today?

Read pages 328–329 on Stanley Hauerwas.

The central question of this chapter has been to consider how theological ethics can engage with issues of the world. Bonhoeffer's life and thought illustrate how this might be possible in the circumstances of his own time. But are his ideas applicable today in **post-Christian**, multi-cultural and globalised Western societies?

(a) Can his ethics address global politics?

Many critics today argue that as Bonhoeffer's ethics were developed at a particular time under Nazism, they only really work in similar extreme circumstances. For example, he compromises Christian pacifism only because in his extraordinary situation absolute pacifism is untenable. Furthermore, his ethics focus on a single threat to humanity whereas in today's globalised world, the threat from terrorism, power struggles between USA and China, Middle Eastern conflict and threats to Western society are far more complex and multi-faceted than Bonhoeffer's more localised notion of politics. Finally, some argue that theology is not equipped to deal with life in stable, liberal democratic societies.

On the other hand, his ethics of engagement with the world gives a place for Christianity as a moral/spiritual conscience in the state's involvement in world politics. Stanley Hauerwas, for example, argues that Bonhoeffer's concern for *truth* in politics is a much needed challenge to the pragmatism of Western democracy. Here is a place for the Christian church to play a special role in global politics as it reminds political leaders not to confuse tolerance with lack of engagement with truth. As Hauerwas has commented, a society which only practises tolerance for pragmatic reasons without any idea of truth quickly falls into indifference and 'indifference leads to cynicism'. In other words, as Bonhoeffer frequently noted in his own situation, liberal societies can undermine the truth creating a 'void' which is quickly filled by totalitarian powers.

(b) Are his ethics compatible with plural moral societies?

It is generally thought that there is no one moral code in contemporary post-Christian societies. Moral pluralism suggests that as each person or group pursues its own ethical code the notions of right and wrong are not absolute but relative to that person or group depending on its situation. Plural societies do though assume pragmatically that each person should be tolerant of other people's moral values up to the point where they are seen to cause harm to others. In many ways, Bonhoeffer appears to support this view — that is certainly the way he was interpreted by Joseph Fletcher.

Fletcher refers to the example given by Bonhoeffer of Mother Maria who volunteered to sacrifice her life to save a Jewish girl in a concentration camp. Fletcher uses the incident as the reason why killing innocent people cannot be an absolute wrong because the rightness or wrongness of killing can only be judged relative to the principle of Christian love. Fletcher greatly approves Bonhoeffer's argument that telling the truth depends on the situation and place, concluding that Bonhoeffer 'is as radical a version of the situational method as any Christian relativist could call for' (*Situation Ethics* p. 149).

On the other hand, some consider that Fletcher's interpretation of Bonhoeffer's ethics is completely wrong. Bonhoeffer is not a **moral relativist** because in his view Christian ethics are formed outside secular society and developed within the discipline and practice of the Christian community. Truth is not relative, as Fletcher considered. On the contrary, truth is absolute but has to be applied in each situation directed by faith and conscience. Telling a lie is still a lie even if it *has* to be told — as, for example, when telling the truth would cause the break-down of a relationship. In this respect, Bonhoeffer is deeply critical of liberal plural moral societies because in relativising moral values they have undermined the very idea of truth.

Although this presentation of Bonhoeffer's ethics would appear to make his views incompatible with contemporary moral pluralism, many argue that in fact his ethics are even more necessary as a constant reminder of whether society, in trying to be non-judgemental of different moral viewpoints, has lost sight of what a truly just community really is.

(c) Are his theological ethics compatible with multi-faith societies?

Despite Bonhoeffer's work to defend and protect Jews from the Nazi regime, many argue that his belief that Jews should eventually convert to Christianity makes his theology incompatible with contemporary multi-faith Western societies. Even though Bonhoeffer was not aggressive in this aim and considered that it was the state's duty to give equal rights and protection to all its citizens, his critics consider that his theology would cause resentment and even mistrust.

On the other hand, in his essay from prison, 'After Ten Years' (that is, ten years after Hitler's rise to power), addressed to his co-conspirators, he wrote about the lessons learnt from experiencing life 'from below' — the suffering and marginalisation of the outcast and the powerless. He had come to understand the experience of sympathy in a new way. Sympathy

---

Read pages 167–170, 331 on Joseph Fletcher.

Read Fletcher *Situation Ethics* (1966), pp. 74–75.

Key term

Moral relativism The belief that there are no moral absolutes or that moral values are relative to very general human values such as happiness or love.

is not merely tolerance, but the experience of what it means to belong to a faith community which is either on the receiving end of prejudice and discrimination or, as the dominant religion, is the source of power and control.

Therefore, all religions but especially Christianity in the Western societies, might find in Bonhoeffer's idea of sympathy as 'costly grace' a guide to developing genuine multi-faith societies as there will be sacrifices and costs. For Christians in particular, Bonhoeffer's teaching on community, discipleship and truth might provide practical ways in which the Church should question its power without losing its integrity as a witness to Christ.

Summary diagram: Dietrich Bonhoeffer

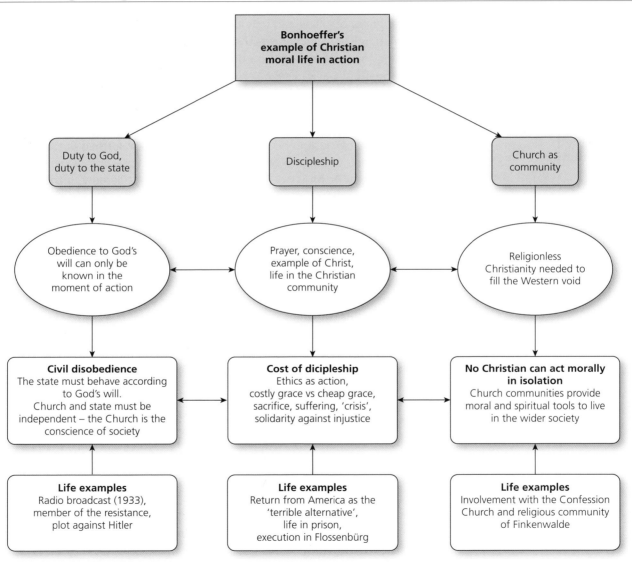

Revision advice

By the end of this chapter you should be able to explain how Bonhoeffer's life, his experience of Hitler and the Nazis shaped his views of Christian ethics and in particular: whether a Christian always has a duty to obey the state or ruler; the role of conscience and obedience to God's will; the significance of the Christian community and the role of the Church in the development of Christian values.

Can you give brief definitions of:
- the world come of age
- the Western void
- no rusty swords
- religionless Christianity
- Jesus as a 'man for others'?

Can you explain:
- what he meant by the 'terrible alternative'
- why he changed his mind about pacifism
- his teaching about the relationship of the state and Church
- the difference between cheap grace and costly grace?

Can you give arguments for and against:
- whether Bonhoeffer is right that obedience to the will of God is liberating
- the claim that Christian ethical decisions are always ones of conflict and action
- civil disobedience?

Sample question and guidance

'Bonhoeffer's most important teaching is on leadership.' Discuss.

The essay might begin by considering Bonhoeffer's teaching based on Jesus' instruction to obey the ruler and St Paul's explanation that obedience to the ruler is because he is appointed by God. The essay might then consider the role of the leader or ruler in establishing order and justice. Attention then might focus on Bonhoeffer's distinction between the idea of the leader and leadership itself and especially his insistence that leadership must represent the will of society (or God). It might be concluded that this is his most important teaching as it is the basis for his teaching on tyrannicide, the problem of the Western void and ethics as obedience to God's will.

On the other hand, the essay might argue that Bonhoeffer's critique of a world or society which has 'come of age', and its implications for Christianity, liberal values and community, are more important than his teaching on leadership.

Further essay questions

Assess the view that Bonhoeffer's teaching on ethics still has relevance today.

'Christian ethics means being obedient to God's will.' Discuss.

To what extent was Bonhoeffer's religious community at Finkenwalde successful?

Going further

Books by Dietrich Bonhoeffer:

Letters and Papers from Prison (Fontana Books, 1959). This is often the book students of Bonhoeffer read first.

The Cost of Discipleship (SCM Press, 2001). This is a very accessible way of finding out about Bonhoeffer's theological ethics and his idea of 'costly grace'.

Books about Dietrich Bonhoeffer:

Joel Lawrence: *Bonhoeffer: A Guide for the Perplexed* (T and T Clark/ Continuum, 2010). A very clear and accessible introduction to Bonhoeffer's central theological ideas.

Eberhard Bethge: *Dietrich Bonhoeffer: Biography – Theologian, Christian Man for His Times* (revised edition, Augsburg Fortress, 1999). The definitive biography written by his friend, worth dipping into.

Other books we've talked about in this chapter are:

- Bonhoeffer D. *Ethics* (SCM Press, 1955/2005).
- Bonhoeffer D. *No Rusty Swords* (Collins, 1965).
- Bonhoeffer D. *The Way to Freedom* (Collins, 1966).
- Fletcher J. *Situation Ethics* (Westminster John Knox Press, 1966).
- von Klemperer K. *The Terrible Alternative* Ed. Andrew Chandler (Mowbray, 1988).

Index

Page numbers in **bold** indicate definitions.

a posteriori **7**, 8, 9
   arguments for existence of God 58, 66, 90
a priori **7**–8, 25, 178
   arguments for existence of God 58, 81, 90
Abrahamic religions **114**, 115
act utilitarianism **171**, 197
acts and omissions **216**
agape 140, **169**, 330
agnosticism 105, **106**
akrasia **255**
altruism **169**, 199
Ambrose 152, 252, 276
Ancient Greece 16–18
animal suffering 199–200
Anscombe, G.E.M. 50, 51
Anselm of Canterbury, Saint 82
   Descartes' development of argument 88–89
   Gaunilo's criticism and response from 86–87
   ontological argument 82–86
   Proslogion Chapter 2 82–84
   Proslogion Chapter 3 84–86, 92
anthropic principle **65**
anthropomorphism **77**
antinomianism **167**
apokatastasis 281
Apollinarius 315–16
apologetics **65**
applied ethics **139**
   see also business ethics; euthanasia
Aquinas, Saint Thomas 34, 59
   appeal to imagination 70
   on conscience 170
   cosmological argument 66–70
   Fifth Way 58, 59–60
   First cause **67**, 68–69
   Five Ways 59–60, 67, 75–76, 289–90
   four tiers of law 148–51, 326
   legacy of Aristotle 45–46
   lux and *lex* **153**–54
   natural law 150, 151–57, 161, 326–27

necessity and contingency 67–**68**, 69–70
   objections to ontological arguments 87–88
   predestination 281
   primary and secondary precepts 154–55
   Prime Mover 34–35, 37, 67, 68
   prudence and natural law 155–56
   soul 45–46
   telos 152–53
   Temple's consistency with 166
aretaic ethics (virtue ethics) 139, **140**, 152
argument from design **290**
Aristotle 5, 38, 58
   Aquinas and legacy of 45–46
   and causation 29–39
   communal aspects of ethics 228–29
   empiricism vs. Plato's rationalism 30–31
   four causes 31–33
   on friendship 203
   objection to theory of the Forms 24
   objections to theories of 35–37
   philosophical views 30–31
   Prime Mover 33–35, 36–37, 68
   Prime Mover vs.Plato's Form of the Good 35
   soul 44–46
assisted suicide 207
atheism 105, **106**
atheological objector **298**–99
Augustine of Hippo, Saint
   on human nature 249–58, 263
   human will after the Fall 254–58
   human will before the Fall 253–54
   interpretation today 258–62
   life of 250–53
   theodicy 116–19
   theodicy, objections to 119–20
authority 304–5
   Jesus' 305, 313
autonomous Christian ethics **330**–32
autonomy **177**
Barmen Declaration **342**
Barth, Karl 295
   debate with Bonhoeffer 343–44
   debate with Brunner 295–97
   on universalism 282
basic knowledge 298
beatific vision **278**–79
beauty and moral goodness 289
behaviourism **50**, 51
   objections to 51–52

belief, knowledge and 10–11
Bentham, Jeremy 194
   act utilitarianism 197
   on animal suffering 200
   classical utilitarianism 192–93
   greatest good of the greatest number 195
   hedonic calculus 194
   hedonism, alternatives to 194–95
   principle of utility 193
   rejection of natural rights 196
Bible
   authority for Christian ethical practices 323–24
   contradictions 325–26
   death and afterlife 266–72
   and life of Church 294–95
   literalism and interpretation 325
   Parable of Sheep and Goats **272**–73
   Parable of the Lost Son **308**
   Protestant ethical heteronomy 328–29
   Richman and Lazarus 269
   use of violence 325–26
Biblicism **324**
Bland, Tony 218
blasphemy **211**–12
body 40
   and soul in Plato 43
   see also mind–body question
Boethius 85
Boff, Leonardo 311
Bonhoeffer, Dietrich 335–50
   Confessing Church 342
   cost of discipleship 343–46
   costly grace 344
   duty to God and duty to state 338–39
   ethics as action 343–44
   Finkenwalde community 342–43
   justification of civil disobedience 340–41
   leadership 340–41
   life of 335–38
   obedience to God's will 339–40
   relevance today 346–48
   religionless Christianity **341**–42
   role of Church as community 341–43
   sacrifice and suffering 344–45
   solidarity 345–46
Book of Revelation **267**, 268, 269, 270
Breivik, Anders 248, 249
Brümmer, Vincent 96
Brunner, Emil 295
   debate with Barth 295–97

Buddha 309
business ethics 224–45
    applying ethical theories to
        232–33, 235, 241–42
    corporate social responsibility
        228–31
    development in Britain 225–28
    globalisation 238–42
    good for business 236–38
    principles for good 229–31
    whistle-blowing **233**–36
Calvin 280–81
Calvin, John 288
    Barth disagrees with Brunner on
        296–97
    on conscience 289
    on faith 293
    the Fall and human finiteness 292
    grace 293
    innate human sense of God 288
    knowledge of God in Jesus
        Christ 294
    order of creation 290–91
    tensions in theology of 295, 296
Calvinism 280–81
caritas **253**
categorical imperative **181**–85
category error **48**–49
causation
    Aristotle and 29–39
    Hume's criticism of 68
cave, simile of 22–23, 300
chance 74–75
Christ-event **319**
Christian moral action *see* Bonhoeffer,
        Dietrich
Christian moral principles 323–34
    autonomous ethics and practices
        330–32
    heteronomous ethics and practices
        326–30
    theonomous ethics and practices
        323–26
Christianity
    Augustine's conversion to 252
    and Plato 44
    religionless **341**–42
Christology **314**
Cicero, Marcus Tullius 146–47,
        250, 289
civil disobedience, justification for
        340–41
common good 156–57, **229**–30
community
    person and 135
    role of Church as 341–43
concupiscence **256**

Confessing Church 342
conscience
    Aquinas on 170
    Brunner on 296
    Calvin on 289
    Fletcher on 170–71, 172–73
    Hell and 273
consciousness 40, 41, 46, 51, 52
    as basis for quality of life 214–15
consequential ethics **340**–41
consequentialism 216–18
continence **255**
contingency, necessity and 67–**68**,
        69–70
contradictions **84**
    and theonomous biblical ethics
        325–26
conversion **97**
    experiences 105–6
Copleston, F.C. 72–73
corporate experience **101**–2
corporate social responsibility
        228–31
cosmological arguments 58, **67**, 75
    Aquinas' 66–70
    developments in modern 71
Cottingham, John 52, 72, 76, 109
    ontological argument 90–91
Council of Chalcedon **313**–14
covenant **324**
cupiditas **253**
Dante Alighieri 274
    vision of heaven 278
    vision of hell 274–75
    vision of purgatory 276–77
Darwin, Charles 64
Dawkins, Richard 51, 77, 259, 293
dead donor rule **218**
death and afterlife 266–85
    Barth on 282
    Christian eschatological teaching
        273–78
    election 279–82
    Hick on 282
    New Testament foundations
        266–72
    Parable of Sheep and Goats
        272–73
deductive arguments 6
defining predicate **89**
deism 114, **115**
Dennett, Daniel C. 51–52
deontic ethics **139**, 140
deontological ethics **140**, 180
deontological theories **148**
    and euthanasia 216–18
    and teleological theories 141

Descartes, René 48
    Cottingham's critique 52
    development of Anselm's argument
        88–89
    Kant's critique 89
    Ryle's critique 48–49
    and substance dualism 47, 48
design argument **60**, 290–91
    and Aquinas' Fifth Way 59–60
    criticisms 62–65
    and evolution 64–65
    Hume's criticism 62–63
    Mill's criticism 63–64
    modern versions 65–66
    of Paley 60–62, 291
divided will 255–56
divine command theory **139**,
        140, 151
divine decree **280**
divine law **149**–50, 327
divine likeness 121–22
docetic **316**
dockers strike 225–26
double predestination **280**
dualism **46**
    and monism 46
    substance 46–48, **47**
duplex cognitio Domini **290**, 292
duty
    to God and duty to state 338–39
    Kant's moral teaching 179–80, 186
dysteleological **123**
    evil 123, 125, 128
ecumenism **70**
efficient cause 31, **32**, 33
    objections to 36
egoism 140
election 279–82
Emmet, Dorothy 69
emotivism 138–**39**
empirical **217**
empirical knowledge **8**
empiricism **25**
empiricists 25, **30**
employment contracts 234–35
Enlightenment **60**, 61, 62, 177, 192
environment and ethical theories 242
Epicurean thesis **63**
epistemology 4, **5**, 6–8
eschatology **266**, 268, 270
    developments in Christian 273–78
esoteric **250**
eternal law **149**, 326, 327
ethics **5**, 134–45
    as action 343–44
    autonomous Christian ethics and
        practices **330**–32

ethical life 135–38
and globalisation 240–41
heteronomous Christian ethics and practices **326**–30
person and community 135
theonomous Christian ethics and practices **323**–26
theories of 138–42
see also business ethics; Kantian ethics; situation ethics
ethos **231**
eugenics **210**
euthanasia 207–33
Catholic ethical autonomy and 331
definition 207–8
Küng on 331
law and 208–10
natural law and 219
non-voluntary 208, 218
physician aid in dying 208, 209–10
quality of life principle **212**–15
sanctity of life principle 210–12
situation ethics and 220
slippery slope **209**–10
voluntary 208, 215–18
evil 113–31
defining problem 114–15
didactic 125–27
dysteleological 123, 125, 128
evidential problem 114
inconsistent triad **114**–15
moral **114**
natural **114**, 118, 122, 125
non-moral **114**
responses to problem 115
soul-making theodicies 120–**28**
theodicy of St Augustine 116–20
evolutionary theory 64–65
excluded middle 6
exegesis **318**
Existentialism 36, **139**, 275
faith
formed and unformed 293
and God's grace 292–93
history and 318–19
and situation ethics 168–69
the Fall 117–18, **253**
and human finiteness 292
human will after 254–58
human will before **253**–54
interpretation today 258–60
fallacy of composition **36**, 73–74
fideism **299**
Fifth Way 59–60
Final cause 31, **33**, 34, 59
Finkenwalde community 342–43
Finnis, John 156

First cause **67**, 68–69, 71, 75
first form of the categorical imperative **181**–82
Five Ways 59–60, 67, 75–76, 289–90
Fletcher, Joseph 165
on Bonhoeffer's ethics 347
on conscience 170–71, 172–73
on euthanasia 220
objections to situation ethics of 171–74
situation ethics 167–69, 331
and Temple 165–67, 168
forgiveness 308
form of life **307**
Form of the Good **20**, 24, 135
and Prime Mover 35
formal cause 31, **32**, 44
formed faith 293
the Forms **19**–20
hierarchy of 20–21
objections to theory of 24–25
four causes 31–33
Francis, Pope 242
Frankena, William K. 141
fraternity **230**
free market economy **232**
free will **179**, 253
defence 118, 120, 122, 124
and predestination 257–58
Saint Augustine and 118–19, 120, 254, 257–58
freedom and knowledge 123–24
Freud, Sigmund 262
Friedman, Milton 224
friendship and sex 253–54
Gaunilo of Marmoutiers 86–87
Geach, Peter 49, 51
Gehenna **269**
Gifford Lectures 97, 98
globalisation 238–42, **240**
Glover, Jonathan 214–15
Gnosticism 116
God
duty to state and duty to 338–39
obedience to will of 339–40
God's existence, arguments based on observation 56–80
Aquinas' cosmological argument 66–70
criticisms of design arguments 62–65
design argument of Paley 60–62, 64
Fifth Way of Aquinas 58, 59–60
leap to transcendent issue 75
Leibniz and principle of sufficient reason 71–74

modern versions of design argument 65–66
objections to arguments from experience 74
sheer chance 74–75
teleological argument 59–62
God's existence, arguments based on reason 81–94
Anselm's ontological argument 82–86
objections to 86–89
a priori and *a posteriori* proofs of God 90
God's existence, knowledge of 286–303
Alvin Plantinga 297–99
Barth–Brunner debate 295–97
knowing 286–87
natural 286–87, 288–91, 299–300
natural–revealed theology debate 295–300
revealed 286–87, 292–95
true knowledge 287, 296
Gospel of Matthew **269**
grace **258**, 292–93, 344
greatest good of the greatest number 195
Gregory of Nyssa 273, 276
Griffith-Dickson, Gwen 109–10
Grotius, Hugo 147
Gutiérrez, Gustavo 310, 311
Hades **269**
happiness 213–14
Hauerwas, Stanley 328–29, 346
heaven 277–78
Hedley, Douglas 300
hedonic calculus 194
hedonism **194**
alternatives to 194–95
hell 273–76
Heraclitus 18
heresy **116**, 120, 121
heteronomous Christian ethics **326**–30
heteronomy **179**
Hick, John 51
'experiencing as' 96
on intermediate state 277
on mind–body question 50
response to Phillips 128
on teachers of wisdom 309
on universalism 124–25, 282
version of Irenaean theodicy 122–23
Hobbes, Thomas 96, 153, 249
Hooker, Richard 146
human dignity 136, **229**
human law **150**–51, 327

human nature 248
    Augustine on 249–58, 263
    human potential 248–49
    interpreting Augustine today
        258–62
humanitarian principle **260**
Hume, David 62
    criticism of causation 68
    criticism of design argument
        62–63
hypothetical imperative 180–**81**
The Idea of the Holy 103–4
identity 6
Ignatius of Loyola, Saint 106
imagination
    appeal to 70
    and natural theology 300
immanence **295**
immanent **32**, 295
immortality and God **184**–85
incarnation 211, **315**
inconsistent triad **114**–15
incorrigible facts **287**
ineffability **98**, 108
infinite regress **70**
innate human sense of God 288–89
inner purity 308
instrumental good 123
instrumentalism 125, **128**, 212
intrinsic **328**
intrinsic value **211**
Irenaean theodicy 120–22
    Hick's version of 122–23
Irenaeus, Saint 120, 121, 122
James, William 97–99, 105
Jesus Christ 304–22
    affirmation of life 306–7
    authority 304–5, 313
    birth and incarnation 315–16
    Christ-event 319
    Christology **314**
    history and faith 318–19
    knowledge of God 314
    the liberator 310–13
    miracles 314–16
    moral teaching 307–9
    resurrection 266–67, 316–18
    revealed knowledge of God in
        293–95
    Son of God **313**–18
    teacher of wisdom 306–9
    uniqueness 318–19
John XXIII, Pope Saint 240–41
Judas Iscariot 275
judgement day 270–71
Kant, Immanuel 89, 178
    critique of Descartes 89

Kantian ethics 140, 141, 177–90
    applied to globalisation 241
    and business ethics 232–33,
        235, 241
    categorical imperative 181–85
    duty 179–80, 186
    hypothetical imperatives 180–81
    immortality and God **184**–85
    moral teaching 179–80
    objections to 186–87
Kenny, Anthony 64, 158
King, Martin Luther, Jr. 326
kingdom of ends (third form of
        categorical imperative) 181, 184
Kingdom of God 268–69
knowledge
    basic 298
    and belief 10–11
    and freedom 123–24
    a posteriori **7**, 8, 9
    a priori **7**–8, 25, 178
    theory of 6–8
    true 287, 296
    see also God's existence,
        knowledge of
Kolbe, Maximillian 248, 249
Kotarbinski, Tadeusz 25
Kuhse, Helga 210
Küng, Hans 115, 330–31
language and ethics 137
Laozi 309
leadership 340–41
legalism **167**
Leibniz, Gottfried Wilhelm 71–74
Leo XIII, Pope 227
lex **153**–54
liberal principle **214**
liberal societies **341**
liberation theology 310, **328**
libido **262**
limited/unlimited election 279
Locke, John 212, 213
logic **4**, 5
logical principles 6
love
    governing Christian practices 330
    sufficiency of 332
    will as 253
loyalty 234, 235
Lucifer **274**
Lund, Frank 207
lus **153**–54
Luther, Martin 139
Macquarrie, John 319
Magisterium **327**–28
major premise **5**
Manicheism **250**–51

Manning, Henry 227
manualist **148**
manuals 147–48
Maran atha **270**
marginalised, Jesus as liberator of
        312–13
martyr **267**
material cause 31, **32**
materialism 46, 50–52, **51**
metaethics 138–**39**, 166
metanoia **308**
metaphysics 4, **5**, 11
Mill, John Stuart 64, 141
    liberal principle **214**
    objections to design argument
        63–64
    on personal liberty 196
    rule utilitarianism 197–98
millenarianism **271**
mind–body question 41, 46
    Anscombe on 50
    Hick on 50
    objections to theories of 52–53
    Ryle on 48–49
    substance dualism 46–48, **47**
minor premise **5**
miracles 314–16
monism **46**
Moor, Dr David 215–16
moral evil **114**
moral goodness 289
moral pluralism 347
moral principles *see* Christian moral
        principles
moral relativism **347**
moral responsibility, collective
        260–61
moral teaching
    of Jesus 307–9
    of Kant 179–80, 186
mortal sin **276**
Moses 307, 309
motion 34, 36–37, **67**
Muhammad 309
mysterium tremendum et fascinans **103**
mystical experiences **103**, 104–5, 107
mysticism **103**
natural evil **114**, 118, 122, 125
natural law 139, 146–63, **150**, 289,
        326–27
    application to euthanasia 219
    Aquinas' 150, 151–57, 161, 326–27
    and business ethics 226
    lus and *lex* 153–54
    and manuals 147–48
    modern development 156–57
    objections to theories of 158–60

primary and secondary precepts 154–55
    principle of double effect **157**–58
    prudence and 155–56
    and telos 152–53
natural rights 136, 156–57, 196–97, 202
natural theology 286–**87**, 288–92
    challenges to 299–300
    innate human sense of God 288–90
    order of creation 290–92
    –revealed theology debate
        295–300
necessary being **68**, 70, 75, 84, 85, 86
necessity and contingency 67–**68**,
    69–70
neo-colonialism 241
Neoplatonism **251**–52
Nestorius 315, 316
New Testament on death and
    afterlife 266–72
    Kingdom of God 268–69
    problems 269–72
    resurrection of Jesus 266–67
Newton, Isaac 60–61, 62, 192
Nicene Creed **44**
Nichols, Vincent 229–30, 231
Niebuhr, Reinhold 260–61, 337
'no rusty swords' **342**
noetic quality **98**
non-contradiction 6, 84
non-moral evil **114**
non-voluntary euthanasia 208, 218
normative ethics **138**, 139, 143
notes, making 11–13
numinous **103**
Ockham's razor **66**
omnipotence **119**
ontological argument **81**, 90
    Aquinas' criticism 87–88
    Cottingham on 90–91
    Descartes development of
        Anselm's 86–87
    Gaunilo's criticism and Anselm's
        response 86–87
    Kant's critique of Descartes 89
    objections to 86–89
    a priori and *a posteriori* proofs of
        God 90
    of Saint Anselm 82–86
ontological theories 11
ontology **257**
order of creation 290–92, 297
ordinary and extraordinary means
    210, 217
Origen 273, 276
Original Sin 119, 256–**57**
    interpreting the Fall and 258–60

Otto, Rudolf 103–4
Paley, William 60–62, 291
    Hume's criticism of 62–63
palliative care **208**
Pannenberg, Wolfhart 317
Papal encyclical **327**
Parable of Sheep and Goats **272**–73
Parable of the Lost Son **308**
parousia **267**, 269–70
passive euthanasia 208, 219, 220
passivity **98**
paternalism **214**
Paul, Saint, conversion of 105
Pelagianism **121**, 252–53
Pelagius 252–53
per genus et per differentia **30**, 35
perdition **280**
persistent vegetative state (PVS)
    208, 215, 218
person
    in community 135
    and ethics 136–37
personal religious experiences 103–6
personal responsibility 308–9
personalism **167**, 168, 220, 331
Pharisees **266**
Phillips, D.Z. 77, 115, 173
    Hick's response to 128
    on soul-making theodicy 127–28
philosophical doubt 9–10
philosophy **3**
    branches 4–5
    conversation 2–4
    metaphysics 11
    sense experience and problems
        9–11
    vocabulary 4–8
physician aid in dying 208, 209–10
physician aided suicide 208
Pinker, Steven 259
Pius XI, Pope 230
Plantinga, Alvin 297–99
Plato 16–28, 136
    background 16–18
    body and soul 43
    and Christianity 44
    Form of the Good **20**, 24, 135
    Form of the Good vs. Aristotle's
        Prime Mover 35
    the Forms **19**–20
    hierarchy of the Forms 20–21
    objections to theory of the Forms
        24–25
    rationalism vs. Aristotle's empiricism
        30–31
    reality, understanding of 19–23
    Realm of Appearances 20

    Simile of Cave 22–23, 300
    Simile of Divided Line 21–22
    soul 42–44
Platonism **251**–52
point of contact **288**, 297
poor, Jesus liberator of 310–11
Popper, Karl 25, 142, 243
positive law **160**
positivism **168**, 220, 331
post-Christian society **346**
post-Enlightenment **260**
post-Lapsarian **256**
postulate **184**
practical reasoning and ethics 135–36
pragmatism **98**, 167, 220, 331
precepts **191**
    primary and secondary 154–55
predestination 257–58, **279**
    election and 279–80
    single and double **280**–81
predicate **7**, 88, 89, 92
preference utilitarianism 198–200, **199**
preferential option for the poor **310**
Pretty, Diane 209
pride and disobedience 254–55
Prime Mover **34**, 37
    Aquinas and 34–35, 37, 67, 68
    Aristotle and 33–35, 36–37, 68
    vs. Plato's Form of the Good 35
principle of accommodation **290**–91
principle of credulity **99**
principle of double effect **157**–58,
    216–18
principle of sufficient reason 71–74, **72**
principle of testimony **99**
    Swinburne on 99–100
principle of utility 193
priority of ends (second form of the
    categorical imperative) **181**,
    182–84, 233
problem of other minds 100
process theology **291**–92
Proslogion
    Chapter 2 82–84
    Chapter 3 84–86, 92
Protestant
    ethical autonomy 331
    ethical heteronomy 328–29
prudence and natural law 155–56
psyche **43**
purgatory **271**–72
    and intermediate states **276**–77
purposive **33**
    universe 36, 37, 152, 160
Pythagoras 18
QALY **217**
Qatar World Cup 237

quality of life principle **212**–15
Rahner, Karl   77
reality, understanding of   19–23
reciprocity   **230**
redemption   **259**, 276
reductionism   **50**
reformed epistemology   **297**–99
regeneration   **292**
relativism   139, 166, **167**–68, 220, 331
   as distinct from situationalism   142
   teleology and   193–98
religion, ethics and   137–38
religionless Christianity   **341**
religious experience   95–112
   conversion experiences   105–6
   corporate   **101**–2
   nature of   97–99
   objections to theories   107–10
   personal   103–6
   personal testimony and convincing
      others   99–100
   problem of other minds   100
   types   100–106
   ways of understanding   107
repentance   276, 308
Restrepo, Camilo Torres   310–11
resurrection   266–67, 316–18
revealed theology   286–**87**, 292–95
   faith and God's grace   292–93
   knowledge of God in Jesus
      Christ   293–95
   –natural theology debate
      295–300
Richman and Lazarus   **269**
Roman Catholic Church
   beatific vision   **278**–79
   ethical autonomy   330–31
   ethical heteronomy   326–28
   predestination   281
   purgatory   277
Ross, W.D.   172
Rousseau, Jean-Jacques   249
rule utilitarianism   **197**–98
Russell, Bertrand   36, 70, 73, 96, 107
Ryle, Gilbert   48–49
the sabbath   308–9
sacrifice and suffering   344–45
Sadducees   **269**
Samaritans   311–12
sanctity of life principle   210–12
   rejection of   212–13
Sanders, E.P.   318
Sartre, Jean-Paul   109, 275–76
secular pacifism   **337**
self-determination, right to   209
sense experience   **7**
   problems of   9–11

sensus divinitatis   **288**, 298
Sermon on the Mount   149, **307**–8,
   324, 325, 328–29, 332
sex
   and friendship   253–54
   and human nature   261–62
Sheol   **269**
si integer stetisset Adam   **292**
Simile of Cave   22–23, 300
Simile of Divided Line   21–22
simplicity   66
sin
   and collective moral responsibility
      260–61
   mortal   **276**
   Original   119, 256–**57**, 258–60
Singer, Peter   198, 241, 242
   preference utilitarianism
      198–200, **199**
   quality of life principle   212–13
single predestination   **281**
situation ethics   140, 164–76, **165**
   application to euthanasia   220
   Fletcher's   167–69
   four working principles   167–68, 331
   objections to Fletcher's theory   171–74
   six propositions   168
   Temple and Fletcher   165–67, 168
situationalism   151–**52**, 165–66
   as distinct from relativism   142
Skinner, B.F.   51
slippery slope   **209**–10
Smart, Ninian   103, 104
Socrates   4, 17, 18, 21, 42, 43
solidarity   **230**, 345–46
Solomon, Robert C.   224, 231
Son of God   **313**–18
soul   41–42
   Aquinas and   45–46
   Aristotle and   44–46
   Descartes and   47
   Hick and   50
   objections to theories of   52–53
   Plato and   42–44
soul-deciding theodicy   **118**
soul-making theodicy   120–**28**
   of Hick   122–25
   of Irenaeus   120–22
   Phillips on   127–28
   of Swinburne   125–27
Soul One and Soul Two   51
sports, business ethics and   236–37
stakeholders   **228**
Stoics   151
strong sanctity of life principle   **210**
   argument against euthanasia
      210–12

subjectivism   **139**
subsidiarity   **230**
substance dualism   46–48, **47**
   Descartes and   47
   objections to   48–49
suffering   **114**
   minimising   199–200
   sacrifice and   344–45
sufficient reason, principle of
   71–74, **72**
suicide   207, 208
Suicide Act 1961   208
sustainability   **230**–31, 242
Swinburne, Richard   65
   didactic evil   125–27
   simplicity   66
   testimony   99–100
syllogism   **5**–6
tautology   **7**–8
teleological argument   **59**
   criticisms   62–65
   for existence of God   37, 58, 59–62
   Hume's criticism   62–63
teleological theories   33, **140**, 148,
   168, 193, 201
   and deontological theories   141
   difficulties with   186
   and relativism   193–98
teleology   **33**
telos   152–53
Temple, William   70, 138, 141, 173,
   227, 233
   and Fletcher   165–67, 168
Ten Commandments   137–38, 150, 324
Tennant, F.R.   65
Teresa of Avila, Saint   104–5, 107
testimony, principle of   **99**
   Swinburne on   99–100
theodicy   **116**
   objections to Saint Augustine's
      119–20
   of Saint Augustine   116–19
   soul-making   120–**28**
theology of crisis   **345**
theonomous Christian ethics   **323**–26
theory of knowledge   **6**–8
theotokos   **315**
third form of the categorical
   imperative   **181**, 184
thought experiments   **300**
Tillich, Paul   71, 275
Tolstoy, Leo   306
Torah   **307**
Toronto blessing   101, 102
transcendent   **32**, 75, 103
transience   **98**
Trinitarian view of God   **294**

true knowledge   287, 296
tyrannicide   **340**
underside of history   **310**
unformed faith   293
universal consent argument   289
universalisation (first form of
        categorical imperative)   181–82
universalism   124–25
    and election   281–82
unlimited/limited election   279
usury   **225**
utilitarianism   **140**, 171, 191–206
    act   **171**, 197
        applied to globalisation   241
        Bentham and classical   192–93

and business ethics   232, 235, 241
    objections to   200–202
    Peter Singer and preference
        198–200, **199**
    rule   **197**–98
    teleology and relativism   193–98
utopia   **337**
validity   **5**
The Varieties of Religious Experience
        97–99
Vecera, William   106
virtue ethics (aretaic ethics)   139,
        140, 152
vitalism   **208**, 210
Vivekananda   309

vocabulary, philosophy   4–8
Voltaire   71–72, 74
voluntary euthanasia   208,
        215–18
vulgar relativism   **139**
weak sanctity of life principle   **212**
Western void   **341**
Westminster Confession of Faith   **280**
whistle-blowing   **233**–36
wholly other   **103**
Williams, Rowan   95
Williams, Sir Bernard   202
Wittgenstein, Ludwig   96, 306–7
world come of age   **341**, 344–45
zealots   **310**

Photo credits